Moving On

Young people and Leaving Care Schemes

Nina Biehal, Jasmine Clayden, Mike Stein, Jim Wade

LONDON : HMSO

CONTENTS

LIST OF FIGURES

LIST OF TABLES

LIST OF ABBREVIATIONS

A level	Advanced level certificate in education
B Tec	Business and technology education council
CEP	Centre for economic performance
CH(E)	Community home with education
DHSS	Department of Health and Social Security
DoH	Department of Health
DSS	Department of Social Security
EWO	Education welfare officer
FE	Further education
GCSE	General certificate of secondary education
GNVQ	General national vocational qualification
LEA	Local education authority
LMQR	Labour market quarterly report
NACAB	National association of citizen's advice bureaux
NCB	National Children's Bureau
NNEB	National nursery examination board
NVQ	National vocational qualification
OPCS	Office of population and census surveys
SILP	Semi independent living project
SPSS	Statistics package for social scientists
SSD	Social services department
SSI	Social services inspectorate
TEC	Training and enterprise council
VOL	Voluntary
YT	Youth training

ACKNOWLEDGEMENTS

Without the help and cooperation of numerous individuals, local authorities and institutions our research would not have been possible. We would like to thank everyone in our participating local authorities who helped and advised us during the course of this study. In particular, we are grateful to the staff of the leaving care teams who not only gave time for interviews but coped patiently with our persistent demands for information; to all the social workers who were involved with us and to our project groups, whose advice and guidance has proved invaluable over the past four years.

A special thanks goes to Janet Barton who, with dedication and good humour, organised our office and meticulously transcribed many hours of interviews. Also to Philip Raws, who stepped into the breach for several months to organise and conduct interviews with care and sensitivity. Thanks also to our colleagues at the Child Care Research and Development Unit at Leeds University; in particular to Nick Frost, Liz Johnson and Lorraine Wallis whose advice, support and encouragement was much appreciated.

Funding for our research was provided by the Department of Health. We are grateful for this assistance and also for the considerable help of our research liaison officer Dr. Carolyn Davies. Additional thanks to Chris Sealey, Martin Harrison and Bryan Hopper.

Most of all we are indebted to the young people who participated in our study. Without their honesty and willingness to share with us both personal and painful aspects of their lives, this book could not have been written. We hope that we have been able to do justice to their views and that the ideas presented here may, in some small way, contribute to improving the services available to young people leaving care in the future. It was their wish and it is also ours.

PART 1

INTRODUCTION

This section gives a brief description of the four leaving care schemes and provides some contextual information about the local authorities in which they are situated. It outlines the methodology adopted for our survey of 183 care leavers and for our interviews with a follow up sample of 74 care leavers. A profile of aspects of the care careers of the follow up sample is included to set the scene for subsequent chapters.

CHAPTER 1

INTRODUCING THE STUDY

The research context

"I wanted to leave and I didn't want to leave . . . but it had to be done sooner or later. I had to leave sooner or later."

"When you come out (of care) it's hell after. You don't know what you're doing or where you're going. It's just like taking you from one country and putting you into another."

Each year thousands of young people leave the substitute homes provided for them by local authorities and, if unable to return to their families, seek a place for themselves as young adults in the community.[1] The vast majority move on from care between 16 and 18 years of age.[2] The comments made above by two young people as they embarked on this journey capture the complex and ambivalent feelings experienced by many making this transition. A sense of loss at the breaking of established ties and, for many, of a secure home base often blend with a desire for greater autonomy and a more adult identity. For others, inbuilt expectations of moving on create feelings of resignation and, for those least prepared, the experience of transition can equate with the powerful imagery of migration, of standing alone in a potentially hostile environment without the skills and language needed to survive.

Concern at the vulnerability of young people leaving care to live independently in the community has grown from the mid 1970's. Our research into the support being offered to them by leaving care schemes has been influenced by a number of related developments which have contributed to the 'awakening of leaving care in the professional and political consciousness' (Stein 1991).

First, a body of findings from small scale surveys and qualitative studies has highlighted the range of problems faced by young people leaving care and made

---

1. Although there are no national figures, it is estimated that about 10,000 16 and 17 year olds leave care to live independently each year. In the year ending 31 March 1990, 6239 young people were legally discharged on reaching 18 in Great Britain (NCB 1992).
2. Throughout this book we will continue to use the terms 'care' and 'leaving care'. Although since the Children Act 1989 they no longer have the same legal currency, 'leaving care' is a more succinct expression than its more accurate alternative – 'ceasing to be accommodated and/or looked after'. They also remain in popular usage amongst accommodated young people themselves.

some connections between these difficulties and the quality of their pre-care and in-care experiences.[3] Although the detailed messages arising out of these studies will be explored in our subsequent chapters a few pointers offered here in summary form will help to identify some of the major themes. These studies have highlighted the diversity of the care experience and shown that care leavers are not a homogeneous group in terms of their pre-care experiences, their care histories, their needs, or their cultural and ethnic backgrounds. Care may have been valued by young people and helped them but it may also have contributed to other problems. They were likely to have experienced further movement and disruption during their time in care. For those in care longer term there existed a tendency for their links with family, friends and neighbourhood to weaken. Allied to these problems, the stress of dealing with family rejection and/or extended separation and loss often created identity confusions. Young people often lacked a detailed knowledge of their pasts, a convincing narrative of who they were and why events had taken the course they had, and these feelings could be amplified for black young people brought up in a predominantly 'white' care system if they became detached from family and community supports. Given these difficulties it is perhaps not surprising to find that young people in care tended to do poorly at school and lacked the qualifications they would need for later life.

Upon leaving care, a lack of adequate preparation coupled with the early age at which care leavers are expected to assume adult responsibilities, have tended to mean that loneliness, isolation, unemployment, poverty, homelessness, movement and 'drift' were likely to feature significantly in many of their lives. The social work support and financial assistance they received was shown to be variable and inconsistent and many local authorities lacked formal leaving care policies and consistent procedures that could guarantee young people an equal chance of accessing services.

A significant contribution of the qualitative research was to provide an empirical and 'ordered' underpinning to the views of young people and this was complemented by a second development – young people living in care coming together to talk about their experiences. From the mid 1970's, the growth of local 'in care' groups, the Who Cares? Project, Black and In Care, and the National Association of Young People in Care all contributed to an increased awareness of the connections between the quality of life experienced by young people in care and their lives after leaving care (Stein 1983). The confidence and self belief engendered through the self organisation of young people led to the articulation of a series of demands for reform. These ranged from an end to bulk purchase and the use of order books in children's homes which denied young people dignity and the chance to develop their life skills, to demands for greater participation in decisions affecting

---

3. See for example: Bonnerjea 1990; Stockley 1990; Barnardo's 1989; Randall 1989; Randall 1988; First Key 1987; Stein and Carey 1986; Klein 1985; Lupton 1985; Stein and Maynard 1985; Kahan 1979; Godek 1976.

their lives and for improved practical and financial resources to assist young people leaving care. The voices of young people were and are influential in persuading practitioners and policy makers of the need for improved services.

A third related development has been the reform of child care law. In relation to 'leaving care' this included the 'Continuing Care' recommendations of the Social Services Committee Report on Children in Care (Social Services Committee 1984), amended by The Review of Child Care Law and included in the 1987 White Paper 'The Law on Child Care and Family Services', which formed the basis of the relevant sections of the Children Act 1989 (DHSS 1985b; HMSO 1987). Our research, then, has been carried out during the first three years of implementation of the new Act which has given local authorities both new duties and wider discretionary powers in relation to leaving care. It has placed duties upon local authorities to prepare young people for leaving care (Section 24.1) and to advise and befriend young people to the age of 21, where they left care after their sixteenth birthday (Section 24.2). It also gives them discretionary powers to offer financial assistance to young people in relation to housing, education, employment or training (Sections 24.6.1 and 24.8). In addition, the Act also embodies other duties and powers in relation to the accommodation of young people, inter-agency working to meet the needs of care leavers, the publicising of services available and representation and complaints procedures.[4] While the Children Act has helped to raise the profile of leaving care and to stimulate the further development of services, the balance between the duties and powers within it has meant that regional and local variations in the level of services available to young people persist (Broad 1994; First Key 1992).

Finally, and emerging in tandem with the above developments, has been the growth of a range of policy and practice initiatives at the local level designed to respond to some of the acknowledged problems experienced by care leavers. From humble beginnings a range of projects designed to offer accommodation and support to young people emerged through partnerships established by social services departments, voluntary agencies, housing authorities and associations. By 1986 these initiatives included the very first specialist leaving care schemes. Research based upon these innovative schemes raised a number of questions that required further investigation (Bonnerjea 1990; Stein 1990; Stone 1990).

- First, what different scheme models and approaches to leaving care are developing and what services do they provide?

- Second how effectively are schemes able to support young people leaving care? What are the 'outcomes' for young people of their involvement with schemes?

- Finally, how do the outcomes and experiences of young people who use schemes compare to those not being assisted by schemes?

---

4. For a more detailed discussion of the powers and duties contained within the Act see Stein (1991); DOH (1991b).

Designing the study

The main purpose of our study was to investigate different leaving care schemes and approaches to leaving care in three local authorities. We took as our starting point the view that leaving care is a *process*, not a single discrete event, and that it involves young people in making a number of *transitions*. The concept of transition offered a useful framework for our research, leading us to consider the transitions that care leavers make in different areas of their lives – from (substitute) home to independent accommodation; from school to the labour market; from living with carers to living alone, setting up home with a partner or becoming a parent. Taking this youth transitions framework as our starting point led us to draw on the existing sociological and social policy literature in this area, in addition to the literature on child welfare, in order to evaluate how leaving care services were assisting young people in different areas of their lives. It also enabled us to make some comparisons between our sample and the transitions made by young people in the general population.

Our aims were therefore to improve our knowledge of the transitions made by young people leaving care and to evaluate the ways in which different types of leaving care schemes helped them to make these transitions. We also aimed to evaluate the outcomes achieved by leaving care schemes in their work with young people.

We therefore decided on a two stage study. First, a survey of *patterns* of leaving care in three local authorities – City, County and District. Second, an in depth qualitative study of the *process* of leaving care and of the support offered to care leavers by the four leaving care schemes in these authorities. These two studies were intended to be complementary. The first provided empirical information on young people's transitions and the support available to them. The second, building on this empirical information, allowed us to explore the social processes involved in moving on from care, an evaluation of the support offered by schemes and a comparison of the outcomes attained for a group of young people receiving help from schemes with outcomes for a comparison group of young people without scheme support. Our two stage research design was not intended as a method of triangulation, as we were not using the second part of the study simply to check the validity of the first. The aim was to explore how the patterns uncovered by the survey related to what young people and the professionals working with them thought and did, and to look for explanations of these patterns (see Mason, 1994).

Collaborative research

From the outset we thought it was important to ensure that our research was sensitive to local needs and agencies in the three authorities studied and, most importantly, that we were accountable to participants in the research. Project groups were therefore established in each local authority with representation from young people, leaving care schemes, social services management, field social workers, foster and residential carers, housing and research. These groups met twice yearly and served as a forum for developing approaches to the research, testing out research instruments and sharing problems and concerns. They provided an opportunity to bring together different perspectives and interests in order to develop research questions relevant both to care leavers and to those working with them. The project groups also provided a helpful setting in which to test out initial findings.

We realised that it would be difficult for young people to participate fully in a forum of this kind, surrounded by more powerful professionals. We tried to deal with this by inviting several young people along together, for mutual support, and by keeping agendas and the conduct of the meetings informal and jargon free. In one authority, some 'pre-meetings' were held with young people just prior to the project group meetings to give them an opportunity to test out their views in a less threatening setting before putting them to the full meeting. However, despite discussions with young people about the ways in which we might facilitate their full participation in the project groups, in most cases they were not fully involved. These difficulties, together with the reality that some of these young people were unable to maintain their attendance at the groups due to the unsettled nature of their lives, meant that involving young people in the project groups was not an unqualified success.

Involving young people

Despite these difficulties, involving young people remained central to the research. In the most basic sense, young people were directly involved during out qualitative study. Young people's views form the core of this study, as we interviewed 74 young people about their experiences in care, on leaving care and about the support they received thereafter. These young people were contacted through their social workers or leaving care scheme workers and asked if they wished to be involved in the research. We felt it would be easier for them to say no to a third party than if approached directly by ourselves. At the end of each interview we requested their permission to interview the profesionals working with them, in order to give them further control over the research process.

We also thought it important that care leavers should be involved in framing the questions the research would address, so in the early stages of the study we arranged meetings with groups of care leavers in each of our project authorities. At these informal meetings we asked young people what *they* would like researchers to investigate about the process of leaving care. These lively discussions helped us to develop the research questions included in both our survey and our qualitative study.

The survey

Our survey aimed to collect information on all young people aged 16–19 leaving care in our three local authorities during a six month period in order to chart patterns of leaving care. Questionnaires were completed by the social workers of all young people who left care in this period. The response rate was high, with information collected on 183 young people, representing 91% of those leaving care during this period. This high response rate was achieved through intensive work to raise the profile of the research in the authorities, involving meetings with local area managers and many individual conversations with social workers uncertain about involving themselves in the research.[5]

Using the entire local populations of care leavers as our sample, together with the high response rate we obtained, went some way to ensuring that our findings were representative. However, methodological problems arose from our decision to employ a broad definition of leaving care, including young people who moved from a care placement to independent accommodation as well as those who were legally discharged from care. This wider definition made it more difficult for us to identify our survey population and raised the issue of consistency, since the social workers completing the questionnaires could have had different opinions as to what constituted leaving care in this broader sense. We tried to ensure consistency by breaking down broad conceptual categories such as 'independent accommodation' into precise, detailed descriptive categories (lodgings, bedsit, hostel etc) on the questionnaires. Our aim was to be as unambiguous as possible in order to minimize potential errors by social workers in completing the questionnaires and by ourselves in coding them (see Hoinville and Jowell et al, 1987:27). Piloting the survey enabled us to iron out a few ambiguities that had crept in.

A further problem arose from the fact that the questionnaires were completed by social workers rather than by care leavers themselves. This meant that information was not always complete. Social workers were not always sufficiently informed about all aspects of young people's lives covered by the survey. However, this was interesting in itself. For example, the fact that a fifth of the social workers did not know whether young people had any qualifications tells us something about the degree of attention given to education. We tried to ensure the accuracy of social worker responses by asking precise factual questions about young people's lives rather than questions that required expressions of opinion. During coding, questionnaires were checked for internal consistency and, where inconsistencies arose, the social worker was telephoned for clarification. The survey was analysed using the statistical software package SPSS-PC.

The survey provided us with a context to guide our next steps, particularly as regards the 'outcomes' for young people in the critical first few months out of care. This included important contextual data and pointers in relation to the use of leaving care schemes, accommodation, support, assistance, family links, education, employment and care careers. The findings of the survey were published in 1992 (Biehal, Clayden, Stein and Wade 1992) and are also drawn upon in the discussions

---

5. See Biehal, Clayden, Stein and Wade (1992) for a discussion of the methodological issues involved in the survey.

which follow. However, the principal focus of this book will be on the findings from our subsequent qualitative study.

The qualitative study

Our qualitative study began with a period of participant observation of scheme work, interviews with scheme staff and social services managers, and the analysis of policy documents. Our aim was to identify the distinctive features of the four schemes and to construct initial scheme profiles. Both County and District each had one leaving care scheme, whereas City authority possessed two – one managed by a voluntary agency, City (vol), and another managed directly by social services, City (ssd).[6] The use of there different types of local authority (see chapter 2) and, within them, four distinctive types of leaving care schemes, not only enabled us to explore different models of provision but also to take account of the impact of different contexts, policies and services on leaving care careers.

After this preparatory work, we defined and identified our sample of young people. The sample comprised two groups – a 'participating' group who were receiving key worker support from the schemes and a 'comparison' group of non-scheme young people. Our total qualitative sample was 74 young people: 30 from County, 27 from City and 17 from District. Of these, 42 (57%) were included in the participating sample and 32 (43%) in the comparison sample. The structure and breakdown of the total sample is discussed later (see Chapter 3). Due to the different sizes of our authorities, the numbers of young people who moved to independence varied during our recruitment period.

In order to avoid the over-representation of certain groups of care leavers and to facilitate comparison we used stratified random sampling (May, 1993). We therefore attempt to stratify both the participating and the comparison sample by gender, ethnic origin, last substitute care placement and time in care (less then two years/ more than two years). Initially, each young person leaving care was assigned to the appropriate category (for example: female, white, in care less than two years, leaving from a foster placement) until each category was full.

However, stratification was difficult to sustain in view of the small size of the sampling frame, which consisted of all those leaving care placements or legally dicharged from care in each authority. The number of young people included from District, the smallest authority, was only attained by taking **all** the young people that we could identify who moved to independence or were legally discharged during this period. In this sense they were not subject to the same stratification criteria as those in City and County. Gender also proved difficult to manage in practice. The preponderance of young women who moved on at this time, particularly in County, led to a disproportionate number included in the research. Our research time scale

---

6.   Brief profiles of the four schemes are provided in Chapter 2.

precluded further delay in order to recruit more young men. Similarly, the vast majority of young people using the City (ssd) scheme left care from residential placements so a decision was eventually made to abandon stratification by last care placement for the City authority.

In addition, the small numbers of black young people that we were able to identify resulted in us including all of these young people in our sample, a total of nine, regardless of whether the appropriate category for stratification was full. We felt justified in doing so in view of the importance of exploring the experiences of black care leavers, as so little research exists in this area (see First Key, 1987; Black And In Care, 1984). The reasons for their under-representation remain unclear. However, we did make strenuous attempts, including discussions with leaving care scheme staff and with black social workers in the authorities, to identify more black young people for inclusion in the research, unfortunately without success. For similar reasons, the very small numbers of care leavers with special needs led us to include in our sample all of those we could identify – just six young people, most of whom had mild or moderate learning difficulties and one of whom had a serious mental health problem. As numbers in these two groups are so small, some caution is needed in extrapolating from our findings, but we feel that the accounts of these young people nevertheless provide valuable information about experiences of care and leaving care for black young people and those with special needs. These are discussed in some depth in chapters 11 and 13.

It was also not possible for us to maintain completely separate 'participating' and 'comparison' samples. Patterns of scheme usage are complex. As we anticipated, some young people ceased to use schemes or used them intermittently while others, originally in our 'comparison' group, began using schemes at a later point. A triumph of reality over methodological purity! Further problems of comparison arose from the fact that, in a sample size feasible for an intensive qualitative study, precise matching between a participating and a comparison sample proved impossible to attain, as a far larger sample would have been needed to take account of all relevant variables. These problems of comparison are explored in more depth in chapter 20.

After piloting our interview schedules with young people already using the schemes (who would not be included in our research), we carried out semi-structured in-depth interviews with young people using leaving care schemes, their leaving care workers and their social workers (particpating sample) and young people not using schemes and their social workers (comparison sample).

Three complete sets of interviews (T1, T2 and T3) were carried out between January 1992 and January 1994, a total of 426 interviews. Each interview was tape recorded and then transcribed. In addition, policy interviews were carried out towards the end of the study with leaving care project leaders and, where appropriate, senior managers responsible for leaving care policy. In order to facilitate analysis of empirical data, a brief questionnaire was completed at the end of interviews with young people at all three stages of the research.

Semi-structured interviews were used to enable us to gather rich data on experiences, opinions and feelings while providing a clear enough structure to allow comparisons to be made. Questions for each subject area were specified but interviewers would often follow up answers, seeking clarification and elaboration. In both the specified questions and the improvised follow up, interviewers took care not to ask leading questions. However, where it was clear to the interviewer that through the provision of a simple piece of information (for example, about entitlement to benefits or the existence of a local service) the research could 'give back' something to respondents, this was done once the interview had ended. In doing so, we were guided by feminist critiques of disengagement in the interview process (see, for example, Oakley 1990).

A great deal of attention was paid to putting the respondents at ease and establishing trust before the interview began, particularly with the young people. However, in many cases it was the professionals who were more anxious about being interviewed than the young people themselves. The fact that all three researchers had had practice experience in working with young people in care was certainly an advantage. Care was taken to emphasise the researchers' independence and to guarantee total confidentiality. In most cases the same interviewer was involved with each respondent throughout all three stages of the research, which led interviewees to appear noticeably more comfortable with us as the study progressed.

We built in a number of safeguards to ensure reliability. First, the semi structured nature of the interview schedules and our conduct of the interviews aimed to ensure that young people and the professionals working with them were dealt with consistently. Interviewing both young people and the professionals working with them at each point in time provided a means of comparing and cross checking answers, in order to understand different perspectives on events. The longitudinal nature of the study also made it easier for us to unravel the pattern of events in young people's lives since, as Bullock and others have suggested, deception is difficult to sustain over several meetings which were, in our case, six to nine months apart. (Bullock et al, 1993). All interviews were carried out by members of the research team to ensure greater consistency in the material. However, self report studies in areas such as drug/alcohol use and offending are prone to misreporting, either due to concealment or exaggeration (Smith and Nutbeam 1992). We hoped to overcome some of these problems through the checks and balances outlined above. Finally, in our primary emphasis on recent and specific events, problems of inaccuracy arising from generalisation and recall over a long period were minimised.

Measuring outcomes

Outcome measures were constructed to assist in the evaluation of scheme services. Using qualitative data from our interviews together with the questionnaires completed at the end of interviews with young people, outcomes along a range of dimensions were analysed: accommodation, life skills, education, career paths, social networks, relationships, identity, drug/alcohol use and offending. An assessment was also made of the overall outcomes achieved by each scheme. The measurement of outcomes raises substantial methodological problems which are discussed in full in chapters 20–22.

Data analysis

Our qualitative study was analysed by means of a content analysis of the interview transcripts and a quantitative analysis of the questionnaires completed at the end of the interviews. The analysis of the questionnaires made it easier for us to analyse patterns across our interview sample. In order to familiarise ourselves with the range and diversity of qualitative material generated from our interviews an initial analysis of a sub-set of the data was carried out. Key issues were identified and a set of categories were devised which were used to code the data set of individual interviews. Our aim was to search out patterns and relate these to existing theories and knowledge. As a check for consistency, transcripts were read twice by different team members.

The entire data set was then analysed using this coding scheme and each theme was explored across all cases. New themes that emerged during the course of the analysis were incorporated into the coding framework. Brief pen pictures of the young people, completed after each interview, were used to ensure that this thematic analysis did not lose sight of individual circumstances. Further analysis was then undertaken to draw out associations between professional interventions and behaviours and to tease out the complex relationships between different variables.

Our qualitative study provided us with empirical data both on processes and on young peoples' and professionals' perceptions of these processes. Although causal explanations are rarely possible in the social world, our data enabled us to analyse critically the social relations of care leavers in respect of their families and friends, the care system, leaving care schemes, social workers and other agencies. In consequence, we have been able to explore the ways in which existing policies, practices and social contexts affect care leavers' lives and structure their experiences and choices.

Presenting the findings

It is now ten years since the last major qualitative and longitudinal study of young people leaving care was conducted (Stein and Carey 1986). It followed a group of young people from one authority and charted their experiences as they attempted to establish independent lives for themselves in the community. Ten years on transitions are occuring in a new context. Major social policy changes affecting social security and housing have influenced the possibilities for young people. Youth labour and training markets have been restructured. Local authorities are operating within tight financial constraints and, in relation to social services, social workers have had to contend with major reorganisations of services and with new legislation affecting

City (vol): This scheme is the oldest in the authority and was established in 1986. It is directly managed by a voluntary agency operating in partnership with the local social services department. The scheme is jointly funded by the agency and the department on a purchaser/provider basis and working arrangements are consolidated in a service agency agreement. The voluntary agency takes responsibility for scheme policy and for the management, support and training of staff.

The scheme has remained small in size with a project leader and four project workers supplemented by the use of students and some volunteer befrienders (see Appendix figure 1). The scheme offers an accommodation based service to the local authority for limited numbers of young people. Scheme services centre on the provision of shared trainer flats for up to 20 young people and intensive support is offered for 12–18 months with the aim of preparing them to move on to independent accommodation. Support is offered through a mix of individual and group work and links with housing agencies help to ensure a flow of move on accommodation. Once young people move on further help is available, but usually at a less intense level. The scheme priority is to focus on those undergoing preparation.

City (ssd): This scheme was launched in 1989. It is funded and managed directly by the social services department. The scheme's brief is to offer a universal service open to any young person preparing to leave care or already living independently in the community. However, in part, its origins lay in a review of children's homes within the authority and most staff are from residential backgrounds. The scheme's links with children's homes meant that during our research period most of its work was with young people moving on from residential care. Developing at a time of profound reorganisation of departmental services, for much of our research the scheme lacked a clear policy, managerial and procedural framework within which to operate. In consequence staff were largely required to carve out a direction for themselves.

The scheme has ten staff including a unit manager, two senior care staff and seven care staff. The support available to young people has involved helping to prepare them prior to their move from care, arranging accommodation and providing practical support through the transition from care. The scheme manages a four bed semi-independence unit.

Although there were no clear arrangements for collaboration and joint planning between the two schemes during the research period, recent organisational and policy changes within social services are laying a firmer foundation for co-operatic

County

County is also a very large authority with a population of 865,100 on 199 night. Just under a third of its residents live in the city, which is situated at of the county, and is surrounded by villages and small towns form councils. The resident population is predominantly white (88.9%) b

from 99.2% in the north west of county to 71.5% in the city. The city district itself has the highest population of 'black' ethnic groups outside of London and the eighth highest in Great Britain. The proportion of county's population from minority ethnic groups was just over 11% compared with 5.5% for Great Britain. Different minority ethnic groups include Indians (8.4%), Pakistani (0.3%), Bangladeshi (0.2%), Black Caribbean (0.6%), Black African and other black groups (0.4%), Chinese (0.2%) and other Asians (0.4%).

County's economy partly reflects its traditional roots in textiles, footwear, clothing and engineering as well as more recent high technology industries. A third of its employees work in these old and new manufacturing industries. However, like city, the service sector is the major employer with concentrations in similar bodies, institutions and industries. In 1991 the unemployment rate was 7.5% for all ages and 8.8% for 16–20 year olds and 4.2% of 16–20 year olds were attending a government scheme.

County leaving care scheme

This scheme also aims to provide a service to all young people leaving care and those living independently within the county. It is the oldest of our participating schemes and was established as a specialist scheme in 1985. It is directly funded and managed by social services. As it has grown, it has taken on a brief to develop and co-ordinate leaving care services for the county as a whole.

The size of the authority and the complexity of its administrative divisons has led this scheme to develop a more specialised staff structure. Specialist roles have developed in response to its focus on developing a range of accommodation options for young people leaving care. These include directly managed hostels (one for young people with learning difficulties), supported lodgings, a 'floating support' scheme organised as a dispersed hostel and formal agreements with statutory and voluntary housing agencies to ensure a stream of individual tenancies. There are 12 staff members: a team leader; four 'generic' social workers to support young people living independently; two 'accommodation' social workers to manage the supported lodgings scheme and five 'project' workers who manage the hostels and dispersed scheme.

Different levels of support are available to young people, reflecting the need the scheme has to ration its resources explicitly. Those entering supported accommodation are offered a comprehensive package of support whereas for those entering their own accommodation the support offered tends to be less intensive and rationed according to need. For those not receiving ongoing support from the scheme, a priority is placed upon a formal duty service to ensure that young people and their social workers have, at a minimum, access to advice and information. All support work is undertaken on an individual basis and, apart from the duty service, in young people's own homes and placements. The scheme's base in a large city centre social work office means that more informal and group work services are not possible.

District

District, with a population in 1991 of 194,000 is one of the smallest local authority areas in England. Its population is made up of one large town (84,538) and seven smaller towns spread throughout the district. The resident population is mainly white (95.4%), 4.6% being of minority ethnic origin compared to 5.5% for Great Britain. Different minority ethnic groups include Pakistani (3.3%), Indian (0.3%), Bangladeshi (0.2%), Black Caribbean and other Black groups (0.2%) and Chinese (0.1%).

Over half the workforce is employed in the fast growing service sector including public services, banking and insurance. By contrast employment in manufacturing industries, particularly textiles, metal goods and electrical engineering is contracting. In 1991 the unemployment rate was 9.5% for all ages and 10.4% for 16–20 year olds. Five per cent of this age group were on Government schemes.

District leaving care scheme

Established since 1986, this scheme is managed by a voluntary agency working in partnership with the social services department. Since 1992 the local authority has assumed full responsibility for direct revenue costs, although the voluntary agency provides the project building and meets some indirect costs (staff support/training and running costs at the project base). The voluntary agency has responsibility for scheme policy and for the management, support and training of staff. Liaison and co-ordination with the authority is maintained through regular joint meetings.

This scheme also provides a universal service to all care leavers in the authority but, given the relatively small size of the authority, the scheme has remained quite small with a project leader and three and three quarter (equivalent) project staff. From its inception, part of the scheme's brief has been to provide a drop-in centre for young people living independently. The siting of the project base in the centre of the principal town makes it accessible for most young people and, alongside structured individual programmes of support in young people's own homes and placements, it has been able to develop a distinctively 'community based' approach. A range of open access services are available at the project including groups, a daily drop-in and duty service and organised activities/holidays. Young people are therefore able to pop into the centre for advice and to participate in social activities for as long as they wish to use it.

In addition to its direct work, the scheme has also invested in promoting accommodation resources for care leavers. It manages a supported lodgings scheme, and links and joint ventures with local housing associations have been aimed at providing a range of good quality permanent tenancies.

CHAPTER 3

A PROFILE OF OUR FOLLOW UP SAMPLE

Children and young people looked after by local authorities are not a homogeneous group. Differences in their family backgrounds and experiences, their personal characteristics and abilities and the pattern of their care careers influence their progress through care and their life chances upon leaving. This pattern of diversity was apparent in the sample of 74 young people who agreed to participate in this stage of our research. In this section we will offer a brief profile of their care careers and, through selected case studies, illustrate the implications of differing careers both for young people's lives and their perceptions of their care experience. This account will enable us to set the scene for subsequent chapters that will explore their experience of transition and chart their attempts, over the first 18–24 months of independent living, to establish their lives as young adults in the community.

Of the 74 young people, 29 were male (39%) and 45 were female (61%). All were aged 16–19 years when recruited to the research. The overwhelming majority of the sample were white (88%), although nine black and mixed heritage young people were included in the research (12%).[1] In addition our sample included six young people with special needs. Five had moderate learning difficulties and four of these had been statemented as having special educational needs while at school. The sixth was a young man with serious mental health problems.

Care careers

The majority (56%) of these young people entered the substitute care and accommodation of our authorities when already teenagers. Table 3.1 shows the age distribution upon entering care.

---

1. We prefer to use the term 'mixed heritage' to describe young people of 'mixed origin'. Although as a concept it retains some ambivalence, it is a more positive alternative that alludes to the complex cultural heritage of young people who have a black and a white parent. The problems we encountered in trying to recruit more black young people have been mentioned earlier.

Table 3.1 Age at entry to care (n = 74)

	n	%
0 – 4 years	18	24
5 – 10 years	15	20
11 – 14 years	28	38
15 – 17 years	13	18

This pattern is broadly similar to that found in our survey, 62% of that sample having entered care between 11 and 17 years of age (Biehal et al 1992).[2] This tendency for a large proportion of young people to enter care in their teenage years has also been highlighted by other recent research (Garnett 1992; Rowe et al 1989; Stein and Carey 1986).

Although many may have initially been accommodated on a voluntary basis, as their careers progressed most became subject to court orders. Three quarters (55) were in statutory care prior to their move to independence. For some young people care had constituted a relatively short episode in their lives, although the disturbance it created may not have been minor, for others it represented their main life experience. Two fifths of the sample had been accommodated for ten years or more and a further quarter for between four and nine years.

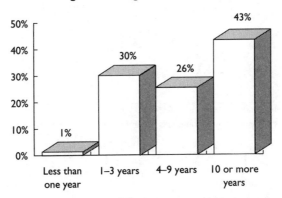

Figure 3.1 Length of time in care (n=74)

Since our sample, by definition, includes all those for whom a return home was not negotiable at an earlier stage of their care careers, the weighting towards longer-term care is perhaps not surprising. It is, however, of

2. 113 young people first entered care between 11 and 17 – 62% (n = 183).

significance that the majority spent most of their formative childhood and teenage years in care. Most, in consequence, were dependent on social services and professional carers to provide them with a stable and secure support base, to equip them with the practical and social skills they would need to manage as independent adults, to help repair their often fragile and damaged identities and to encourage their educational progress – all crucial to their future life chances. The degree to which this proved possible will form the substance of later sections of this book.

The dynamic picture of patterns of placement use, residential and foster, afforded by a care careers approach has highlighted the continuing centrality of residential care as a resource for teenagers (Cliffe and Berridge 1991; Stone 1990; Rowe et al 1989). The last placement in care for two fifths of this sample was in residential care as Table 3.2 indicates. A slightly higher proportion left from foster care and only a few young people were placed with parents or relatives prior to independence or legal discharge. Of course, last placement in care is only a crude indicator of a young person's placement history and many of these young people had experienced both types of provision during their care careers.

Table 3.2 Last 'care' placement (n = 74)

	n	%
Residential care*	30	41
Foster care	33	45
With parents	5	7
With relatives	6	8

* Residential care includes children's homes/assessment centres/independence units/CH(E)s

We have pointed to the importance of stability and security as a fundamental base for a positive experience of care. Completed research has stressed the tendency for young people in care to experience movement and disruption to their lives (Stein 1990; Berridge and Cleaver 1987; Millham et al 1986). Our survey found that fewer than one in ten young people remained in the same placement throughout their care career, two fifths made four or more moves and one in ten moved more than ten times (Biehal et al 1992). A similar pattern emerges for this follow up sample.

Figure 3.2 Movement in care (n=73)

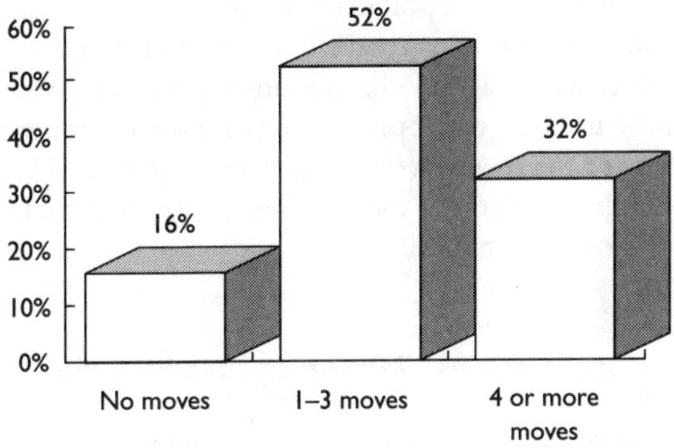

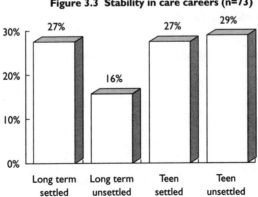

A third of this group made four or more moves during their time in care and only 16% remained in the same placement throughout.

Where placements break down young people are often left with a sense of loss and responsibility. A further move also involves them in having to negotiate relationships with a new set of carers and can involve disruption to school and family/friendship networks. Multiple moves can lead to a sense of instability and loss of constancy in young people's lives. The influence of movement for family and friendships, young people's emerging identities and especially for educational attainment will be a focus of attention in later chapters. Equally, stability in itself did not always equate with happiness and contentment for these young people. Some, whilst stable, continued to feel 'different' from other family members or were treated differently, a few experienced abuse and/or exploitation in their placements and others never recovered from the unhappiness of family separation or rejection.

In order to show the diversity of these young people's lives in care, we have grouped the sample into four categories – long-term settled and unsettled and teenage entrants both settled and unsettled.

Figure 3.3 Stability in care careers (n=73)

Although similar proportions of both long-term and teenage entrants had a stable care experience, our data points to two tendencies.[3] First, that those who entered care at an earlier age and remained in care long-term were more likely to find a settled placement, only 16% having unsettled careers and, second, that it proved more difficult for a greater proportion of those entering care as teenagers to find a stable base for themselves. Their lives were more likely to have been punctuated by further movement and for these moves to have been compressed into a relatively short time period.

Illustrations of differing care histories

Our discussion of the patterns of care careers for these young people cannot, however, do justice to the complexities and connections between their pre-care and care careers. To give greater depth to both the diversity and the realities of living in care we have selected a sample of case illustrations that correspond to the four career types outlined above.

Long-term settled – foster care

Lee entered care at two years of age as his mother could no longer cope with caring for him. Although retaining some contact with his father throughout care, he lost touch with his mother. He remained with the same foster carers throughout, found them very supportive and encouraging and felt included as part of the family. He viewed them as his real parents and felt he had experienced a 'normal' family upbringing.

"I regarded me foster parents as real parents and their kids as my brother and sister, so we were just like a real family."

---

3. A stable care career does not imply that young people made no moves, simply that their overall pattern was stable. Indeed that this was how they themselves viewed their experience of care. In addition, for teenage entrants, two or three moves compressed into a short space of time could prove very unsettling.

Long-term settled – relatives

Stephanie, her sisters and brother were abandoned by their mother when she was six years old. She and her sisters were taken in by her grandmother and a fostering arrangement was established. She remained with her gran until 17 years old when her gran died, thereby precipitating a move to her own accommodation. Living with her family, Stephanie did not regard herself as having been in care. From her perspective she had experienced a family upbringing and had little to do with her social worker until her gran's death. Conscious of not wanting to feel different to other children she perceived contact from her social worker as intrusive and resisted his involvement with her school and family life. Contact in her own right only commenced:

". . . ever since me gran died, that's when I got to talk to them (social services) meself because normally me gran used to do all the talking for us. She used to ask them for us but I can do it meself now."

Long-term – unsettled

Persistent physical abuse by his parents led to Mark entering care at nine years of age. Deeply troubled by his experiences and scapegoated while living with his family, he rejected any further contact with them. His disturbance was manifested in behaviour problems at school and in care and a pattern of truancy was established that influenced his involvement in offending and substance abuse. Care offered little stability and he experienced eight moves in the next seven years, including two secure units, and changed schools eight times. He felt that the culture of the children's homes he was in affected his pattern of offending, drug use and absconding. He had not entered for offending but others had and he felt a pressure to conform. With the exception of one children's home where "it were just like a family", he had been unhappy in care and ran away frequently:

"I couldn't handle being there. It weren't that I were getting picked on or owt . . . it were just atmosphere there, I couldn't handle it. Everywhere you went there were kids shouting and bawling."

Teenage – settled

Hannah referred herself to social services at 14 years of age after a sustained assault by her mother. Unstable pre-care and kept off school to care for her younger brothers and sisters, she found her first stability in a children's home. With positive support and encouragement from carers her school attendance improved, she made friends and felt that her experience in a semi-independent unit had helped prepare her for her future life. She felt that at each stage she had been consulted and her views listened to by her social worker and carers:

"You got to say what you wanted to happen in the future and what you wanted to do and how you wanted it to happen."

Although wary and nervous about the expectation that surrounded moving on at 17, she reflected that care had been a very positive experience for her:

"It's been a very good experience . . . I don't call it a children's home, I just call it home."

Teenage – unsettled

Jane entered care when 14 years old. A pattern of truancy and running away had placed her beyond the control of her mother. This pattern continued in care and over the next three years she had six placements in children's homes, including two out of authority placements. Unable to accept controls or the authority of adults her perception of care was that it "felt like being in the nick". Although considered 'bright' and 'articulate' she obtained no qualifications at school. She felt powerless to shape her life and that consultation was tokenistic:

"Whoever I spoke to, they always said to me, we don't know what's going to be happening, it depends on you. We got into the review and they decided they knew what was going to happen and they knew what was best for me and they knew where I was going to live and what I was going to do with my life."

Angry and confused, she was unclear why she persistently ran away and felt that staff failed to explore this with her:

". . . and then when they got me back to kid's home, I'd be grounded and all me privileges stopped . . . and that'd be it. Then three or four days later I'd be free to go out again."

Her behaviour and, despite concern from staff and social worker, the failure of care to resolve the feelings which underlay it, left her unprepared for moving on.

These illustrations should help to bring to life the perceptions of young people that follow in later sections and form a prelude to our discussion of their experience of transition from care to the community.

PART 2

This section explores our young people's experiences of transition from care to the community. It charts their attempts, over the first 18–24 months of independent living, to establish their lives as young adults in the community. It also indicates some of the ways in which schemes and social workers supported young people in different areas of their lives.

CHAPTER 4

MOVING OUT

This chapter asks when, how and why these young people made the transition from their final care placements to their first independent accommodation. It outlines the range of accommodation they moved on to and the support offered to them by leaving care schemes in planning and making this transition.

Transitions

"I loved it. It got lonely, you know, the first few days but it felt so great. I felt grown up."

"You're on your own. It's lonely. And there's nowt to do."

(YOUNG PEOPLE'S PERSPECTIVES ON MOVING TO INDEPENDENT ACCOMMODATION)

Leaving the family home to move to independent accommodation is typically one aspect of young people's transition to adult status, a marker of new adult responsibilities. Similarly, care leavers' transitions from substitute homes to their first indepedent accommodation are an important element of their broader transition to adult responsibilities and may overlap with other changes in their lives, such as the transition from school to work, or from practical and financial dependence on adult carers to greater independence in these areas. Changes in one area of a young person's life may influence the nature and pace of other transitions he or she may make. For example, in the general population those young people who make early transitions to employment are typically ahead of their peers in making personal life transitions (Banks et al, 1992), and unemployment may delay young people's transition to independent housing (Jones, 1987).

Transitions need to be understood in terms of the context in which they take place, so in order to understand the transitions the care leavers made, we need to consider the interaction between two chains of events, one belonging to the individual young people and one belonging to wider society. These two chains of events interact to structure the life histories of individuals (see Cohen, 1986).

This approach – a life course analysis – aims to tease out the ways in which the young people's transitions are structured both by their personal histories and relationships and by the broader social and economic context in which their lives take place. The transition strategies of young people leaving their last care placements are deeply interwoven with their own personal histories, the nature of their family relationships, their relationships with former carers, their economic circumstances, and the local availability of appropriate and affordable housing. The following discussion considers some of these influences on care leavers' transitions to independent accommodation and looks at the role of leaving care schemes in assisting them with this transition.

We define independent accommodation as accommodation which, unlike children's homes and foster homes, does not provide 24 hour staff cover under the direct supervision of Social Services and is not in the parental home. The majority of the young people in the sample moved on from their final care placement. Only one sixth (12) formally ceased to be looked after but made no move at this stage.

This chapter considers not only when, why and how young people move on from their final care placements, but how these questions interrelate. In her analysis of two large surveys of young people in the population as a whole Jones argues that: 'The reason for leaving home is likely to govern the age at leaving and the means by which it is done' (Jones 1987). Similarly, for some care leavers at least, the age of leaving their final care placements and the housing destinations they move on to are influenced by the reasons they choose (or are constrained) to move on at this point.

When?

The majority made the transition from (substitute) home to their first independent accommodation far earlier than other young people in the general population. Most of the young people we interviewed moved on from their final care placements at the age of only 16 or 17. Only three young people moved straight from their final care placement to live with a parent. If we exclude these three, we find that 24% of the sample (18) moved to independent accommodation at the age of 16 and 61% (45) had done so before the age of 18. Our earlier survey of 183 care leavers found a similar pattern: 29% moved to independence at the age of 16 and 60% had done so before the age of 18 (Biehal et al, 1992). Other studies have also drawn attention to the early age at which care leavers move to independence (Stein and Carey, 1986; Department of Health 1991; Garnett 1992).

The stark contrast between the transitions care leavers make from their substitute homes and the transitions from home made by young people in the general population is highlighted by a large study of young people in Scotland, which shows that the median age of leaving home is 22 years for men and 20 years for women (Jones, 1987). If we compare care leavers to young people in the general population, therefore, we see that they make an accelerated transition and have to shoulder adult responsibilities at a much earlier age than most other young people.

Figure 4.1 Median age of transition to independent accommodation in years

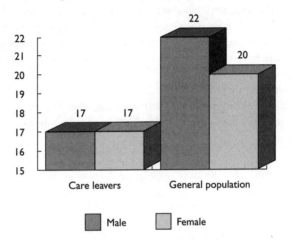

Focusing solely on the age at which social service's formal involvement ceases does not give a true picture of the number of care leavers who have to manage independently. In many cases, the young people moved on before they had formally ceased to be looked after. Two fifths of the young people we interviewed moved to independent accommodation such as flats, hostels and bedsits while they were still formally 'looked after'. This group of 'looked after' young people has to cope with greater responsibilities and potentially has equal, if not greater, support needs than their peers in foster and residential homes. Accordingly, planning for care leavers must take account of the numbers moving on from their final care placements while still 'looked after' and of the early age at which many of them do so.

How?

Among the 74 young people in our qualitative study, moves to first independent accommodation followed three broad patterns: planned moves, crisis moves and unplanned sudden moves by young people. The last group was small comprised of six young people who simply walked out of their final placements suddenly, though not in crisis situations.

Planned moves

Nearly two thirds of those who moved made planned moves from their final placements. Planning the move usually involved the young person, the social worker, the leaving care team (if involved) and foster parents or residential staff. This gave the young people an opportunity to think through the available options and consider whether they wished to move to supported accommodation, such as hostels or supported lodgings, or to fully independent accommodation. In most cases planning for the move had started between three and twelve months earlier. Where schemes were involved at an early stage, they helped to bring about transitions to independent accommodation that were well co-ordinated and showed evidence of focused planning for leaving care. As well as assisting with planning for leaving care, in a number of cases scheme workers worked with young people in their final care placements preparing them for the move. This work could range from training in practical skills and budgeting to discussing the difficulties in taking greater responsibility for their lives and strategies for coping with loneliness.

Andy's leaving care scheme worker and social worker worked closely together to plan his move out of care. His scheme worker visited him regularly in his children's home during the six months prior to his move, discussing the issues that arise for young people living out of care and giving practical preparation in domestic and budgeting skills as the children's home were failing to provide this. He agreed a programme of work with Andy and offered him a choice about the kind of help he wanted. An agreement was drawn up between Andy, his scheme worker and his social worker regarding the tasks each would undertake and the professionals' work was closely co-ordinated throughout. When Andy moved to the scheme's dispersed hostel, his scheme worker visited him regularly and assisted him in developing skills in budgeting and in negotiating with other agencies. He also helped him to extend his social networks, while his social worker counselled him about family issues. At an early stage his scheme worker began to work with Andy to plan for his eventual move to follow on accommodation.

In many cases the planning process required great sensitivity on the part of the professionals as it foregrounded questions about the young peoples' relationships with their families or foster carers and made rejection, or simply a lack of long term commitment, more explicit. For example, a few said that they wished to live with a parent or remain with a foster carer, only to be refused. In some ways, considering questions about their future could make vulnerable young people painfully aware of the lack of support actually available to them from non-professional sources. A skilled approach was also needed when some young people opted for fully independent accommodation while professionals felt they would be unable to cope without an earlier stage in supported accommodation. Ultimately, the decision lay with the young person in every case, but professionals sometimes had the sensitive task of trying to persuade some young people to make the transition to unsupported accommodation more slowly, without undermining their confidence.

Crisis moves

A substantial minority of our sample (17) left their care placements in a crisis situation. Over half of these crises arose from the breakdown of foster placements. In many cases these were long term placements which broke down as young people reached their mid-teens. In fact, well over a third of those who left foster placements to move to independent accommodation did so as a result of placement breakdown, confirming the observation by Rowe et al that 'adolescence is a risky time for foster placements' (Rowe et al, 1989). Taking all those placed in foster care (including those who remained in their foster homes once they ceased to be 'looked after'), we found an overall fostering breakdown rate of 33%, a little lower than the rate of 38% found by both Berridge and Cleaver and Rowe et al (Berridge and Cleaver, 1987; Rowe et al, 1989). For a further three young people, the move to independent accommodation was precipitated by the breakdown of a placement with parents or relatives.

It is clear, then, that many young people do not remain in long term foster placements once they reach their mid-teens and placements with parents or relatives do not necessarily offer continuing support. Indeed, young people may be asked to leave with only a few weeks' or even days' notice. For a few young men tensions with relatives or foster carers crystallised around their apparent lack of motivation in looking for employment. In some cases conflicts with carers arose over the degree of autonomy demanded by the young people as they grew older and in one case long term foster carers asked a young woman to leave when she became pregnant. In two cases an accommodation crisis was precipitated when young women walked out of unhappy or abusive foster placements.

A further five had to leave residential placements at very short notice, in four of these cases due to unacceptable behaviour, including assault and arson. One young woman, who had been given two weeks' notice to leave her children's home because staff thought her behaviour was deteriorating, felt that:

> *"leaving were like a rush job. I felt that they didn't want me . . . why are they doing this to me?"*

Leaving care schemes played a vital role in assisting the majority of those who left care in crisis situations to find accommodation, often at very short notice. Over a quarter of the young people allocated key workers by the leaving care schemes had left their final placement in a crisis situation and required urgent help with finding accommodation. This was a particular problem for the leaving care schemes in City, as nearly half of the young people they worked with had had to move on from their final care placement in a crisis. Providing emergency assistance to young people leaving care in a crisis was therefore a significant aspect of the service provided by schemes.

> Denise was thrown out by her foster parents when she became pregnant. Her social worker contacted the scheme for assistance in finding emergency accommodation and Denise was placed in a shared trainer house (dispersed hostel) with another young mother. Her scheme worker not only assisted her with the move, but worked with her on the day to day problems of living in independent accommodation and helped her arrange move on accommodation. She also worked with her on parenting skills, on managing relationships and developing greater assertiveness. Work was closely co-ordinated with Denise's social worker throughout. Denise very much appreciated having someone to turn to as she learned to adapt to two significant transitions in her life – the transitions to parenthood and to living in an independent household. It was important to her "just to know they're there if anything goes wrong."

Why?

The breakdown of foster placements and, to a lesser degree, of placements with parents or relatives and of residential placements, accounted for the early move to independent accommodation for half of the 16 year olds and for a third of all those under 18. All but one of those who left their final placement in a crisis situation was under 18. This group, therefore, had little choice over the timing and nature of their move.

For the rest of the sample, the underlying reasons for moving on were more complex. If we take the group of six young people who simply walked out of their final placements, for example, reasons for leaving varied. Four left to move in with the families of their boyfriends or girlfriends or to live nearer to them, and the other two walked out of foster homes in which they had been unhappy to stay with friends. All but one of these young people were under 18. None of these arrangements lasted very long and for most of these young people a period of instability followed as they made frequent moves.

Some young people chose to move on because they were keen to move to what they saw as total independence as quickly as possible. In these cases, the young people themselves gave the main impetus to the move. One young woman, whose foster carer was keen for her to stay, explained:

"I wasn't really getting on (with foster carer), I just wanted like to spread my wings and such and move on a bit, cos I've always wanted to do things for myself."

Most felt a mixture of excitement and anxiety about the prospect of moving on:

"I was happy because I'd have me freedom and you know, I could be up and out and about whenever I wanted, but like, I was a bit sad because I didn't know how it would be living on me own, and like, I wouldn't have me (foster) mum and dad there."

A few left before they felt ready and were unwilling to move on, or were ambivalent about the move:

"Well I thought . . . I couldn't leave (children's home) because I wouldn't be able to cope on my own. When I told (residential worker) that I'd like to stay for the rest of me life she says, well you can't."

"I wanted to leave and I didn't want to leave . . . but it had to be done sooner or later. I had to leave sooner or later."

The assumption that young people in residential placements had 'outgrown' their placements was common and was given by a number of professionals as the main reason for young people moving on when they did. As one leaving care worker put it:

"rather than looking at the needs of the young person, is this person ready for moving on, it's the old stereotyped thing. When they reach 16, 17, ship 'em out."

Several social workers also complained of this pressure to move young people out of residential placements before they were ready. As the social worker of one 17 year old woman, who lacked most social and practical skills and had minimal family support, explained:

"My feeling was that she was far too young emotionally to be let loose to live on her own, but the policy is, of course, that children of that age in care have to go out and get somewhere to live."

Young people themselves were aware of this expectation:

"You're not allowed to be there over 17 really. It's not that you're not allowed, it's more like they start giving you advice on how to look for flats and places, you know. 'Cos basically, everyone moves out round about 16, 17."

In some cases, older residents were seen as disruptive to the home's regime, demanding more autonomy and requiring a different approach from staff. Some were accused of bullying younger children or of being a bad influence on them. Others were thought to have outgrown their placements because they needed greater privacy as they grew older. Some young people also expressed the view that they had outgrown their placements and were keen to move on:

"I was too old to be there . . . I felt like a little kid."

Underlying the view that some young people had to move on when they did because they had 'outgrown' their placements lies a real difficulty faced by residential staff. If they are to provide stability for young people who remain long term in residential placements, they must cater for a wide age range that includes young people in their late teens. Yet it may be very hard for staff to meet both the needs of this group of young adults and those of younger residents, particularly when the former are sometimes disruptive and may be seen as a bad influence on children in the home. However, while moving young people on to transitional accommodation that caters solely for an older age range, such as separate semi-independence units, offers some advantages, it may build more movement into the care system, increasing the instability in the lives of these young people.

A few foster carers also made it clear that they expected young people to move on at a pre-ordained time. One young man who had lived with the same family since he was two years old had always known that they expected him to leave once he reached the age of 16 and a young woman was expected to move on from the foster home she had lived in for ten years once she reached the age of sixteen, even though this happened in the middle of her exams. Two other young men, both with learning difficulties, who had lived with the same foster carers for most of their lives, moved on reluctantly at 18. Although both had always felt 'part of the family', their foster carers were not prepared to let them stay once boarding out payments ceased. However, for one fifth of those in foster placements, foster carers were more flexible and supportive, and let young people stay on with them for several months or even longer until they had arranged accommodation and felt ready to leave, often assisting them with arranging this accommodation and moving into it.

In the majority of cases, young people making planned moves from their final placements were willing to move on and felt the mixture of excitement and anxiety described above, a desire for greater independence mixed with an understandable fear of the unknown. The timing of their moves was influenced by a mixture of a natural desire for greater autonomy and, for some, the culture of the establishments they were leaving, with their assumptions about the 'normal' age for leaving.

The momentum of the planning process itself also played a large part in determining the time at which young people moved on. Where applications to hostels or for tenancies were made, the time of moving on was governed by the time that this accommodation became available, which was out of the control of the professionals working with the young people. This could be sooner than expected, leading to a hurried move, sometimes before the young person was ready. For other young people, keen to move on, the wait for a tenancy could be much longer than expected, leaving them in placements longer than planned and sometimes feeling both children and adults in the community. All these factors have an impact upon the transitions of young people from care, help to structure their life chances and affect the levels of support that can be made available to them to ease the journey.

Part 2 of our book picks up these themes and, looking across our whole sample, explores the experience of transition for these young people in the early 1990's. In turn we cover key dimensions of their lives – their attempts to establish a home, to start a career, to construct secure identities and networks of social support for themselves as young adults in the community – and make connections between the problems they encountered during their first 18–24 months of independent living and their experiences prior to and during their time in care. Our aim is both to explore the support being made available to them from carers, social workers and leaving care schemes and to highlight the key policy and practice issues that arise from this discussion.

This provides a crucial context to the more detailed examination of leaving care schemes that forms the substance of Part 3 and to an understanding of the difficulties and challenges facing schemes as they attempt to support young people leaving care. In Part 3 we focus on those young people receiving support from schemes and evaluate the impact that their involvement had upon their lives. We profile each of the four schemes in turn, identify distinctive models or approaches and show how these influence the shape of the services they offer. We then end with a discussion of the key themes and issues that arise from our research and which situates the place of leaving care schemes within the totality of leaving care services.

Concerns about quality and the need to monitor the effectiveness of social work services have grown in recent years. This is particularly pertinent to specialist services such as those provided by leaving care schemes. Part 4 grapples with the problems inherent in constructing a realistic methodology for evaluating outcomes for young people using scheme services. Mindful of the range of influences that structure young people's life chances, we develop a 'holistic' appraoch that connects the different starting points of young people – their differing experiences, skills and abilities – to the outcomes of their scheme involvement at the close of the study. Overall outcomes for those young people using schemes are also compared to those for a 'comparison' group of young people in each authority without key worker support from a scheme. In today's contract culture it is important for schemes to develop effective ways of monitoring services and of evaluating the outcomes of their interventions. We conclude by stressing the importance of involving young people themselves, as users of the service, in the construction of service objectives and of monitoring procedures.

Our concluding chapter, in summary form, draws together some of the central themes running through the book and highlights some key elements essential to the development of effective leaving care services.

CHAPTER 2

THE THREE AUTHORITIES AND THEIR LEAVING CARE SCHEMES

The research was carried out in three very different local authority areas: **CITY** – a large northern Metropolitan District; **COUNTY** – a large Midland County Council; **DISTRICT** – a small Metropolitan District centred on a northern industrial town.[1]

City

City is one of the largest Metropolitan Districts in England with a population of 715,000. As well as the city itself, the authority includes extensive suburban and rural areas and smaller free standing towns. Its population is predominantly white (94.2%) just under 6% being of ethnic minority origin compared with 5.5% for Great Britain. Different ethnic minority groups include Black African and Black Caribbean (1.6%), Indian (1.5%), Pakistani (1.4%), Chinese and other groups (1.2%) and Bangladeshi (0.3%).

Its economy, historically rooted in the ready made clothing and engineering industries, has witnessed a major growth in the service sector since the 1950's. In 1991 just under three-quarters of its employees worked in this sector with significant concentrations in local and central government, the National Health Service, universities and colleges, banks, insurance companies, accountancy, law firms, retailing, hotels and catering. By contrast twenty per cent of employees worked in manufacturing firms making a wide variety of products including beer, battle tanks, board games, pharmaceutical and toiletries. During the 1990's City's unemployment rate has been about 9%. In 1991, 10.7% of 16–20 year olds were unemployed and 3.9% were attending government schemes.

Leaving care schemes

The City authority contains two leaving care schemes, **City (vol)** and **City (ssd)**.

---

1. The data on the three authorities in this section is extracted from the 1991 census (OPCS 1992).

frustrated because their friends had moved on but they were left behind. Giving only a two or three weeks' notice of a tenancy makes long-term preparation plans and a smoothly co-ordinated transition difficult to achieve. Closer co-operation and joint planning between housing departments or housing associations and social services regarding the timing of offers of tenancies to care leavers is therefore needed.

Where?

This section provides a 'snapshot' of the different types of accommodation to which these young people first moved. The aim is to provide a picture, albeit a static one, of the first stage of their transition. A more dynamic picture of their early housing careers will be given in the next chapter.

One fifth (20%) of the young people in our sample moved directly into council, housing association or private tenancies, 53% to intermediate households, 12% to parents/relatives and 15% made no move. However, while 20% of these care leavers became independent householders by 19 years of age, in the general population only 0.5% of those aged 16–19 are independent householders (OPCS 1993b, Table 12). While moving to tenancies of their own immediately on leaving care offered potential stability, it also brought enormous responsibilities which required a considerable degree of maturity from the young people at a very early stage in their adult lives.

Figure 4.2 Independent accommodation (n=74)

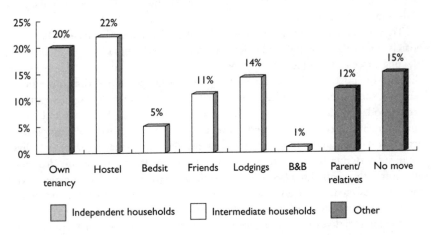

Where, then, do most other young people in this age group live? An Economic and Social Research Council (ESRC) study of 5000 young people in Great Britain found that 90% of those aged 16–17 years were living in their family home, and that this figure increased for the same cohort to 93% by the time they reached 17–18 years as many young people return to live at home again (Banks et al, 1989). Yet in our sample only six young people (8%) either moved to live with a parent on leaving their final placement, or remained with a parent with whom they had been placed once they ceased to be 'looked after,' for three or more months.

If we extend the definition of living in the family home to include living with other relatives such as grandparents, siblings, step-parents or aunts and uncles for three or more months, the proportion of care leavers who initially moved to live with parents or relatives rises only to 12 per cent. Even if we include those who stayed for brief periods of time, ranging from overnight to just a few days or weeks with a parent or other relative while waiting to move on to other accommodation or because they were homeless, the proportion of care leavers who returned to their families for any period of time at all in the first nine months after leaving care rises only to 36% of the sample. This disparity between the patterns of early household formation of care leavers and that of young people in general demonstrates the vast difference not only in the responsibilities faced by these two groups but also in the family support available to them.

Research has shown that a proportion of young people move to intermediate rather than final housing destinations when they initially leave home. Intermediate household status includes hostels, bedsits, bed and breakfast accommodation and other furnished accommodation. Analysing a large sample of young people from the General Household Survey, Jones found that by age 20–24, 13% of young adults were living in these types of transitional accommodation, although this was less common among working class young people. Even by this age, the vast majority (85%) were living with parents (Jones 1987). Among our sample of care leavers the picture was quite different, with 53% of the young people moving initially to transitional accommodation.

Transitional housing that was *supported* could offer many advantages. Dispersed hostels run by the City (vol) and County leaving care schemes offered wide-ranging 'floating support' to young people living in individual or shared flats and houses (see chapters 17 and 18 for a fuller account of these). Together with more conventional hostels for young people, transitional housing offered semi-supported accommodation as a bridge to greater independence. Some found these environments served as a useful preparation for a move to unsupported accommodation, giving them greater responsibility for managing their own lives while still offering back up support. A few were not yet ready for this degree of autonomy: three left either because they were unhappy or were fleeing violence and three were evicted. Although a number of care leavers have strong aspirations to live independently, they may nevertheless have serious problems in adapting to a lack of structure in their lives. One young woman described the difficulty of adapting to the greater freedom available in a hostel:

"I just wanted a bit more independence, but when I got to the hostel I think at first I had a bit too much independence 'cos I just like went wild at first, you know."

Supported lodgings, available in County and District at the time of the research, could also offer a useful transitional stage for young people moving out of substitute care or accommodation. However, most of our sample made only short term use of them. Of the eight who moved initially to supported lodgings, only three remained there for a period of months rather than weeks, and for these the lodgings provided a useful intermediate stage which allowed them to adjust to taking greater responsibility for their lives while still having an adult to whom they could turn for support. In addition, for three other young people who remained in their former foster homes once their care orders expired, the foster placements were converted to supported lodgings placements and continued to be funded by Social Services, a straightforward means of allowing the young people continuing stability in placements they regarded as their home.

Of the seven young people who moved to unsupported transitional accommodation – bedsits, bed and breakfast accommodation or board and lodgings – six moved following placement breakdown. This was primarily used as emergency accommodation and most of the young people stayed only a short time. This accommodation offered little stability and usually no support. Finally, all but one of the eight who moved initially to stay with friends, lived with the families of their boyfriends or girlfriends. In most instances, these arrangements were short-lived and for most of these young people a period of instability followed during which they made several moves.

Nearly three quarters of the young people moved initially to shared accommodation. However, even a move to shared and supported accommodation could feel very lonely. As a 17 year old woman, who moved abruptly to a hostel when her children's home closed down, reflected:

> *"At first when I left (children's home) it was really, really difficult because, like, I was used to having everybody around me all the time, you know. Just living by myself, it was awful. I hated it. But now it's alright . . . I cried when I left (children's home)."*

The nature of the first accommodation that the young people moved to was governed by a mixture of their personal circumstances and the support available to them. The local availability of different types of supported accommodation varied across our three local authorities, and this variable provision, together with differences in local housing markets, also governed the choices made by care leavers. Those young people in contact with the leaving care schemes were more likely to move to supported accommodation, as they were able to benefit from the specialist knowledge and resources of the schemes. Schemes offered these care leavers the opportunity to consider a range of possible accommodation options, depending on their specific needs at the point of transition from care. They also offered much needed support to those who struggled to adapt to their new circumstances. Many of the young people felt unprepared for coping with life out of care and found it much tougher than they had expected.

> *"Well they could have told me it was going to be a bit harder, living on your own. 'Cos it ain't exactly easy."*

> *"I thought it would be easier but it hasn't been. It hasn't been as easy as I expected."*

And one young man who had lived a very sheltered life in a Catholic children's home for many years could not cope with the transition to his own house at all. His leaving care worker commented:

"He never had food in when I went . . . it's come as a great shock to him."

Whether young people moved to supported accommodation or to independent households, their difficulties in coping with the practicalities of life in independent accommodation were compounded, for many, by loneliness:

"Well the worst of it is not having someone I really know to talk to."

"Well it's just there's no-one to talk to when you've got a cold or something, or when you're feeling poorly there's no-one there."

For young people such as these, experiencing difficulties in adapting to living in independent accommodation, support from key workers after they had made their initial transition was just as important as scheme assistance in planning and preparing for the move.

Staying on

Eleven young people in our follow up sample (15%) made no move, remaining in placements with parents, relatives or foster carers after their care orders were discharged. Four of these were living in placements with parents or relatives. Of the other seven, who had all been in foster placements, four had lived with their foster families long term, most of them since babyhood. These young people saw themselves as 'part of the family' and this view was shared by their foster carers. As one young man who had been placed with the same family since he was two explained, it was 'common sense' to remain at home until he felt ready to leave. There was simply no question of him making a transition that was in any way different from his peers who had grown up in their birth families. One of these long term foster placements was funded as supported lodgings after the young person's 18th birthday because the young man in question had moderate learning difficulties and needed continuing support from his former foster carers.

Three young women who had lived with their current foster families for only two to three years were also able to remain with them past their eighteenth birthday. All three planned to move into their own flats soon and there was an understanding between them and their foster carers that they would remain only short term. One of these placements was funded as supported lodgings.

Overall, then, only a fifth (21%) of those whose last placement was with foster carers remained in their foster homes for at least a few months once they formally ceased to be looked after at the age of 18. Our earlier survey of 183 care leavers found a similar percentage (18%) remaining with foster carers, although the National Foster Care Association found that only 5.5% of care leavers continued to live with their former foster carers (Biehal et al 1992; NFCA 1992).

Why, then, did the vast majority move on from their foster homes? As we have already seen, 33% (11) of the young people whose last placements were in foster care left as a result of placement breakdown and in another four cases foster carers expected the young people to move on once they reached the age of 16 or 18, even though the young people were reluctant to do so. In three cases young people moved on because their foster placements had been intended as a short term bridge to independence and had lasted as long as planned. Five other young people chose to move on, either because they wanted to move to independent accommodation or because they were unhappy in their foster homes, and a further four left their foster carers because the foster families moved to another part of the country.

If we consider placement breakdowns, pressure on young people to leave foster homes before they felt ready and young people's departure due to unhappiness as negative reasons for leaving, we can see that half of those whose final placement was in foster care left for negative reasons – an indication that many teenage foster placements are problematic and that a high level of support is needed. The duration of a foster placement was not an indicator of whether a young person would have the option of staying on in their foster homes after 18 years of age. Some of those who had been in the same foster home since early childhood were expected to move on immediately funding stopped, while others who had been with foster carers only since their mid-teens were allowed to stay on until they found suitable move-on accommodation. Whilst pressure on placements and problems with funding lie at the heart of some of these movements, it nevertheless remains the case that the majority of young people whose last placement was in foster care could not rely on their foster carers to continue to offer a home once they had reached their eighteenth birthday.

Moving on: scheme support

As we have seen, in most cases young people made planned transitions to their first independent accommodation. Where leaving care schemes were involved, planning and preparation for the move began up to a year earlier. Schemes were able to offer valuable advice on local accommodation resources, help with deciding on the most appropriate form of move on accommodation and help with finding this accommodation. In some cases schemes offered comprehensive preparation for leaving care, including assistance with practical skills, budgeting, negotiating skills and the development of social networks in the community. For those who left care in crisis situations, schemes played a vital role in finding accommodation in emergency situations and supporting care leavers in their transition to this accommodation. Young people benefited most where schemes and social workers agreed a clear division of roles and responsibilities and closely co-ordinated their work. The schemes' continuing support to young people in the early stages after they had moved to their first independent accommodation was highly valued by many of the young people.

Schemes were not only able to offer specialist knowledge of local housing options but in some cases had developed links with local housing agencies. Some schemes also played a valuable role in developing local accommodation resources for care leavers and were able to offer supported transitional accommodation in specialist hostels, dispersed hostels or supported lodgings. Where supported transitional accommodation of this kind was not available, or not desired by the young people, schemes assisted young people in finding accommodation in the private, voluntary and public sectors of the housing market and supported them in making these transitions to independent households.

However, for a number of care leavers, transitions from care were problematic, and these raise issues that require further consideration.

• Summary Points •

Nearly two thirds of the care leavers made their transitions from (substitute) home to independent accommodation before the age of 18, and of these a quarter had moved to independence at the age of 16. Care leavers are required to cope with adult responsibilities at a far earlier age than other young people in the general population.

- There is need to challenge informal practices and formal policies which create pressure for young people to move on before they are ready to do so. Moving on should be 'needs' and not 'age' related.

The breakdown of foster placements and, to a lesser extent, residential placements and placements with parents, precipitated a significant minority into a hurried, crisis move to independence. The duration of foster placements was not a predictor of their stability once young people reached their mid teens. Where foster placements had broken down, young people were deprived of potential continuing support from foster families once they moved into the community.

- Particular attention should be given to supporting foster placements as young people reach their mid-teens, as even long term and apparently stable foster placements are at risk of breakdown at this stage.

- In residential placements, there was often an assumption that young people should move on once they reach the age of 16 or 17. In part, this arose from the difficulty of catering for the needs of a wide age range within one establishment. However, moving young people on to specialist accommodation builds in yet more movement to care careers that in many cases have offered little stability. These difficult questions require further attention.

- Where young people wish to remain in foster placements beyond the age of 18, consideration should be given to changing the status of this accommodation to supported lodgings thereby enabling social services financial support to continue. Arrangements for foster carers to provide continuing support of other kinds should also be formalised and supported.

- In some cases, the momentum of the planning process itself led to rapid and early moves to independent accommodation when tenancies were offered earlier than expected. Closer co-operation and joint planning between housing departments or housing associations and social services regarding the timing of offers of tenancies to care leavers is therefore needed.

Care leavers are a diverse group with different needs. Some wanted to move directly to independent tenancies but for others, who were not yet ready for this, transitional housing that was *supported* could offer many advantages. This included hostels, dispersed hostels and supported lodgings.

- As a group, care leavers need a range of different types of accommodation, offering varied levels of support.

Leaving care schemes played a valuable role in planning transitions from care, in preparing young people for these transitions and in providing follow up support. They also played a vital role in assisting those young people whose transitions from care occurred in crisis situations. Schemes offered specialist knowledge of local housing provision and in some cases developed links with housing providers or themselves provided supported transitional accommodation. Well planned transitions involved the provision of wide ranging preparation and follow on support, and good co-ordination with social workers and with other agencies.

CHAPTER 5

EARLY HOUSING CAREERS

This chapter discusses the different types of accommodation young people moved to in the first 18–24 months after leaving care. It examines the reasons for the instability in their early housing careers and considers the support they received.

For many young people leaving home is a gradual process. They may leave and return on a number of occasions (Jones 1987; Banks et al, 1992). For most young people moving away from home is usually a matter of choice. Young people may move to go to college, to get a job, to set up home with a partner, with friends or perhaps alone. Yet as we saw in the previous chapter the majority of care leavers are expected to leave their (substitute) homes to live independently before the age of 18, paradoxically far earlier than most young people leave home. The parameters within which they may exercise choice about when to move on are set by the very fact that they are in care.

This chapter will consider the early housing careers of these young people. The concept of a housing career is similar to that of an employment career – a dynamic concept which looks at an individual's movement through different kinds of accommodation over a period of time. In considering the types of households that the young people moved to and the degree of movement in their early housing careers, we will see how far their housing careers were shaped by choice or constraint. In fact, there is not a clear dichotomy between the two: opportunities available to the young people may be limited by constraints such as local housing provision, the level of family support they can rely on, or their economic circumstances. Choices may be influenced by personal circumstances such as parenthood, the desire to cohabit with a partner, willingness to live alone or to live in shared accommodation. The type of professional support available from leaving care schemes or social workers may also have an impact on the range of choices available to the young person. Social class is also a major indicator of the extent to which constraint may modify choice (Jones, 1987). So opportunities and choice in young people's housing careers may be structured by both individual and social factors.

Major social policy changes and the changing housing market in recent years helped to structure the early housing careers of the care leavers in our sample by making it more difficult for all young people on low incomes to live independently of their families. The 1980's saw a marked decline in the availability of low cost rented housing, with the supply of private rented housing declining by 65% between 1971 and 1985 and a decline of 80% in new local authority housing between 1978 and 1988 (Jordan, 1992). The 1988 Housing Act also made it more difficult for young people to gain access to low cost housing, with a reduction in protection for tenants and the ending of rent restrictions in the private sector.

During the same period, the 1986 and 1988 Social Security Acts brought a switch from 'needs' to 'age' related assessments, a withdrawal of entitlement to income support for 16 and 17 year olds and a reduction in support to those under 24 years of age, although some short term discretionary support is available for young people estranged from their families. The underlying assumption is that young people can turn to their families for support. Care leavers, however, often do not have this option as many of them cannot rely on the same level of family support that may be available to their peers in the general population. The impact of these policy changes provides a context for the following discussion.

Households

By the time of our final interview, 18–24 months after the young people had first left care, a much smaller proportion of them were living in *intermediate households*.

Figure 5.1 T3 Intermediate households (n=53)

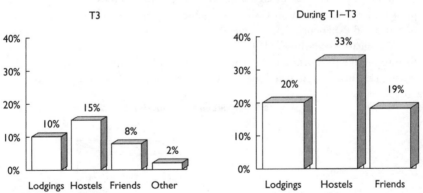

Overall, the proportion staying in these intermediate households had dropped from 53% when they first left care to only 35% of those remaining in the sample. However, this 'snapshot' of where the young people were living when last interviewed under represents the actual use made of these forms of transitional housing. If we consider the 'flow' of their early housing careers we can see that during a period of up to two years after they left care, a third stayed in hostels of some kind, a fifth stayed in lodgings (either in supported lodgings or ordinary board and lodgings arrangements) and a fifth stayed with friends at some stage.

The types of hostels varied enormously, including specialist hostels for care leavers, homeless hostels, mother and baby hostels, hostels for women fleeing violence, a hostel for young men with learning difficulties and one for young people recovering from mental illness. Many of those staying in supported accommodation found the support they received invaluable. For example, a young woman in County highly appreciated the specialist hostel for young mothers she was staying in, which required residents to pursue further education or training and provided a crèche to enable them to do so. This young woman was enthusiastic about the opportunities it provided:

"I've got it made here, I've got it made and like, I'm going to get everything I can out of it. My son's in a beautiful crèche, what more do I want? It gives you friends here as well, so, say you're in trouble and that, you've got someone to turn to."

A young man staying with an older woman friend and her family also recognised that he needed some support at this stage in his life, having lost his council tenancy and then spent several months in custody. He felt that his friend was a stabilising influence and that he was not yet ready to live in a tenancy of his own again:

"I just prefer to stay 'cos I don't think I can cope on me own. I'd probably end up going round nicking cars again and stuff . . . I'd still let me mates come round and like it'd still be noisy and stuff like that."

A few, however, were so ill-equipped that they could not cope even in supported accommodation and were evicted or rapidly moved out. For these young people, the pressure to leave care at an early age together with the effects of their personal histories and experiences led to severe problems.

Turning to those who lived in *independent households*, we see that, corresponding to the drop in the proportion of intermediate households, within 18–24 months after leaving care many more care leavers had become independent householders.

Figure 5.2 Independent households

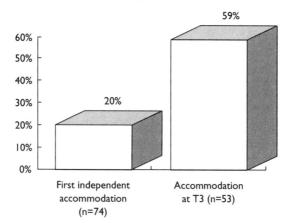

The proportion of young people now living as independent householders had trebled since they had first moved out of care, rising from 20% in council, housing association and private rented flats or houses (n=74) to 59% of the remaining sample by the time the research ended (n=53). All but one of these young people was aged 19 or younger, yet, as we saw in the previous chapter, in the general population only 0.5% of 16–19 year olds are independent householders, compared to 59% (31) among this group of care leavers. If we consider the movement in their early housing careers it becomes clear that, although the majority managed reasonably well, a substantial minority were ill-equipped to do so. A third of the young people who moved to council or housing association tenancies during their first two years after leaving care subsequently lost or gave up these tenancies. Some either lost or moved out of their tenancies because they could not cope with so much autonomy, found it hard to budget or to maintain reasonable relations with neighbours. Others left through loneliness, because the property was damaged or due to harassment. After years in care where their day to day life was supervised and controlled, which was especially the case for those who had spent long periods in residential care, many experienced real problems in adjusting to living alone. As one young man commented when explaining his decision to give up his flat and go travelling. "I couldn't get used to being by myself, I were finding it hard." He added that he missed the structure of living in his children's home and would have liked to return there:

"It was the system. There was a routine every day and you knew what was happening and you knew what were coming."

A common problem was difficulty in controlling their own space, as in a number of cases groups of other young people would virtually take over a young person's flat or house, using it as a drop in centre at all hours. This could cause problems with neighbours and could make it difficult for young people to establish a reasonable routine which would enable them to establish or sustain a place at college, training establishments or in employment. A leaving care worker in District felt that young women were particularly vulnerable in this respect:

"We've had more problems with young women being taken advantage of, having their flats taken out of their hands practically by local youths who use it as a dropping in centre. We've had that happening more with young women than with young men."

In addition, three young people who were in private tenancies had to move on due to problems with security of tenure. Although private tenancies can provide flexibility, they may be insecure or temporary and do not offer the same potential stability as tenancies in the public or voluntary sector. Insecurity of tenure meant that these young people were likely to need further assistance in finding accommodation. So, while the availability of independent tenancies, (particularly council and housing association tenancies), can provide a welcome stability for care leavers, it is important to remember that many continue to have considerable support needs if they are to maintain their homes successfully.

Loneliness was a problem for many of the young people living alone. Several sought to resolve this by moving closer to other family members or to districts with which they were more familiar. The lack of social networks was particularly difficult for a number of young mothers who complained of feeling 'cooped up' or isolated on estates where they knew nobody. As one isolated young mother explained, she was unhappy living on a council estate in an unfamiliar area because "It's not my area, I wasn't brought up here."

Parental/family households constituted the third type of household that the young people stayed in. When last interviewed only two young people were staying with a parent or other relative, but during the research period nearly half of the young people had stayed with parents or other relatives at some stage. However, in most cases these stays were only very brief stops, ranging from a few days to a few weeks. For those who stayed only briefly, the majority did so because they were homeless and looking for alternative accommodation. For them, staying with relatives constituted a brief emergency stop. Only a sixth (12) lived with relatives for three or more months during this two year period. In contrast, Jones' analysis of the housing careers of a large sample of young people found that over two thirds were still living at home by their nineteenth birthday (Jones, 1987). Other studies have also shown that many young people who first leave home later move back to live with parents (Banks et al, 1992; Jones, 1987). It is clear from this that most care leavers are not able to rely on the level of family support available to many of their peers.

For many of these young people families offered a respite from the vagaries of the housing market, not a home. Reasons for this varied. In some cases, the young people themselves did not wish to return home for more than a very short time because of long standing difficulties in family relationships or because reconstituted families now contained new members they found hard to accept. In other cases, families made it clear that they were not prepared to allow the young people to move back on more than a very short term basis and, in some cases, overcrowding was a problem. As one young man who had been in long term foster care explained, his father did not want him to stay, but would not have put him out on the street. Eventually, he explained:

> *"I had to move away from my dad's because he didn't want the responsibility at the end of the day."*

The assumption that care leavers staying with parents are living in a stable situation is questionable and individual circumstances need to be assessed in every case.

Movement

There was a high degree of mobility among the young people in the early months after they left care. It is important to distinguish here between positive and negative reasons for movement. Some moves by young people of this age may be positive –

they may move to find a job, to be closer to their families, to set up home with a partner and/or a baby. So some degree of mobility is normal for this age group. In the general population young people usually move progressively towards better quality and more secure forms of accommodation during their early housing careers (Jones 1987). However, other moves may be for negative reasons – perhaps due to crises in the young person's life, insecure tenure in the private rented housing sector, or an inability to sustain a tenancy resulting in eviction.

By the time of our first interview, which took place in the early weeks or months after leaving care, many young people had already moved on from their initial accommodation. This high degree of mobility persisted throughout the research period.

Figure 5.3 Movement since leaving care

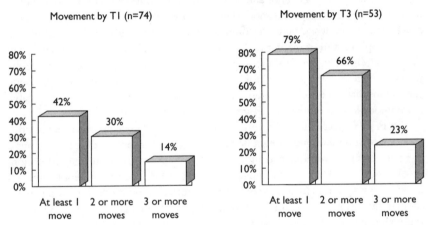

Within only a few weeks or months of leaving care, nearly a third had already made two or more *additional* moves since leaving care and nearly a seventh had made three or more moves. Indeed, 18–24 months after leaving care over half had made two or more additional moves and a sixth had made five or more moves. Our earlier survey of 183 care leavers also found a high degree of mobility in their early housing careers. 39% had made one or more moves in the first nine months after leaving care and 11% had made four or more moves (Biehal et al, 1992)[1]. Early housing careers were therefore unstable for many of the young people.

There was no clear association between mobility in the early months after leaving care and movement while the young people were in substitute care or accommodation. Also, at this stage, there was no significant difference in the degree

---

1. This may be an underestimate as it was based solely on information provided by social workers, but in nearly a quarter of the cases social workers said they did not know how many times young people had moved.

of mobility between young people receiving help from leaving care schemes and those who were not. However, for many of those who had key workers at leaving care schemes, scheme workers provided much needed assistance in finding alternative accommodation when they had to move on in difficult circumstances. Within two years of leaving care, three quarters of those with very unstable early housing careers, that is, those who had made three or more additional moves were being assisted by the schemes. For many of these young people the scheme workers' extensive knowledge of local housing resources proved invaluable.

In a few cases (9) young people moved initially to relatives or friends, then moved on to hostel, tenancies or supported lodgings when these became available. These might be construed as moves for positive reasons, as they were moves to better or more stable accommodation. Nevertheless, these cases beg the question of why the young people were not able to remain a few more weeks or months in their final care placements until this more stable accommodation became available. Some moves were made when better accommodation became available. For example, 31 young people moved from intermediate households to tenancies of their own during this period, although not all of them stayed in these tenancies. Some of the moves by young women may be accounted for by the fact that, within 18–24 months of leaving care, almost half had become parents and most had therefore made a move to stable accommodation, in most cases council or housing association tenancies.

Of more concern are those young people who made several moves within this short space of time for what might be seen as negative reasons, leading to disruption in their personal lives and making it hard for them to sustain further education, training or work. Many of the moves came about because young people with no stable accommodation (neither short term supported accommodation nor tenancies of their own) moved to or from temporary stops with friends or relatives. A third of the young people did this at some stage and some of them moved between a succession of short stays with friends or relatives because they had no suitable alternative accommodation at the time. Some of these young people had initially moved to supported lodgings or hostels when they left care, but had moved on to stay temporarily with friends or relatives because they had been unhappy or had been asked to leave. However, a number of the others had made their initial transition from care placements to accommodation with friends or relatives which proved to be only of a very short term nature.

For many of the young people moves were generated by crises. Within two years of leaving care, over a quarter of the young people had left their accommodation at some point because of a crisis, half of them because they had been evicted and the rest because they were fleeing harassment or violence. Looking more closely at the group of twelve who made five or more moves, of whom two thirds were young men, the reasons for this high number of moves appear to vary by gender. For most of these young men the high degree of movement was associated with behaviour problems or depression, and for half of them their involvement in criminal and drug-related sub-cultures required them to keep moving on, often to avoid violence. Two of the young men, one of whom had moderate learning difficulties, were particularly vulnerable to harassment and exploitation. As for the young women, their initial accommodation had broken down for a variety of reasons (in two cases due to violence by a boyfriend or relative), and they had moved through a succession of short stays with friends, relatives or in private rented housing, unable to find a secure tenancy.

Those who made a higher number of moves (three or more) moved most often from short stays with friends or relatives, from bedsits or from private rented flats and houses. Moves from hostels and from council or housing association tenancies were less common among this group. This may suggest a need for greater use of hostels and supported lodgings for young people who need to spend a transitional period in supported accommodation, together with easier access to council and housing association tenancies for care leavers who are ready to become independent householders.

Homelessness

There has been growing concern in recent years about the association between a care background and subsequent homelessness (Young Homelessness Group, 1991; Randall, 1989 and 1988). Research by Centrepoint in 1988 found that 34% of the young homeless had been in care at some point in their lives (Randall 1988). During a six month period in 1993, 29% of all young people seen by Centrepoint had been in care and nearly half of these were only 16 or 17 years old (Strathdee and Johnson, 1994). The percentage of those no longer 'looked after' who subsequently become homeless has therefore dropped only slightly since the implementation of the Children Act.

Our study approached this issue from a different perspective, looking at what proportion of a cohort of care leavers subsequently experienced homelessness within an 18–24 month period after leaving care. Of our sample, 22% (16) were homeless at some point during this period and a few experienced homelessness on more than one occasion. As all the three authorities studied had leaving care schemes, a significant part of whose work was both individual assistance with accommodation and the development of housing initiatives for care leavers, our figures may possibly underestimate the true scale of the problem across the country as a whole.

Nearly two thirds of those who became homeless stayed in hostels for the homeless and/or slept rough for a while. The rest could be described as the hidden homeless, moving between a succession of brief stops with relatives or friends because they had nowhere else to stay. There was an association between homelessness and leaving care at an early age, as four fifths of the young people who were homeless had left care before the age of 18. Half of the young people became homeless at the age of only 16 or 17, a figure close to Centrepoint's finding that 42% of homeless care leavers were 16 or 17 (Strathdee and Johnson, 1994). Even for young people in the general population, leaving home under 18 is an age of great risk as the numbers of homeless people are increasing fastest among the 16–18 age group (Jones, 1993). For care leavers, leaving care at only 16 or 17 clearly increases the risk of homelessness.

Young men were more likely to be homeless than young women, as by the end of the study there were nearly twice as many young women in the sample as young men, yet more than half of the homeless were young men. Although in the general population people from black and other minority ethnic groups are more likely to experience homelessness, in our study this was not the case, (see Strathdee and Johnson, 1994). The ethnic origin of the young people was not associated with risk of homelessness, although numbers of black young people in our sample were very small so it may be unwise to draw firm conclusions from this. In one case, though, racism was indeed a contributing factor to the eviction of a black young woman. Homelessness among care leavers appeared to be more of a problem in City and County, as the homeless were evenly distributed between these two authorities. In the much smaller authority of District, only one young person became homeless, a young man with moderate learning difficulties whose family vandalised his flat.

What, then, were these young people's routes into homelessness? First, over a third became homeless following eviction, either as a result of noisy and disruptive behaviour or due to theft of property from the owners of the accommodation. Half of the young people were accommodated in tenancies or bedsits of their own before they became homeless but lacked the personal and social skills to sustain a tenacy, either finding it hard to cope with the lack of structure in their lives or allowing their accommodation to be taken over (and in two cases vandalised) by others, leading to a breakdown in relations with neighbours and landlords or to the young person leaving their accommodation on impulse because they felt unable to cope. For three, the need to flee violence contributed to their becoming homeless and in one case severe depression was a factor. A quarter of the homeless had to leave temporary accommodatin with their families because relationships had broken down. Over half of these young people lacked the personal resources and social skills needed for independent living and a third had chaotic lifestyles, in a few cases associated with involvement with drugs or crime. On the other hand, for a quarter the primary reason for homelessness was their difficulty in finding affordable and stable accommodation coupled with the impossibility of living with their families for more than very brief periods.

While *triggers* to homelessness were associated in many cases with emotional and social difficuties experienced by the young people, it should be recognised that one of the reasons that these problems *resulted* in homelessness was because the young people were subsequently unable to find accommodation. Their problems, therefore, were compounded by a lack of affordable accommodation for young single people. Also, some of those who became homeless disappeared for a while, so that social workers and scheme workers were unable to help them.

Income and employment status are also of relevance here. In their study of young people living away from home Kirk et al identified clear links between youth homelessness and the decline in the youth labour market (Kirk et al 1991). The effects of homelessness and unemployment on one another can work both ways as losing a job or persistent unemployment can contribute to young people losing their accommodation, and a lack of stable accommodation can make it impossible for a young person to find a job or take up further education or training. Several young people commented that finding stable accommodation was, to them, a pre-requisite for putting other aspects of their life in order. Understandably, they found it hard to focus on employment or training while they were preoccupied with finding accommodation. Over two thirds of those who were homeless were also unemployed. Of the others, three young women were caring for their children and only two (one eighth) were in employment or education.

The support needs of homeless care leavers are enormous, particularly as the reasons for their homelessness are so complex. Two thirds of the homeless were in contact with leaving care schemes and most of these were receiving help from a keyworker. Leaving care schemes clearly have a vital role to play here, one which addresses not only the accommodation needs of the young people but also the emotional, social, family and employment issues that contribute to their homelessness.

Markets and money, policy and practice

Local housing markets played a part in shaping the housing careers of the young people. Kirk et al have noted how changes in housing policy in the 1980's, with the gradual shift towards home ownership, and the decline in the private rented sector in recent years, have worked to the extreme disadvantage of youth (Kirk et al, 1991). The young people in this study certainly felt the impact of this contraction in the private sector. A number of young people found it hard to find accommodation in the private rented sector and were obliged to move between a number of short stops with friends or relatives. Yet despite difficulties of access over a fifth of the care leavers stayed in private rented bedsits, flats or houses at some stage. At the close of our study, however, only four young people were in private tenancies. For some of these young people there were particular difficulties with insecurity of tenure and high rents which forced them to move on again. While the private rented housing market can be a useful source of transitional accommodation for care leavers, the shortage of affordable properties and insecurity of tenure pose considerable problems for them and, indeed, for any young people on low incomes.

Local public and voluntary sector housing policy and practice and the local availability of council and housing association tenancies also had an impact on the young people's housing careers. In County, council housing stock in rural areas was far more limited than in the principal city. This could pose problems for young people who applied to be housed near their families. As at least one young person found when she applied for housing near her family in a small town that she would have a very long wait for accommodation in that area, despite her particular need for family support. There could also be problems in implementing the Children Act at local level in local authority housing departments. Although the central Single Strategy section of City's housing department showed a real commitment to the needs of care leavers and worked closely with the leaving care schemes, a City social worker complained that her local housing office seemed to be oblivious to the spirit of the Children Act in failing to take account of the needs of a deeply depressed and isolated young man, living alone in a private rented house, who wanted to move across to the other side of the city to be near his father.

The choices available to care leavers looking for accommodation were therefore structured by a variety of factors. Crucially, the economic resources available to them modified their chances of finding accommodation. Poverty, unemployment and the lack of affordable housing all had an impact. Local housing markets in the public, voluntary and private sectors also structured the choices they could make.

At a more individual level, the types of household the young people lived in were also determined by the stage the young people had reached in their transitions to adult life, in particular their marital/partnership status and their parental status. Gender also played a part, as many more young women became parents and some had to flee violence from partners. Young people's readiness to cope with independent living, their particular abilities and motivation, and the level of family support available to them all influenced the degree of movement in the young people's early housing careers.

Support to care leavers

In our three local authorities, social services and leaving care schemes intervened to improve care leavers' opportunities in the housing market. Through developing links with statutory and voluntary housing providers, to varying degrees, the schemes were able to ensure a flow of permanent tenancies for care leavers. In District and County, joint ventures undertaken with housing agencies helped to ensure a wider range of options. In these two authorities social services were funding care leavers' accommodation indirectly through supported lodgings placements and, in County, through partnership arrangements with housing associations for leaving care hostels and a dispersed hostel. County also funded workers in hostels around the county, in return for negotiated access for a quota of care leavers. On an individual level, scheme assistance to care leavers to help them find and sustain placements or tenancies helped them make the transition to living in independent accommodation. Equally important was support to care leavers who needed to find new accommodation at times of crisis. Through a variety of initiatives, schemes were therefore able to increase the range of accommodation options available to care leavers and support them in sustaining tenancies.

• Summary points •

Only a sixth of the sample lived with family members for three or more months after leaving care, although nearly half had brief stays with parents or extended family at some stage. These arrangements were often unsatisfactory. For most, a return home to live with their families for more than a few days or weeks was simply not an option.

Extensive use was made of transitional forms of accommodation such as hostels, lodgings and stays with friends. Many of the young people who were not yet ready for independent accommodation found an intermediate stay in supported accommodation to be a helpful preparation for greater independence but stays with friends were usually short lived. A few could not cope or were unhappy in supported accommodation and rapidly moved out or were evicted.

A fifth (20%) moved to independent tenancies in the public, voluntary or private sector when they first left care and this figure rose to 59% 18–24 months later. Some were ill-prepared for living in an independent household and one third subsequently lost or gave up their tenancies, unable to cope with this degree of autonomy. Loneliness was a problem for a number of those living alone and, for some, finding a tenancy close to family members was very important. Problems with security of tenure and high rents made tenancies in the private sector more difficult to sustain. Many of those in independent accommodation needed considerable support in order to sustain their tenancies.

There was a high degree of mobility, with over half making two or more moves and a sixth making five or more moves within two years of leaving care. For those who made several moves, movement was often precipitated by a crisis or by their inability to cope with living indepedently, even in supported accommodation. Just over one fifth (22%) became homeless at some stage.

Leaving care schemes provided valuable support in helping care leavers find accommodation, often in times of crisis, and in helping them sustain their tenancies. Indirect support to care leavers was also given through the development of supported lodgings schemes, directly managed hostels and a variety of partnership arrangements with housing providers.

- The high level of mobility in the early housing careers of many care leavers means that many will continue to require help with accommodation for some time after they have made their initial move out of care. Help is required both in finding accommodation and in sustaining tenancies. Many of those living in independent households need continuing support in order to prevent the breakdown of these tenancies.

- Social services should facilitate access to a range of both supported and unsupported accommodation, to meet the varied needs of different care leavers. There is a need for flexibility and a recognition that some may not find it easy to settle straight away and may need access to different types of accommodation at different times. Partnership arrangements with housing agencies to provide hostel places or tenancies for care leavers and the development of supported lodgings schemes may extend the range of options for care leavers.

- Access to council and housing association tenancies should be facilitated as these provide greater security of tenure than tenancies in the private sector. Within local authorities, there is a need for co-ordination of the work of social services and housing departments to meet the accommodation needs of care leavers.

- Care leavers should have opportunity to return to care placements if necessary, just as other young people may leave home and return to their families on a number of occasions before finally leaving. Flexibility is needed, instead of a rigid division between provision for young people in substitute care or accommodation and services for those who have left care.

- Continuing support from social workers and schemes should be wide ranging. Success or difficulty in other life areas – for example, practical and social skills or careers – act reciprocally on young people's ability to maintain their homes.

CHAPTER 6

SCHOOLING AND CARE

In this chapter we will explore some of the factors which
influenced the in-care educational progress of the young people in
our sample and their attainment at the end of schooling.
We will also point to the importance of attainment for their
future life chances.

As we have seen, the transition from care to independent accommodation tends to
be accelerated for 'looked after' young people and to overlap with other key
dimensions of transition, in particular with their attempts to negotiate a successful
route from school to work. For most care leavers, without the security of the parental
home, gaining entry to youth labour markets is a priority and success or failure in this
area may act reciprocally on other aspects of their lives; for example, their ability to
manage their accommodation or to sustain friendship networks and an active social
life.

In relation to education, the mid teenage years represent a time for consolidating
past experiences and achievements and making choices about future career
directions. However, as a life course approach would suggest, these choices are not
unconstrained. They are made within definite and limiting structural contexts.
Recent research has pointed to the continuing impact of social class and family
background, region, gender and 'race' on the shaping of career routes and identities
(Roberts 1993; Banks et al 1992). This major study of 5000 young people found that
qualifications earned by the age of 16 ". . . proved the best single predictor of the
direction that individuals' careers would then take", but that the ability to acquire
qualifications at this stage was profoundly influenced by social class background
(Roberts 1993 p.230). The study also emphasised that paths taken at this stage
tended to be decisive. By the age of 19 ". . . career patterns have crystallised into the
routes to permanent destinations in the labour market" (Banks et al p.2). They have
developed a certain fixity from which it is hard to recover.

Given the significance attached to attainment at this stage, young people entering
care are likely to be disadvantaged. They are overwhelmingly drawn from the most
deprived working class families (Bebbington and Miles 1989; Social Services
Committee 1984). Accumulated evidence suggests that the disadvantaged social

class origins of these young people will have a major influence upon their educational attainment (Coleman, Hofler and Kilgore 1981; Halsey et al 1980). For many young people entering care, the disturbance and stress related to their damaging pre-care experiences including neglect and physical, sexual and emotional abuse will also have a major impact on their educational careers (Heath et al 1994; Stein 1994).

However, consistent concern has been expressed that, rather than helping to compensate for poor pre-care educational experiences, the care process itself has tended to compound them (Report to the Social Services Committee 1984). Educational development has tended to have a low profile for social workers relative to meeting the welfare needs of accommodated children (Aldgate et al 1993; Jackson 1988/9). As the Department of Health sums up in its guidance document 'Looking After Children':

". . . just being in care is not usually in itself a primary cause of educational failure. It is rather that children bring their educational problems in to care with them and too often care experience does little to ameliorate these deficiencies"

(DEPARTMENT OF HEALTH 1991A: P.9).

Attainment

Completed research in this area has tended to confirm official concerns about the poor educational attainment of young people in the care system (Aldgate et al 1993; Jackson 1988/9; Heath et al 1989). Samples of care leavers have also shown that the vast majority left school without recognised qualifications (Garnett 1992; Stein 1990; Stein and Carey 1986). Our survey found that, out of a sample of 183 care leavers, two thirds had no qualifications at all, only 15% had a GCSE ('A-C' grade) or its equivalent and only one young person possessed an A level (Biehal et al 1992). These findings are consistent with Garnett's survey of care leavers which found that three quarters failed to obtain qualifications (Garnett 1992). For our follow up sample attainment at the end of schooling was also poor. Forty (54%) had no qualifications, only one young person attained an A level and, while 19 others (25.5%) had one or more GCSE's at 'A-C' grade or its equivalent, only three young people (4%) had three or more. Those who did attain some qualifications were overwhelmingly female (85%) and from fostering backgrounds (70%). Only three young people whose last placement was in residential care attained any qualifications at the end of schooling.

Overall these findings compare very unfavourably with both national and local figures on the qualifications obtained by young people generally. Whilst recognising the socially disadvantaged pool from which care entrants are drawn, the differences are sufficiently striking to warrant some comparison. School attainment tables for 1992 show that, of those 15–17 year olds enrolled that year, 38% attained five or more GCSE passes at 'A-C'. For our three authorities approximately one third of pupils attained at this level (Department for Education 1992).[1] As regards A level (or Scottish equivalent), in 1990/1 25% of boys and 29% of girls attained at least one pass (Social Trends 1994, Table 3.18). In effect then, whereas at least a third of young people are managing to obtain five GCSE's, for care leavers the pattern is reversed. Between one half and three quarters, depending on the particular sample, are leaving school without any qualifications, very few attain five GCSE's 'A-C' and even fewer appear to reach A level standard.

Given our earlier observations about the central importance of qualifications at 16 years as a key predictor of future career options and paths, young people with care backgrounds seem particularly ill-equipped to enter increasingly competitive youth labour markets. The need for young people to have the opportunity to make good educational progress whilst accommodated is therefore paramount. However the care experience of our sample points to some barriers or learning hurdles that tend to impede that progress.

Barriers to progress at school

Previous research has highlighted the damaging discontinuities for young people's lives created by movement and disruption in care (Stein 1990; Jackson 1988/9; Berridge and Cleaver 1987; Millham et al 1986). It has also highlighted the low priority often given by social workers to school moves when considering placement changes and the impact of this, not just educationally, but for young people's emerging identities, their sense of themselves, and for their friendship networks. To rebuild their lives after moving requires enormous emotional energy and strength and this for a group of young people who have already experienced disturbance and stress in their past lives. Successive movements can amount to an "assault on personal identity" (Stein 1993).

In our survey we found that only one in ten young people had remained in the same placement throughout their time in care; two fifths had made between one and three moves; nearly a third four to nine moves and one tenth had moved more than ten times. We also found an association between movement in care and poor educational attainment – three quarters of those who made four or more moves had no qualifications compared to only half of those who made no moves (Biehal et al 1992).

For our follow up sample movement was also a prominent feature of their lives in care. Only 12 young people (16%) made no moves and nearly one third (31%) made four or more moves. For nearly one fifth of the sample disruption had damaging implications for educational progress and attainment. One young woman who experienced multiple placements and four different schools during her time in care, says this of her experience:

---

1.   For District 32.6%; City 31.2% and County 33.2% attained five or more 'A–C' passes that year.

"Well it (care) didn't do much for me school work for a start because . . . I was always moving . . . I'd have to take a lot of time off school and I . . . ended up not taking my exams through it all."

Another spoke of feeling disorientated and unable to focus at school:

"I didn't know what was going on inside my head because I was moving around so much and I had to start on different pieces of work."

For others the feelings of insecurity created by disruption either compounded earlier behaviour problems and patterns of truancy or, for some, created new ones. In addition two of the black young people in the sample mentioned the disruptive effects of racism on their educational careers. One, who was the only black child in her primary school, was kept off and taught at home by her mother because of racist attitudes by other pupils and the other, whilst remaining at her school, felt isolated and marginalised as one of only seven black children in the school.

Perhaps not surprisingly the vast majority of this group of young people failed to find stable work or training on leaving school. Over two thirds at the first interview were either unemployed or in casualised work and only two had managed to continue in education or find work. The former, a young woman who made three moves in 2½ years, and whose grades dipped with each move, was aided by positive support from her foster carers, social worker and teachers. Although failing her GCSE's, she stayed on into the sixth form to retake them and start a B.Tec National course. This may suggest that, for some young people, consistent and active support can overcome the barrier of instability.

For some the stress and unhappiness of being in care made it difficult for them to focus on school work. In some cases this linked to being unhappy in placements, even where long-term, in others to coping with rejection or the need to be at home. The utter despair of one young man, unable to cope with rejection by his family and its implications for schooling, was captured in these lines:

"They said I never used to do any work, I . . . went into total decline if you like. Just sat there doing nowt, staring into space."

Accounts of young people's lives in care have highlighted a feeling of being 'different', marked out or labelled as troublemakers (Stein 1994; Stein and Carey 1986). A significant minority (12) spoke in these terms about their school life, although there were subtle differences in the way it had impacted upon their lives. First, where young people were in stable placements with foster carers or relatives and felt part of the family, they often wanted minimal social work involvement in their schools, to avoid being seen as 'different'. Home visits were often experienced as intrusive, affecting their everyday lives. Most social workers respected this, left school links to carers and often limited themselves to boarding out visits unless problems arose. However, the findings from a recent study into the education of young people in stable long-term foster care both points to a continuing pattern of poor progress and attainment and to the need for intensive compensatory inputs if these young people are to be offered the chance to catch up with their peers (Heath et al 1994). Given the link between school attainment and future career routes that we have identified, perhaps this tendency to adopt a laissez faire approach to schooling, even though it may help to promote a more 'normal' family life, does these young people a disservice in the long run. Not all made good educational progress at school, some faced limited career options and had regrets about not being pushed to attain.

Second, some felt they had been affected by labelling and the low expectations of teachers. For example, one young woman who had experienced three placement moves and five different schools and, in consequence, found adapting to new syllabuses and the different rhythms of school life hard, felt unsupported and frustrated in the lower stream:

"I mean you get dumped with all the trouble makers or no hopers because you can't do the work because the teachers won't give you a chance, so you get, what's the word, guilty by association. But it's their fault for dumping you with 'em."

Finally, and in contrast, a few mentioned equal embarrassment at teachers' attempts to over-compensate for them being in care. Over-concern can be experienced negatively by young people, particularly where, as for some, care had offered a better quality of life than their former homes. Although difficult for teachers, the right balance needs to be struck between concern and sensitivity to the needs of young people not to be marked as 'different' from their peers. One young woman captured both sides of this problem in the following way:

"People was asking me questions about why I was living at the (children's home) and things like that . . . and it just did me head in . . . And the teachers was always asking me if I was alright and . . . making me stand out in a crowd and . . . I didn't like that . . . That's another reason why I didn't go (to school)."

Non school attendance represents an obvious barrier to learning and truancy punctuated the schooling of one third of our sample (23). For one half (12) of these a pattern of truanting had been established before entry to care. For some this was linked to boredom or not being pushed to attend by parents, for others it was linked to family movement, parental relationship breakdown or physical/sexual abuse. A number mentioned a connection between truancy, 'hanging out' with peers and trouble which further compounded their problems. For ten of this group entry to care seemed either to make little or no difference to this established pattern or made it worse. Obviously not all truancy was care related. One or two in stable placements developed a penchant for selective attendance, depending on whether they liked a particular teacher or subject. Others talked of school culture and falling in with the 'wrong crowd'.

Although many of the factors associated with truancy have already been outlined – movement, stress, labelling, unhappiness in care – there were some additional ingredients. For four young people entry to care marked an onset of truancy. All were placed in residential care and, whilst other factors were clearly involved (for example, one had experienced several care moves and all degrees of family rejection), all mentioned that pressure from their peers and a culture of non-attendance contributed to their truancy. Indeed a further eight young people spoke of this as influencing their pattern of truancy, abscondions and involvement in drugs and crime. Some of these young people felt that it appeared 'normal' for young people not to attend school and, while there were also examples of positive encouragement and support for achievement, that in certain homes non-achievement was covertly sanctioned. Clearly some staff were presented with real dilemmas. Speaking in hindsight some young people clearly regretted that they were not more strictly controlled but, what is equally clear, is that at the time they were very resistant to change. However, one young woman said that part of the reason that underlay her truancy was to demonstrate her need to be controlled, for staff to show they cared. Others felt they were socialised into bad behaviour because of the other young people resident, although at that age they may have been willing victims. As one young woman expressed it, the children's home:

> *". . . was alright, we had a laugh there and that but . . . it weren't me really, 'cos I always got in trouble there 'cos there were other kids there who were on remand and everything, and I just started doing things that they were doing which didn't do me any good at all."*

For some young people there was clear evidence of pro-active support by residential staff and social workers to re-establish a pattern of schooling – including taking them to school, exploring alternatives to school and home tuition – but once a pattern of non-attendance was established it seemed very hard to break, especially if other young people were not attending. If young people were sufficiently resistant it seemed that staff would eventually give up. As one young woman said:

> *". . . in the end they just used to let us stay in bed . . . and not bother going to school . . . I used to be able not to go. I don't know why."*

Perhaps not surprisingly the vast majority of this group were facing uncertain and insecure futures (19 out of 23). Two had become parents by the first interview and just two managed to return to full-time education. One was encouraged to return to college by foster parents and the other through concerted support by her social worker and leaving care worker. The remainder were facing futures marked by unemployment interspersed with periods on training schemes or in casualised work.

The need for pro-active strategies to create a positive culture that promotes educational progress and attainment in children's homes is therefore apparent. Where such strategies have been tried, including homework clubs, individual progress plans being drawn up with children and the appointment of liaison teachers to link homes with schools, evidence suggests that progress can be made (Fletcher-Campbell 1990; Jackson 1988/9). In a sense, wherever young people are placed, a better balance is required between the traditional 'welfare' focus of social work, with its emphasis on meeting children's physical and emotional needs, and the need to prioritise educational aims and make these a central part of child care planning. It is in this context that the development of age related schedules by the Looking After Children Project to aid such planning and review are important (Parker et al 1991). The schedules attempt to focus the attention of social workers and carers on areas of children's development that are usually neglected where the parenting role is shared between several adults and, for 'looked after' young people, this has tended to be true of education.

However, if the active support and encouragement of young people's schooling is an essential element of these strategies, it is of concern to note that, looking across our entire sample, fewer than a third of the young people spoke positively about this being a prominent feature of their care experience. While a few spoke with anger and regret about a perceived failure of carers and social workers to actively support their progress, a majority appeared to feel that their school life had simply not been the major concern. These perceptions are indicative of the distance that has yet to be travelled.

Those who attained qualifications

More light may be shed on some of the ingredients that help to promote relative 'success' by looking at those who did manage to obtain some qualifications. At the first interview 20 young people had attained some GCSE 'A-C' or equivalent passes. An examination of their care careers produced some interesting associations. Three quarters (15) had been able to establish themselves in stable placements where they felt well supported and encouraged to achieve at school. To varying degrees care offered a new or continuing context in which they could develop and build upon their strengths. The majority were in foster care (14 out of 15), although for one young woman entry to a children's home offered her a first sense of stability after enforced pre-care non-attendance at home. Nine of those in foster care were in long-term placements of more than six years and the other five between one and three years. For the majority placement stability enabled a stable and continuous experience of school. These findings add further confirmation to those of earlier studies that have highlighted the importance for educational success of placement stability offering continuity of care and schooling in the context of a supportive and encouraging environment for study (Stein 1994; Aldgate et al 1993; Jackson 1988/9). From this stable group of 15, a majority (8) either continued in education or found stable work or training after leaving school.

Of those with less stable care careers (4), two managed to find some stability in the latter part of their schooling, one with foster parents and one with an aunt. However the influence of disruption in their early lives remained open. At first interview three had failed to find a stable career path and one was a parent.

For five young women in the stable group above, care was able to compensate for pre-care patterns of non school attendance. All had been kept off school by parents to carry out domestic tasks and/or care for younger brothers and sisters. Entering care proved to be a liberating experience educationally. For one young woman it was the first time she had experienced stability, praise and encouragement – "I took a whole different view to school and I went and really tried". The transition was usually hard:

> *"Well, it was a bit of a struggle at first, but then it got better . . . 'cos I were used to not going to school. But then, you know, I pulled me socks up really and started going full-time."*

The key for them was finding a stable and supportive placement where they were encouraged by carers and could harness their own motivation (five in fostering and one in a children's home). In each case social workers were also active both with the young person and in linking with school and teachers. Teachers too had a prominent role in supporting the young people with sensitivity and through attending reviews. One case illustration can link many of these aspects of positive practice.

One young woman entered care when just 15 having disclosed to the educational welfare officer at her school that she was being sexually abused by her stepfather. Prior to this, school attendance had been very erratic as she was kept off to care for younger siblings. Once settled in a foster placement she flourished. Now able to attend regularly her grades improved along with her self-image and confidence and she was able to build sustaining friendship networks for the first time. Her carer and social worker were encouraging and liaised closely with school about her progress. The role of the school EWO was crucial, providing key on-site support, counselling (3/4 hours per week initially) and through respecting confidentiality – most of the pupils and teachers were not fully aware of her circumstances. After a year she was able to return home and her social worker helped negotiate a contract with her mother that would respect her right to study (having her own room in a crowded house, privacy and support for her work). By the second interview she had passed some GCSE's and settled into a full-time college course.

All five of these young women managed to get sufficient qualifications at school to enable them to continue in education (4) or training (1). If care is, as the Department of Health suggests, to 'ameliorate' the deficiencies of poor pre-care educational experiences, to offer compensatory help, then it is clear that the demands on social work time are likely to be quite heavy. A pro-active approach is required to find and maintain a stable and supportive care placement, to monitor, encourage and review progress and, through linking with schools, to coordinate networks of support for young people. Education needs to have high priority even where young people are placed long-term with relatives or foster carers and, most particularly, aspects of positive practice in children's homes need to be encouraged to promote a culture of achievement.

• Summary points •

Young people entering care tend to come from the most disadvantaged family backgrounds and, for many, the stresses of their pre-care experience have lasting effects on their educational progress. For the majority of our sample care was unable to offer a sufficiently compensatory experience for them to establish a successful pattern of schooling. Over half left school with no qualifications and only three attained three or more GCSE's 'A-C'. For a significant minority care compounded their educational difficulties. The effects of movement and disruption, labelling, feeling 'different' and of patterns of truancy all had a negative impact on their educational careers. The majority of these young people failed to establish themselves in education, work or training upon leaving school. Those who did attain qualifications and go on to start positive employment careers tended to be those who had experienced a positive and settled care career. Mostly female and from fostering backgrounds, care had enabled a continuous pattern of schooling to be maintained or renewed. They had been positively encouraged to achieve by carers, teachers and social workers and the latter had been actively involved in close school liaison.

- Placement stability enabling continuity of schooling is a pre-requisite for attainment. Education needs to have a high priority from the point of entry to care and to be an integral part of child care planning. Progress aims need to be targeted, monitored and reviewed.

- If young people are to have a chance of catching up with their peers intensive compensatory inputs will be necessary. Those who did attain did so because of the interest, concern and encouragement shown to them by carers and social workers.

- Close liaison with schools/teachers is necessary and teachers should be helped to be conscious of the impact of care on young people in order to avoid a dual problem of labelling and over-compensation, both of which mark young people as different from their peers.

- The prioritisation of 'welfare' above educational concerns needs to be questioned. Where young people are in stable long-term fostering arrangements with carers or relatives the low key role of some social workers, predicated on a belief in promoting 'normal' family life, can do them a disservice. Many of these young people failed to attain and later regretted not being pushed.

- Children's homes need to adopt strategies to promote a positive culture of educational achievement. Only three of those from residential backgrounds attained any qualifications and most faced an insecure future.

CHAPTER 7

EARLY CAREER PATHS – EDUCATION, EMPLOYMENT, TRAINING AND INCOMES

We have highlighted the poor educational attainment of most of these young people at the end of schooling and pointed to some aspects of their pre-care and care experiences which influenced this. Here we will explore their attempts to establish a career for themselves over the first 18–24 months of independent living and draw attention to the influence that their diverse experiences of care and support from carers, social workers and leaving care workers may have had upon their career routes.

Since the late 1970's both the context and the nature of transitions from school to labour market have been profoundly restructured. The proportion of young people making a direct entry to work from school fell from 53% in 1976 to 15% in 1986 (Wallace and Cross 1990) and in 1990 only 17% of 16 year olds directly entered employment (LMQR 1992a). This route, favoured in the past by a majority of working class young people, has been replaced with a range of 'transitional economic statuses' based around education and training (Jones and Wallace 1992). The proportion of 16–18 year olds participating in Youth Training increased from 5% in 1981 to 15% in 1990 (Social Trends 1994, Table 3.13). Participation in full-time education has mushroomed, with 73% of 16 year olds and 58% of 17 year olds continuing in education in 1993/4 (CEP 1994). A number of factors that influenced this restructuring can be identified. The rapid decline of the youth labour market engendered by recession in the early 1980's, the decline of manufacturing and the emergence of new service industries with a perceived need for better training in flexible and transferable skills and the rapid expansion of vocational courses in schools and colleges have all had an impact (Banks et al 1992). In consequence, new pathways to transition have opened up, transitions have become more protracted as entry to work is deferred and young people are faced with more formal choices about their future direction. However, individual decisions are being taken by young people in the context of shrinking and intensely competitive youth labour markets.

Despite this new context, in the last chapter we emphasised the continuing importance of qualifications gained at 16 as a key predictor of future career routes and of the period between 16 and 19 as one in which these routes take shape, gain fixity and lead to ultimate destinations in the labour market. Qualifications gained at school influence the likelihood of avoiding unemployment and also, if continuing in education or training, the kinds of courses or schemes that young people can join (Banks et al 1992). We also emphasised that between one half and three quarters of care leavers complete their schooling with no formal qualifications and are therefore ill-equipped to enter this contest.

Early career patterns

Completed research into the post care careers of samples of care leavers has highlighted their over-representation amongst the unemployed (Stein 1990; Stein and Carey 1986). Data from our survey (Biehal et al 1992), our follow up sample at the first interview and from a recent survey of leaving care schemes (Broad 1994), both confirm these high levels of unemployment and the under-representation of care leavers in education.

Table 7.1 Education/Employment Status

	Survey (n = 182) %	Follow up sample (n = 74) %	Broad survey (n = 859) %
School/FE	8.5	12	19
F-T work	13	16	9
YT	13.5	15	13
Unemployed	36.5	50	49

These snapshot findings compare very unfavourably to those of the 16–19 year old population at large. Although nationally unemployment amongst 16–19 year olds has been consistently higher than that for other age bands since 1986, in 1993 22% of males and 16% of females in this age band were unemployed (Social Trends 1994, Table 4.20). This compares to between one third and one half of the above samples of care leavers. Although, as we have seen, direct entry from school to work has fallen dramatically for most young people, participation in continuing education for these samples of care leavers was very low. We have indicated that around 15% of 16–18 year olds were participating in youth training (similar to the above samples) and well over a half continuing in education, but for these care leavers participation in education was dramatically lower. For them the failure to obtain qualifications at school, coupled with the difficulty of establishing themselves in the community at an early age, had made gaining a foothold on the career/further education ladder extremely difficult. Particularly so when the assumption that underpins YT and much of further education is that young people will be participating from the security of the family home.

However, if we take a more dynamic approach and look at the early career routes of our follow up sample over the first 18–24 months of independent living the picture becomes more complex. To do this we have grouped them into three main routes: 'academic', those who continued in full-time post compulsory education (school or FE); 'work', those in full-time permanent employment or on a stable YT programme; and 'insecure', those unemployed, in casualised work or unstable YT (i.e. recently started or with several failures behind them). These routes have been adapted from a typology of the main post-school routes developed by Roberts (1993). Table 7.2 gives an overview of the early career routes for these young people.

Table 7.2 Career Routes

	TI (n = 74)	T2 (n = 67)	T3 (n = 53)
Insecure	45–61%	36–53.5%	19–36%
Work	15–20.5%	12–18%	12–22.5%
Academic	9–12%	6–9%	5– 9.5%
Parent	5– 6.5%	13–19.5%	17–32%

The T2 total includes those not interviewed at T2 but contacted again at T3 (8); the parenthood figures do not represent all parents, merely those with full-time child care responsibilities.

At the first interview nearly two thirds of the sample were in the insecure route and, as we have seen, one half of the sample were unemployed. By the final interview, 18–24 months later, all but one of the young people in this route were unemployed. Indeed this significantly under-represents the degree to which, once young people entered this route, their careers took on a fixity from which, at least during the research cycle, it proved hard to recover. First, of the 21 young people lost to the study at the final interview, four fifths (81%) had been unemployed at the last point of contact. Second, of those who became full-time parents during the course of the study (32% at its close), only one had not been in this route prior to parenthood. It was the movement from insecurity to parenthood that represented the most marked feature of early post-care careers. Although motivations for early parenthood are complex, the failure to attain at school and find a positive direction represents part of the context in which decisions about early motherhood are made (see chapter 12 for a more detailed discussion of these issues).

The need to find stable work, education or training at an early point after leaving school is highlighted by looking at those who entered the academic and work routes. Nine young people in the work route remained stable in the same work or training throughout the research. This was also the case for four in full-time education; a further three successfully completed their courses and found work. During the research cycle, only three young people were able to make a definite recovery from unemployment; two returned to full-time education and one successfully joined a YT scheme. The very limited numbers who were able to escape the cycle of unemployment punctuated by episodes on training schemes or in casualised work once this pattern became set, points to the degree of difficulty and the extent of the challenge facing workers trying to help care leavers back into employment. Even those who embarked on courses, training or work remained vulnerable to unemployment, five later became unemployed, and those who remained stable were mostly engaged in low level courses or forms of employment. However, it needs to be stressed that we were only able to chart the post-care careers of these young people over a relatively short time period, perhaps a longer-term follow up may result in a more optimistic scenario.

Those in education, work and training

Those who did gain entry to the academic and work routes were not high flyers. Those in education were undertaking B.Tec. or City and Guilds level courses in catering, social care, business and tourism. Only one young woman had aspirations for higher education. Those on YT schemes were gaining skills in social care, printing and office work and those employed were working as care assistants, receptionists/secretaries, warehouse packers and one as a garage attendant. Three of these young people had moderate learning difficulties and, while comprehensive support enabled them to continue to build their skills and confidence, their longer-term career prospects remained uncertain.

Five of these young people gained further qualifications during the course of the research, four were at foundation level (GNVQ level 1). Three of these were continuing at the next stage and the fourth found work. One young woman completed an NNEB and found a full-time nursery job. In total eight young people successfully completed a YT scheme. Of these, five found work with the same employer, one with a different employer and one moved on to college. Only one became unemployed and two were continuing youth training at the close of the research.

Three quarters of this group were female and the vast majority were pursuing gendered careers in social care or office/reception work. Evidence does suggest that girls tend to fare better than boys up to and including GCSE level and this was the case for our sample. Gendered divergences tend to occur at this point with girls having a more restricted gender-specific range of options available to them and fewer progressing to higher education (Banks et al 1992; Redpath and Harvey 1987). Black young people are more likely to stay on in education but those entering the labour market are more likely to experience unemployment and for longer periods than their white counterparts (LMQR 1992b). Although there were only nine black and mixed heritage young people in this sample, they appeared to be doing slightly better in their early careers than the white young people. Three remained in the academic and work route throughout and two recovered from unemployment, one entering full-time education and the other a YT scheme.

A brief look at the care careers of those who managed to establish themselves in education, work or training reveal many of the ingredients associated with educational success identified in the last chapter. Two thirds had stable and positive care experiences, the overwhelming majority in foster care. Although their stays in care were not necessarily long-term, ranging from 1 to 16 years, stability enabled a continuous pattern of schooling to be maintained or renewed. Virtually all felt they had been encouraged and supported to attain by their carers. For those who entered education, eight out of nine had also received a positive through care package of support and encouragement from professionals (carers, social workers and, in some cases, teachers). Social worker links between young person, placement and school had been close and well co-ordinated. For those entering YT or work the social worker role appeared more patchy. Although several mentioned active careers help from carers and advice from teachers and the school careers service, a majority made no mention of having received advice about career options from social workers. The majority, with the support of carers, had negotiated entry to YT or work for themselves.

Nearly three quarters of those who entered these routes did so from the shelter of supported accommodation – either they remained with foster carers or family/relatives or were in supported hostels and lodgings. Although most moved on during the research period, perhaps it points to the need for young people to have a supportive base from which to launch their initial careers. While all these young people needed reserves of confidence, motivation and self-discipline to keep to their chosen option, for those living independently and without close family support the discipline required seemed immense. As one young woman in her own tenancy and pursuing a college course commented:

> *"It's just me who has to make my own decisions. There's not really somebody like me mum to say, 'oh come on girl go to college, do your assignment before you go out'. There's none of that. I've got to use my own initiative and say . . . I can't go out, I've got to do my assignment . . . I've got to go to sleep so I can get up in the morning. I mean it's hard, really hard."*

Although quite secure and having good links with her extended family, the low key support offered by her social worker was crucial. She had helped her look at college options and assisted with application forms; had visited the college with her and arranged SSD funding to cover rent and maintenance. Funding would last until completion of the course and could be extended if she wanted to continue in education and regular contact was being maintained. Five of those following full-time courses were being fully funded by social services and another started to receive funding once she left the family home for a hostel. For all those in education there was evidence that carers, social workers and, where involved, leaving care workers had been active in offering young people advice and assistance about course options, applications, funding and were involved in college liaison. This support was not necessarily intrusive, respecting the need of young people for autonomy, but was there for back up and to offer assistance if problems arose.

The need for a stable home base was evident. Nearly all of those who lost jobs or dropped out of courses did so because of an inability to manage their lives and, in particular, their accommodation. For example, one young man gave up both job and flat when he found the pressure and isolation of living alone too great. Despite support from social worker and scheme he felt unable to cope and went travelling. Another, unable to control his space was taken over by friends and eventually lost his YT place and his flat. Continuity in support was crucial, especially for those with less stable post-care careers. In District, a young man with learning difficulties was able to retain his job despite three moves including a housing breakdown due, in large part, to the continuous and intensive support of his leaving care worker. For another young man with learning difficulties, networking to create employment opportunities was necessary. Having completed a special needs YT, his leaving care worker linked with a specialist employment agency in order that he could remain productive and continue to build his skills and confidence. He continued gaining work experience in a hospital placement.

As we have indicated, only two young people managed to recover from unemployment to return to full-time education, both female. The following case illustration summarises some of the elements of support that are required and points to the need for careers help to be part of a well planned and co-ordinated transition package. This young woman entered a children's home when 15 years old. Rejected by her mother, influenced by the peer culture in the home and the stigma of being in care, she truanted for the last two years of school. Bright and without qualifications, she had immediate regrets. Her move to a council flat was planned by the home, her social worker and leaving care worker. The latter focused on stabilising her in her new home and establishing systems for helping her to manage her life. Her social worker advised about college options and went with her to careers and college. The LEA refused her grant application on the grounds that social services were in loco parentis and, although the decision was challenged by her social worker, she arranged social services funding for the duration of the course. With continuing support she was able to pursue her college career. In this case the demands on social work time had been increased by the failure of the local authority *as a whole* to adopt a corporate approach to meeting her financial needs.

Only one young woman made a definite transition from unemployment to the work route. For her, the move from foster care to a supported hostel managed by the County leaving care team had been unsettling. She was unemployed and uncertain about her future. As part of a comprehensive package of support, her leaving care worker discussed options and arranged a meeting with a specialist careers officer and, in consequence, she chose a YT scheme in social care. Despite a further move to her own flat, her confidence grew as she found she could manage and her immersion in the world of work and college, she was studying for a City and Guilds qualification, had broadened her horizons. As she said, "there's a lot more I can do than I realised". Success in both areas of her life had become mutually reinforcing.

All three of these young women were able, quite secure in themselves and had positive relationships with extended family and friends. They had personal resources upon which the support they were offered could build. The third was able to return to college after moving into a supported hostel for young mothers. For two, therefore, the support and encouragement available in supported environments was important to their recovery and, for the third, a focus on her career needs as part of a well planned transition was crucial. At the final interview only one other young man with a more unstable past appeared to be making a fresh start in employment terms. His care career had been marked by absconsions and involvement in drugs and crime. The key for him was a renewal of the relationship with his mother. After a period in custody he had just returned to live with her and was starting a YT in computing. His new sense of belonging and security had helped give him the determination to try again.

The insecure route

As we have shown, nearly two thirds of our sample entered this route and, once there, very few escaped other than through parenthood. Seventeen (23%) were continuously unemployed up to our last point of contact with them and, at the final interview, all bar one of those in this route were unemployed, the exception being the young man above. A typical pattern included one or more failed attempts at YT and episodes of short-term or casual employment followed by lengthening bouts of unemployment. Given the shaping of routes that occurs between 16 and 19, their failure to establish themselves in work or training meant that their long-term futures were very uncertain.

The young people in this route were more likely to have had a less stable care experience, including the disruption of placement moves. Truancy was more likely to have figured prominently in their pre-care and care careers and, since a greater proportion were from residential care backgrounds, for this pattern to have been reinforced by peer cultures in children's homes. Also clustered more heavily in this group were those who had experienced parental rejection. In consequence they were often more isolated, lacking in self-esteem and confidence, had more difficulty relating to others and in organising their lives. Although young people with these characteristics were more heavily represented, some in this route had experienced a positive and stable care career, they simply had not been able to find stable work or training. Insecurity was, after all, the pattern for the majority.

The principal qualities that employers tend to look for when recruiting young people include qualifications, punctuality/reliability, confidence, a willingness to learn and to work as part of a team (Smith 1994). The vast majority of these young people lacked qualifications and many had personal deficits which made them less attractive to potential employers and inhibited their chances of launching a career.

Those lacking informal family and community supports were further disadvantaged, since these informal networks have tended to be a major access route to employment for working class young people (Sone 1994; Banks et al 1992). Some young people felt that the stigma of care, in particular its perceived association with trouble, had also followed them into the world of work:

"I don't know . . . I think for the rest of me life people will hold against me being in care. I think they'll say, 'oh well, she was in care, can we sort of trust her', . . . I think it gets held against you."

Indeed this mark of care seems equally to affect practitioners attempting to promote opportunities for care leavers with employers; they appear to need considerable reassurance (Sone 1994).

The failure of these young people to start a career did not necessarily equate with a lack of professional support. Rather more it pointed to the fact that, where experience of care had been unable to resolve past deficits in young people's lives and provide a platform for attainment, these problems were extremely difficult to resolve at this point without intensive help, especially where young people were also having to cope with the pressures of independent living. Most social workers and leaving care workers were aware of the importance of work and training both to young people's futures and to positively reinforce other aspects of transition. Although the support offered was variable, for most restricted to advice and information about career options or encouragement to find work, for around a third, even though unsuccessful, it was more practical and focused. This was particularly the case where young people entered supported accommodation managed by schemes or where careers help formed part of a planned transition package.

To give an example. One young man who had been abandoned at birth and experienced 19 different care placements entered a trainer flat managed by the City (vol) scheme. Although insecure, prior to the first interview he was on a YT scheme but struggling to retain commitment to it. His worker viewed this as a priority and attempted to encourage him to retain motivation and develop a daily routine. When this proved unsuccessful she tried to explore other career options. Although his involvement in a local drugs culture required him to leave the flat, a brief period of stability in his own flat enabled her to help him start college. However his inability to manage his life and control relationships led to further instability and college was abandoned. Continuity from the scheme prevented a descent into homelessness but had been unable to bear fruit in career terms.

Another young woman, unhappy at being rejected, truanted for the last two years at school. She moved into a house supported by the City (ssd) scheme. After two YT failures, help from her leaving care worker and social worker got her started on a third scheme. She found it hard to sustain and lost several placements through unreliability. Links between the workers and YT scheme enabled her place to be kept open for several months but, despite encouragement, she eventually lost her place and became unemployed.

Although ultimately unsuccessful, support for these young people had been pro-active and structured as part of a wider package of support. However, where support was restricted to advice and information, it often proved insufficient for young people who were confused and uncertain about their futures and their abilities. For example, one young man returned to County after several years fostered out of authority. In part this represented an attempt to reconstruct his identity and re-establish links with his family. He started college but found the course difficult and the stress of rebuilding his life too great and dropped out. Despite advice about careers from his social worker and the leaving care scheme, he remained unemployed and made several moves before settling with his brother at the end of the research. At the final interview his social worker recognised that a more structured approach might have helped:

> *"I think now, going down to the careers office or something, actually going with him might have helped him. I think every time he got sent he probably did go and had a cursory look round and then left again, perhaps not able to . . . sit and talk with someone about courses or whatever was available. I think had I done that with him . . . there might have been a different outcome."*

For a minority support had simply been absent and this was particularly true where social workers had failed to refer young people to schemes. Once social work support ended they were left to cope with unemployment alone. One young woman, apart from a brief YT episode, had been unemployed continuously. Her social worker had not offered support, indeed had rarely visited, and the case was closed a year before the close of the research. Not aware of the leaving care scheme, she had no obvious source of help. Bored and frustrated, she had lost motivation and blamed herself for her predicament:

> *"I used to have loads and loads of plans, but they just seem to have all gone . . . I think I've just got a bit lazy."*

A number of workers mentioned lack of motivation by young people as a barrier to the help they could offer. It seemed to be an issue for just over a quarter of the young people in this route and was an ingredient in the cases discussed above. For some young people this was clearly connected to emotional damage in their lives but, for others, it was mentioned in the context of young people either having moved to an area of high unemployment or having friends who were unemployed. It was felt that they lacked role models of 'industry' and, in consequence, failed to respond to support. Clearly this is a problem that extends beyond care. Young people growing up in areas of high unemployment, where parents and friends may be out of work, where few options are visible to them, are quite likely to become disillusioned and fatalistic. For our sample, where these structural factors overlay personal histories marked by disturbance and stress with its implications for self-identity, the problem appeared more acute; especially for those living independently and without someone to push and encourage.

Many young people who were unemployed appeared to recognise the problem themselves. They were bored, had little money to visit friends and their days had lost any semblance of structure and routine. In order to survive some had reversed the clock, sleeping by day and staying up at night. This pattern affected their ability to find work and attend interviews:

"Sometimes you can't be bothered going 'cos you're used to being set in all day, you're not used to getting up early to go to interviews."

Although some remained sceptical of the merits of education and training, many who had truanted regretted their past failure to attend school, to focus harder on their work and to attain qualifications. Most had also missed any careers advice that schools were able to offer. They were painfully aware of how disadvantaged this had made them:

"I just feel I've wasted five years of me education, 'cos I didn't used to learn nowt."

"I'm looking round for jobs . . . but it's hard to get in without qualifications."

We have pointed to the importance of a secure and stable home base to enable young people to establish a pattern of work and training. Most of those whose post-care careers were marked by instability and movement ultimately failed to avoid unemployment. At the final interview, those young people who had made four or more moves were three times more likely to be unemployed than in full-time work. Several young people spoke of the need to find stable accommodation as a pre-requisite for normalising other areas of their lives, including work and training. Reciprocal links between homelessness and unemployment have been identified (Kirk et al 1991; Randall 1989). Our survey also pointed to the same association, with nearly two thirds of the homeless in that sample being unemployed (Biehal et al 1992) and exactly the same ratio was apparent for this follow up sample. Two young men lost their supported lodgings as a direct result of unemployment and, for several others, it was a contributory factor in housing breakdown. This mirrors the findings of other studies of care leavers where a clear association was identified between unemployment and the ability of young people to manage other areas of their lives, including their homes (Stein 1990; Stein and Carey 1986).

Supporting careers

We have seen that those who attained some qualifications at school and went into employment, training or work tended to share certain characteristics. Their care careers were more likely to have been stable, to have enabled a continuous pattern of schooling to be maintained or renewed. They were disproportionately female and to have come from foster backgrounds in which they were shown interest, concern and encouragement to attain by carers and social workers; a base from which they could harness their own motivation. They were more secure, less rejected and more likely to have positive relationships with extended family and friends. The majority also started on their career path from the shelter of supported accommodation and most, especially those in education, continued to receive practical, financial and emotional support from social workers and, where involved, leaving care workers. As we have seen, the three young women who did recover from unemployment also shared some of these characteristics.

The challenge facing leaving care schemes (and social workers) is to develop strategies capable of enabling those for whom care was unable to offer a sufficiently compensatory experience an opportunity to return to learn, train or work. As we have seen, the initial destination of nearly two thirds of our sample was the insecure route. The vast majority of these young people lacked qualifications and most had personal deficits linked to their pre-care and care experience that made them less attractive to employers and training agencies. For those unemployed, continuing rejection had lowered self confidence and motivation and many young people were uncertain about their own self worth, strengths and abilities. The reciprocity between productive employment and management in other life areas reinforces its importance as an area of work.

Our four schemes were very much aware of this challenge and were assisting young people, in a context of limited opportunities, in relation to employment. Most of the work undertaken was individually based with young people and, as we have indicated, included exploring options, offering advice and information, advocacy and liaison, helping with job search, strategies to build confidence and motivation and arranging finance. Help was at its most intense when young people were living in supported accommodation managed by schemes or when part of a planned transition package.

The value of group work or drop-in settings as a context in which young people can build their practical and social skills for employment in an environment of mutual support has been recognised (Smith 1994). Of the two schemes with group work or drop-in facilities at the project base, District and City (vol), neither had specific groups with an employment focus, although City (vol) had run a job club in the past. District had a careers officer run regular surgeries at the project and City (vol) was setting this up in the later stages of the research. However the access available to young people at these schemes meant that help was on hand to assist with job search; young people had access to papers, job centre vacancies and phones.

The need for young people with past deficits to be made aware of their past achievements, to have their own achievement profiles as a basis for building their confidence, for planning work on strengths and weaknesses and preparing them for employment has also been highlighted (Smith 1994). This is particularly important where young people have previously failed or missed large parts of schooling (Sone 1994). For our schemes most of this work was happening informally and only District had educational assessment forms to be jointly completed by staff and young people as a basis for future work.

Although most leaving care workers had informal links with colleges, careers and training agencies and were active in liaising on behalf of young people, none of our schemes had developed more structured and formal arrangements, especially with employers, to promote wider opportunities. District and City (vol) were attempting this towards the end of the research. For all schemes the developmental priority up to this point had been to develop accommodation and financial resources. Smith (1994) gives examples of how some schemes have entered into quite elaborate arrangements with employers to promote opportunities and tapped into funding sources to employ specialist employment workers on schemes.

However this discussion does raise a dilemma for schemes. Whilst networking to promote opportunities is of obvious importance, the direct provision and management of services around employment and training raises more questions. It can offer schemes greater control and help to ensure that services are appropriate to the needs of its care leavers, however it also runs the risk of separating these young people further from their peers, of maintaining a continuing institutional link and of duplicating services in the mainstream. Whether it is better to run direct services or facilitate more appropriate services in the mainstream sector will be a matter of continuing debate.

Incomes

The extended nature of the transition from school to work now undertaken by most young people has increased their continuing financial dependence upon their families (Jones and Wallace 1992). Youth training allowances and discretionary awards for further education are not sufficient to enable young people to live independently. The vast majority participate from the security of the family home. The majority of care leavers, as we have seen, move to independence between 16 and 18 and, given their career patterns identified above, have to manage this difficult transition on very low incomes.

Of the sample included in our survey, over a third were living on less than £30 per week, over half on less than £50 per week and only 7% were earning over £70 (Biehal et al 1992).[1] A similar pattern was apparent for the follow up sample (Table 7.3).

Table 7.3 Incomes

	T1 (n = 73)	T3 (n = 51)
Less than £35	31–42.5%	18–35.5%
Less than £50	49–67%	26–60%
£51–80	16–22%	10–19.5%
Over £80	8–11%	15–29.5%

DSS income support applicable amounts were raised from £33.60 to £34.80 during the research cycle.

1. 62 (36%) were managing on less than £30; 97 (56%) on less than £50 and 12 (7%) on more than £70 (N = 172). Income support applicable amounts were £28.80 at that time.

Two fifths were having to manage on less than £35 per week at the time of the first interview and even some 18 months later a third were coping at this level of income. Only one in ten were earning over £80 per week soon after leaving care and although the proportion with this level of income had increased to nearly a third at the final interview, this was mostly accounted for by the increase in young parents. All the parents who had their children living with them were dependent on state benefits.

The vast majority were living at or near the poverty line and the stress of trying to budget and run their homes on low income impacted heavily upon their lives. As one young mother commented, coping "was a struggle, a real hard struggle". A study of poverty amongst young people living away from home in Edinburgh found that poverty was not just a matter of low income but of the degree to which there was easy access to other forms of support, particularly family resources (Kirk et al 1991). Care leavers are less likely to be able to rely on their families in this way and, given that financial independence is not a realistic option for most, they continue to rely on the state for their income – whether through benefits, training allowances or education grants.

Major social policy changes during the 1980's have acted as a disincentive for young people to leave the family home and have reduced the disposable income available to them. The 1986 Social Security Act introduced a switch from 'needs' to 'age' related assessments and the removal of a separate householder addition for those under 25 years of age. Income for those under 25 was paid at a rate 25% lower than for those over 25, regardless of circumstances (Craig 1991). The 1988 Act saw a removal of entitlement to claim for most 16 and 17 year olds, although in certain circumstances young people 'genuinely estranged' from their families could claim 'severe hardship' payments. However these payments are only available for limited periods and contain no right of appeal (NACAB 1992; Craig 1991). One consequence of these changes has been that, for care leavers living independently, social services have been obliged to use Section 24 funds under The Children Act 1989 to provide financial support to young people. In some cases, where claims for income support were refused, this would take the form of basic income maintenance.

All three of our authorities were using funds in this way. Our data suggests that where young people were living independently but still subject to a care order they were often refused income support on the grounds that social services were in loco parentis. Those who had been accommodated appeared more likely to have claims for income support accepted on the grounds of 'estrangement'. Where claims were refused social services would fund both income and, in many cases, rent where housing benefit also refused claims. If social services took responsibility for income they would also therefore be likely to have to bear the **full cost** of supporting young people in the community. The divisions between departments at the local level – social services, the benefit agency and housing benefit – were therefore creating inconsistencies for young people based on their status (whether they had been accommodated or in statutory care) rather than upon their current needs.

More positively, as we have seen, Section 24 funding was used to finance young people in full-time education and to provide incentives to work and train; top ups were available for young people participating in youth training or in low waged work. At the first interview 42% (31) of the young people were receiving financial assistance and for half of them (16) it was their primary source of income – either they were unemployed or at full-time college. For those unemployed financial assistance ended when they could claim at their 18th birthday. For those in education or training funding would continue until their courses ended. Eight young people (15%) were still receiving financial assistance at the close of the research.

Section 24 provisions regarding financial assistance are discretionary. The permissive nature of these powers has meant that this assistance has become subject to marked regional and local variations. The kinds and amounts of financial help that young people can expect to receive will depend on where they happen to be in care. A survey of 102 local authorities found that only 42% offered an automatic leaving care grant, the remainder either operated a discretionary system or failed to provide one (Lowe 1990). Garnett's study of three authorities discovered distinct differences in the rules of eligibility for financial help and in the amounts that were then allocated (Garnett 1992). Tackling discretion was an issue for our authorities. Decisions whether to fund personal income top ups were taken by local social work offices. In order to reduce inconsistency arising out of a decision making process that is discretionary, all three authorities had issued guidance to social workers about amounts and circumstances in which financial payments should be made. In County, the leaving care team had a lead role in developing policy for the county around financial assistance and, in conjunction with the Children's Rights Office, was attempting to steer the principles underpinning financial assistance towards a more rights based approach.

Our findings suggest the need for central government departments to develop a co-ordinated and corporate approach to meeting the financial needs of this vulnerable group of young people. Initiatives need to be taken to encourage inter-agency and corporate policies at the local level; to draw together social services, the Benefit Agency, housing benefit and education authorities. We have already mentioned the failure of one education authority to offer a grant *because* a young woman was in the care of social services. Although discretionary awards are scarce, to offer them to this group would enable social services to use its funds constructively to top up the grant to a level at which young people could manage their homes. In another case the refusal to accept a claim for 'severe hardship' jeopardised a young man's move to a new flat. His past had been marked by movement, instability and offending. While social services challenged the decision he was left with £15 to live on and little furniture. He was dependent on his extended family for food and at great risk of breakdown and a return to crime. The need for co-ordinated and consistent decision making at the local level, based upon young people's current needs, is essential if young people leaving care are to be offered the best chance of making a smooth and successful transition.

• Summary points •

The failure of the majority of these young people to attain qualifications at school had left them facing an uncertain future in the labour market. One half were unemployed within a few months of leaving care and nearly two thirds were in the 'insecure route' and facing periods of short-term or casualised work interspersed with episodes of training and unemployment. Once in this route very few escaped during the research cycle other than through parenthood. Most were managing at or near benefit levels. Those who did move into education, work or training were disproportionately female and tended to have had positive and stable care careers, the majority in foster placements. Most also started their careers from the shelter of supported accommodation. Those whose post-care careers were marked by movement and instability rarely avoided unemployment and their failure to find work impacted upon their ability to manage in other life areas.

- Post care career patterns reinforce the need for educational attainment and progress at school to be an integral part of individual child care planning from the point at which young people enter care. Qualifications gained at school are the key to a positive initial destination in the youth labour market.

- A structured and pro-active approach to career planning needs to be an integral part of a well planned transition to independent accommodation. Success in different life areas can become mutually reinforcing for young people.

- Offering continuity in support is important both to encourage, support and motivate young people engaged in work and training and also to help those unemployed to return to learn/earn.

- Leaving care schemes have an important role to play in assisting social workers in this area. Their developmental brief puts them in a strong position to build links with employers, colleges, TECs and training agencies in order to promote opportunities for care leavers. They have a role in helping to prepare young people for a return to education or training – to help young people recognise their past achievements, to identify strengths and weaknesses and to help them choose a next step that is appropriate to their needs and interests. Groups and drop-in services that schemes offer can also be helpful in enabling young people to gain ready access to advice and in promoting their practical and social skills for employment. However, the degree to which schemes engage in the direct management and provision of services or focus on facilitating appropriate provision in mainstream sectors is a matter for some debate.

- The limited incomes available to young people have led our authorities to use Section 24 funds to meet subsistence needs. Funding has been used to enable young people to undertake college courses and to top up incomes for those in youth training or low waged work. It has also been necessary where claims for income support and/or housing benefit have been rejected. Where these claims were refused for young people living independently, decisions appeared to be based more on the status of young people (whether they were still subject to a care order) than on their current needs. A corporate approach at both national and local level is required to ensure that the financial needs of care leavers are adequately met.

CHAPTER 8

FAMILIES, FRIENDS AND FOSTER CARERS: SOCIAL NETWORKS AND SUPPORT

In this chapter we will explore the range of informal supports available to our young people to help ease their transitions into the community. We will look at patterns of family contact across the sample and at young people's perceptions of their families. We also explore other forms of informal support including foster carers, partners and friends.

Patterns of family contact

When they first left care only a tiny minority of the young people (8%) returned to live with a parent or continued living with a parent with whom they had been placed while being 'looked after'. Only one young person was living with a parent by the end of the study. In fact, during the first 18–24 months after leaving care, only 12% of the young people returned to live with one of their parents for three or more months at any stage. If we also include stays with other relatives, we find that only half returned to their families for any length of time during a period of 18–24 months after leaving care. In some cases, relationships with parents had virtually broken down but they were able to return home for a few nights during a crisis, when they had nowhere else to go. In a substantial minority of these cases, the situation broke down rapidly, as in one case where a young woman was raped by the brother she was staying with.

Patterns of return for the total population of children and young people who are 'looked after' generally show that most young people return home. In a follow up study of 450 children who were 'looked after', Bullock et al found that 82% had returned to their families within five years of being accommodated and predicted that almost all children in care will eventually be returned to their families (Bullock et al, 1993). Our research suggests that there is a relationship between age and patterns of returning home. Patterns of return for 'looked after' children of all ages are different from the pattern for this particular sub-group of that population; that is, for those young people who continue to be 'looked after' until the ages of 16–18. Our findings indicate that the majority of young people who remain in substitute care or accommodation until the ages of 16–18 are those for whom a return home has not been negotiable.

Although very few were reunited with their families, the majority (81%) did have some contact in the early months after leaving care and two thirds saw family members at least weekly at this stage. This is similar to the pattern established in other studies. Our earlier survey of 183 care leavers found that 79% were in contact with their families (Biehal et al 1992), while Rowe et al's study of nearly 6000 'looked after' children (all ages) found that about 60% had contact with their families at least once a month (Rowe et al 1989). However, frequency of contact alone can tell us little about the quality of these family relationships, how supportive they were to the young people, the diversity of family members with whom young people maintained contact, and the significance of these relationships for the young people.

Positive family relationships

Defining the quality of relationships for a sample of this size is difficult, since each family relationship is a unique web of shared histories and experiences. We have therefore based our assessment of the quality of relationships on the perceptions of the young people themselves, taking account of the views of professionals who knew them well. In the following discussion, positive relationships are defined as those where the young people perceived their relationship with family members to be of good quality and to offer them support in the broadest sense and where this view was confirmed by their social workers or leaving care workers.

In these terms, less than a third of the young people could be said to have reasonably positive, supportive relationships with one or both parents during their transition from care. However, within 18–24 months of leaving care there was a rapprochement between a number of the young people and their parents and, by the end of this period, one half could be said to have reasonably positive relationships. While most parents did not offer the young people a home (or the young people did not wish to return), a number of the young people felt that the quality of their relationships with their parents had improved.

Those with positive relationships with parents valued having somewhere they considered to be their home base, even if they did not actually live in the family home. They needed to know there was somewhere they could go if they felt lonely, or during a crisis. It was important for them to feel that a parent would 'be there' for them if they needed them. A young man who had found it hard to cope with the loneliness and lack of structure he experienced living alone in a bedsit was relieved when his father at last began to offer him support once he became homeless:

"'Cos like he never saw a lot of me when I was in care . . . it's like he wants to see me now. 'Cos he knows he made a mistake then, so I don't really mind sleeping on the settee. It's a base, innit."

Another young man, whose mother re-established regular contact while he was in custody and later offered him a home, explained the difference this had made to his outlook on life:

"When me mam started visiting me in nick, I knew then, I didn't feel lonely then. From then on I knew me mam, she'd always be there for me."

A number of the young people were anxious to find accommodation near their families. Some of those with positive links were living in the same neighbourhood as family members, seeing them regularly either through visits or, in some cases, through regular contact at the local social club. Living nearby made it easier for them to maintain or renew family links of some kind, enabling them to pop in regularly for company and sometimes for meals. One young man explained how he felt that his family gave him 'a bit of encouragement' and how, as they lived just around the corner, "if I need owt I can pop up and see 'em". In some cases relationships improved after a young person moved to the same neighbourhood as a parent.

For some, the initial period after leaving care was a time when they attempted to renegotiate relationships. Most young people involved in this process of renegotiation did not actually move back to the parental home, but leaving care was a time when they re-evaluated their relationships with parents or made attempts to renew contact. A few recognised that they could sustain reasonably positive relationships with parents as long as they did not live under one roof:

"Me mum's good, do you know what I mean? The best mum in the world, it's just that we can't live together."

For a few young people there were reconciliations. These young people had felt hurt and angry about their past experiences, but the loneliness, stresses and crises they experienced on leaving care prompted them, or their parents, to attempt a rapprochement. These young people showed a poignant need for reconciliation and cautiously responded to parental overtures despite having experienced years of rejection, as in the case of one young woman who had been sexually abused by her stepfather:

"I mean at Christmas she really opened up to me about me stepdad and it's the first time she's done it. I started crying. I think it were tears of relief more than anything because it were the first time she's actually admitted to me that she believed me about what happened between me and me stepdad and she apologised for taking his side against mine. But it's like she said, it were a case of him or me and I couldn't support her and five kids . . . I don't trust anybody at all. I don't even trust me own mother."

Despite the young people's understandable caution, crises such as homelessness, the death of another family member or, in the case of two young people, a complete mental breakdown, sometimes brought them closer to parents. The young woman who had been raped by her brother and had suffered a subsequent breakdown became reconciled with her mother in the ensuing months, after having been 'looked after' for most of her life:

"It used to be, I don't know, like visiting a distant relative you didn't know, just sitting there making polite conversation. But now it's totally different. You know, I sit down and talk to her about most things and it's getting a much stronger bond, I think."

Others gave similar accounts of the strain that separation had placed on relationships and of the gradual process of re-establishing a *modus vivendum*:

"It just felt weird, you know, your mum coming to see you and not knowing what to say to her after so long being with her, you just feel scared of talking to her, you know. You have to grow to know your mum again and grow to know your brother and sister again."

Several young women found that their mothers showed a renewed interest in them once they had a baby:

"It's a lot better now than it was because I've got (baby) to think of and they're all around me."

They felt they had a new status in the eyes of their families and that consequently they were viewed with more respect. Some, however, were ambivalent or even bitter about their mothers' increased contact with them, feeling that it was the baby they were interested in rather than them.

The renewal of relationships with parents sometimes proved to be a disappointment as past difficulties in relationships surfaced, or new problems emerged. In particular, a number of young women complained that although they had renewed contact with their mothers, they were disappointed to find that they were not being sufficiently 'parental'. They were dismayed to find that their mothers were behaving 'more like a sister' or 'more like a friend' or 'more of a teenager than a mum':

"There are still problems. Like, she's too nice, she doesn't tell me off enough, it's just like friends, you know what I mean? It's not like a mother/daughter relationship, it's weird."

It seems that separation had made it hard for these mothers to find a role for themselves vis-à-vis their daughters. These young women were dismayed to find that they did not really respect their mothers and these disappointments sometimes brought back to the surface old grievances about what they saw as parental failures leading to their initial entry to care.

Most of those who were well supported by their parents also had links with members of their extended family and these links were very important to them. But for a fifth of the young people, their extended family was their *primary* source of support – aunts, uncles, siblings, grandparents or step-parents all had an important role to play. This group of young people had no contact with their parents or, despite maintaining some contact, found their parents very unsupportive. Siblings were a particularly important source of emotional support and for nine of the young people their closest and most supportive relationships were with brothers and sisters. For a few young women, their relationship with older sisters had a parental quality and they would rely on them for support, advice and guidance. Recent research has shown that even since the Children Act 1989, with its emphasis on contact, work with sibling groups has remained a neglected area of practice. Maintaining contact between siblings who are separated and, where possible, placing 'looked after' siblings together, can have very important implications for them later in their lives when they leave care. However, three quarters of sibling groups are separated in care (Bilson and Barker 1992–93). Contact between siblings can play a part in helping children and young people develop a secure sense of their identity and sibling bonds are often particularly strong when parenting is not effective (Ward 1984; in Bilson and Barker 1992–93).

Some young people had been cared for by members of their extended family and had developed close bonds with them, seeing them as additional or surrogate parental figures. A few had lived with grandparents at some stage of their lives and maintained a positive relationship with them, which they found very helpful. As Rowe et al have also observed, promoting involvement by grandparents is often very beneficial to children who are 'looked after' (Rowe et al 1984). For others, contact with siblings, grandparents, aunts, uncles and cousins did not offer clear support but fulfilled an important symbolic role for young people who sought contact with extended family members to meet their need for a sense of belonging and identification with their families. However, for young people who had suffered severe parental rejection this identification with the wider family could not fully meet their needs.

Poor family relationships

Sadly, well over a quarter of the young people either had no contact at all with family members or had poor relationships with both their parents and their extended families. Relationships were characterised by conflict, a lack of interest by family members or only infrequent contact. Some young people saw their parents regularly but did not experience this contact as supportive; parents were either reluctant to see them, were uninterested in them or conflicts regularly occurred during visits.

Patterns of rejection established before they were separated from parents continued once the young people had left care and remained a source of considerable distress to them. Almost a third of the young people interviewed had experienced rejection by one or both parents. Some of these young people attempted to renew contact with parents after many years, only to have their advances met yet again with outright rejection, with parents making it clear that they wanted no contact. Two young men (both with moderate learning difficulties) were not only rejected by their parents but were exploited by their siblings, who either tried to extort money from them or stole all their belongings from them. Rejection from an early age remained a source of considerable inner conflict and distress which these young people were still struggling to resolve at the point of leaving care. Not surprisingly, special occasions made their estrangement even more painful:

> *"It were just a family I saw in the park once. Christmas day. So I went out for a ride on me bike, sat on a park bench watching these kids play. They were flying a kite so I went up to them and says 'what's it like Christmas with your family?'"*

A few had brief reconciliations with parents they had not seen for a long time which rapidly fizzled out due to lack of parental commitment. These episodes left the young people feeling still more hurt. Two brothers who had moved from their home area with their foster parents some years earlier returned to their home town when they left care hoping for a reunification with their family. Although various family members provided temporary accommodation these situations soon broke down and, in a town that was no longer familiar and with no accommodation of their own, they turned to acquaintances for help. They were deeply disappointed by their family's lack of commitment to them:

> *"I expected me family to mean more, think more of me and try to support me more . . . You see, it's the people that aren't related that seem to care more for us, which seems funny."*

Many of the young people with poor family relationships (including the group who spoke of clear parental rejection) developed strategies to help them deal with their distress, either through seeking to distance themselves from their families or through constructing idealised images of their parents. The first group were distressed, angry and resentful about abandonment, rejection or past abuse. One young man who had been abused and rejected was clearly still very angry and hurt:

> *"If anybody mentions me family I just say I haven't got none. I don't want to know 'em.'*

Similarly, a young woman who had been in and out of care most of her life expected little from her family, explaining that 'they've never really acted like parents'. Others said that they chose not to see their parents at all. Not surprisingly these young people's feelings about their families were complex, full of conflicts and ambivalence, and even those who said they 'chose' estrangement from their families were clearly deeply distressed by this.

Some young people who had been consistently rejected by parents for many years had built up idealised pictures of them, constructing explanatory narratives of their lives which sought to exonerate parents or rationalise their behaviour, sometimes by blaming themselves or by blaming social workers. They tried to reconstruct their parents' actions in positive ways, or tried to construct narratives which would explain why parents had given them up or failed to maintain contact without tarnishing their image of the parent. These conflicts led some to blame themselves for the abuse or rejection they had suffered and left them confused about relationships in general. Others cherished fantasies of rebuilding relationships with rejecting parents and became angry if any suggestion of blame was attributed to a parent, even after suffering serious physical or sexual abuse at their hands. A young woman who wanted to trace her father hoped that he would "be there, a dad to look up to", and a young man who had not seen his parents for nine years imagined how different life could be:

> *"I just wish I had a family from when I was young. Things wouldn't be so complicated . . . I want to see them regularly. Yeah, be involved with them, do things with them, like a family."*

For many of the young people who continued to be 'looked after' until their late teens and had had poor relationships with their families before they were separated from them, these had not improved while they were being 'looked after'. Even where relationships had been less problematic, separation sometimes created additional strains, leaving young people feeling they didn't really know their families any more. In such cases, the prognosis for support from their families once they ceased to be 'looked after' was poor.

Maintaining family contact

The level of contact maintained with their families while they were being 'looked after' was a good indicator of the level of support the young people could expect from them after leaving care. Of the 21 young people who had positive relationships with their parents when they first left care, all but one had maintained regular contact during most of the time they were being 'looked after'. Contact had been welcomed and encouraged by social workers and carers. Even though regular access did not lead to reunification with parents, in these cases it at least allowed the child and family to keep in touch. It enabled them to maintain and, in a few cases improve, their relationship. For those young people for whom we have evidence that regular family contact was not maintained in care, the majority had poor relationships with parents on leaving care. In looking specifically at young people who leave care in their late teens we see the *consequences* for many young people of low levels of contact with their families during the time they are 'looked after', whatever the reasons for this lack of contact. In this our findings add further weight to earlier research which has emphasised the importance of maintaining family links for children who are 'looked after' (Millham et al 1986; Fanshel and Shinn 1978).

Foster carers

Of those who were fostered, one quarter felt a very strong identification with their foster families. They felt a sense of belonging, that they were treated as part of the family, 'like a son' or 'like a daughter'. This group, particularly those who had been with the same family from an early age, felt that they belonged to their foster families rather than to their birth families. As one young man put it:

"I regard them as me real parents, so far as I'm concerned, so far as they're concerned, I'm their son."

Even some of those who had moved to live with their foster carers more recently felt that they offered more emotional support to them than their birth families:

"I keep in contact with her because she's more of a mum to me than my own mum was."

These feelings were not always reciprocated. Conflicts sometimes led to a breakdown of relationships, or in some cases foster parents showed little interest once their formal involvement ceased. And, as we have already seen, for a third of those who left care from foster placements their transition to independent accommodation was precipitated by placement breakdown. A young man with learning difficulties who had lived with the same foster carers for seventeen years wanted to stay beyond his eighteenth birthday but was asked to leave immediately boarding out payments ceased and the foster carers had no further contact with him. Another young man who had also seen himself as 'one of the family' found his foster carers made little effort to maintain contact once he left, "they just sort of leave it up to me". For young people who felt they 'belonged' to their foster carers' family, the breakdown of relationships with foster carers created a terrible sense of loss, as two young women explained:

"They treated me more like a daughter than my own did . . . and I gained sisters and a grandma and grandad you know, everything that I didn't have they did, and I had it . . . and I just lost it all, it was awful."

"Them foster parents that I had, to me they will always be mum and dad, because that's what they were for three years. They helped me out a lot. I call them a lot of names a lot of the time but deep down I do love them and I wish that I could have regular contact with them, but I can't."

Only a third of those who had been fostered continued to receive ongoing support from foster carers when they first left care and within 18–24 months this figure had fallen to less than a fifth. Earlier studies have found similar patterns of continuing support from foster carers. Our earlier survey of 183 young people found that 36% of those who had been fostered received continuing support from foster carers up to nine months after leaving care, while the National Foster Care Association found that 34% of foster carers remained in contact with children who had left their care (Biehal et al 1992; NFCA 1992). Only a tenth of those who had been fostered continued to live with former foster carers after the age of 18 and, for most of these, foster carers continued to receive financial support from Social Services through redesignating the accommodation as supported lodgings. However, all but one had moved on by our second interview a few months later. Whilst pressure for places and problems with funding lie at the heart of some of these movements, it nevertheless remains the case that, for the majority of those fostered, their placements did not provide a substitute home base that they could rely upon in the long term.

Partners

Several of the young people began to cohabit with partners within a very short time of moving to independent living. Nearly one eighth were living with a partner within a few months of leaving care, either in independent accommodation or with their partner's family, although most of these relationships had ended a few months later. Within 18–24 months over a third of the young people we were able to contact were living with partners and two of these were married.[1] This is a far higher proportion of young people cohabiting than is found in the general population. In her analysis of data on over 4000 young people, Jones found that only 5% were living in partnership households (Jones 1993). Not surprisingly, living with a partner could help to combat loneliness, as one young woman explained:

> *"It was nice to have someone there, you know, not being on my own all the time. It was nice to come and be getting something ready for when he came home."*

For three young women, though, living with partners was less positive, bringing violence rather than companionship.

Many of this group had families who were either rejecting or were otherwise unsupportive to them, and five young women depended entirely on their partners for emotional support and were isolated from family or other social contacts. In some cases young people appeared to 'adopt' their partner's family as an alternative family, compensating for their own lack of family support. This raises the question of whether loneliness and lack of emotional support from their families precipitates some young people into setting up home with partners at an early stage of their lives.

Friends

Many were isolated and felt lonely much of the time:

> *"I'd like to go out and socialise a bit more and make a few friends, 'cos I think you are a different person if you've got friends. If you've got no friends I think it's, I don't know, it makes you low."*

---

1. Of the young people remaining in the sample by the final interview (n=53), 19 were living with partners. This represents a quarter of the original sample, but we do not know the household status of the 21 who were lost, some of whom may also have been cohabiting by this point.

The majority of the young people who had poor friendship networks also had poor relationships with parents, characterised by rejection, conflict or simply a lack of parental interest and support. Some saw parents infrequently or not at all. On the other hand, two thirds of the young people who had positive relationships with parents also had good networks of friends. The association between having a poor or non-existent relationship with parents and having poor social networks on leaving care suggests that those young people whose difficulties in relationships with parents persisted into their late teens may have particular difficulties in building and sustaining other social relationships. Young people whose family relationships had made it hard for them to trust anyone, found it hard to make and sustain friendships. As one young woman, who said she had been repeatedly let down by others, commented:

"If I want a friend, I don't have any problem finding friends. It's just that I have a problem committing myself to that friendship and that's why I've not looked for a friend."

Several of the young people felt that they had a circle of 'mates' but no real friends. There was sometimes a gender dimension to this, as one lonely young man explained:

"I mean lads, they're not really ones for close knit friendships are they, not like girls are . . . So they just go out in a big group and they don't really know each other much. That's what I find, anyway."

Some vulnerable care leavers were exploited by other young people, their homes used as places to drop in day and night and sometimes virtually taken over. Often loneliness and insecurity prompted them to acquiesce to this, with the result that their lives became chaotic, they had problems with neighbours and found it hard to establish themselves in employment or training.

Professional support

The vulnerability of some care leavers to exploitation by friends and acquaintances was widely recognised by leaving care workers, who tried to help them learn strategies for managing their relationships with other young people and to protect themselves from exploitation and, in some cases, harassment. Leaving care schemes were generally well aware of the importance of helping care leavers establish and maintain a circle of friends. Some tried to encourage the young people to develop leisure interests and linked them into local clubs and activities for young people. Their detailed local knowledge and links with local youth provision were an invaluable resource here. In addition, the District scheme and both the City schemes ran a variety of groups, some purely social and recreational and some developmental/educational, all of which could offer a focus for establishing and developing the young people's social networks. The group setting served as a useful arena for helping young people improve their social skills and their ability to manage relationships with others. Although there is a danger that such groups may encourage care leavers to become ghettoised, in the absence of alternative networks they do provide a network of contacts and, in some cases friends, together with an opportunity to develop social skills in a supportive setting. In general, social workers were less well informed about the nature of the young people's friendships and only very few of them attempted any work with them on social skills or on widening their social networks.

Another helpful route to widening friendship networks was further education, which naturally provided a pool of other young people of similar ages. Several young people found that they were beginning to make new friendships once they began courses in further education. Assisting young people to apply for college courses and to maintain their places there can serve an important social function as well as an educational one. Support from social services to young people continuing their education was therefore extremely important. Of course, financial support is of key importance, but encouragement, interest and concern from social workers and scheme workers played an important part in supporting those who continued their education.

Apart from some workers on the City (vol) scheme, work on family issues was not a primary focus for leaving care workers. Even for many social workers, work on family issues was not a priority at this stage in the young people's lives, although many of the young people themselves felt considerable distress about the quality of their relationships with their families. Less then a third of the social workers were working on family issues with care leavers, although it must be borne in mind that in some cases the young people were unwilling to discuss their families. Of those who did address family issues, some were involved in counselling young people, assisting them in dealing with conflicts or in managing family relationships. In several instances social workers played a mediating role, helping young people repair links with parents or other relatives or brokering a return home. In some cases the work focused on maintaining links with siblings still in care or on key members of their extended families. In others, where certain family relationships were perceived as destructive, social workers were trying to encourage young people to assert themselves or distance themselves from their families. Some social workers seemed to feel that however negative family relationships appeared to be, a young person would nevertheless benefit from maintaining some contact, however poor the quality of that contact. They would advise 'don't burn your boats' or 'don't sever your links'.

In a few cases, social services formally supported the continuation of help from foster carers by redesignating foster placements as supported lodgings placements. Although not feasible or desirable in every case, this approach is to be welcomed as it provided continuity and stability for the young people, allowing their move to independence to be determined by their readiness to move on rather than by their age.

• Summary points •

Very few of these young people were able to return to their families to live, although four fifths retained some contact in the early months after leaving care. However, fewer than one third had positive or supportive relationships with one or both parents. During the 18–24 months of the research some renewed or repaired relationships with their families and around one half had some positive relationships at the close of the research. For young people this was a time for attempting to renegotiate relationships and for attempts at renewal and adjustment; although for many, this process ended in further rejection. For one fifth links with extended family members or older siblings constituted their primary source of support. Positive family relationships were associated with having had continuing contact through care and with an ability to build and sustain friendship networks.

Over one quarter of the sample had poor or non-existent support from parents and almost one third had experienced rejection. The majority of these young people also had few friends and experienced loneliness and isolation. The failure to maintain or renew family relationships whilst looked after appears to influence young people's ability to build other support networks.

Only one tenth were able to continue living with their foster carers beyond the point of legal discharge, although one third continued to receive support once they had moved on. Within 18–24 months of leaving care over one third of the sample were living with partners and some seemed to have 'adopted' their partners' families as an insulation against loneliness. Work on family links and mediation in family relationships was not a central priority for workers at this stage. Leaving care schemes tended to focus on the individual young person and fewer than one third of social workers were working actively in this area at this time. Schemes were more involved in helping to promote friendship and leisure networks.

- An assessment of the extent and quality of support that 'looked after' young people can expect to receive from their families once they leave care should be made long before they leave their final placements. In most cases their best interests will be served by efforts to maintain or create links with their families while they are being 'looked after'.

- Both while a child is in substitute care or accommodation and *after*, social workers have an important role to play in assisting, where possible, young people with poor family links to improve them through encouraging contact and mediating between them and their families. Even if relationships with parents have irretrievably broken down, other members of a young person's extended family may be able to offer some support. They may not be able to offer a place to stay, but simply by keeping in touch, showing concern and offering emotional support grandparents, aunts, uncles or siblings can make a young person feel less isolated.

- Many care leavers would also benefit if more flexible use was made of foster placements, allowing young people to remain post-18 on a supported lodgings basis if desired. Consideration should be given to the possibility or young people returning to foster families if their first attempts at independent living break down. Imaginative use could be made of foster carers' skills to provide after care services to their young people once they have moved on. We strongly recommend a review of the role of foster carers in relation to leaving care.

- Finally, leaving care schemes have an important role to play in assisting young people to establish and maintain a network of friends. Through the provision of groups to facilitate social contacts and give guidance on social skills, linking young people into local youth and leisure provision and through individual advice on managing social relationships where difficulties arise, they can help care leavers combat isolation and strengthen their resistance to exploitation by others.

CHAPTER 9

DEVELOPING LIFE SKILLS

The practical and social skills we require to live successfully in the adult community are learnt throughout our childhood. Here we explore the influence of the care experience on the ability of these young people to gain essential life skills, the degree to which they were prepared for their future lives and their early attempts to manage their lives in the community and improve their skills.

> *"Care has done quite a lot for me. It's helped me out. Helped me realise what life is all about and how to look after myself."*
>
> *"You just got some toothpaste and soap."*
>
> (TWO YOUNG PEOPLE'S CONTRASTING PERCEPTIONS OF THE CARE EXPERIENCE)

The ability of young people to care for themselves and relate appropriately to others underscores all other dimensions of transition. It influences their ability to manage their homes once they move on from care, to find employment and to construct an active and sustaining social life. However, as we shall see, the relationship between these core skills and success in other life areas is reciprocal. Life events that induce a sense of instability and insecurity can undermine the ability to deploy self care skills that have already been accumulated. Young people's lives can enter a downward spiral.

What do we mean by life skills? We have divided life skills into three broad areas: self care – including personal hygiene, diet and awareness of contraception and sexual health; practical skills – including budgeting, shopping, cooking and cleaning; and interpersonal skills – the ability to manage formal and private relationships, including sexual relationships. Ideally, the acquisition of these skills should be an integral part of our common journey from childhood to adulthood. For many but by no means all young people growing up in the family home, learning these skills is a **gradual** process beginning in childhood and progressing with increasing age and development. It is usually a **supported** and **participatory** process, involving discussion, negotiation, risk taking and trial and error in the context of a stable family and friendship network. It is also a subtly **holistic** process based on a grounded understanding of young people's personalities, needs and abilities. Conflicts can therefore be negotiated and accommodated.

For young people in care this pattern has often been significantly different. Accumulated evidence has tended to emphasise the limited opportunities available for young people to participate in decision making and to take risks; to stress the over-protective nature of many care arrangements (Stein 1990; Stein and Ellis 1983; Page and Clarke 1977). It has pointed to the inflexibility of some regimes in children's homes and the influence of bulk buying, fixed menus and staff changes on limiting opportunities for the gradual development of practical skills (Who Cares? Trust 1993; SSI 1985; Berridge 1985). Also to the tendency for preparation to be compressed into the last years of care and to have a predominantly practical focus, to lack a holistic perspective (Stein and Carey 1986). Finally, while some young people do manage to find a stable and positive base in care, for others patterns of movement and a lack of continuous carer support tend to impede the gradual assimilation of skills and knowledge.

Preparing for life in the community

The pre-care and care careers of the young people in our sample were characterised by diversity. Nearly a third, as we have seen, first entered care when already teenagers and, where they had and retained positive relationships with their families, they were often quite skilled at the point of entering care, having had opportunities to learn in a family setting. Family members then remained a reference point for further support and advice. For the two fifths who had been in care more than ten years and for whom care had been their main life experience, the need to find a stable placement and continuity in support and encouragement from carers and social workers was even more essential. Particularly where they had experienced family rejection and stress in their lives, they were more likely to need a stable platform upon which they could develop their practical and social skills.

Some young people were able to find this, especially where they had been placed in long-term foster care and where they felt 'part of the family' and included in family decision making. In this context they were able to gain skills gradually and 'naturally' over time. They felt confident to ask questions and 'check out' problems they were unsure about with their carers and, as they got older, were able to negotiate greater autonomy for themselves. In these placements the approach to developing life skills was more holistic, integrating the assimilation of practical skills with concern for the wider emotional aspects of psycho-social development and the need to be able to build and sustain a varied range of relationships. Young people were encouraged to make friends, join clubs and participate in after school activities and their friends were made welcome at home.

However this balance was not apparent in all foster placements. While some offered an abundance of care and concern, the young people themselves were over-protected and lacked sufficient opportunity for development; a risk that appeared greatest for those with learning difficulties:

"They did everything for me . . . I didn't have to do anything"

Although young people rarely complained at the time, they were often left with regrets and anxiety when standing at the threshold of their own flats. As one young woman fostered with relatives commented:

"When I lived with me nan I never used to offer to do anything, never used to offer to cook. I had everything done for me, then when you get to your own place it's hard 'cos you think, 'Oh, am I doing everything right?' You worry a lot."

In contrast a few young people, even where placed long-term, felt their placements had been exploitative. Although unhappy, either they had not disclosed this to their social workers or their testimony had not been believed and acted upon. One young woman described her experience as being like a 'live-in slave', having had to do all the chores for the family and having little space for herself. Others mentioned discouragement from going out and making friends and/or resistance to them bringing friends home. Some young people, although stable, never felt able to integrate with the family, remained on edge and, in consequence, the quality of their preparation suffered:

"I never felt at home, never, even when I was with (my foster carers) ten years I never felt at home. I always knew I was in care."

Although the majority of young people in foster care valued the concern, interest and encouragment shown to them by their carers and social workers, there were areas where, for some, communication was more difficult. Studies point to the difficulties most families experience when discussing sexual health and sexuality, most believing it to be the province of schools (Allen 1987). While many young people did obtain advice in this area and most felt themselves to be knowledgeable, even if this knowledge had been culled from a variety of sources (media, school, friends and older sisters were often mentioned), some felt embarassed to discuss this area with carers:

"I mean there are certain things you find you can't talk to your foster parents about and you'd rather talk to an outsider."

Indeed some young people also found approaches from social workers in this area intrusive and too personal. The need to build a close and confiding relationship to discuss intimate issues also affected social workers themselves. Some felt uncomfortable and preferred to leave the responsibility to carers; others provided basic literature but were less available for continuing discussions. Given that truancy featured in the lives of a significant minority of our sample and that, in consequence, young people may have missed out on that source of information, the potential for a serious gap in their education was very real. This appeared equally true for young people in residential care. Although most homes did provide literature and a few ran group sessions on sex and sexuality, most counselling seemed to depend on the quality of relationship a young person had with a particular staff member. Inputs rarely seemed structured or planned.

In overall terms, direct inputs from social workers to young people and foster carers in these key developmental areas were variable. Social work attention tended to focus most strongly where there were discrete problems in placements. Where young people remained stable it was more likely that the central role in developing practical and social skills would be left with carers and social workers would restrict themselves to a monitoring role at reviews. Sometimes they were reluctant to intervene directly, feeling it would be intrusive upon family relationships, in other cases it was simply assumed that young people's skills would progress naturally in that setting. Obviously the constraints and pressures upon social work time make it difficult to offer intensive support directly but, as we have seen, some young people were lacking opportunities to develop skills and build relationships. There was little evidence that guidance or training was being made available to assist carers to develop more structured programmes of preparation nor, in some cases, that a pro-active approach to the development of life skills had been made a central part of the child care planning and review cycle. In consequence when, for some young people, placements broke down at a later point precipitating a move to independent living, they lacked many of the core skills necessary to sustain their new homes.

The experience of young people in residential care was equally varied, as the comments at the start of the chapter imply. Where young people found stability in a children's home, particularly small group homes, they often felt they had been offered opportunities to develop their skills and abilities gradually in a supportive and participatory environment. For some it compensated for an unstable pre-care career.

However, in children's homes this positive environment is more difficult to achieve. Although the daily learning process is informal, based around a trusting relationship with a key worker, where groups of young people are living together the need for a structured and formal framework to set goals and monitor and review progress is more obvious. The shift system and staff changes tended to reduce continuity of support for young people. For young people living in the main home, bulk purchase and catering arrangements reduced opportunities for learning practical skills. Some young people were affected by the stigma of being in a children's home and, in consequence, were more reluctant to socialise outside or invite friends back. Some who did found they suffered a lack of privacy to entertain. Many were also affected by peer cultures in children's homes and, where they established a pattern of truancy, absconding or drug use, they sometimes missed out on structured preparation altogether. This was also true for those who experienced multiple placement moves. For them, self help ultimately proved the only alternative:

"I've not really had a lot of help . . . As I've grown older I've just found it out for myself."

"I brought meself up really."

The difficulties of providing an adequate preparatory experience in children's homes has led to the growth of semi-independence units attached to homes and a number of young people spent their last 12–18 months in units preparing for independence. Again their experience was varied. Many valued the opportunity to practice their practical skills (shopping, cooking, cleaning, handling money) and build confidence in a supportive environment. It enabled them the chance to take risks and make mistakes while support remained on hand:

"They helped you to budget things out and see what it would be like by yourself."

However some young people felt that the environment was too artificial, that, as they later discovered, budgeting in the real world was far harder. It also tended to compress 'independence' skills training into the last years of care, for it to assume the character of a 'domestic combat course' and underplay the emotional and relational dimensions of development (Stein and Carey 1986). Several social workers and leaving care workers were critical of this tendency. They felt that while young people learnt many practical skills they often lacked the 'inter-dependent' relationship skills they would later need. Some also felt that the preparation offered lacked a guiding framework, was often unstructured and that, in consequence, the experience offered to young people was variable.

Our evidence tends to reinforce this view. Where young people were able to establish a bond with a worker, not necessarily their key worker, or where they were seen as responsible, the quality of their experience tended to be better. For example, one young man described a staff member, not his key worker, as being "like a dad to me". He was able to communicate with him and use him as a source of support when he found others, including his key worker, difficult to talk to. While those who had positive relationships with staff were also positive about their experience, some whose care careers were marked by instability and behavioural disturbance felt more negative. For instance, one young man experienced his time in a unit as a form of punishment. Rather than feeling supported he felt under surveillance and was eventually eased out of the children's home to early independence. He felt he had received no effective preparation.

Our data points to the inconsistent and variable nature of provision. Some young people in both residential and foster care found a stable and supportive base upon which they could gradually develop their skills and confidence. For others movement, over-protection, lack of opportunity and the structures of children's homes limited their progress. The young people themselves had different starting points. The impact of pre-care stress and instability often had lasting effects on their intellectual and emotional development and, for some, was manifested in behavioural disturbance. Others were influenced by peer group cultures in children's homes. Some resisted attempts to be constrained or 'trained', preferring to experiment for themselves:

"If you're going to find out, you've got to find out yourself . . . then you live how you want to live."

Finally, the cultural self-care needs of black young people were not always met. While one young woman spoke very positively of her children's home, she had had limited opportunities to learn and practice her own style of cooking. Another was very critical of her social worker's ignorance of her needs for special hair and skin care and her lack of understanding of the additional costs involved.

In circumstances where responsibility for the care of young people is shared between a number of adults, the need for a clear framework to guide the development of skills is necessary. Clear guidance and procedures in our authorities appeared to be lacking, and training and support for carers (especially foster carers) seemed limited. Equally, the progress of skills did not always form a central part of child care planning and review. As a result, where young people were stable and had positive relationships with carers and/or social workers their skills could develop informally, but for others the risk of gaps in their education remained.

The role played by leaving care workers at this stage also varied from scheme to scheme. All schemes valued early referral as it gave the opportunity to plan young people's transitions well in advance, to co-ordinate plans with social workers and carers, build a relationship with young people and identify strengths and weaknesses for future work. However, the degree to which schemes engaged in active support around practical and social skills varied. County, for example, aware of the need to ration its resources across a large authority, usually only adopted an advisory role. District and City (ssd) did offer direct assistance at the preparatory stage, mostly to young people in residential care. City (vol) would also involve themselves with young people who were awaiting a place in their trainer accommodation. Social workers often referred young people where they were unhappy with the support being offered in a children's home or where they felt skills training to be more suited to the specialist role of schemes. While this involvement was invariably valued by young people, not least because they were usually granted a new status and respect as young adults, it was also indicative of how the development of essential life skills can be compressed into the latter stages of the care career. Where involved, young people also had access to the social groups and drop-in services run by the projects. Some had a preparatory focus and offered the opportunity to socialise, develop skills and make social contacts that would be helpful to them once they moved on.

Building skills in the community

As we have seen, the period of transition was one of intense activity for social workers and leaving care workers. Young people, experiencing conflicting emotions, needed help to organise their homes. Help was solidly practical and included arranging leaving care grants, buying furniture, decorating, setting up systems for paying bills and offering advice and assistance around life skills (cooking, shopping, negotiating with agencies). The practical and emotional resources available to young people varied greatly at this point. Just under one third had positive relationships with their parents and could therefore turn to them for advice, information and informal support. Others could turn to grandparents, aunts or older siblings. Some relied on partners' families and, as the research progressed, more young people moved in with partners (one third by the close) and a few relied heavily on them to compensate for their own lack of skills.

At the point of transition nearly two thirds had quite good practical and self care skills, just over one half were able to manage formal encounters with agencies with some success, but only two fifths had good budgeting skills. Between one quarter and a third needed intensive support in most areas. Although they had moved on from care, some to supported accommodation, they lacked the skills to sustain their lives.[1]

The degree to which young people were prepared for their lives in the community related to both age and gender. Previous studies have highlighted the unrealistic expectations that surround the move to independence for most young people in care at 16–18 years of age; an expectation of 'instant maturity' (Stein 1990; Stein and Carey 1986). Several workers in this study were critical of the 'push' factors that launched young people into the community before they were ready to cope.

Even two years later, a smaller proportion of those who left at 16 had good life skills (46%) as compared to those who left at 18 (66%).

The ability to manage was also gendered. At all stages of the research young women were twice as likely to have good skills and to be able to manage their accommodation. This both related to practical skills, especially managing money, and to the ability to maintain reasonable relations with landlords, neighbours and friends; two of the key factors associated with housing breakdown. Although many workers were aware of the greater risk of breakdown for young men, it suggests a need to tackle gender-related assumptions amongst young men (and perhaps carers) at an early stage in their care careers.

The help offered appeared most intensive where transitions had been well co-ordinated and planned over time and, most especially, where young people moved into supported accommodation either directly managed by or linked to schemes. Stays in supported lodgings, hostels or semi-independent flats gave young people who were uncertain of their skills and abilities a further opportunity to practise in a supported environment. In some instances it attempted to compensate for poor past experiences in care and assistance with life and social skills formed part of an overall package of support that reached into most areas of young people's lives. A few young people, insecure and unsettled by their pasts, were unable even to cope with this degree of independence and their situations broke down, but the majority valued the

1.   See chapter 22 for a detailed discussion of the basis for our assessment of outcomes in this area.

practical and emotional support they had received. As one young man summed up succinctly, "it made me see meself differently".

Where young people made planned moves directly into their own flats and help with life skills was available, they also valued the practical assistance. However, even more they appreciated the reassurance, company and positive reinforcement that contact could offer at this time of uncertainty – "she was someone I could talk to as well". In this sense help with practical skills needs to be set in a context of meeting the emotional and interpersonal needs that young people have and central to this is the fear of isolation and loneliness that independence brings. Those who lacked close support and had received insufficient guidance in the past, felt the burden of having to cope alone:

> ". . . like I haven't got a doctor up here yet . . . I don't really want to go in to social services, stand there and talk to somebody and say, look, what's doing this and what's doing that and everything . . . Nobody's ever took me to sign on, I had to go and do it meself and everything."

Others were struggling with financial difficulties:

> "I didn't expect that it'd be as hard . . . If I'd had guidance and someone talking to me . . . but no one told me what to expect."

Some young people felt they needed to resolve problems for themselves, to be independent, and refused to seek help – "you've got to work it out for yourselves haven't you".

After their first 18–24 months of living in the community, life remained hard for most of the young people. Few had made great strides in the practical management of their lives, although, for most, gains in terms of their confidence and maturity had been hard won:

> "I mean it's a challenge having to do stuff for yourself, you're having to learn to cook, you're having to learn to clean . . . I mean, all right, you're not good at it to start with or you can't be bothered, but in time you learn and you eventually do it."

The majority of those whose practical and social skills were competent when they had left care had been able to develop and refine them in the community, they had gained in confidence and, for those with informal and professional support, the advice and support offered had been reassuring. Some of those with poor skills had also taken small steps, usually where offered intensive help in supported environments by social workers and leaving care workers.

Budgeting remained a serious problem for nearly a third of the sample and, for some of those with support, direct debit systems had been set up:

> "If I had me bill money I'd spend it on someat else. I think it's important to pay your bills nowadays 'cos you get cut off."

As we have seen, the very low incomes available to young people had greatly increased the pressure on fragile budgeting skills and upon workers trying to teach skills. Even where young people were living with partners the vast majority were coping at or around benefit levels. Coping with poverty increased stress, threatened the ability of young people to manage their homes and heightened their sense of social isolation. Young parents found it particularly difficult and some had to deny themselves in order to meet their children's needs:

"Sometimes I find myself not eating, not purposely, but I just don't have, you know, I'll save that or whatever . . . I won't have to buy so much next week."

Successfully negotiating encounters with formal agencies was still a problem for around one half of the sample. Many young people in touch with schemes had relied heavily on their support to mediate in their dealings with landlords, housing agencies, social security and employers. Schemes were very much aware of the kinds of skills that young people needed to manage formal and informal relationships in the community and help in this area was a focus of scheme activity. At the close of the research, as support was gradually being withdrawn or reduced in intensity, young people were aware of the need to take greater responsibility in these encounters for themselves. Some felt more confident and assertive:

". . . no problem with anything like that, just tell them the problem and get the job done."

Others, with still limited abilities, required continuing intensive help. Young people valued the accessibility and informality of schemes, especially where they encouraged open access through drop-ins and social activities. It felt reassuring for them to be able to pop in with a problem and receive advice before it assumed the proportions of a crisis. Those who had lacked support had had to learn their negotiating skills the hard way, often learning through the failure of past encounters. Some expressed anger at the lack of support afforded them and the difficulties it had presented:

"I've had to do it, I've had to do it, nobody else was going to do it for me!"

The difficulty with approaches to teaching life skills that rest upon an 'independence' perspective and that focus on practical skills training in the latter years of the care career prior to releasing young people into the community, is that they fail to appreciate the relationship between these core skills and other dimensions of young people's lives. Life events that create a sense of instability and insecurity have a reciprocal impact on the ability of young people to continue learning or deploying skills. In this sense, however good the training, it is unlikely to be successful unless young people feel secure and stable and have their needs met in a holistic way. Equally, it cannot compensate for the need for continuing support as young people are buffeted in their early post-care careers.

We have already pointed to the pressures imposed on young people by unemployment, poverty and isolation and their implications for the strains on young people trying to practice skills. For some young people the pressure proved too great and contributed to their inability to manage their homes. For a few others with quite good life skills, life crises prompted a collapse in their ability to manage. For example, a young parent, whose main support came from her partner and his family, found herself on a downward spiral when the relationship broke down and her supports were lost. Her depression meant that she was no longer adequately able to care for her child or home. Prompted by child care concerns, her social worker negotiated a return to supported lodgings to give her a chance to recuperate. The life of another young woman collapsed after she was sexually abused. Although fearful of going out in public and living from day to day, the counselling offered by her leaving care worker proved, in a real sense, a lifeline for her.

The confidence and assertiveness required to manage a range of formal and informal relationships was also of crucial importance. Several young people were either evicted or threatened with eviction due to a failure to successfully control relationships with landlords, neighbours and friends. The failure to protect their homes from invasion by others created debts, nuisance for those around them and the loss of structure to their lives inhibited attempts to find employment or training. Continuing support enabled some to repair the damage and make a fresh start, for others it precipitated a descent into instability and insecurity.

Where young people lack the level of life skills that they will need to manage successfully in the community, whether through inadequate preparation while in care or their own limited abilities, a range of transitional supported accommodation options needs to be made available. The evidence from our study suggests that they can provide intensive compensatory help to young people. The role of leaving care schemes in developing options, training providers and co-ordinating support is important. Our schemes were investing heavily in this area. The informality of schemes, particularly where they offered group and drop-in facilities, was also valued by young people. Schemes were used both as a source of long-term help by young people struggling in the community and as an arena in which they could make friends, relieve pressure and reduce isolation.

Finally, where, for whatever reason, young people are unable to sustain their skills, there is a need for respite provision. Several young people were able to return to supported lodgings or hostels when their lives were affected by crises. However, these were mostly either young parents, where instability created child care concerns, or young people with learning difficulties who had been unable to cope with the pressures of independent life. Perhaps these facilities needed to be extended to other young people, several of whom were having equal difficulty managing their lives.

• Summary points •

For young people in families the assimilation of practical and social life skills tends to occur gradually throughout childhood. It is a participatory and supported process that is holistic in approach, based on a grounded understanding of the personality and needs of the individual. For these young people in care the experience was more variable. Some, especially but not exclusively in longer-term foster care, found a stable and supportive platform upon which they could gradually build their skills and confidence. A sense of stability and security was essential, as was an opportunity to participate in decision making and to explore a range of relationships outside the home. Constraints in residential care tended to give fewer opportunities and life skills training tended to be more practically focused and concentrated at the latter end of the care career. It sometimes failed to address the wider emotional and relational needs of psycho-social development. Some in foster care were over-protected and even exploited.

- Preparation cannot be left to chance where care is shared by several adults. An overall framework of clear procedures and guidance needs to be developed to ensure consistency; training and support is necessary for carers/social workers and the progress of life skills needs to be a central part of the child care planning and review cycle.

- The particular cultural needs of black and mixed heritage young people should be a focus of attention.

- Many young people lacked essential practical and social skills upon leaving care. This was particularly the case with young men and gendered assumptions need to be tackled at an early stage of the care career.

Most young people continued to struggle in their early post-care careers and the pressures of poverty, unemployment and isolation strained their already fragile skills. Those with informal and professional supports fared better. However, crises generated in other life areas threatened the skill base of young people. For some, their skills collapsed or deteriorated when under pressure.

- For those least prepared and/or able a range of supported accommodation needs to be available – lodgings, hostels and semi-independent flats – and leaving care schemes were playing an important role here.

- Continuity in post-care support is important, as are informal access points for young people to gain help and reduce the pressure of social isolation. For those whose skills break down, respite provision is required to prevent a descent into homelessness.

CHAPTER 10

EMERGING IDENTITIES

Stresses in young people's pre-care lives combined with the loss and disruption caused by separation can have damaging implications for young people's developing identities – for their self image, confidence and self esteem. Where young people fail to find a stable and secure base for themselves within care, these problems may be compounded rather than remedied. Here we look at these young people's attempts to construct a coherent narrative of their lives that can connect past and present and provide a framework for their future lives in the community.

As we have suggested, a 'life course' approach to the study of young people involves situating them within two chains of events – one belonging to the individual young person and one belonging to wider society – which interact to structure their life histories (Cohen, 1986). An individual's identity therefore incorporates elements derived from his or her position within society – which includes their class, gender and ethnic identities – and from their personal biographies. Those aspects of identity and difference which may be seen as 'given', such as gender, ethnic identity and social class, may lead to exclusion and marginalization for some and greater opportunities for self-actualisation for others. Yet these social identities constitute only part of any individual's identity and young people cannot be defined primarily in terms of any one of these. Equally, individual personal histories do not constitute the sole definers of their identity. Self concepts deriving both from an individual's personal history and from his or her social identity are both incorporated into an understanding of the self.

Identity should not be seen as static, but as a dynamic project in which individuals do not 'have' but 'live' a biography. It is a sense of continuity across time and space as interpreted by the individual, but this interpretation is a continuous process whereby narratives of self identity are maintained or subtly revised as life progresses. As Giddens has argued:

"Self identity, in other words, is not something that is just given . . . but something that has to be routinely created and sustained in the reflexive activities of the individual."

If we consider self identity in these dynamic terms, as a 'story' of their lives which individuals routinely create and sustain, we can understand it as a "reflexive project of the self, which consists in the sustaining of coherent, yet continuously revised, biographical narratives" (Giddens 1991). Making sense of the narratives by which they explained their history and 'situated' themselves in the world was very much on the minds of many of the care leavers in our study at this time of major change in their lives.

As they made their various transitions from care placements to independent accommodation, from leaving school to entering the labour market, from changing or leaving behind old relationships to forming new relationships as partners or as parents, their sense of self identity had to integrate these changes into their ongoing 'story' of the self. Transitions in traditional cultures have often been ritualised in rites of passage, but in the modern world individuals have to develop strategies for adjustment and for coping with the losses and the gains, the risks and the opportunities that transitions can bring. For some young people, the transition from the relative security of care placements to an existence no longer determined by structure and routine can be experienced almost as a migration from one country to another:

> *"When you come out (of care) it's hell after. You don't know what you're doing or where you're going. It's just like taking you from one country and putting you into another."*

For a number of young people the stresses of this transition led to a crisis of confidence, a fear that they would be unable to cope with living in the community. Most, though, gradually adjusted after a time, showing great determination to make a success of their lives. One young man aptly described this process of adjustment to the changes in his life:

> *"You've got to be more positive. You've got to be, 'cos if not you end up down and out".*

The way that individuals cope with changes in their lives will be influenced by two main aspects of identity: their sense of who they are (self concept) and their sense of self esteem. These are of course inextricably inter-related, as an individual's 'story' of how they became who they are involves an evaluation of their self worth, and high or low self esteem will help to shape the particular narratives individuals construct in order to understand their lives. We will therefore look first at these young people's understanding of who they were, which involved them in an evaluation of their personal histories and relationships, and second at their sense of self esteem. We will then consider the initial impact of their transitions to independence upon their sense of self identity.

Narratives of history and belonging

> *"In order to have a sense of who we are, we have to have a notion of how we have become and of where we are going' (Taylor 1989, in Giddens 1991). "*

For young people who have experienced at the very least family disruption, separation and, in many cases, a high degree of movement while they were 'looked after', it can be difficult to establish a sense of continuity and of belonging. Most of the young people had been 'looked after' long term – over two thirds for more than 4 years and two fifths for more than 10 years – so they had been separated from their families for a considerable length of time. For those who had experienced several moves during their care careers, attachments had repeatedly been made and broken (see also Stein and Carey, 1986). Over the years, some found it increasingly hard to commit themselves to new relationships. Their experience of disrupted family relationships, compounded by the disruption of relationships that they formed while they were in substitute care or accommodation, made it hard for them to form close attachments or to trust anyone. As one young woman described her experience of care:

"Well it felt really depressing. I couldn't really get emotionally involved and stay in one place all the time, 'cos I can't."

In these circumstances it is perhaps not surprising that for many the need for a sense of continuity in their lives was very strong. Many were trying to find out more about their family and personal history. Some requested access to their files in order to piece together a coherent narrative of their past, others were trying to gather more information about parents they had lost contact with, or never met. A few young people who had lost touch with a parent over the years were trying very hard to trace them again at this turning point in their lives, although sadly in most cases parents could not be traced or, if they were, said that they wanted no contact with the young people. One young woman who was trying to gather more information about her origins was working on her life story book with her social worker and several mentioned having worked on life story books over the years, but while some found this helpful others were less enthusiastic, complaining that they were little more than a list of events which did not explain what the people involved were like or why things had happened. In piecing together fragments of memory with 'official' accounts of past events provided by social workers and carers, young people were trying to construct a coherent 'story' to explain their history, but for some their experiences and relationships were too complex, disrupted or painful to be easily transformed into a single linear narrative. One young woman described this process:

"We used to do (life story books) bit by bit to see how much we could remember and try and fit it all together, which used to help a bit, but not much."

In recent years life story books have been criticised by some for providing 'authorised versions' of a child's life history in a way which tends to foreclose areas of the child's experience which do not fit (Cohen, 1992).

A number of the young people still remained confused about the course of past events by the time they left care. For several of these, however, it was not simply a need to know more about their past that preoccupied them. Some did in fact have an adequate knowledge of past events in their lives, but were still struggling to come to terms with this knowledge, for example by trying to make sense of their parents' rejection of them, and of the ensuing events in their lives. For these, it was not so much a question of *what* happened but *why* it happened, and of the implications of what happened for their sense of identity. Naturally, this was a painful process and the young people required skilled help in working through it. One young woman objected to being described as 'abandoned' when she read her file because of all the negative connotations for her sense of self that this entailed and a young man who wanted "to know more about why me dad gave me up" found it hard to talk about his family at all. Several were struggling to reconcile the rejection they had experienced with their strong identification with parents. Driven by their need to feel they 'belonged' to their families, they devised narratives which explained or excused parents' past behaviour, a process which sometimes involved blaming themselves. Not surprisingly, this process generated conflicts which were not easily resolved, leaving some young people depressed and ill-equipped to cope with the new stresses that resulted from leaving care.

Even where young people experiencing these conflicts in resolving their past received a high degree of support on leaving care, some still found it hard to manage living out of care and experienced a number of crises. For example, one young man who was still struggling to make sense of his father's rejection of him many years ago was very much preoccupied with his past, constantly reworking various explanations for past events in an attempt to create a coherent 'story' of his life that he could accept and live with. The inner conflicts that this process generated left him confused about relationships: "I don't know what's right any more". His preoccupation with his past and his need to repeatedly rehearse his 'story' made it hard for him to accept help from his social worker and leaving care worker in moving forward and making a success of his future. His low self esteem and his expectation that people would not like him made it difficult for him to form relationships or to control the 'hangers on' who virtually took over his flat and would regularly eat him out of house and home. He also found it hard to focus on work or training, to budget and to care for himself. He felt angry but powerless to change anything in his life, despite a high level of support from professionals.

Another young man with a similar history, who had always understood that his parents had given him up when he was two weeks old and had not wanted to see him, was given a different version of events by his grandmother at around the time he left care. She told him that he had been removed by social services against his parents' will and that social services had taken the decision to terminate access. This young man, who had always felt rejected by his parents and who suffered from very low self esteem and an inability to take control of his life, was jolted into a re-evaluation not only of them but of his whole autobiography – the course his life had taken required a revised 'story' with new explanations.

Not all the young people dealt with past events by trying to find out more. One young woman who had suffered sexual abuse wanted to deny painful past events, insisting that she did not want to know and that knowledge of her past had been 'forced' on her by social workers when she was 15. Her account demonstrated her struggle to create and control her own version of her life story and construct a positive self-image against all odds. Fiercely self reliant, her attempt to construct an autobiography which excluded professional versions of events was one strategy she adopted in order to feel she could make her own choices, despite the abuse, stigma, and powerlessness she had experienced in the past.

A need for a sense of belonging was also a feature of some of the young peoples' accounts. One young woman expressed her feelings of exclusion, feelings that were shared by several young people:

"I don't know, it's just my family seems so close and everything and I'm just far apart, just drifting on a raft somewhere . . . I feel everyone's gone and left me, basically."

Those young people who had been fostered by relatives or by long term foster carers who saw them as 'one of the family' did have a positive sense of belonging. As one young man who had been fostered by his aunt for two years explained, when he moved to live with his family he felt "I just fit in". Maintaining links with parents, siblings and other members of their extended families was generally experienced as helpful by most of the young people, even where those relationships were difficult. Only a few said they chose not to see their parents.

As we have seen (chapter 8), contact with families can serve an important *symbolic* function for young people, helping them to maintain a sense of 'belonging' to their families even if relationships are poor, and this may have positive implications for their sense of self identity.

Self-esteem

Self esteem was assessed by means of a qualitative analysis of the young people's accounts of their lives, taking account of how they positioned themselves in their explanations of events. These assessments were also considered in the light of the opinions of the professionals interviewed who knew them well – their social workers and leaving care workers. This analysis showed that many of the young people suffered from low self esteem when they first left care. Not surprisingly, this was particularly the case for those who had suffered rejection by one or both parents, which was the experience of a fifth of the sample. As one young man explained:

"I'd never had anyone close to me all through my life. I'd been moved around all me life, never had me mum and dad and one thing I realised is . . . the feeling I had inside me all the time was hurt, not having anyone to love me or be able to love me."

Low self esteem resulting from rejection by parents could leave young people expecting others to reject them too. One young woman explained how acutely she had felt this:

"Because (schoolfriends) all had their mothers and fathers around them at the time, then they thought "Oh well this girl, her mum and dad don't even like this girl, so why should we.""

It is well known that the experience of sexual abuse is associated with low self esteem and this was also the case for a number of the young women who had suffered sexual abuse in the past (see Finkelhor 1986; and Wyatt 1987). Young people in both of these groups often found it hard to trust others and therefore found it hard to make or sustain relationships. In particular three young women who had not only been sexually abused by their fathers or stepfathers but had also been rejected by their mothers, who took the abuser's side, were socially isolated and had serious difficulties in forming relationships because they felt unable to trust anyone.

The stigma of living in substitute care or accommodation had also contributed to the low self-esteem of some young people, who spoke of how worried they had been about the assumptions they thought others might have about them:

"You know everybody thought, oh yeah you're really going to be bad you know, because you're in care. So I just got a chip on my shoulder that I was bad. So I went out and got on with the job of being bad."

For those who had felt ashamed about being in care, finding an acceptable story to explain their situation was crucial. Even after leaving care, some young people were acutely aware that their experiences set them apart from other young people they met and they very much wanted to be seen as 'normal'. One young woman refused offers of help on leaving care precisely because she did not want to have anything that 'normal' young people would not have and was determined to live a life of total independence from others, unaware that total independence from any adult support is not the norm for most young people.

However, for some young people who had suffered rejection or abuse, care offered some compensation. In these cases carers had offered greater security than they had experienced before and were successful in helping the young people build up their confidence and self esteem. Where substitute care succeeded in compensating for unhappy experiences pre-care, some young people had found they were at last able to settle at school, concentrate on their work and form trusting relationships. Even a few young people who were teenage entrants to care felt they had benefited from the greater security they had experienced in successful placements. These positive experiences left them better equipped to cope with independent living than they might otherwise have been.

Changing identities

During the first 18–24 months of independent living, major changes in their lives had led to shifts in some young people's sense of self identity. Success in coping with living independently gave some of them a justifiable pride in their own achievements and led over time to greater confidence and an enhanced sense of self esteem. A belief in their ability to handle problems, achieve goals and deal with people effectively tends to increase a little for most young people between the ages of 16 and 19 (Banks et al 1992). For these care leavers, who had experienced family disruption and in many cases emotional upheavals, this growing sense of self efficacy was a very positive development. Although many had found the transition to living out of care much harder than they had imagined, for those who felt they were beginning to make a success of their lives the ability to cope with new responsibilities led to growing self confidence. A young woman in City explained: "It's been hard so I've had to build up that confidence myself." Others felt they had learned to be more assertive and to manage relationships better:

"I can stick up for myself now. I'm proud of myself, I am."

"It's been an education ever since I moved out. I've learned a lot and I find I'm a lot more positive. If I want something I'm not going to be shoved out of the way."

Another young woman contrasted her satisfaction in successfully managing independent living with the lack of autonomy she had experienced in her foster placements. Her lack of participation in decisions while she was 'looked after' had, she felt, left her unconfident, unsure about who she was, and ill prepared for living independently. Although she felt lonely living in a flat of her own, for the first time she had the opportunity to make her own decisions and she felt that this had given her growing confidence:

"I don't fully know myself at all. Over the years I've had a lot of decisions made for me and they say you're doing this, you're doing that. I've had no place anywhere for, like, a say. So really I'm beginning to realise who I am, or what sort of person I am, but not totally yet, I'm beginning to get there."

Another young woman who was enjoying independent living explained how satisfying she found it to have greater control over her life and how positive independence had been for her self esteem:

"I feel more of a person now that I'm on me own and I ain't got to go and ask permission from social services for this that and the other. I feel more like myself now, like I'm a normal person.'

Improvements in family relationships also led to increased self esteem for some. As one young man's social worker explained:

"Well I think because his family relationships have improved, so he thinks better of himself, he can feel he is liked and valued by his family."

For some young women relationships with their mothers improved once they had a baby. Even where this was not the case, a number of the young mothers felt that parenthood gave them growing confidence through giving them a clear role and status as mothers.

Vocational identities also had an impact on self esteem. Success in pursuing further education gave some young people increased confidence over time, once they had learned to manage the demands of their coursework as well as the upheaval and responsibilities of moving to independent accommodation. On the other hand, research into young people's employment careers has shown that failing to get a job or losing a job can lead to a temporary reduction in self esteem (Banks et al 1992). It came as no surprise that for several young people in our study – interestingly, mostly young men – the inability to find a job led to a loss of self confidence and in some cases to depression.

For nearly half of the young people remaining in the sample there was no improvement in self esteem within two years of their leaving care. This group included those who were still struggling with unresolved feelings about past rejection or abuse. Many of these still found it hard to trust others and, consequently, they continued to have problems in building or sustaining relationships. A number of them became very dependent on boyfriends or girlfriends but were otherwise quite isolated. A few of those who had experienced abuse or rejection were on a downward spiral, suffering from depression and unable to cope with living in the community, and three had had complete mental breakdowns. The leaving care workers of two young men who had breakdowns thought they were triggered by a combination of isolation and losing a job plus, for one young man, an overwhelming desperation at his inability to trace his mother who had broken off contact many years earlier. For the third, a young woman who had suffered years of abuse in her foster home, a breakdown was triggered by her brother's rape of her when she moved in with him on leaving care.

Conclusions

Forging a new identity as a young adult living independently of parents or carers can be stressful as well as exciting for any young person, especially where they lack a clearly defined status in society – being neither adult nor child (Coleman, 1993). For young people needing to establish themselves at an earlier age than most of their peers, and in many cases lacking a sense of belonging, this status ambiguity can bring additional pressures. They do not 'belong' with their former carers, they may not feel that they 'belong' to their families, yet they have no clearly defined role within society at large, particularly if they are unemployed and not pursuing further education.

The lack of a clearly defined status may be compounded by uncertainty about where they have come from and who they are. For some, the lack of a clear sense of continuity can leave them preoccupied with the past and ill-equipped to deal with the present. It is also widely accepted that an individual's knowledge of their history is essential to the formation of a secure sense of identity (Parker et al, 1991). Not only should 'looked after' children be given clear information about their history, as is widely recognised, but there should be a recognition that children and young people may continue to struggle to make sense of this history throughout the time they are in substitute care or accommodation *and after*, and may continue to require skilled help with this process. Continuing parental contact wherever feasible, as the Children Act recommends, may also help young people make sense of their past, even if the quality of that contact is poor. In addition, contact with parents and with members of the extended family may serve an important symbolic function in giving young people a sense of belonging, however limited this may be. This may have positive implications for their sense of self identity and sense of self esteem. It also leaves the way open for relationships to change and perhaps improve as the young people grow older.

Participation in decision-making while they are 'looked after' and allowing young people increasing autonomy as they grow older can also help to prepare them better for leaving care. As Stein and Carey have argued, a commitment to greater participation can help prepare young people to take greater responsibility for their lives when they leave care (Stein and Carey, 1986). Young people need opportunities to make decisions, take risks and make mistakes while they are still in the relatively safe environment of children's homes or foster homes. Placements in which young people have little opportunity to take part in decision making offer poor preparation for leaving care.

Most leaving care workers recognised the importance of addressing questions of identity. Work on self esteem, confidence building, assertiveness and managing relationships was a feature of the work of all four schemes, but was particularly evident in the work of the City (voluntary sector) and District schemes. These schemes in particular saw work on identity issues as a priority, as they underpinned young people's ability to make a success in many other aspects of their lives. One worker explained how, in his work with a young woman who had been sexually abused, he felt the outcome of scheme help would be limited by her continuing need to resolve issues in her past:

> *"I think there are fundamental things which are preventing her from caring enough about herself and from looking at the future and those are the things I've mentioned about history and family and so on . . . I hope some sort of break can occur in that area because I don't think she's going to allow herself to be happy, I don't think she's going to be able to make relationships or achieve true independence . . . I'd want her to explore those things in the past which have prevented her from trusting."*

All the schemes were attempting to help young people develop more positive self identities through the work being done on practical and social skills. Success in one area of a young person's life could have mutually reinforcing repercussions in others. For example, improvement in life skills or in managing their homes or finding training/employment had implications for developing confidence and self-image.

The young people's identities – including their sense of continuity, of belonging, and of self esteem – naturally had a powerful influence on the outcomes that leaving care scheme workers were able to achieve in their work. Confusion about their origins, or an inability to resolve conflicts they felt about past rejection or abuse, a feeling that they did not belong to a family or a sense of powerlessness and low self esteem could all make it hard for them to manage the stresses and responsibilities of living independently in the community, whatever the level of support they received. Equally, a secure sense of identity, whose components included an adequate knowledge of the past, an acceptance of their history and a reasonable level of self esteem, can contribute to successful outcomes for young people. In this respect, their individual 'starting points' governed the degree of 'success' that leaving care workers could expect to achieve in the short term.

• Summary points •

Our identities are derived from the inter-relationship between our personal biographies and a range of social identities, including social class, ethnicity and gender. They are not 'fixed' but subject to constant renegotiation. For young people in care, the experience of separation from and disruption to family life can lead to a loss of continuity in their lives and, especially where care careers are marked by further movement, repeated breaking of attachments can make it difficult for young people to build relationships and trust others.

For our young people, the point of leaving care was a time in which many were attempting to make sense of their pasts, to trace missing parents, to find greater continuity in their lives and a sense of belonging. They needed a 'story' of their lives that made sense, reduced their confusion about both *how* and *why* events had happened as they did and to provide a more secure platform for their futures in the adult community. Those who had retained family links, even where contact was not very positive, seemed better able to do this. Knowledge of their families, at a minimum, gave a symbolic certainty to their lives. Those who remained confused about their past found life out of care more difficult to manage; they tended to be less able to manage in other life areas. Those with low self esteem had more difficulty managing relationships and were less confident and assertive.

For nearly one half of the sample there had been no noticeable improvement in their confidence and self-esteem after two years of living independently. For others, the struggle to establish themselves had brought growing confidence and a more positive self-image as they found they could gradually take control of their lives. Positive family relationships, establishing an employment identity or parenthood were ingredients that helped here.

- The importance of a knowledge of one's past for a positive self concept is well established. Young people need to be given opportunities to explore their personal histories. It is not a one off activity – many young people were still attempting to construct or refine their 'stories' of their lives *after* they had left care.

- Maintaining family links is of obvious importance. Even where relationships remained poor, it offered a symbolic reassurance to young people and engendered a sense of belonging.

- Whilst in care young people need opportunities to participate in decision making and to take risks in a supported environment. They are more likely to be prepared for adult life if they are gradually able to assume responsibility and a greater control of their lives.

- As young people leave care, schemes have an important role to help young people adjust to the pressures and strains of living in the community. Guidance in all areas of young people's lives can help to reinforce confidence and a positive self image; success in one area has repercussions in other life areas. The social activities that schemes can offer may help young people to develop their social skills and to gain confidence in managing a range of formal and informal relationships.

CHAPTER 11

BLACK YOUNG PEOPLE: EXPERIENCES AND IDENTITIES

In this chapter we examine the care careers and after care careers of black, Asian and mixed heritage young people. The young people's experiences of racism and their perceptions of their ethnic identity are also explored, and professional responses to them are discussed.

Despite our efforts to identify black, Asian or mixed heritage care leavers, we were able to interview only nine young people with this background, of whom only one was male. Four lived in City, four in County and only one in District. As numbers were so small, extreme caution must be exercised in drawing conclusions from this data. However, our in-depth discussions with these young people gave interesting insights into their experiences of substitute care, their experiences of racism, and their views of ethnic identity. Professional attitudes to black young people who are 'looked after' were also explored. Our survey of 183 care leavers included a group of 25 young people of black, Asian or mixed heritage, providing us with more information on care careers and after care careers.

Most of the 'black' young people we interviewed were of mixed heritage. One was of Afro-Caribbean origin, one was of Asian origin and the other seven were of mixed heritage. Four of those of mixed heritage were Afro-Caribbean/white, two were Asian/white and one was Middle Eastern/white in origin. All but one of this group of mixed heritage young people had a white mother and a black father. In our survey, young people of mixed heritage were again by far the largest sub-group, comprising 17 of the 25 'black' young people. This pattern is consistent with other studies of children who are 'looked after'. Bebbington and Miles found that children of mixed heritage were two and a half times more likely to enter care than white children, all other things being equal (Bebbington and Miles, 1989). Similarly, Rowe et al found that children of mixed heritage were the largest sub-group of black children being 'looked after' by local authorities and Garnett found that half the black young people in her study of care leavers were of mixed heritage (Garnett 1992; Rowe et al, 1989).

Care careers

Three of the young people entered substitute care or accommodation before the age of four, one between the age of five and ten and the other five were teenage entrants, all but one of whom had been 'looked after' since the age of 11–14. Time in substitute care correspondingly varied across the group, with three having been 'looked after' for one to three years, three for four to nine years and three for ten or more years. Our survey of 183 care leavers revealed that black/Asian/mixed heritage children were two and a half times more likely than white children to enter substitute care under the age of five and were more than twice as likely to be 'looked after' for ten or more years. We found that this group were therefore likely to enter substitute care earlier and stay longer. Rowe et al's survey of placement patterns also noted that admission to care in the pre-school years was a more prominent feature of black admission patterns than white ones. As Rowe et al argue, these findings belie the popular assumption that black children entering substitute care are more likely to be teenagers (Rowe et al 1989: 181).

Our survey also found that the pattern of care careers for black, Asian and mixed heritage children was broadly similar to that of white children. No differences were observed in the reasons for initial entry to substitute care or accommodation, their likelihood of remaining in care continuously, in patterns of movement in care or in the numbers experiencing multiple admissions. Among the group of nine young people in our qualitative study, most had had relatively stable care careers. Most had experienced both foster and residential placements during the time they were looked after, but their final placement before leaving care was more likely to be with foster carers, which was also the pattern we found in our survey.

The young people's views on how far their placements had met their particular needs were mixed. Within a single local authority, practice could vary. One young woman in County said that resources for hair and skin care had been readily available in the children's home she had been placed in, together with positive images of black people, such as pictures of Martin Luther King on the walls. At the time, though, she had not been very interested in the question of her ethnic identity. Another in the same authority complained that her children's home had not provided the oils and creams she needed for hair and skin care, and said she felt that white social workers should receive more culturally appropriate training. Placements with black foster carers had been important to her, and she had learned Caribbean cookery and patois in this environment. A young woman in City who had also been placed with black foster carers explained why she thought this was the best option for black children who are 'looked after':

> *"It's like catering for their needs and such and to show them their roots and things like that . . . it's just like basic things like plaiting hair . . . a lot of English parents don't know things like that."*

There was also the question of stigma. She felt that if black children are placed in white households, it is more obvious to school friends that they are 'looked after':

"I mean, you being black and they want to know why a white person is bringing you every morning . . . or they come to your house and they want to know why you've got so many white brothers and sisters."

A young man, who had been placed in a children's home in City, also mentioned the importance of black carers, saying that he had valued having a black residential worker. However, he felt he had learned little about his cultural background while 'looked after' and only began to explore this after he had left care, in discussions with workers at a hostel he moved to. However, a young woman of mixed heritage who had been fostered with a white family from birth saw them as her 'natural family' and felt that their ethnic origin was not an issue for her.

Some, though not all, of these young people therefore felt that having black residential staff and black foster carers had been important to them while they were looked after.

Education and employment

At the end of this study, we were unable to trace one of the young people, although we had been able to speak to him during the second stage of interview. Within two years of leaving care nearly half (3) of the remaining group of eight were making good educational progress, compared to only a ninth (5) of the white young people remaining in the sample. Two were attending college working for qualifications and one was completing the second year of her YT training for nursery nursing. One of the young women hoped eventually to go on to university. Our survey also found that black/Asian/mixed heritage young people were more likely to be involved in further education after leaving care than the other young people in the sample, as 20% were involved in full time education compared to only 7% of the white young people. In addition, the survey also found that black/Asian/mixed heritage young people were slightly more likely to have qualifiations than the white young people in the sample (Biehal et al 1992).

Within two years of leaving care, two young women in our follow up sample had become full time parents. Half of the group (4) were in full time education, in full time employment or on a stable YT scheme and two were unemployed, although one of these had been well-established in employment until very recently. This compares favourably with the pattern for sample as a whole at this stage, where less than a third were on a secure career path (as defined in chapter 7). In our survey we found that similar proportions of black/Asian/mixed heritage care leavers and white care leavers were in employment, full time education or on stable YT.

Black/Asian and mixed heritage young people in both our survey and our qualitative study therefore appeared to make slightly better educational progress than the white care leavers and their early employment careers were similar to those of white care leavers. However, these patterns should be seen in the context of the generally poor patterns of educational attainment and insecure employment careers of the care leavers in both samples.

Accommodation

Five of the young people moved initially to transitional, supported accommodation, either to hostels or to supported lodgings. Another two had stable accommodation: one remained in her long term foster home and the other moved to a council flat, although this situation rapidly broke down. The last two moved to accommodation that was unstable, in private lodgings or with friends. During their first 18–24 months after leaving care, two young women in City and one in County lived for a time in specialist hostels catering primarily for black young people. All three hostels offered a good standard of accommodation and good support from hostel staff, and all three felt they gained a lot from their stay there. By the end of the study, over half of the young people were living as independent householders in council or housing association tenancies or in one case in a private tenancy, and three were living in supported accommodation either in hostels or supported lodgings. The proportions in these different types of accommodation were similar to the proportions for the sample as a whole.

Four of the young people had very unstable early housing careers, making three or more moves within two years of leaving care and one of them made over eight moves during this period. However, this pattern was not dissimilar to that for the sample as a whole, of whom nearly a third made three or more moves within 18–24 months of leaving care. Our survey also found little difference in the early housing careers of black/Asian/mixed heritage young people (Biehal et al 1992).

Racism and rejection

Five of the young people mentioned experiences of racist abuse. For some this had happened only occasionally, but for others it was an everyday occurrence and one young woman had had the misfortune to live with an extremely racist stepfather. As another young woman explained: "You get harassment everywhere you go."

For some, problems had occured in children's homes, with racist abuse from other children and in one case racial harassment from a residential worker. Anne had had particular problems at school:

> *"Like the children'd wipe their fingers on me and that to see if my colour'd come off and call me milky bar and blackie and things like that, it was terrible . . . they didn't like me and I was the only black child in the whole school. I hated to go to school so in the end I never used to go, me mum used to teach me at home. I never really went to primary school."*

The situation had improved at high school, where there were a number of other black children. In this context, it is a measure of Anne's determination and achievement that she was one of the few young people in our sample who continued her education after the age of 16. Difficulties continued for some young people once they left care, and there were accounts of racism from a caretaker, in a hostel and on a YT placement.

Some of the young people of mixed heritage also complained of rejection and abuse by black people. Jason, who presented as black but had been brought up by his white mother, said he had experienced a lot of harassment from other black young people because he was different, and Mary said her black boyfriend's mother had disapproved of her because she was of mixed heritage. A young woman of Afro-Caribbean/white origin explained:

> *"I've had some black women coming up to me and like saying, you're neither black nor white, and I don't like that 'cos I class myself, I am a black person . . . some black people can be a bit funny, I mean, 'you're not in our race' and things like that."*

These young people had had particular difficulties to contend with, experiencing harassment or rejection from both black and white people. For all of these young people, the experience of racism was an additional difficulty they had to cope with as they made their transition from care.

'Race', culture and identity

As we saw in the previous chapter for all young people in care there are common needs in relation to the development of a secure sense of identity. There was little perceived difference between black/mixed heritage and white young people in our sample in relation to their degree of self esteem, knowledge of their background and general sense of purpose. Indeed, the black young people in our study were slightly more likely to have a secure sense of identity, in these terms, than the white young people.

The literature on black young people in care has raised concern that where young black people are separated from their families and communities, this can lead to problems of identification and belonging (First Key, 1987; Black & In Care, 1984). We therefore attempted to explore some of the complexities of young black people's sense of ethnic identity.

Only two of the young people had a strong sense of black identity, one of whom was of Afro-Caribbean origin and the other of mixed heritage. Geraldine was of Afro-Caribbean origin and had retained close links with her mother and her extended family throughout the time she was 'looked after.' She had entered substitute care at the age of 13, by which time she had already developed a strong sense of black identity. While 'looked after' she had been cared for by black foster carers and had later moved to a children's home with a black staff member. While in the children's home she had attended four 'Black and in Care' conferences, which may have contributed to her development of a positive sense of black identity. Anne was of Afro-Caribbean/white origin. She had a white mother, a black father she had never met and a black stepfather. She had entered substitute care at the age of nine, but had grown up in black families, fostered with members of her extended family in the Afro-Caribbean district of City. Her mother, whom she had visited regularly throughout the time she was looked after, had consistently advised her to be proud of her black identity. Her view was that:

"I will not be seen as white, I will always be seen as black . . . that's how I see life. Making all my decisions as a black woman."

For both of these young women, close identification with their families, integration within local Afro-Caribbean communities, placements with black carers and reinforcement by parents or peers were key ingredients in their strong and positive sense of black identity.

Three young women completely rejected aspects of their ethnic origin and preferred to pass as white. One was of Asian origin and two came from Asian/white backgrounds. For all three, ethnic identification was closely bound up with their feelings about their families. Balbir came from a tiny Asian community in District. She had entered substitute care at the age of 15 and was completely estranged from her family. Her total rejection of her family, which her social worker believed to be associated with the painful reasons for her entry to substitute care, brought with it a total estrangement from the Asian community in which she had grown up. She was unwilling to talk about her cultural origins with anyone, to the consternation of her social worker, who was concerned about her rejection of her background. As her social worker put it: "she has rejected that part of herself." Balbir refused to identify with her ethnic background, insisting that it meant nothing to her and that she wanted nothing to do with it:

"It's strict and I don't particularly like it . . . very strict, the rules and boundaries that you follow."

She preferred to be seen as white and appeared to have chosen total assimilation into the white community. Estranged from her family and rejecting her cultural background, Balbir was cut off from two key elements significant to her identity. Her denial that these issues held any importance for her and her reluctance to address them led to her social worker's understandable concern about the implications of this denial for her future well being.

For Ellen, whose mother was white and whose father came from Pakistan, rejection of her Asian background was similarly bound up with her rejection of a parent. After her parents' divorce she had been brought up by her father in a traditional Muslim manner, but her father's physical abuse of her and his refusal to let her see her mother led to unresolved feelings of anger and hurt towards him. In rejecting him, she rejected all that he represented. She, too, reacted against her traditional upbringing as a Muslim girl:

"I wanted to be like everyone else, being able to go out and hang around with your schoolmates or whatever, which I were never allowed to do."

As soon as she entered substitute care in her early teens she asked for western clothes and, like Balbir, Ellen preferred people to think she was white. Her social worker also felt that another component to her rejection of her Asian background was a clear choice made on rational grounds: "It's a choice that, if she's does that, it means she'll have an easier life." Her rejection of her backgrond was perhaps also reinforced by the fact that her social worker had been too busy dealing with other issues in her life to discuss this, and her children's home had not had any Asian staff who might have served as positive role models. The importance for young people in care of providing role models and materials that promote positive cultural images has been highlighted in the literature (First Key 1987, Black and in Care 1984).

For Marian, rejection of her Asian background dervied from a strong identification with the white foster family she had lived with from birth, which she described as "my natural family." Her birth mother was white and her birth father, whom she had never met, was Asian, but she had no interest in her ethnic origin and appeared to have absorbed negative stereotypes about Asian people. When asked how she would describe her ethnic origin she answered:

"Terrible . . . I'd rather not be Anglo-Asian or whatever it is, I'd prefer it if he (her father) was a Spaniard or something. I wouldn't want to be considered Asian. Most people think I'm Italian or Spanish and I prefer it that way."

The fact that she had lived all her life with a white family in a rural area with an overwhelmingly white population, and had a strong sense of belonging and loyalty to her foster family, suggests that her choice to be white was in some respects structured by her circumstances. Given that her family originated from the city, which had a substantial Asian population, this perhaps raises questions about the appropriate placement of black and mixed heritage young people.

All three of these young women were clear that they preferred to see themselves as white, and their rejection of the Asian part of their origins was in all cases closely bound up with their identification, or lack of it, with their substitute or birth families. For two of them, the fact that they had little contact with adults of Asian origin while they were 'looked after' may also have contributed to their lack of identification with their Asian backgrounds.

Another three young women, all of mixed heritage, accepted the diversity of their origins. Mary's acceptance of her multi-dimensional ethnic identity appeared to derive from her close identification with both her parents, one black and one white. She had learned a lot about her Jamaican background from her father and identified strongly with what she saw as black culture, but nevertheless saw herself as distinct from black people.

"I just class myself as myself really, I'm not saying that I'm white, I'm not saying that I'm black. I just say 'Look, I'm mixed race and I'm proud of it.'"

Similarly Sandra, who had never met her Middle Eastern father, felt positive about her mixed heritage as it made her feel individual and special:

"It's important to me that I am what I am, I'm not ashamed of what I am. I've got like, mixed race in me so I feel like, different, I feel I'm my own person."

Nicola had been fostered from birth by white foster parents and had assumed she was white until a social worker mentioned, when she was nine years old, that her mother (who was dead) had been Afro-Caribbean/white. She had been surprised and shocked but not dismayed by this revelation. While she was 'looked after' and when she first left care she was uninterested in her ethnic background, but within two years of leaving care she had begun to think more about her origins and had begun to feel very positive about being "someone that comes from a mixed race." Her developing interest in this aspect of her identity was generated partly by her two year relationship with a boyfriend who was black and partly because she had begun to think more about her mother. At this stage she was trying to find out more about her mother and was beginning to feel a strong sense of continuity with her.

Jason, whose background was Afro Caribbean/white, had a more problematic sense of ethnic identity. He had been brought up by his white mother and although he presented as Afro-Caribbean, he felt he was not accepted by black young people and that he could not fit in with the black community. Unlike Jenny, Mary and Sandra, he lacked any positive identification with his mixed heritage and, seeing himself as neither black nor white, felt he did not belong anywhere. Within a year of leaving care he had begun to see himself as black, partly because that was how others perceived him and partly because hostel workers had begun to discuss these issues with him. However, he still felt he had nothing in common with other black people. Also, he felt his identity was both more individual and more multi-faceted than a uni-dimensional definition of 'black' or 'white' could capture: "Everybody's different, aren't they? Everybody's like got different situations."

It is clear that, within even such a small group of young people of black, Asian or mixed heritage, there is enormous diversity in self-definitions of ethnic identity. All except Jason were very clear about how they saw themselves and how they wanted to be seen and most felt comfortable with the ethnic identities they had chosen. Only Balbir, both of whose parents were Asian, had entirely denied her ethnic origin, the others having chosen to identify with either white, black or both parents. Tizard and Phoenix also found that young people of mixed heritage were comfortable with a variety of definitions of ethnic identity. In their interviews with 58 15–16 year olds of mixed heritage, they found that three quarters felt proud of their mixed heritage and thought of themselves as 'mixed' or 'brown', or in one case 'white' (Tizard and Phoenix, 1993: 61). In our study, both the young people with a strong sense of black identity had grown up in a black environment and held politicised views about black issues. As Tizard and Phoenix also found, defining their identity as black was related to holding more politicised views about racism, and those young people who looked white tended not to think of themselves as black (Tizard and Phoenix, 1993: 64).

It is also clear that in all cases ethnic identification was closely bound up with young people's identification with their families, or, in some cases, their rejection of a parent. In this respect, it was linked to the young people's sense of belonging which, as we saw in the last chapter, was an important element in all the care leavers' sense of identity. For at least some of these young people, the choice of a particular ethnic identity was part of the process of constructing a positive sense of self-identity in a wider sense. For Sandra, for example, her desire to know more about the Middle Eastern father she had never met and her strong identification with his ethnic identity was one aspect of her attempt to build a coherent account of her life, which also involved requesting access to her file. She was struggling to build this ethnic identity into her sense of self, feeling that it made her "different" and special in a very positive sense. In this respect, her attempt to develop a sense of cultural identity based on her father's origins served as a means of self affirmation.

On the other hand Geraldine, who had been very assertive about her black identity, had begun to feel this was less important to her within two years of leaving care. She reflected that the primacy of her black identity in her sense of self had helped her compensate for a general feeling of insecurity, in giving her a clearly defined sense of self identity and some confidence in who she was. Now that she was older she had other social identities that were equally important to her. Her views about her black identity had changed as new developments occurred in her life, her confidence grew and she began to accept herself more:

"I find now my culture doesn't really matter much to me because when I was pregnant I knew, how can I put it, I found the real me, myself, and I started to like myself as a person. And like, once you hit that mark, your culture can just come in afterwards. It's not so important as I thought it would be . . . because finding out about my culture then was important to me, and it's not really so important now because I've got my proper identity and now I know it and I've got what I wanted. I've just moved on, yeah."

As her confidence grew and she became more comfortable with other aspects of her self, Geraldine no longer wished to define herself solely in terms of her black identity. As Stuart Hall has argued, in his discussion of cultural identity, 'black' identity is not single or unified: it exists as one identity alongside a range of other differences (Hall, 1992: 309).

Geraldine's account also indicates the way in which identities are subject to change. For several of the young people, self-definitions were complex, sometimes contradictory, and shifted over time. As we have seen, Geraldine's sense of black identity became less important to her over time. More dramatically, Balbir and Ellen moved from being closely integrated in Asian communities to rejecting all that these communities represented. In contrast, both Mary and Alison had been uninterested in their ethnic identity while in substitute care, even though Mary had been placed in a children's home which gave particular attention to the needs of black children. At the time, as Mary explained:

"I didn't even think about it, no. I didn't even think about being a black person."

Yet over time both young women began to see themselves as black, or of mixed heritage, and to consider this aspect of their identity as increasingly important to them. There was also evidence of ambivalence in aspects of some young people's identification with others of black, Asian or mixed heritage. Jason began to see himself as black, but continued to feel he had nothing in common with other black people. Anne strongly identified with the black community, but resented the assumption by her housing association that she would necessarily want to live in the Afro-Caribbean quarter of City. She saw her pursuit of education as a means of eventually escaping the material deprivation in this area and wanted the housing association to offer her the same choices they would offer anyone else. Sandra, while wanting to identify with her father's Middle Eastern background, distanced herself from the local Asian community in County, perhaps because she had absorbed stereotyped views about people of Asian origin in the white environment in which she had grown up.

For most of these young people then, their sense of ethnic identity was not fixed and stable, even within a relatively short period. As their circumstances changed, as relationships with families or boyfriends developed or were ended, their views about their ethnic origins changed and their sense of ethnic identity was subtly transformed. In Tizard and Phoenix's study of a much larger sample of young people of mixed heritage, some reported changing their self-definition according to the context they were in, depending on whether they were with friends or family (Tizard and Phoenix 1993: 160). Just as all identities may contain shifting and contradictory elements, these young people's sense of ethnic identity shifted as their responses to their individual histories, families, cultures and environment changed over time. If identities are not fixed entities but are subject to change as life progresses, then we should not be surprised if 'racial' identities shift over time just as other social identities do (see Tizard and Phoenix, 1993: 171). Hall argues that people:

". . . assume different identities at different times, identities which are not unified around a coherent 'self'. Within us are contradictory identities, pulling in different directions, so that our identifications are continuously being shifted about. If we feel we have a unified identity from birth to death, it is only because we construct a comforting story, or 'narrative of the self' about ourselves"

(HALL, 1992: 277)

Some of the social workers and leaving care workers involved with these young people appeared to hold a somewhat different view of 'racial' identity, tending to see it as a fixed biological/cultural attribute that the young people possessed. For young people of mixed heritage, their black or Asian origins were sometimes seen as the primary definers of ethnic identity, although the young people's own view of their identity was often both more subtle and more complex.

For example, one young woman who also presented as white explained how her social worker, once he had discovered that she was of mixed heritage, had tried to encourage her to see herself as black and feel positive about her black identity, even though she saw herself as 'mixed race' rather than black: "He thinks it's right exciting." Similarly, Mary's social worker believed that she had a strong sense of black identity and identified predominantly with her black father, whereas her own view appeared to be more complex:

"I can either be white or I can either be black. No-one can ever say to me you're a black this and you're a white that, 'cos I'm in between . . . I have to put across to them that I'm not black, I'm mixed race."

The situation was somewhat different for Balbir, who was of entirely Asian origin but presented as white. In rejecting her Asian background she was rejecting all aspects of her ethnic identity, not choosing one aspect rather than another. Her social worker was very concerned about her total estrangement from her community of origin and had wanted to work through this issue with her, but Balbir categorically refused to discuss this. Her social worker explained:

"She knows we think it's an issue. She says it isn't. It's not right for us to impose any more (identity) work on her and she's suspicious that we give her black social workers because she's black."

Owusu-Bempah argues that social workers often hold the stereotyped view that black children have a negative self concept and that this is at the root of any problems they might display. In his study of student social workers' responses to black children he suggests that social workers' pre-occupation with 'identity work' with black children arises from the fact that black children are:

"predominantly seen as having a pathological self-identity, or identity crisis, which in turn influenced the respondents' treatment of the children's behaviour."

(OWUSU-BEMPAH, 1992).

The working assumption that black identities are fixed for all young people who have any black or Asian ancestry, and are the only possible identities for these young people, is common within social work. As Tizard and Phoenix have argued, this is founded on implicit theories of race which see people as divided into distinct biological groups, each with their own fixed psychological characteristics (Tizard and Phoenix, 1993: 3). Similarly, in his discussion of the debates around transracial adoption, Gilroy has suggested that:

"The definition of 'race' which informs these arguments elides the realms of culture and biology in the same way as the volkish new right preoccupation with kith and kin" and is linked to *"mystical and essentialist ideas of a transcendental blackness."*

(GILROY, 1987: 65)

Within social work, these attempts to give varied ethnic identities a single, unified content have their origins in two positions. One is the view that grouping black, Asian and mixed heritage identities as 'black' is a necessary political response to the fact that, even though they are not the same, they will be treated the same, as 'other', by white society (see Hall, 1992). These approaches have also arisen from the struggle to put the basic needs of black children who are 'looked after' on the agenda, a struggle which has included a call to pay attention to the cultural needs of these children. Yet this project to address children's need to preserve a sense of continuity and develop a sense of identity which is inclusive of their ethnic identity has sometimes tended to position mixed heritage children in fixed 'black' identities, which are seen as the primary definers of their identity.

Many social workers have argued that children of mixed heritage 'should' see themselves as black, since this is how others will regard them, and that to do otherwise is to deny reality and will cause psychological damage (see Tizard and Phoenix, 1993: 46). This view appeared to be shared by at least some of the profesionals working with the nine young people of mixed heritage in this study. Yet as we have seen, some of the young people of mixed heritage appeared to hold a subtly different view of their ethnic identity, at once more complex and more fluid, and in most cases they were comfortable with this sense of who they were. It may be that young people such as these would welcome a more open attitude by professionals which accepts that their own self definitions have strength and validity. Anne succinctly expressed the view that greater flexibility and consultation by professionals would be helpful:

> *"They're not thinking, they're not asking what we want, what we need, what we think's right. They're just assuming all the time . . . and that's why we always get the wrong end."*

As for the question of psychological damage that is presumed to result from the rejection of a black identity, we have seen that for this small group of young people acceptance or rejection of black or Asian origins was closely bound up with identification with or rejection of their families. Where the rejection of black/Asian identities is so closely bound up with family estrangement, it would be difficult to disentangle the relative impact on a young person of family conflict and the rejection of black/Asian identities. If young people in these circumstances are 'damaged,' this may be as much the result of problems of family identification as of problems of 'racial' identification. Equally, if they identify with a white parent as well as, or instead of, a black parent, denying the white part of their identity may also have its costs:

> *"People of mixed heritage have argued that to deny the white part of their inheritance is psychologically damaging, and in their view involves accepting the discredited racial theory that everyone belongs to one of three or four distinct races. In their view individuals should be able to claim simultaneous membership of whichever group they choose to identify with."*

(TIZARD AND PHOENIX, 1993: 3).

Alongside policies designed to ensure that black, Asian and mixed heritage children who are 'looked after' have access to black or Asian role models and positive continuity with cultural practices in their families of origin, a more open attitude to questions of ethnic identity for 'looked after' young people of mixed heritage may be helpful in assisting them to explore these complex issues.

• Summary points •

By far the largest group of 'black' young people in both our survey and our qualitative study were young people of mixed heritage.

Black/Asian/mixed heritage young people tended to enter substitute care at an earlier age and stay longer than white children. Apart from this, there was little difference between the care careers of black/Asian/mixed heritage young people and white young people.

For these young people their experience of care was variable. Some were placed with black foster carers or children's homes which offered positive role models, images and resources. However, one young person felt that her cultural and practical needs had been neglected by her social worker.

Patterns of educational attainment were poor for all care leavers, although among the young people interviewed black/Asian/mixed heritage young people were slightly more likely to make good educational progress after leaving care than white young people. Early employment careers were similar for both groups.

Ethnic origin appeared to make no difference to early housing careers.

The majority of the black, Asian and mixed heritage young people interviewed had experienced racist harassment and abuse. Some of the young people of mixed heritage also felt that they were not accepted by black people either.

Self-definitions of ethnic identity were varied and shifted over time. Identification with a particular ethnic group was strongly related to young people's identification with or rejection of family members. Professionals tended to hold more fixed views of ethnic identity than the young people themselves.

- The cultural and self care needs of 'looked after' black and mixed heritage young people should be a focus of attention. Access to positive role models, images and resources is helpful.

- A more open attitude to young people's self-definintions of ethnic identity may be more helpful than approaches which position mixed heritage young people within fixed 'black' identities. Young people of mixed heritage who do not see themselves as black should not be pathologized as suffering from 'identity confusion'. However, for some young people, where rejection of cultural origins is linked to family rejection/conflict, confusions and tensions may arise and young people may well need help and counselling to explore these.

- Ensuring that black, Asian or mixed heritage children and young people have positive contact with others of similar origin while they are 'looked after' would offer them the opportunity to maintain some continuity with their ethnic background. This approach would help to keep questions of ethnic identification 'open' for the young people. Some mixed heritage children, particularly those who have been brought up solely by a white parent, may see this as less important to them and, where comfortable with their identities, this view should be respected. Placements in locations that reduce the possiblity for cultural continuity should be avoided.

CHAPTER 12

EARLY PARENTHOOD

Recent surveys have highlighted a tendency for early parenthood
amongst samples of care leavers. In this chapter we will focus on
those who became parents either during or soon after their time
in care. We will look at how they were managing their lives
in the community and at the informal and professional supports
available to them.

*"I've gone from leaving school to running a house with a child already and I've just not
had a chance to take it slowly, so that's what's hard."*

(YOUNG MOTHER REFLECTING ON THE RAPID CHANGES IN HER LIFE)

For care leavers, aspects of the transition from childhood to adulthood are both
accelerated and compressed. As we have indicated, transitions from school to labour
market and from dependent to independent householders occur at an early age and
often overlap. For a sizeable minority, especially young women, these are
accompanied by an early transition to parenthood. As the comments by the young
mother suggest, coping with multiple responsibilities in adverse circumstances is
extremely 'hard', particularly so for young people who themselves may have
experienced rejection, poor parenting, disruption and stress in their early lives.

Two recent surveys have highlighted the large numbers of young women leaving
care who are either already parents or pregnant. Our survey found that one eighth of
the young people had children at the point they moved to independence or were
legally discharged from care. This represented almost one quarter of the young
women in that sample (Biehal et al 1992).[1] Another found that one in seven young
people were pregnant or had children at the point of legal discharge (Garnett 1992).

---

1. Out of a sample of 183 young people, 23 were parents at this point (12.5%). Three were male and
20 female (total females 87).

Similar patterns are apparent for our present sample. At first interview, shortly after moving to independence, one tenth (8) of the young people had children; seven were young mothers and one young man had just become a father. Of the young women, one had become a parent prior to entering care and the other six whilst being 'looked after'. However, within 18–24 months of leaving care, one third of the young people had become parents and nearly one half of the young women were coping with early parenthood. All were aged 19 or under when their babies were born and, given that we had lost touch with 21 young people at this stage, these figures could be an under-estimate.[2]

These patterns contrast sharply with those for the population as a whole. In 1991 only 5% of young women aged 15–19 had children and only 2.8% were lone mothers at 19 years of age (OPCS 1993a, Table 37). The average age for becoming a first time mother in the late 1980's was 26.5 years (Kiernan and Wicks 1990). Despite a current public discourse which constructs teenage parenthood and especially lone mothers themselves as a social problem, some studies of young mothers have emphasised the social context in which mothering takes place, in particular the financial dependence it entails, as being at the root of the problems experienced by them. Where young mothers had sufficient supports, especially from *their* mothers, the majority were nonetheless able to cope in difficult financial circumstances and provide good quality care to their children (Phoenix 1991; Sharpe 1987). Although for many of our sample parenting was a recent experience – at the final interview children's ages ranged from one week to five years – the vast majority displayed a real commitment to caring for them and two thirds appeared to be managing quite successfully. Very few were coping alone and support was being conjured from a variety of sources including family members, partners and their families, ex-carers, friends, social workers, leaving care workers, hostel staff and lodgings providers. Despite struggling on low incomes and coping with the restrictions and loss of teenage freedoms that early parenting involves, they were trying to be 'good' and caring parents.

Preparing for parenthood

Concern about the numbers of teenage mothers leaving care has led to questions being raised about the adequacy of personal and social education available to young people in care (Biehal et al 1992). Department of Health guidance emphasises, as a central part of preparation, the need for young people to be helped to develop and maintain relationships with others, both general and sexual (DOH 1991b). It appears

---

2. At this stage 24 were parents, 21 female and three male. This represents 32.5% of our original sample (N = 74) and 46.5% of the females within it (total 45). Another male was about to become a father any day.

to be part of a wider problem. Studies have highlighted the distinct reticence of parents to comunicate with children about sexual health and relationships, believing it to be the province of schools (Allen 1987); others to the patchy, haphazard and narrow curriculum in schools which condemns many young people to learning about sex from peers and the media (Hudson and Ineichen 1991). For young people in care, disruption through movement, problems with truancy and the tendency for them to lack one consistent figure through their care careers capable of inspiring trust, it may mean that they miss much of what is on offer (Audit Commission 1994; Rickford 1994).

Just over one half of the parents in our sample said that their pregnancies had been unplanned (13) and nearly two thirds (8) of these were in the younger age range (17 years or under). Whilst most felt they knew about contraception, their 'education' came from a variety of sources. School, media, friends and family members (particularly older sisters) were most often mentioned. Some had advice and literature from carers, residential workers and social workers, although there did appear to be a tendency for social workers to assume that carers would deal with this area and, for some, a degree of discomfort in discussing sex with teenagers. Even if aware, their failure to protect themselves points to psychological factors that can inhibit the use of contraception for teenagers. Safe sex requires an ability to communicate between partners and where young women have had poor chances for developing trust, confidence and a positive self identity, relating to young men in a confident and assertive way can be difficult (Hudson and Ineichen 1991).

Perhaps more surprisingly, given the focus in recent debates on unwanted teenage pregnancies, over one third (9) said that their pregnancies had been planned. Most were older (18/19 years of age) and eight had jointly planned their child with a partner with whom they were already cohabiting. They were setting up home together and starting a family. Perhaps this points to an important feature of care leavers' accelerated transitions. Having to move to independence early, with the threat of loneliness that this can involve, can create a more urgent need to select a partner and start a family, particularly if young people have been rejected by their own families. Indeed three quarters of the young parents (18) moved in with partners and, although 10 lasted throughout the research, more than two fifths (8) of these relationships subsequently broke down. Three were violence related and precipitated further instability for these young mothers. However, while most relationships remained stable, not all were problem free nor were male partners necessarily supportive in relation to child care. Only six young mothers lived as single parents throughout and two out of the three males were with partners; one losing contact with his son when his partner moved on without informing him.

The motivations that might underpin a choice for early parenthood are complex and insufficiently understood. Early parenting has a class cultural context; most young single parents tend to come from larger and poor working-class family backgrounds, have failed educationally and have limited employment prospects. In consequence, there appear few benefits to deferring motherhood and it can offer an opportunity to gain a sense of purpose in life. Without clear alternatives it is one means of accessing a more socially valued adult identity (Musick 1993; Hudson and Ineichen 1991; Phoenix 1991). Whilst our young mothers did not speak explicitly about their limited options, it did seem pervasive in their decision making. Of those who became pregnant after leaving school, very few had qualifications of any kind and only one was employed. Most were unemployed and a few had casual or part-time work. The new status and respect hoped for as wife and mother was expressed by one young woman:

"In six months I will have had my baby, so I'll be learning to be a respectable mother, I'll be a wife".

For many the need to belong, to love and be loved, to have something of their own and the chance to compensate for the poor care they experienced, seemed to be prominent. The following comments make the complexity of these needs and desires apparent:

"Me and me boyfriend don't own much at all and we haven't got families that love us and this is hard. You know, we wanted something that was ours, give our love to him that we never got."

". . . so I've got somebody to be more closer to than just sitting here on my own . . . I've got somebody to look after and I've got something that no one can take away from me. I know it's mine and I know I'll love it . . . And I know when it grows up it'll love me for what I've done and how I've treated it. So it's not like my family is with us, one day we can speak, the next day we can't speak . . . (I'll) give it a nice childhood which we missed out on."

Support to help young people prepare for parenthood came from a variety of sources. Eleven had mostly positive relationships with one or more family members. For some their mother was a key figure offering advice and support, for several their sole positive family support was from an older sister. Where they had children, skills were learnt through watching their care and babysitting. Extended families were also important. One young woman felt helping care for her aunt's children had given her a "rough idea what I was letting myself in for". For some (7) pregnancy brought a renewal of family relationships and increased contact, although some young people felt ambivalence, as past suspicions and conflicts once again rose to the surface. Five young people, without family support, depended upon their partners and his/her family, some living with them until permanent accommodation could be found. One young woman subsequently lost that support when her relationship broke down, precipitating a crisis in her ability to care. A further four appeared to depend primarily upon their partners and lacked other informal supports.

In addition to these informal networks, many received positive help from professionals to prepare. Some received help from social workers and foster carers, one young woman in District being able to remain with her carer on a supported lodgings basis until making a planned move to a flat with her boyfriend. She was also receiving help from the leaving care scheme and able to attend their ante natal group at the project base. One young woman in County who became pregnant whilst at a supported hostel managed by the leaving care scheme had to move, since they lacked child care facilities, and chose a specialist unit for young mothers. She felt that support from staff and other residents helped her focus on the realities of motherhood:

> "*Well, when I moved in here I see that you do go through your rough patches and have good patches and you just manage through it.*"

Most who became pregnant in care moved to specialist mother and baby units, although their experiences were variable. Four in County moved to a unit managed by social services and, although requiring a further institutionally driven move, all were positive about the support they received once settled. However, one young woman sensitive to advice and criticism, did feel that staff tended to 'preach' at them rather than support. The only young woman to use a unit in City was unhappy, feeling there was no toleration of mistakes and that she was under critical surveillance. Her social worker negotiated a return home to her mother. District, a small authority, lacked a specialist resource and one young woman, with an unstable past and prone to absconding, was sent to a unit 150 miles away when pregnant. Despite appreciating the support there, she remained angry and resentful and, after returning to a children's home with her son, felt fairly unsupported. The home was not geared up to meet her needs; her son was the only baby there. Unable to cope with parenting and the restrictions it imposed on her life, she eventually gave care of her son to her grandparents. Finally, one young woman in City required to leave her foster placement when pregnant, moved into a trainer flat run by City (vol) leaving care scheme and received a positive package of support, of which helping to prepare her for parenthood was a part.

A substantial minority (9) appeared to miss out on important aspects of preparation. For some this was linked to instability in their lives and/or absconding from placements; for others to discontinuities through changes in carers or social workers. However, for a few it was also connected to the failure of social workers to offer pro-active help. One young woman who felt she lacked advice from her social worker says, "it would still have been nice for someone to tell me what I were like getting myself into". The unevenness in support arrangements identified here is of concern, given the particular support needs of young parents, and needs to be the subject of more focused research.

Coping with parenthood

The onset of parenthood was a time of pride and optimism for virtually all the young parents and, as we have indicated, two thirds seemed to be managing quite successfully. Even where pregnancies were unplanned the children were almost invariably wanted. The depth of investment made in their children was apparent and, in some instances, assumed an almost tragic quality as young parents attempted to balance their own needs and desires for security, identity and love with their determination to provide all the aspects of caring that they themselves missed:

> *"She just makes my life . . . and I enjoy that responsibility and I'm glad that I'm a parent."*

One young woman, mentioning her abandonment by her own mother who had a serious drinking problem, said:

> *"She did love us, she must have loved us, but she got in so much debt. That's why I'm never going to get in debt, 'cos I don't want to end up like me mam. I want to give my kids all that my mam could never give me."*

Only in one case was all contact between parent and child lost. This young man, profoundly unstable in his own life and unable to live with his girlfriend, maintained twice weekly contact with his son until she moved away without informing him. His sense of loss was felt acutely:

> *"Just every day you wonder where he is and what he's doing and where they're living and that, but you don't know. Like I've still got Xmas presents wrapped up for him and I can't give 'em to him 'cos I don't know where he is."*

A number of young people, in particular those with wilder and more unstable pasts, felt that the onset of parenthood had been a stabilising influence and helped them centre their lives. One young father with a history of involvement in offending and drug use, settled down with his girlfriend and baby. Abused and rejected by his family, he was committed to creating his own:

> *"Since I've had my daughter, it's like all the instincts of committing crime has just gone . . . If I do it and get caught I've got nowt to gain but I've got . . . my flat, my girlfriend and my daughter to lose through it."*

For all it represented a crash course in growing up and taking responsibility. Although many felt parenthood had occurred too soon in their lives and experienced frustration at the restrictions it imposed, very few regretted having a child. Taking responsibility and gaining maturity, whilst enforced, was also a source of pride and satisfaction as parents found they had the resources and resilience to cope with the pressures of a multiple transition:

> *"I've grown up a lot. I don't know, I think it's the responsibility more than owt. You have to grow up . . . it's because you're on your own and you just have to do it, don't you? You can't say 'I can't cope', because it's a case of having to cope when you're on your own and you've got a baby to look after."*

Of pressing importance to these young parents was the need to establish a secure home base for child rearing. Five young mothers who made planned moves from care placements to permanent tenancies remained stable throughout the research. A further 10, especially those planning parenthood with partners, moved from transitional forms of accommodation (supported lodgings, hostels, relatives or partner's families) to their own tenancies either prior to or after the birth of their babies. In all, within 18–24 months of leaving care, nearly three quarters (71%) of parents were living in permanent tenancies. The support of social workers and, in particular, the access of leaving care schemes to accommodation resources was important. The majority were helped to establish a secure home base.

Where early housing careers were marked by significant instability some young mothers, fairly secure in themselves, were able to continue offering positive care to their children and support was available to help them re-stabilise their lives. For example, violence from her partner forced one young mother to flee her accommodation in County. Help from her social worker and leaving care worker enabled a negotiated return to a social services run mother and baby unit until a new flat could be found in a different part of the city. Once there she was able to make a fresh start with her child. Another who, with social worker help, had only settled in a second flat towards the close of the research, was aware of the strains that her pattern of movement had placed upon her son. "It was unsettling for him but I tried to make him feel really secure". One social worker spoke with some admiration of the ability of a further young mother to provide quality care despite a 'chaotic lifestyle'; ". . . she makes sure he gets fed, she has him well clothed, he gets lots of love". For her, with two small children at the final interview, violence from her partner created further instability and, once again homeless and staying temporarily with her mother, she was receiving help from her leaving care worker to look at future options.

In only five cases did crises in the ability to provide care lead to explicit child protection concerns. Inevitably the particular circumstances of these young mothers were unique but some associations were apparent. None had positive relationships with their own families and all were quite insecure, unassertive, lacked confidence in themselves and had difficulty making and, in particular, controlling relationships with others. For the majority, limited practical skills and abilities compounded these difficulties. For one young mother, heavily dependent on her older husband for support, concerns centred on past allegations of abuse from his older daughters and her ability to protect the child from him. For another, reliant on her partner and his family, the breakdown in this relationship and loss of family support precipitated a crisis in both her ability to care and manage her accommodation. Although reluctant, she returned to a mother and baby unit and was receiving intensive help backed by an emergency protection order to give social services more control. To give a third example, a young mother, after a stay in a trainer flat managed by the City (vol) scheme, made a planned move to a flat with her boyfriend. Despite an intensive package of support including social worker, scheme, health visitor and Homestart, a second pregnancy led to a crisis. Lacking confidence and assertiveness, her flat was being taken over by her partner's friends about which she was able to do little. She refused to return with the new baby and, after giving temporary care of her older son to his paternal grandmother, was receiving ongoing help in a supported lodgings placement.

In all five cases the child protection focus was structured, concerns made explicit to the young women and intensive help offered to develop their abilities and confidence in parenting. Three were enabled to return to more sheltered accommodation to gain respite; the third being a young mother in City who found stability at a young mothers' hostel after a very unstable post-care career. In only one case was an emergency protection order used to receive a child into temporary care and, in this case, attempts were being made to reunify the family.

It is understandable that in such circumstances the primary focus of intervention becomes the child. However in none of these cases was a second social worker allocated for this purpose. Rather the focus of social work involvement tended to switch from mother to child and the mothers themselves ran the risk of losing support *in their own right* as care leavers. Where schemes were involved a more holistic input to the mother herself was more easily maintained and, with close collaboration and a clear division of responsibilities, schemes have a valuable role to play in this area.

This discussion also points to a wider problem. Even in cases where there was no evidence to warrant child protection concerns, there was a pervasive tendency for some social workers to become more concerned with monitoring the child care of young mothers than with meeting their needs as young adults *who were also* mothers. It may be understandable that this becomes part of the social work equation where mothers are both young and vulnerable, but it was by no means clear that many of these young mothers had been made aware of the dual nature of this role, of its potential dangers for them, nor in consequence were they able to make an informed choice about whether to continue accepting this support. In contrast some social workers were very clear that the additional support being offered from themselves, health visitors and others, was due to the age of the young woman and not because she herself had been accommodated and had experienced poor parenting in the past.

We have pointed to poor educational attainment and limited career opportunities as being one factor that may influence early parenthood through the search for a valued social identity. Motherhood also usually involves a period of financial and social dependence on partners and/or families for practical support. A further influence upon parenting has been the impact of recession on the ability of partners and families to provide that support (McRobbie 1991). In her study, Phoenix (1991) found that partners and parents were usually unemployed and as poor as the young mothers themselves and that, since poverty represented a principal constraint on mothering, these mothers required considerable resilience and resourcefulness to manage.

All the young parents in our sample who had their children with them were having to manage on state benefits. Only one partner managed to find employment during the course of our research and, earning a low wage, their switch to family credit had if anything worsened their financial circumstances. As this young mother said, managing was a "struggle, a real hard struggle". All were finding it 'hard'; some ran up debts to ensure their children did not go without and a few sacrificed some of their dietary needs. Those with informal family supports were able to obtain some practical assistance from them, others had to manage for themselves. Once eligible for benefits, none received further regular financial assistance from social services. However some were able to receive help in kind. The District leaving care scheme ran a second hand exchange in baby items. One young mother in our sample obtained a pram, pushchair and clothing from that source. Workers also helped some with charity applications for essential things. Occasionally Section 17 payments available for preventive services to children 'in need' were used on a one off basis. Despite these examples of an imaginative use of resources their lives remained difficult.

Some were happy with their new identities as mothers and some wanted to defer further employment or training until their children were older. Others wanted work, both to find more money and to reduce the frustrations and social isolation that relative poverty can cause.

> *"It gets me down but not to the point where I feel suicidal, just to the point where I feel like roaring. But I'm alright, because I've got me friends . . . and me family, they always come round and see me . . . But sometimes I feel a bit down."*

As with this young woman, most single parents felt subject to a 'poverty trap'. They were aware that most jobs available to those without qualifications were low waged; child care would be expensive if families were not available and, although more compatible with child care, they often felt that part-time work was not economic given the reduction in benefits that would follow. In a few cases leaving care workers had discussed opportunities for further training with young mothers. They had explored options and discussed the possibility of social services funding courses and arranging child care. Although none had yet taken up the offer it was clearly important in expanding their horizons, in enabling them to think that their aspirations for a return to learn were realistic.

Only one young mother managed to return to learn during our research cycle. She had moved from a supported hostel managed by the leaving care scheme in County when pregnant. Given a tour of alternative options by her leaving care worker, she chose a supported hostel for young mothers that had an expectation that all residents would resume full-time college. With her own flat in the complex, support from staff and residents and a staffed crèche for her baby, she successfully resumed her studies. She felt that college was not only important for a future career, about which she was ambitious, but that it also enabled her to retain her identity as an independent young woman, to maintain a sense of balance in her life:

> *". . . 'cos I feel me again, when I'm at college I feel like I've not got any kids and when I come home I'm a mother."*

The more young mothers feel supported and able to get an occasional break from the responsibilities of care the less they are likely to feel dissatisfied with parenthood (Phoenix 1991). For a significant minority of our sample, lacking informal sources of support, the failure to obtain a break from care greatly increased the pressures and frustrations of motherhood. In some instances they felt their own identities had been subsumed into that of being a mother. They had no time for themselves, limited social contact and little energy to care about their own appearance. As one young mother of two and with a third on the way commented wistfully:

> *"I don't miss going out, I don't mind missing that, it's just having my own quality time."*

Struggling financially and unable to get a break from child care, despite the support of her partner, she looked forward to this third child with a mix of trepidation and resignation; "we'll cope . . . you've got to ain't you?". Several single parents also missed out on playgroup provision due to the stigma they felt attached to single parenthood; they felt too uncomfortable to give it a try:

> *"I thought it was all like women with husbands and that and I thought, no, I ain't going. I ain't being the only single parent there."*

For this young woman, quite isolated and frustrated with the pressures of full-time care, all professional help ended a few months after leaving care when no concerns about her child care skills were apparent. She had never been referred to a leaving care scheme and clearly had needed help to break into this potential source of support.

In general leaving care workers and many social workers recognised the need to reduce isolation and promote support links for young parents in the community, especially where they lacked family support. In District and City groups run by the schemes, including young parents' groups, were an important source of support. In County, where the scheme offered no group work, some individual workers attempted to link mothers with playgroups and parents' groups in the community if they wanted this. The advantages of group situations for young mothers are evident. They can offer a release from stress and isolation, an opportunity to share anxieties, help with parenting skills and with managing relationships with partners and, for the children, a chance to socialise and play together (Rickford 1994). However, given the unhelpful social climate that surrounds single parenthood, not all young mothers will be able to take advantage of these forms of provision without being encouraged and reassured.

For some young parents groups will not be appropriate and more individual solutions are needed. In a couple of cases the Homestart agency was involved to help with parenting skills and to reduce isolation and links with health visitors were encouraged in a similar way. Where young parents, especially those with positive family links, were managing quite successfully it appeared that regular low key visits from leaving care workers or social workers were sufficient to offer reassurance. For young mothers it meant that, should practical problems arise, they knew support would be available for them. Those who lacked contact appeared to feel the burden of responsibility more keenly and were less certain about possible future sources of help.

Already in this report we have pointed to the importance of promoting links between young people and their families both during and after the time they are looked after. We have highlighted its role in offering both practical support and symbolic reassurance to young people and pointed to an association between positive family relationships and young people's ability to make and sustain other friendships. These informal sources of support were particularly important to young parents. Although partner selection was sometimes problematic and friends were not a primary source of practical help, they did help to reduce a sense of isolation and frustration. Positive links with immediate and extended family members were more crucial and, for some, a close link with a mother, sister or aunt represented a mainstay in their support.

For seven young women, their new status as mothers brought increased contact with families. Mostly this was welcomed, in some instances had been longed for, but was seldom unproblematic. Some ambivalence relating to past conflicts and rejections were almost inevitable and, in a few cases, renewed interest was treated with suspicion. In one instance this was due to a fear of a cycle of sexual abuse being repeated and in another to resentment that it had taken her pregnancy for her mother to reappear on the scene after years of rejection; in this case she felt an understandable mix of anger and jealousy. In only two of these cases were workers available to offer either a mediating role or counselling to assist young people to work through their feelings. In general terms, as we have seen, active work on family issues appeared less of a priority once young people had moved to independence with fewer than a third of social workers offering direct assistance in this area. Given the tendency to early parenthood identified here and the importance of informal supports to young parents, counselling and mediation remains an important area of work.

• Summary points •

For young people leaving care there is a marked tendency to early parenthood. Within 18–24 months of leaving care one third had become parents, representing nearly one half of the young women in the sample. While over one half of pregnancies had been unplanned, over one third were planned with partners, reflecting a pattern of early family formation for care leavers. Three quarters of parents lived with partners at some stage.

- These findings point to gaps in the level of personal and social education available to young people in care and, perhaps as significant, to difficulties that young women in care may experience in communicating with male sexual partners. Safe sex requires a level of confidence and assertiveness that most teenagers find difficult.

- Preparation for parenthood was uneven. Some had informal support from family members, partners or partners' families; others relied upon carers, social workers and leaving care workers. The experience of those pregnant in care of specialist mother and baby units was variable; although for most the experience and specialist support was helpful.

- A range of accommodation options needed to be available and here the specialist role of leaving care schemes was important. For those less confident, remaining with foster carers or moving to supported lodgings or hostels provided valuable transitional support. For those more confident, good quality permanent tenancies were needed. Nearly three quarters were in permanent tenancies at the close of the research. Respite provision was also important. Several young mothers whose post-care careers were marked by instability influencing their ability to care were offered respite in lodgings or hostels.

- Where, in a small minority of cases, serious child protection concerns arose the support offered was generally positive. However no young parents were offered a second social worker for the child. Support tended to switch from mother to child. Even where there were no concerns, there was a pervasive tendency for the social work role to focus on monitoring child care. Where leaving care schemes were involved a more holistic approach to supporting the mother *in her own right* could be maintained.

- Although two thirds of the parents appeared to be managing quite successfully in adverse circumstances, poverty was a central problem and, for those without informal supports, it compounded their sense of social isolation. None, once eligible for income support, received financial help from social services. A few received help in kind, one scheme ran an exchange for second hand baby items, and some were helped with charity applications. Perhaps further thought could be given to the imaginative use of Section 24 and 17 funds to help parents to meet their children's needs.

- Schemes have a crucial role in encouraging and informing parents of the possibilities to return to learn. Most parents were aware of the poverty trap that limited their opportunities. Only one parent, through a specialist hostel with child care facilities, returned to college. Three others had been advised by schemes of this possibility, including social services funding and child care. Further initiatives in this area could be valuable.

- For some young mothers, contact with their families was renewed once they became parents and raised complex memories and feelings for them. Most young parents depended heavily on informal supports. Continuing mediation and counselling is required if these relationships are to prove supportive. Our evidence suggests that active support in these areas declined once young people left care.

- For those without informal supports, access to social and parenting groups in the community or to those run by schemes offered the chance for a break, to socialise and receive advice and reassurance. Networking to provide supports of this kind was important and a number of young parents needed encouragement to attend, being conscious of the stigma that currently surrounds early motherhood.

CHAPTER 13

YOUNG PEOPLE WITH SPECIAL NEEDS

In this chapter we will chart the progress of a small number of young people with special support needs. We will look at their preparation for leaving care, their early housing and employment careers and at the informal and professional sources of support available to them.

Young people with physical and/or learning disabilities looked after by local authorities and attempting to make the transition to adulthood are at a critical turning point in their lives. Recent legislation and guidance relating to children and adults returning to the community places new responsibilities upon local authorities to: develop individual and flexible care plans that adequately prepare them for transition and which involve them in decision making about their futures; help them maximise their potential for independent living – including housing options, future careers and support networks in the community; plan for a smooth transition to adult services where continuing support is required; and ensure that these support packages are integrated and co-ordinated on an inter-agency basis (DOH 1991c).

Although published research on the careers of accomodated young people with special needs is scant, our snap shot survey of 183 care leavers in these three authorities did point to a worrying tendency for those with special needs (particularly those with emotional and behavioural difficulties) to be over-represented amongst the unemployed and homeless in that sample (Biehal et al 1992). The findings from our follow up sample, whilst more optimistic, relate to just six young people who were designated as having special needs and none had an EBD statement. Three were from District authority, all young men with mild to moderate learning difficulties, and three were from County, a male and a female with learning difficulties and one young man with a serious mental health problem. Only the three young men from District were receiving support from a leaving care scheme throughout the research period. With such a small group the need for caution is evident, but we can chart their early post-care careers, give an indication of the support being made available to them and offer some pointers for further research.

Preparation

We have suggested that practical and social skills need to be developed gradually through care and that this process should be supported, participatory and holistic in approach. For young people with disabilities, whether cared for within the family home or substitute care, there exists a tendency to over-protect. Societal discrimination and their own vulnerability can inhibit carers from enabling them to become more independent and take risks (Fry 1992; Richardson and Ritchie 1986). The ethical dilemmas for workers attempting to balance 'risk taking' and 'protection' are very real (Stevenson and Parsloe 1993). However, for accomodated young people the need for structured preparation programmes is particularly crucial, given their need to move on at some point.

For four of this group the opportunity to develop skills and relationships in care appear to have been limited. In District, two young men in stable long-term foster care were considered over-protected. Most things were done for them and neither were encouraged to make friendships or invite friends back. Both were isolated, had problems making relationships and, according to one leaving care worker, one was uncommunicative and spent most of his time in his bedroom. Both were asked to leave by their carers on reaching 18 and a more structured package was offered once both had made planned moves to supported lodgings. The third, after an unstable care career, received little structured help in these areas while at his last children's home. More intensive help was offered when he moved to sheltered accommodation.

Finally, the case of the young man with mental health problems points to the lack of appropriate resources for his needs. Despite an earlier care episode, he lived with relatives until having a profound breakdown when 15. Upon discharge from hospital he was reluctantly accepted by an ordinary small group home. He never settled and the home was unable to cope with his behaviour. In consequence, after four months, he was 'pushed out' into a private flat. Over run by 'friends' and unable to cope he suffered a relapse and, after being hospitalised, moved to a supported hostel where he remained through the research. His social worker sums up the problem:

"I don't think . . . (it) . . . was an appropriate resource for him. At that stage . . . he had already been diagnosed as schizophrenic and so he had very particular needs . . . and (it) . . . just wasn't geared up to meet them . . . but that was the only resource there was. (So he) found himself stuck in a home that wasn't appropriate for him and being pushed out of the door because it wasn't . . . appropriate."

The experience of the other two young people was more positive. They were less sheltered, encouraged to take responsibility in practical areas despite their limited abilities and to participate in local youth and church clubs as a means of building their relationship skills. However, in the case of one young man stable with his long-term foster mother throughout the study, she, despite working full-time, was expected to carry the load of teaching him these skills almost single handed.

Preparing young people with disabilities to attain greater independence can be a difficult and lengthy process. The tendency to over-protect and care *for* is understandable. This discussion points to the need for more support and training to be made available to carers, including the use of outside resources to ease the burden on over-stretched carers, if social workers are unable to make an effective input themselves. Indeed, if social workers felt the opportunities for these young people were limited, it does beg the question of what they were trying to do to influence progress. A danger is that young people's development, rather than occurring through a gradual accumulation of skills, becomes telescoped at the point when plans are being made for them to move on. For young people with physical and learning disabilities this could be potentially disastrous.

Early housing careers

Turning first to the three young men in District, a feature that links these cases is the attempt to provide an integrated and inter-agency approach to meeting their differing needs. All three made well planned moves to their initial accommodation, although one stayed with friends for a few weeks in between. Two moved to supported lodgings and, for them, early referral to the leaving care scheme enabled them to make positive choices about the move and gave time for intensive support plans to be laid. The third moved initially to sheltered accommodation provided by a voluntary agency but, after a few months, he decided he wanted more autonomy and left. After a number of uncertain moves he tried his own flat. It was only when he was clearly not coping that his social worker referred him to the scheme. Despite intensive help from his social worker, the scheme and a crisis support team, his situation broke down when his flat was ransacked by family and 'friends' and arrangements were made for him to move to a specialist supported hostel.

In all three cases specialist resources were drawn upon to help assess needs, to offer support and the work was well co-ordinated and planned. For example, for one of those in supported lodgings, despite intensive help from his provider, scheme and social worker, it was apparent that his skills were too limited for independent living. A worker from the Young Adult Team (learning difficulties) was asked to do a formal assessment and, in consequence, he made a planned move to a specialist hostel where he could stay longer term. The young man was happy with this arrangement, felt he had sufficient autonomy at the hostel, had developed a close relationship with his key worker there and felt his skills and confidence were improving. For the young man above, despite an unstable start, his period at the hostel offered a chance to recuperate, regain his balance and begin to rebuild his self-confidence. At the final interview plans were being laid for him to try again in a new flat near to his one good friend. The scheme were co-ordinating the support package which would involve visits several times weekly for the first few months. Both these young men had made a smooth transition from child to adult services during the course of the research although, for the latter, this assessment only took place once he had failed in his flat.

Formal care assessments recognised their need for continuing long-term support and both changed to social workers from the Adult Team.

A brief look at County raises a number of issues concerning support, planning and accommodation resources. First, the young woman in supported lodgings spent a positive year there developing her skills and confidence. Continuity in support was offered by her social worker. A planned move was made to a council flat near her mother, upon whom she was heavily reliant, and support plans were being arranged by her social worker and the scheme to ease her transition. Despite her limited practical skills, immaturity and vulnerability, her learning difficulties were assessed as insufficiently severe to warrant transfer to adult services. A question mark remained about her ability to continue managing when her current support eased back, as was likely to happen in the not too distant future. Might young people in this situation be the ones most likely to slip through the support net?

The situation of the young man with his foster mother points to the twin dangers of over-burdening carers and of failing to plan for the future. Although they had received positive support from a long-term social worker, a change during the course of the research saw that support plummet. At the final interview only two contacts had occurred in nine months, an introductory visit and a review, and she was thinking of closing the case. No plans were being laid for his future and his carer, struggling to cope with the demands of an over-dependent young adult, was being expected to carry the entire load. Research has pointed to the tendency for carers, especially mothers, to become isolated from social and community life (Hubert 1990) and, whilst committed to offering care, she was becoming increasingly frustrated. This social worker had assumed that everything was fine and had not given thought to his future needs:

> *"You don't get that close to a person . . . if it's a very stable boarding out . . . You don't get that relationship very easily unless . . . (you're) going to do some pieces of work with them."*

The stay of the young man with mental health problems at a health authority run hostel highlights the appropriateness of some resources and problems of inter-agency working. Throughout the research he was based there and spent two days per week with his grandmother, his main support. Without friends, he consistently found his time there 'depressing'. His days lacked structure, he was at a loose end with no money and 'nothing to do'. His medication coupled with loss of motivation and focus made it hard for him to take the initiative – "I live in a dream world all the time, 'cos the drugs they make you daydream". Both his grandmother and social worker were critical of the lack of structure at the hostel and its failure to offer a proper programme of independence training, its explicit aim. Critical at reviews, the social worker felt powerless to intervene between times. Day to day support was their province and, systemically, professional boundaries were inhibiting joint-working. It appeared that her role in preparing him for a future life had become residual and there was apparently no other resource to which he could be moved. In a sense he had become trapped.

His circumstances do not appear unique for adults with serious mental health problems. Surveys of service users tend to reveal sizeable minorities dissatisfied with their accommodation and wanting alternatives, but finding difficulty articulating their needs and feeling powerless to exercise choice. Reflecting the circumstances of this young man, one survey concludes that for empowerment to have meaning for this disadvantaged client group a greater range of choices needs to be made available (Hatfield et al 1992).

At the close of our research housing outcomes for most of these young people seemed quite positive. Although for some further moves lay ahead and the future remained uncertain, continuity of support had enabled them to avoid a descent into homelessness which, for several, had been a real risk.

Education/employment

Department of Health guidance has highlighted the need for training and employment opportunities to be promoted for young people with disabilities (DOH 1991). In highly competitive youth labour markets this group is most vulnerable to exclusion. Carers and practitioners have pointed to the need for strong advocacy to promote life chances, whether through carers, social workers or 'unaligned befrienders' (Fry 1992; Russell and Flynn 1991). Although the future careers of these young people were very uncertain, we can offer clear evidence of attempts to offer positive encouragement and of networking to promote opportunities.

Four of the young people had been statemented as having special educational needs. Two attended special schools and two remained in mainstream education but with additional help from special needs tutors. None of the sample attained qualifications at the end of their schooling. Only two young men remained unemployed throughout, one from each authority. The circumstances of the young man with mental health problems has been described above. For him, his illness and loss of motivation combined with a lack of structure and opportunity. For the other, his unstable post-care career and abuse by his family left him too insecure to consider opportunities at this stage.

Three young people, encouraged by teachers, carers and social workers completed special needs YT schemes. As part of a comprehensive package of support for one young man in supported lodgings in District, his leaving care worker then negotiated access to a specialist employment agency for young people with learning difficulties. He continued there and was gaining part-time work experience in a hospital. In County, when the young man in foster care completed his multi-skills YT his carer and social worker helped him gain entry to a two year college course in catering. Although thought unlikely to gain an NVQ qualification, he had additional support from a special needs tutor and liaison was maintained to press for extra help. However, as we have indicated above, once his social worker changed liaison ceased and his carer was left to worry about his future. Lastly, the young woman completed a YT in social care gaining work experience at a private elderly home. Since she was happy there, despite fears of exploitation, her social worker negotiated a contract with the home for her to stay on in a training post. Built into the contract was a three monthly review to assess progress and monitor the training component of the job.

It is evident that the foothold these young people had on the employment ladder was precarious and that their long-term prospects for financial independence remained poor. However it was clear from the interviews that they valued the work they were doing. Several workers highlighted its importance in giving structure to their day, in building skills, confidence and self image and in promoting social contacts outside the home. Finally one young man managed to obtain and keep full-time employment in a factory throughout the study, despite periodic crises in his life. Access to the job was provided through a 'linkage' friend, an ex-sessional worker from his children's home whom he had known and had a close relationship with for 10 years. She worked at the same place and was able to support him on a daily basis. Encouragement to maintain motivation was also offered by his leaving care worker.

Developing informal support networks

Successful inter-dependent living in the community requires a network of family and/or friendships that can offer security and a positive sense of self. Social isolation tends to figure prominently in the lives of those with learning difficulties and mental health problems. All these young people were isolated in differing ways. Only two had links with family members that were positive and another, as we have seen, was exploited by his family. The other three had been profoundly rejected. All had difficulty making and sustaining relationships, had few or no friends their own age and were dependent upon carers and workers for support. In addition, all were considered immature for their age and lacked awareness around sexuality and sexual relationships. The young woman, having been sexually abused, found relationships with men particularly difficult.

Although progress is slow and difficult and may only involve, as one leaving care worker said, "subtle slight changes", the befriending role offered by leaving care schemes can help in this area. All three young men in District were involved with the scheme. Its open access services including a drop in, social group work and group holidays were used by two to relieve isolation and build their social skills and contacts. One also took part in a men's group with a focus on personal and social education, health and sexual relationships. In addition he joined a group run by the Young Adult Team to build social skills and promote leisure interests. The third felt too unconfident for a group but individual support from the scheme was exploring similar areas. All three found scheme staff approachable and friendly and, for the two living independently, the links it offered meant that they knew where they could turn for help in a crisis. However uncertain their steps, all felt more confident and positive about their lives at the close of the research.

Of equal importance is the need to ensure that when young people move to their own flats they are close to the supports that they have. One of these young men, whose first flat broke down through exploitation from 'friends', was transferred to another close to his brother (from whom he had been separated in care and only recently renewed contact) and his 'linkage' friend. He viewed her as a substitute mother and for years had been spending most weekends with her. In County, the young woman moved to a flat near her mother and older friends from her church. Although heavily dependent on her mother, their relationship was tense, and her social worker was actively involved in a mediating role. Vulnerable to exploitation, part of the support package being drawn up by her social worker and leaving care worker included help to widen her social network, particularly with peers, and counselling around sexual awareness and male relationships.

The stability afforded to the young man with his carer meant that the difficulties that independent living would bring were some way ahead. To him this was his home and he was aware that he lacked the skills and maturity to survive outside. However, as we have indicated, his social worker had no plans to offer him the help that could make this step more realistic. She had no idea what specialist resources might be available to help him and his carer develop his practical and social skills. As she herself said, "I haven't got a clue". Aware of his sexual naivety she felt unable to help – "I wouldn't know where to begin to be honest". Clearly this raises questions that go beyond her particular competence. It suggests the low priority that can be given to young people and carers in apparently 'stable boarding out' situations and it also questions the direction and supervision being offered to her by management.

Despite good quality physical care and the possibility of interacting with others at the hostel, the young man with mental health problems felt isolated, lonely and depressed. The two days he spent with his grandmother were the highlight of his week. Some improvement in his health had given him greater clarity by the final interview but this had accentuated his depression. He was more aware of his own limitations:

"I can't see much future . . . sometimes I get depressed, I think there's no future for me."

His social worker was offering him counselling about his medication, the prognosis and his future but, for him, the things he most wanted, in particular a return to his gran, appeared out of reach. For his social worker, having to straddle a divide between health and social services to deliver a service had proved frustrating. She candidly admitted that "I don't honestly think I've achieved anything". Despite the enterprising examples of positive practice outlined above, it was the sadness of his situation that seemed most poignant.

• Summary points •

Six young people in our sample were considered to have special support needs; five with learning difficulties and one with a serious mental health problem. Only the three in District were receiving continuous support from a leaving care scheme.

Three young men with learning difficulties had been over-protected in care and given only limited opportunities to develop practical skills, sexual awareness and to build friendships. Their preparation accelerated with moves to supported lodgings and a hostel. Although the tendency to care *for* and protect is understandable, their preparation was compressed into the latter end of their care careers.

- Young people with physical and learning disabilities need opportunities to gradually acquire skills and confidence. It needs to be a central focus of the child care planning and review cycle with mechanisms for setting goals and monitoring and reviewing progress.

- For some carers the responsibility for preparing young people rested with them. Support and training should be made available to meet the particular needs of their young people and social workers need to draw on specialist resources to assist carers and ease their burden. In at least one case this possibility had not been considered.

For the young man with mental health problems the lack of an appropriate in-care resource led to a disastrous attempt at independent living. Both he and another young person were unable to manage their flats and were exploited by others.

- A formal assessment of skills and abilities to manage independently is required prior to leaving care. For these two, community care assessments, enabling a transition to adult services, were only made after their lack of skills became painfully apparent.

- Long term advanced planning is necessary if a more independent living situation is to be a realistic prospect. While this was the case for some young people, for one young man stable with his foster carer no plans were being laid for his future.

For most of these young people a well co-ordinated inter-agency approach to meeting their needs once they were moving on was evident. The specialist knowledge of schemes was helpful here. Their role in identifying supported accommodation was important, either through directly managed supported lodgings or through links with specialist agencies for sheltered accommodation Networking to promote training and employment opportunities was also apparent. Social workers and leaving care workers were informally involved in linking with colleges, training agencies and employers on behalf of young people. Continuity in post-care support was crucial, for some whose initial housing situations broke down it prevented a slide into homelessness.

The befriending role of schemes was also valued by young people. The open access services in District (drop-in, groups, holidays) were heavily used by two isolated young men to make social contacts and build their interpersonal skills and confidence. For those not involved in schemes, most social workers were also active in promoting links with family and helping to extend social networks.

Finally, in one case, professional boundaries between health and social services were inhibiting an inter-agency approach to meeting this young man's needs. Day to day responsibility for his care rested with staff at a health authority run hostel and his social worker, although unhappy with its lack of structure and training in practical skills, felt powerless to intervene. These boundaries appeared to combine with a lack of appropriate alternative resources to leave him trapped in a situation with which he was unhappy.

CHAPTER 14

GETTING INTO TROUBLE: DRUG USE AND OFFENDING

Popular perceptions often link being in care with being in trouble. Here we will explore the extent to which these young people were involved in drug misuse and offending and the impact of these behaviour patterns on their lives. Given the paucity of data that exists in these areas, we will also offer some pointers for further research.

Recent years have witnessed societal concern about perceived rising levels of crime, drug and alcohol misuse amongst the young. For young people 'looked after' by local authorities, a popular common sense understanding that associates their situation with 'trouble' has been persistent. The stigma of 'care' punctuates the accounts given by young people themselves (Stein and Carey 1986). It is a burden many feel they carry into their post-care adult lives. There are no official data collated on crime, drugs and alcohol misuse as it relates to young people in care – merely a few disturbing fragments that will be mentioned below.

The findings from our study appear quite optimistic but point, above all, to the need for further focused research in this area. Our findings need to be treated with caution. First, they only chart the early post-care careers of young people; their first 18–24 months of independent living. Second, we have selected three authorities that have leaving care schemes for study and this factor could influence more positive outcomes for young people. Third, problems concerning the reliability and validity of self report studies in this area have been raised. Illegality and disapproval may lead to under-reporting and, conversely, bravado or the need to conform to perceived peer norms can lead to over-reporting (Smith and Nutbeam 1992). As a check on young people's accounts we also sought the views of social workers and leaving care workers as to the existence of problems in these areas.

Drug use

"I'm not one of those that'll just go out and spend it on drugs, I'll buy me food in and stuff first."

(YOUNG FEMALE RECREATIONAL USER)

"Every time I felt down I always had summat to cheer me up, solvents and glue and that. That's the only good thing I can say about drugs, that they cheer you up when you're feeling down."

(INSECURE YOUNG MAN UNHAPPY AND DEPRESSED IN CARE)

These comments capture the dimensions of drug use, positive and negative, for the young people in our sample who have tried them. Table 14.1 gives an overview of usage.

Table 14.1 Experience of drug use (n=74)

	n	%
never/no mention	36	48.5%
experimental/recreational	25	34%
problem usage	13	17.5%

Almost one half of the young people had never used drugs or, if they had tried them briefly in the past, chose not to tell us. In all these cases their professional workers felt that drugs were not a part of their lives. One third admitted having experimented with drugs and a proportion of these continued to use them in recreational settings, often linked to local rave and club scenes. Fewer than one fifth perceived themselves or were perceived by workers to have more serious problems attached to their use of drugs. Of this group only five continued to use drugs heavily throughout the research. Most, often with the support of social workers and/or leaving care workers, found ways of limiting and controlling their behaviour. There was little variation between the three authorities in relation to proportions who were not using drugs or were using them recreationally, although there was a higher concentration of those with problem usage in the City authority.

Comparisons with other groups of young people are difficult given the paucity of research data on drug use amongst the young. However current research following a group of 770 teenagers in the North West over five years has reported that, at 15/16 years of age, 47% of the sample admitted having experimented with drugs at least once (Francis 1994). Another study of 2239 15–16 year olds in Wales pointed to a lower figure of 21%, with one tenth having taken a drug in the past month (Smith and Nutbeam 1992). Allowing for regional variations and the older age range of our sample, our finding that one half were not involved in drug use appears broadly consistent.

Some recent studies have pointed to the growing centrality of 'soft' drugs in the social lives of young people (cannabis, ecstasy, amphetamines etc). Often these are preferred to alcohol due to price, their perceived lack of side effects and the availability of an extended menu for different social settings. It is suggested that drug use is no longer an isolated aspect of young peoples' lives but is becoming part and parcel of growing up in contemporary Britain. Its illegality and role in demarcating different youth identities are part of the pleasure and excitement of escape from restrictions (Coffield and Gofton 1994). Amongst the one third who had experimented with drugs these perceptions were apparent. Several mentioned the association of drugs with a good time and escape from troubles. One says that her use was linked to "just going out to a rave and forgetting all me worries". Another was involved "just 'cos it was fun, a good time". Some related experimentation to peer group cultures at school or in children's homes. In relation to the latter, whilst most young people willingly participated some felt pressured to conform to what seemed a 'normal' pattern of behaviour. One young woman, who had been heavily involved in solvent abuse, looks back with some disgust at the 'crazes' which swept her home:

"I went through a phase where a few of me friends were going out glue sniffing every day and the thought of it makes me feel sick now . . . I don't know how I could have done it . . . If we couldn't get a tin we were sort of devastated for the day . . . I can't actually say it was to get away from real life 'cos, no matter what people say, it don't have that effect on you."

Whilst for some young people, as with this young woman, experimentation was firmly in the past, others continued to use drugs on a regular basis, mostly at weekends with their friends, and all felt themselves to be reasonably in control of their lives.

For those with more serious problems, drug and alcohol use linked to wider patterns of insecurity and instability. One young woman who had been sexually abused by a relative post care relied upon them to help her get through the days as she struggled to recover, supported by her leaving care worker. Another young man, a heavy user from the age of 12, suffered a mental health breakdown (diagnosed as drug related schizophrenia) and, after hospitalisation, remained in a specialist hostel which shielded him from the drug culture to which he remained vulnerable. For a core group of seven young men in the City authority, susceptibility was rooted in feelings of rejection stemming from parental break up or family abuse. For them distress and personal insecurity were manifested in sometimes violent and disruptive behaviour in school, truancy and, once in care, all failed to find stability and experienced multiple placement moves. Drug use became inter-connected with criminal activity and, for most, continuing instability post-care led to a continuation of this pattern.

Some of these young people did manage to regain a measure of control over their lives. Two gave up drugs after witnessing friends dying through overdoses. A further two found that relationships with girlfriends and imminent parenthood brought a new sense of responsibility and a reason to sort themselves out. Another left the area to start a new life. Those who continued to drift, experiencing unemployment, periods of homelessness and sustaining few relationships, seemed to lack the bearings from which they could reassess their lives.

Where serious problems were identified support from social workers and, where involved, leaving care workers was available. In the majority of these cases advice and counselling was offered and leaflets on harm reduction made available. Two were referred to specialist agencies, although neither kept up attendance. Advice was not always accepted and this points to difficulties in offering support in this area. One young man recounted his social worker distributing leaflets to him and his friends in their children's home. The information "made us laugh"; at that stage at least it failed to match their lived experience. Some social workers found it hard to engage young people as they concealed their behaviour from them. Unless young people themselves recognise a problem and the need to change, support to stop drugs is likely to be unproductive. As one young man remarked:

"I had to sort it out meself, nobody else can help me . . . 'Cos if I still wanted to take drugs and somebody coming in and telling me it's wrong, it won't stop me from doing it".

A number of support and training issues arise from this brief discussion. First, recent research and project experience point to the limitations of 'just say no' campaigns (Coffield and Gofton 1994; Francis 1994). As the comments above suggest, young people will experiment with drugs and, unless ready themselves, support to stop is likely to be ineffective. However, appropriate advice with an emphasis on harm reduction may be effective. Second, for the minority of young people in care with more serious problems, drugs misuse appears to be a symptom of a much deeper sense of insecurity and instability which needs to be resolved. Third, the authority relationship between young person and social worker can impede a need to confide. Some authorities have adopted an inter-agency approach to delivering services to young people. For example, it is reported that one SSD has contracted a voluntary advice agency to offer direct counselling services to young people and awareness training to residential staff and foster carers (Francis 1994). On a smaller scale, as with our authorities, health authority staff can be brought in to talk to groups of young people in children's homes. A recent report by The Advisory Council on the Misuse of Drugs (1993) suggests the development of broad health educational programmes in children's homes is necessary, given that placement moves and school changes lead many young people to miss out on more standard programmes. Finally, recent evidence has highlighted the need for staff training in this area. It suggests that drugs and alochol training has had a low priority on qualifying courses and that many professionals are ill equipped to identify and offer appropriate support to clients with alcohol and drug related problems (Alaszewski and Harrison 1992). These needs were echoed by one leaving care worker who candidly admitted to feeling 'unconfident' in this area. Without training he was unsure "how to deal with it" and did not "really know the signs to look out for anyway".

Offending

Despite the popular association between care and 'trouble', there is little official data nor any research studies that focus on the relationship between care and crime. Whilst the need for us to know more is a matter of some urgency, given the stigma which attaches to care, a few disturbing statistics are available. For example, a Home Office study found that 23% of adult prisoners and 38% of young prisoners appear to have experienced local authority care at some point in their lives (cited in NCB 1992). Obviously this represents a much broader group than the care leavers who form the basis of this study; many may have had short episodes when young and others may have been remanded to care *for offending*. Although our cautionary words at the beginning of this section need to be borne in mind, our findings appear more optimistic and point to a reality that, for the vast majority of young people, their entry connects with the inability of their families to provide adequate care.

Table 14.2 gives an overview of offending patterns for our sample.

Table 14.2 Offending patterns (n=74)

	n	%
never	42	57%
minor past	18	24%
more serious past	3	4%
problems post-care only	5	7%
'career'	6	8%

The picture our data offers is one in which over one half of our sample have never had any involvement with the police. A further quarter had 'minor' problems with the police in their pre-care or care careers but have had no involvement since moving on. Offences ranged from criminal damage, fighting and shoplifting to being driven in stolen cars and none warranted more than a caution or conditional discharge. Three young people were involved in either more serious or a greater quantity of offences during the time they were looked after. All were linked to their time in children's homes; none had offended since leaving and the most serious disposal was an attendance centre order for a young man with four convictions for 'joy-riding' and burglary. Although our study could only follow their early post-care careers and some were lost during the course of the study (our assessment is made at the last point of contact), it would appear that for around 85% of the sample their early careers were not marked by criminal activity. Obviously some caution is needed here. Some young people may have committed offences for which they had not been caught and about which we and their workers remained unaware and some were using illegal drugs.

A further five young people committed first offences after moving on from care. Two committed arson, one of whom ran away after a warrant was issued and was lost to the study; one young woman received a probation order after a one-off assault at a hostel and two insecure and unstable young men committed minor offences – shoplifting and fighting. Apart from the runaway, all were receiving support from social workers or leaving care workers to help them re-stabilise their lives. For three of these young people their offences connected with a wider sense of instability. For example, a young mother with limited abilities who set fire to her own and a neighbour's flat, was struggling to cope with both independence and parenthood. Real concerns about her ability to care for her child meant that, at the final interview, her child was being fostered on an emergency basis and intensive social work help was being offered to help her reconstruct her life.

It is important to distinguish between those who have had limited involvement in criminal activity and those who appear to be developing an incipient criminal 'career'. Whilst such assessments must remain uncertain, there were only six young people in our sample where connections between pre-care, care and early post-care experiences suggested this to be the case. All were male and, as our earlier discussion about drug behaviour indicated, for five out of six (all in the City authority) drug use and crime became closely interwoven. Although not causal – life for most of our young people remained difficult in and after care, struggling as they were to cope on low incomes and with distressing past experiences – some clear associations seemed to connect these cases.

For five of these young people, insecurity and stress created by parental break up or physical abuse was manifested through running away or truancy and violent or disruptive behaviour at school. One young man linked truancy to the start of his 'career'.

> *"It were just when I started knocking off school and then I'd knocked off school that long I'd run out of things to do, so that's when I started a life of crime."*

Stress and unhappiness at parental separation had contributed to a sense of failure at school. Truancy had created boredom and opportunity for crime, to find something he felt 'good' at – "as I got older the crime got bigger and I thought, crime's for me, I can do this". A majority had difficulty making relationships and were variously decribed as 'dour', 'solitary' or 'sad'. Care provided neither solutions nor stability, most made multiple placement moves (some linked to their behaviour) and compounded feelings of rejection:

> *"I didn't really care what happened then 'cos I were already in care and I didn't think they could do nowt else more, so I just kept on doing it and doing it."*

Whilst many young people mentioned the peer culture in children's homes as a factor influencing criminal behaviour, some sharing the excitement of infringing laws, others felt pressured to conform. One of these young men, having entered care after being physically abused, only found acceptance once offending:

> *"Well it were just atmosphere I were in and lads I were with . . . You were just sat there and everybody were going out pinching cars and burgling houses . . . and you weren't doing owt . . . They (were) like tormenting you and . . . so I just ended up doing it meself."*

Five were heavily involved in a drugs culture both in and after care. One made its link with crime explicit:

> *"It got that bad, when I had no money I were going out burgling or robbing people in the street for . . . the money to get it."*

For four of these young people post-care instability led to a continuation of these problems. Two, supported by social workers and leaving care workers, found initial stability in their flats but both found transition hard. One lost his flat and job and, moving between friends and family, resumed shoplifting and burglaries to 'survive'. The other, after a period travelling, returned to his father and childhood area and became immersed in a local drugs/crime culture. Two others never found stability, a succession of moves interspersed with periods of homelessness offered little chance to review their lives.

Some did manage to regain some control over their lives at least temporarily. One young man gave up offending when he realised that a stable relationship with his girlfriend and imminent parenthood gave him much to lose. At the final interview he gave voice to this commitment:

> *"So I see it as if I'm not committing crime I ain't going to get locked up. If I ain't going to get locked up I've got a relationship and a daughter and a flat."*

A sense of stability and the need to have a stake in society are obviously crucial. Research into young people leaving Youth Training Centres pointed to the importance of later reunification between young people and their families in providing some physical and emotional security; small successes in this area sometimes engendering greater stability, acceptance and improving employment prospects (Bullock et al 1993). For two young men rapprochement with their mothers enabled a later return home. One, who returned there after a sojourn in custody, started a youth training scheme and the other found stability for several months until relationships once again broke down.

Outcomes for the six were mixed. Although two had had brief spells in custody on remand, none were in prison. The young father above had no further involvement in crime. One, for whom cars had always been an 'addiction', was on a probation order and another was on a supervision order for similar offences. The young man back with his mother was attempting to build a new life and two were lost to the study after the second interview.

Attempts were made by professionals to support most of those young people involved in crime but, as with support around drug misuse, success is difficult to achieve unless young people themselves feel able to take responsibility and seek solutions. Two of those with car offences had been referred to motor projects and one other to an alternative to custody scheme and, while the young people valued their involvement in these projects and the practical help offered, these strategies, in themselves, had proved insufficient to prevent further offending.

The accounts of young people in Stein and Carey's (1986) study suggest that they felt themselves not to be fully in control of their actions, that they were at the mercy of circumstances and distanced themselves from personal responsibility. Whilst more focused research is needed in this area, these perceptions were also apparent amongst this group of young people. Indeed, for the very small number of more serious persistent offenders, their lives did seem to be out of control and their offending part of a much wider set of insecurities that the care system had been unable to address effectively.

• Summary points •

Although popular perceptions connect care with trouble, there is very little official or research data with which to confirm or refute this association. While caution is needed, our findings appear quite optimistic. Nearly one half of our sample had never used drugs, a similar proportion to other recent studies of young people at large, and one third had experimented, some continuing to use drugs recreationally. Fewer than one fifth either perceived themselves or were perceived by workers to have had problems in this area and ony five young people remained heavy users throughout the study.

Our findings on offending confirm that the vast majority of young people in care are there because of the inability of their families to provide adequate care. Over one half had never had involvement with the police. A further quarter had minor skirmishes with the police either prior to or during their time in care. Around four fifths of the young people's early post-care careers were not marked by criminal activity. There were only six young people where connections between their pre-care, care and post-care experiences suggested that they were developing an incipient criminal career.

Offending for this very small group (all male) was connected with heavy drug use and to a wider pattern of instability and insecurity which their time in care had been unable to resolve. Associations between family rejection/abuse, school behaviour problems/truancy, instability and movement in care and a continuing pattern of instability post-care existed for this group. Those who managed to regain control of their lives did so when they found an incentive to stabilise their lives in society – for example, parenthood or rapprochement with a parent. Although support was available from professionals where young people were perceived to have difficulties with drugs or offending, it was unlikely to be very successful unless young people themselves recognised the need to stop.

In relation to drugs and alcohol:

- Awareness training is required for carers and social workers that emphasises harm reduction strategies; not all were confident about tackling these issues;

- Problems associated with the authority relationship between young people and social workers suggest that an inter-agency approach could be helpful. Some authorities are using specialist voluntary agencies to provide direct services to young people and run staff training;

- Problems with movement in care and truancy suggest that children's homes, possibly drawing on health authority staff, have a key role in promoting health education programmes for young people;

- Leaving care schemes have an important role in providing individual support to young people, liasing with other agencies and promoting awareness through activities at the project base.

With regard to offending:

- Our findings suggest that popular perceptions that connect care/leaving care with offending behaviour are unwarranted. The vast majority of young people entering care do so because of the inability of their families to provide adequate care. Assumptions about the associations between care and 'trouble' need to be challenged.

PART 3

This section has a focus upon the four leaving care schemes and the young people in our sample receiving support from them. Each scheme is profiled in turn. We will explore their distinctive approaches and show how these help to influence the culture of schemes, the way services are structured and the relationship of young people to the schemes. The final chapter will highlight the themes and issues that arise from our discussion of different models of provision.

It is important to note that our discussion does not offer a national picture of the support available to young people leaving care. Despite the resource constraints confronting local authorities today, our three authorities, through the funding of specialist schemes, have a commitment to providing quality support services for care leavers. In this sense, a national picture would be likely to reveal greater disparities in provision.

CHAPTER 15

DISTRICT LEAVING CARE SCHEME

Background

Our first scheme operates within one of the smallest metropolitan district authorities in the country and was launched in 1986. It is based in a large terraced house in the centre of the main town. Although space is tight it offers a kitchen/dining area for young people to relax in and a large meeting room on the top floor for group discussions and more private chats. The centre is lively with young people popping in and out to obtain help and socialise together. It remains a small scheme with a project leader, three and three quarter equivalent social work posts and an administrator (half time).

The scheme is directly managed by a voluntary agency working in partnership with the local social services department. Since 1992 the local authority has assumed full responsibility for the scheme's direct revenue costs, although some indirect costs are met by the voluntary agency. The latter include staff support, training and the running costs of the project base. The voluntary agency has responsibility for policy development within the scheme and for the management, support and training of staff (see Appendix Figure 1). Social services management meet with the project leader and agency management on a regular basis to facilitate joint-working procedures (see Appendix Figure 2). Both the agency and social services monitor the scheme's progress annually and the scheme has developed internal systems for evaluating scheme usage and impact. The scheme also has a local advisory group – including representation from social services, councillors and a housing manager – as a forum for policy discussions and service co-ordination.

The voluntary agency and the scheme have developed formal policy statements covering leaving care services and there are agreed local authority and scheme procedures to cover referral, planning and review processes. In addition there is an easy to read guide for young people that outlines the services available locally and both the agency and the social services department have complaints procedures that young people can use. The scheme also produces a regular newsletter for all interested parties.

These arrangements have given the team a clear framework to operate within, an opportunity to develop a coherent approach to service provision and to build links with other service providers (for example, housing, Careers, colleges and training agencies) to promote opportunities for young people.

Approach

At its inception, a joint agency and social services planning group produced a policy document that asked the scheme to provide "training, a drop-in centre and an accommodation resource". Also that the scheme should be available to all care leavers in the area and assist them from the preparation phase until they no longer need support. The scheme has developed a distinctive 'community based' provision centred around it's busy project base. It offers a combination of individual key worker support reinforced by more 'open access' services at the base, including a range of groups, a daily drop-in and a duty service. (See Appendix Figure 3). It attempts to be flexible and informal and to give young people a choice about the intensity of their involvement with the scheme. It is also open-ended. Structured individual support is available through transition for those who need or want it but, where young people appear to be stable in the community, withdrawal of key worker support may be negotiated. When this occurs it remains open for them to sue the scheme's more informal services for as long as they wish, including support and advice from staff. The variety of ways in which young people use the scheme is apparent in our sample and the range of social activities at the base give it a strong project identity.

The scheme's work is influenced by a perspective that recognises the interdependent nature of adult life. Whilst finding appropriate accommodation and helping young people develop the practical skills to maintain it are obviously important, it emphasises the need for emotional security, developing a positive self image and confidence in relationships with others. It is felt that by staying with young people and providing constant positive reinforcement it is possible to see changes in these areas over time.

Profile of scheme users

Given the small size of the authority, we included in our research **all** the young people that we could identify who either moved to independence or were legally discharged during the first eight months of 1992, 17 in total. At this point eleven were receiving support from the scheme and six were not. Perhaps reflecting the varied pattern of scheme usage that 'open access' permits, by the final interview some eighteen months later, eight of the original eleven were still in touch with the scheme. Four were still receiving regular key worker support and four were using the centre for advice and social activities. Two young people had opted for only short-term involvement and only one young woman felt that she had received a poor service. In addition, by the end of our research, all but one of the remaining six had made some contact with the scheme; two for leaving care grants, two for longer term support and one, who had been in a stable supported lodgings placement, was just being referred at the end of the research for help with planning her transition. It would seem that the size of the authority, the well established nature of the scheme within it and sound referral procedures have enabled the scheme to reach out to virtually all these young people in some capacity.

Returning to the original eleven, their care careers, abilities and past experiences were diverse. Six were female and all were aged 17–18 at this point, although for some, scheme involvement had started much earlier. Two of the young men had learning difficulties and a third was referred shortly after our first interview. Length of time in care was very varied, ranging from one to 18 years and, whilst five had found stability in care with no placement moves (four in foster placements), movement had figured more prominently in the lives of the other six, with three making six to eight moves during their care careers. Half the sample had come from fostering backgrounds and, of the others, some had experienced a mix of foster and residential care.

The practical and emotional resources available to these young people varied greatly. Most were struggling on low incomes – six were unemployed and four were in full-time employment, although mostly in low waged work. Although a majority had quite good or fairly reasonable life skills, all were finding the budgeting and negotiating skills they needed difficult to acquire. Two had good supportive networks of family and friends to sustain them, a further four had some community supports but the remainder were quite isolated, lacking in confidence, finding difficulties in making relationships and, especially for those with learning difficulties, were heavily reliant on professional support. This diveristy is reflected in the differing use young people made of the scheme's services.

Access and rationing

Formal access to the scheme is secured through the referral process which, in District, is clear and well structured. The team accepts referrals directly from social workers, carers or young people themselves (two of our sample were self referrals). A set of procedures have evolved within social services that require a leaving care planning meeting to be held within two months of a young person's sixteenth birthday review. At this point a decision is taken as to whether a referral to the scheme is required. (see Appendix Figure 4). If so, referral forms are completed by the social worker specifying the services requested. Scheme staff then meet young people to explore their needs and explain the range of services on offer. Young people are always offered access to all services, individual and social, but if they choose not to use them then involvement may be short-term, as was the case with two of this sample. Both were helped to find and settle into their flats and neither wanted further help, although the door was left open should they need it. For eight out of the eleven, referrals were made some time before their move to independence, ranging from six months to two years for a young man with learning difficulties. This enabled the scheme to build relationships, assist with preparations and help to plan the moves.

Where young people are referred early, the assessment process can be quite informal. If young people want long-term support, time is spent building a positive and trusting relationship as a basis for gradually identifying needs and an overall plan to meet them. However, where necessary the process is given structure and forms are available to enable more formal assessments of skills and abilities to be undertaken jointly with young people.

As we have indicated, the scheme offers a service to all care leavers in the authority and to those already living in the community through a mix of individual support and a range of 'open access' services at the project base. These include a daily 'drop-in' from 12.00–2.00pm where young people can socialise, arrange social events and obtain informal advice from staff; a duty service from 2.00–5.00pm for young people to obtain more structured advice from a staff member and a range of group activities both social and educational. The team runs a weekly social group with activities organised according to demand. These have included sports, aerobics with a volunteer tutor, cookery, judo, mother and toddler and ante-natal groups and a men's group to explore personal and social education. Other services have included an exchange for second hand baby items, sessions run by a Careers Officer and regularly organised group holidays for young people living independently. The 'drop-in' and duty system are serviced by one staff member on a rota basis and, whilst young people are free to see them, contact with their key workers is usually by appointment.

The strength of this approach is in offering young people an informal and flexible service; they can dip into the services they want to use, when they want to use them and can choose the degree of intensity of their involvement with the scheme according to their needs. It is also open-ended, they can maintain contact with the scheme for as long as they need and without necessarily having a problem to discuss.

The use made of these services is evidenced in our participating sample of eleven; five were using the groups and 'drop-in' service on a regular basis and a further three were dropping in occasionally for advice and social contact. In overall terms access to the scheme and its support appears good, given that only one young person in the entire sample failed to gain access during the research period. His situation was the product of extremely poor social work planning. He returned home from his children's home at two days notice and, despite being on a care order for a further year, received no social work help. Unhappy at home with his severely ill mother and wanting a flat, he had simply been given the scheme's telephone number. Perhaps not surprisingly, his poor experience of social workers and the lack of a proper introduction meant that he never used it.

The 'open access' services create both direct informal access to the scheme for young people and, at least potentially, more difficulties in managing a scarce resource. A potential problem for this model of provision, where inevitably a substantial proportion of its work is demand-led, reacting to problems young people bring with them to the project, is to ensure a continuing effective use of scarce resources. Staff need a sufficient allocation of time to plan individual programmes of support effectively, to make regular home visits and to retain a pro-active approach to their work. During the course of the research, as numbers involved with the scheme increased, the team introduced some rationing mechanisms to help maintain this balance. The 'drop-in' had originally been available all day and this was rationalised in the manner described above, both to create more space for staff and because it was felt that it acted as a disincentive for young people to use their day more constructively. The team also introduced a waiting list to be used if it was felt more numbers would inhibit the overall quality of service. If young people were considered a priority they would still take them on, if not they would be placed on the list pending a key worker vacancy. Usually this would apply to young people whose move to independence was some way off.

Developing options

Accommodation

A commitment to providing a range of good quality accommodation options for care leavers has meant that the scheme has invested considerable energy in this area of development. So far it has taken two main forms. First, the development of a supported lodgings scheme to provide transitional accommodation for young people not ready for independent living. Second, the development of inter-agency links with housing providers to ensure a stream of individual tenancies of reasonable quality.

The supported lodgings scheme is managed directly by the team, although other lodgings are found independently by area social workers. All supported lodgings have to be approved by the Fostering Panel and the team undertakes an assessment of all applicants, including a home visit, references, police checks and a health declaration. Placements are funded through a combination of housing benefit and social services and/or young person contributions according to means. In 1993 there were 14 places available. It offers young people who feel unready to assume a tenancy the opportunity to gain skills and confidence in a supportive environment. Daily help is offered by the provider and this is reinforced by key worker support from the scheme. Four young people in our sample were able to take advantage of this provision for a period of time. Two made planned moves on, one to a supported hostel and the other to a permanent tenancy, both young men with learning difficulties. However two situations broke down – one having fallen foul of the requirement to undertake work or training. He lost his youth training place and the pressure of him being at home all day proved too much for the provider. For both, a period of uncertainty staying with friends or relatives was resolved by the scheme helping them to find permanent tenancies.

In addition, there does seem to be provision for young people to remain with foster carers when settled through re-designating the placement as a supported lodgings. One young woman was able to do this thereby retaining stability and continuity of care. She only moved on when she wanted to move in with her boyfriend and managed to retain the support of her carers. A consistent theme of groups working with carers has been for local authorities to use their resources imaginatively in order to fund continuity of care; to enable young people to move on

when they feel they are ready and to fund carers to continue with post-care support (NFCA 1992; Lowe 1990).

From its inception, the scheme has focused on building links and joint-working arrangements with housing providers to ensure access to individual tenancies. Half of these are provided by local housing associations. Access is available to their existing properties and joint bids for housing corporation funds, in which the housing association carries out its landlord functions and the team provides support to young people, have enabled access to refurbished properties and to new build schemes. In addition, a priority scheme has been negotiated with the council enabling care leavers (and those whose situations break down) to be allocated maximum points for rehousing. These links have helped to gain access to good standard accommodation in a range of areas and it is rare for young people to need to venture into an expensive private market. Our data tends to reinforce this perception. There do not appear to have been undue problems finding accommodation for these young people, even in emergencies, and there was evidence of successfully negotiating transfers for young people experiencing difficulties. Finally, towards the end of our research, the scheme negotiated the tenancy management of nine further housing association places.

Financial assistance

The scheme works to policies developed by the Social Services Department. Leaving care grants of up to £1245 (July 1994) – index linked – are available for young people moving to independent accommodation and those in supported lodgings receive a part payment. However these are discretionary and linked to length of time in care. Young people who enter care after their sixteenth birthday and those eligible for a community care grant through the Social Fund may receive lower amounts. A range of discretionary top ups are also available for young people unemployed and unable to claim, those on youth training schemes, in low paid work or at college. With the exception of those completing college courses or schemes, top ups usually end at 18. All applications are processed through district social work offices. The authority has a policy that no young person should become homeless through lack of money and payments are calculated on an individual assessment of means. Nearly one half of our sample (5) received income top ups – four of these were unemployed and unable to claim – and all who moved to tenancies were given leaving care grants.

Careers

Relative to the above developments, initiatives to promote employment and training opportunties for care leavers were more modest. Although not always successful, careers help formed part of the planned individual programmes of support with young people and the scheme was actively involved in networking with Careers, colleges and training agencies on behalf of individual young people. For instance, in relation to a young man with learning difficulties, links established between his leaving care worker and a specialist training agency enabled him, upon completion of a special needs YT, to continue building his skills and confidence and gain work experience in a hospital setting. In addition the flexibility afforded by the scheme's 'open access' services enabled young people to drop in for advice, to check job vacancies and use the telephones. Although there were no groups with a focus on promoting young people's employability, a careers officer did hold regular surgeries at the project. Only towards the end of the research was the scheme looking at the possibility of developing more structured and formal arrangments, especially with employers, to promote wider career opportunities.

Scheme support

We have indicated that the scheme attempts to offer a flexible range of services that can meet differing needs and that young people can choose the degree to what they make use of them. For most young people, intensive key worker support is available through transition and, for those who require and want it, this can be long-term. For others, once settled in the community, withdrawal of this support is negotiated and young people remain free to use the 'open access' services at the centre. Some opt for short-term involvement, either because they feel they do not need further support or they refuse it. Later access to scheme services also appears good. Five out of six of our 'comparison' group began using the scheme in differing ways during the research period.

Key worker support

Eight of the original eleven young people in our participating sample received long-term key worker support from the scheme. Of these, three continued to receive this support throughout the research period whilst, for five, a negotiated withdrawal or reduction of this role had taken place, although they remained in touch with the scheme. All had been referred some time prior to their move for assistance with preparation and planning for independence. Where early referral occurs the team will assist with preparation and planning for the move, although primary responsibility remains with the carers. It represents an opportunity to build relationships with young people, carry out an assessment of their abilities and support needs, organise housing applications and, where it proves possible, to establish joint-working arrangements with social workers – an issue to which we shall return below.

In consequence four of these young people were able to make well planned transitions to their initial accommodation – three moved to supported lodgings and the other was able to remain with foster parents on a lodgings basis. Although their lives remained difficult and further moves lay ahead, continuity in support from the scheme and, in one case from a social worker, ensured that all these young people eventually found a stable home base.

Frank, a young man with learning difficulties, had few skills and was heavily reliant on professional support. He spent one year in supported lodgings developing his skills and confidence. When the family were planning to move he decided to try his own flat. A planned transition was made to a flat close to friends he had made at the scheme, but he eventually lost control due to threats and extortion from local youths; he was the only one working and his wages were being taken from him. The scheme then negotiated a transfer to an outlying town close to his brother and other supports and, with consistent help, he was re-stabilising his life there.

For John, also with learning difficulties, his time in supported lodgings was used to assess his skills for independent living and he eventually moved to a specialist supported hostel where he could stay long-term. He was receiving daily support from the hostel staff and, in consequence, his leaving care worker negotiated a reduction in her role. No longer his key worker, the friendship was retained and he was dropping into the project two or three times weekly for a chat, to see his friends and discuss his problems.

Finally for a more able and confident young woman, Janice, stable with her foster carers but without continuing social work support, the scheme helped her move to a flat with her boyfriend when expecting a baby. She settled in well and key worker support was continuing, focusing on budgeting and debt problems. Although not a regular group user, since she had friends, she had found the ante-natal group and help with parenting valuable and the drop-in had enabled her to meet more people.

For those whose initial transitions were traumatic and uncertain a similar pattern emerged. All four had, by the end of the research, apparently found a stable home base for themselves with partners and, by this stage, three were parents.

Jean, who had been pushed out of her children's home at two week's notice into lodgings, was left feeling confused and rejected. The lodgings broke down within a month and, after stays with friends and relatives, the scheme found her a flat, but in a different area. Although receiving help to settle in she was unhappy and insecure. A transfer was arranged and, once she was settled, key worker support was withdrawn. She continued to use the groups and drop-in to maintain her social network and, at the last interview, was planning a return to college with scheme help.

For all these young people the help offered seemed wide ranging and needs-led. It included arranging accommodation, settling young people in and establishing easy payment systems for bills, work on life skills for those needing it, careers help and, in keeping with the scheme's philosophy, an emphasis on building confidence, self-esteem and social networks – either through activities at the base or by helping to promote family and friendship links outside. The help offered was not always accepted nor successful and, as the young woman returning to college acknowledged, although consistently encouraged, it was only now that she was finding the self-motivation to return. Of the past she said, "I didn't listen . . . I had that attitude I can't be bothered". All had benefited in some way from their involvement with the scheme, gradually gaining in skills, confidence and maturity, although, for those with more limited ability, the steps taken had sometimes been small and uncertain. The comprehensive packages of support available to those with learning difficulties, including networking to draw on specialist resources, seemed particularly impressive. For some, continuity appeared to have prevented a downward spiral into homelessness.

The young people themselves were positive about the help they had received. Some emphasised the practical support they had been given:

"What's best is the advice and help they give you. You know when you're leaving (care), like getting me own flat, it were my (leaving care worker) got me this and got me signing on".

Others appreciated the quality of relationship and informal approach; some contrasting this with the more 'parental' concerns of social workers:

"They don't treat you like a kid no more".

"They treat you like an adult".

"They're friendly and you known they're there if you need help".

For those who took advantage of the groups and drop-in services, they offered easy access to help, the possibility of continuing contact on their terms and a chance to socialise with others, as the following comments suggest:

"If I'm stuck for anything I can come down and ask 'em questions and they'll help me out if they can. It's good to know there's somebody around to help yer, definitely".

"If ever you want to talk about owt, you can just go up and sort of see 'em".

"I go to have a chat with all the kids and talk to (a worker) if I need help".

Joint working with social workers

Our data suggests a tendency in this authority for social work support to fall away either prior to or recently after transition and in some cases whilst young people were still on care orders, as was the situation with the young man who never gained access to the scheme. Looking across the entire sample of 17, there were nine cases where social workers had either ended their involvement or were inactive at this time, suggesting that a low priority is being given to the needs of care leavers in this authority. For five young people in our original participating sample of 11, case management had been passed to the scheme, sometimes with negotiation and sometimes by default. Some social workers mentioned pressures of child protection work and staff shortages as being responsible, another the effects of reorganisation. Some were reluctant to relinquish control and had been pressured.

Whatever the reasons, it does raise some complex issues for schemes. First, it tends to inhibit the possibility of a through care approach to supporting young people in transition, of offering continuity of support by primary carers and social workers with whom young people may have established relationships. It reinforces the separation of care from aftercare. Second, as others have recently commented, it leads schemes to take on a primary care role rather than enabling them, as a specialist resource, to supplement the care provided by others (Community Care 11–17 August 1994; Stein 1991). However, some young people do want to make a fresh start and, for them, that choice should be available.

Where joint-working proved possible, arrangements appeared structured and well co-ordinated with a clear division of roles and responsibilities. Social workers valued the scheme's independence, their specialist knowledge and young person centred approach. One felt that it gave her young person another valuable outlet:

"I've certainly found it helpful to have them here, to help (her) . . . They are another person, apart from the social worker, who the youngster might feel they can talk to better. They seem a bit more independent than us, which is good I think".

Others expressed a typical relief at having someone else with whom they could share the load:

"*. . . taking some of the hassle and stress out of moving kids on*".

Short term involvement

The remaining three young people from our original participating sample only received short-term help from the scheme. For two this was by choice and the third was quite angry that she did not receive the service expected.

Dean, referred whilst still in a stable foster home, wanted accommodation. The team helped him move into a flat and arrange his finances. Although offered the full range of services he decided he did not need further help. He remained settled in the flat with his girlfriend and, although he did not contact the scheme again, he felt he would if he needed anything.

Sharon, an unstable young woman with a disrupted care history, wanted to go it alone once settled in her flat. Angry and rejecting help, her leaving care worker maintained an 'arms length' relationship for a time before she disappeared with her boyfriend and, unfortunately, was lost to the study.

Karen felt she had received a poor service from social services generally. Although a capable young woman living in a stable foster placement, despite asking for help, she had received no counselling around her past sexual abuse and for her last six months there had no social worker at all. She attempted to reconcile herself with her family who were living abroad and, when this failed, she returned home. Feeling rejected, isolated and having nowhere to live, she turned to the scheme for help. Although offered supported lodgings, she found herself a private flat and, after initial help with her leaving care grant and finances, contact ceased, despite a promise of regular visits and an introduction to the centre for social contact. Although she managed, finding a job and gradually reparing relationships with her mother, she felt her struggle to reconstruct her life had been made much harder through lack of couselling and help with her home:

> *"I think both of those would have made a difference to my life. I would have been able to get on with my life a lot quicker if I'd have got counselling and I'd have probably been able to settle in on my own if I'd have got help with me flat as well".*

Whilst what went wrong from the scheme's point of view was not clear, she most definitely did slip through the net.

Later access

As we have already mentioned, five out of the six young people who had no contact with the scheme at the start of our research later gained some access to its services. For two the contact was brief and linked to help in applying for leaving care grants. Another, living in supported lodgings, had just been referred by her social worker at the close of the study for help with planning a move on. The fourth, referred by her social worker when her lodgings placement seemed unsettled, decided to move into her boyfriend's house. Apparently settled and working as a care assistant, her social worker and leaving care worker maintained a watching brief in case difficulties arose with the relationship, having bi-monthly joint meetings with her.

> Finally Danny, another young man with learning difficulties, was referred shortly after the first interview and the comprehensive package of support offered to him was similar to those outlined above. He was already living in a flat and finding it difficult to cope. Despite intensive help from his social worker and leaving care worker, his situation broke down irretrievably when members of his family and 'friends' ransacked his flat and stole his possessions. At the final interview, after eight months recuperation in a specialist supported hostel, he was planning a second attempt in a different flat. Tight support plans were being drawn up to include his leaving care worker, social worker, hostel key worker and a specialist social worker to try and ensure a better chance of success. Given his limited skills, difficulties in making relationships and the likely prospect of long-term unemployment, his future remained insecure. However the support available meant that he had been cushioned and that he still had choices that he could make.

In conclusion, for most of the young people in our sample, the scheme had been a positive influence in their lives. Given their mix of backgrounds and abilities, the flexibility and informality of this 'community based' model seemed to be able to respond to a diverse range of needs. For those needing intensive long-term help the key worker system seemed structured and positive; for those apparently settled in the community the scheme's 'open access' services appeared reassuring. The social activities, important for young people living alone, made access that much easier. While many of these young people's lives remained difficult and insecure, nearly a third were unemployed and three were coping with the pressures of early parenthood, most did know where they could get help if they needed it.

CHAPTER 16

CITY LEAVING CARE SCHEME (SOCIAL SERVICES)

Background

City is the most recent of our four schemes, having been launched in 1989. It evolved out of a review of the city's children's homes and has developed against a background of major changes in the social services department's organisational structure. At its inception, little guidance was given by the department regarding the priorities and organisation of the scheme and formal leaving care policies and procedures were not introduced in City until the end of 1993. This meant that it was only towards the end of our research that clear referral, assessment, planning and review processes were introduced (see Appendix Figure 4 for current procedures).

Initially the scheme was based in a semi-detached house, formerly a small children's home, in a residential area not far from the city centre. This building provided an office together with a large living room and kitchen used as a group centre for young people and, upstairs, a four bed semi-independence unit. At the weekly social evenings the house came alive as young people from around the city called in to share in the preparation of a meal and to meet with one another and scheme staff. During the course of the research the team was instructed, at very short notice, to merge with the staff group of a children's home that was closing down. Its main project base moved to the home's large institutional building on the outskirts of the city, which was less accessible for many young people, but it continued to provide 24 hour staff cover at the semi-independence unit and to use this original site as a group centre.

The scheme is funded and managed directly by the social services department. Ten staff were employed during the research period, including the project manager, and nearly all came from a background in residential child care (see Appendix Figure 1). The abrupt merging of the original leaving care team with staff from a residential child care team initially led to some tensions and difficulties which had inevitable implications for staff morale and the organisation of the service.

Approach

The focus of the scheme's work is two fold: individual work with young people in their own tenancies and support work and skills development in its semi-independent accommodation project. At the beginning of the research, scheme staff also worked with young people in children's homes who were preparing to leave care, although it gradually withdrew from this area. In 1991 staff produced a statement of aims which were "to assist young people in leaving care and gaining independence in the community". These aims were to be achieved by means of three types of activity. First, by practical assistance, preparation, training and information for young people to acquire practical skills for independent living. Second, by helping young people to take up a full and active role in their community to enable them to combat loneliness, isolation and institutionalisation. This was to be achieved by encouraging the development of relationships with family and friends and by encouraging young people to find out about and use community amenities. Third, by assisting young people in gaining the personal skills and qualities required to cope with living out of care, through helping them to build up their self-esteem, develop communication skills and find ways of acknowledging and dealing with past experiences. They also aimed to help young people learn to build constructive relationships.

Although the scheme's aims are wide ranging, in practice the main focus of its work has been on practical assistance and the development of practical skills, centred around finding accommodation and supporting young people in sustaining their tenancies. Through this practical and skills based work, staff aim to build positive and facilitating relationships with young people in order to address the wider personal and social issues referred to above. The initial lack of clear direction from the social services department as to the scope and purpose of the scheme and the scheme's early development from a residential model of service provision has meant that direct work with young people has been its core activity. A wider role for the scheme in developing local resources for care leavers in the city has not evolved. The development of a wider remit for the scheme and of a planned use of the semi independence unit was further hampered in the early years of the scheme's development by the ad hoc use of the scheme's accommodation by the department's senior managers, who used it as a stop gap for young people on remand or whose living situations had broken down. In her evaluation of leaving care schemes Stone has pointed to the need for schemes to pursue a planned, slow and systematic development; for coherent and consistent management structures to offer support, guidance and training to staff and to the damaging implications of rapid and ad hoc growth for proper planning and service delivery (Stone 1989). These observations are pertinent to City, where the department's initial failure to plan the scheme's role and function within the totality of child care services, and to work together with scheme staff to develop policies and priorities for a city wide leaving care service, made it difficult for the scheme to develop planned and integrated provision for care leavers.

Profile of scheme users

Eleven young people were included in the sample, of whom six were male and five female. All were aged 16–18 and all were white, apart from one young woman of mixed heritage. Nine had backgrounds in residential care and only two were from foster care. The length of time they had been accommodated ranged from two and a half years to twelve years, the majority having spent three to five years in care. Movement and disruption featured strongly in the care careers of most of the sample, as only three had remained in a stable placement throughout. Two had moved twice, one had made five moves and another had moved seven times in seven years!

It is notable that eight of this group had experienced profound rejection by their families, either having no or only occasional and unsatisfactory contact. For all these young people, to differing degrees, rejection had implications for their personal and emotional development – few had strong friendship networks, most had difficulties developing relationships, had low self-esteem and lacked confidence. About half also lacked the practical skills they would need to manage independently. This brief picture indicates the complex and multiple difficulties that young people were trying to overcome and the difficult task facing leaving care workers trying to help them re-integrate into the community. However, at first interview, most of the young people were confident and optimistic about succeeding even if only, as one young man put it: "to show 'em all I can make a go of it".

Access and rationing

Prior to the introduction of formal procedures in 1993, referrals to the scheme were often dependent upon informal links. The referral process reflected the scheme's roots within residential care in its focus on building links with young people in children's homes. Scheme staff were linked to each of the children's homes in the city and made contact with young people approaching their sixteenth birthday or were invited to post-sixteenth birthday reviews. As a result, the team's work has been predominantly with young people leaving residential placements although they are equally willing to accept referrals from foster care. Nine of our sample were from residential backgrounds and were referred by social workers or residential workers during a period ranging from a few months to one and a half years prior to their eventual move. The only two from foster care were emergency referrals at the point of breakdown. Our study confirms the advantages of early referral and continuity in that seven of these young people were able to make smooth, well planned transitions to their initial accommodation, supported by social worker, leaving care worker and residential worker.

A lack of formal policies and procedures meant that many social workers and fostering workers lacked clear information about the operation of the scheme. In some cases social workers requested help with preparation and transition plans or, equally commonly, help with finding accommodation when care placements appeared to be breaking down. However, several social workers commented taht they were unaware of what the scheme offered, how it worked with young people or how long its brief lasted. Referral patterns were therefore somewhat haphazard, depending on individual social workers' knowledge of the scheme or on the scheme's links with the residential sector (but not with the fostering service).

On referral, young people were usually approached informally and invited to the project base to discuss the scheme. In those cases where scheme link workers approached young people informally on their visits to children's homes, young people would be invited to come along to the weekly social group. Before the introduction of formal procedures the assessment process was therefore mainly informal and piecemeal. This, linked to the general lack of clarity about the work of the scheme, resulted in confusion amongst referrers. Where referral to the scheme was made early and scheme staff had time to build relationships in an informal way, the assessment process appeared to work quite well. The lack of formal procedures was most clearly exposed where referrals were made for young people in crisis or breakdown situations.

During most of our research this scheme had no explicit mechanism for rationing or targeting their resources at the point of referral. The service was open to any young person who was leaving or had left care and there were no procedures for managing or rationing the flow of young people onto the scheme. However, rationing seemed to be happening by default. Our data suggests that quite intensive support was offered to young people prior to and during transition but that, in some cases, regular visiting patterns appeared to fall away quite soon afterwards to be replaced by a response mode of support. The onus then became placed on the young people to contact the scheme if they needed anything. Where visiting did continue the lack of rationing procedures affected the ability of workers to develop individual support plans with young people and see them through systematically. Visits often became checks to see if the young person was managing as other crises on the worker's caseload took precedence.

Several leaving care workers mentioned an increase in crisis response work as a proportion of their time, inhibiting opportunities for planned work with young people. One was very explicit in explaining why there had been no contact with a young woman who had moved into a flat a few months previously:

"It's just because (she) hasn't actually made any demands on us that she's been left".

The assumption was that she was therefore managing quite well (and in actual fact she was). Another young man recently moved to a bedsit was unclear what support might be on offer and thought the leaving care scheme's role might largely be over now that they had found him his flat:

"he keeps bobbing in every now and again to see if I'm all right and that's it. You know, he's done his job".

Once young people have been referred to the scheme, informal direct access is still available to them in addition to more formal access through appointments with their key workers. Most of the scheme's work is on an individual basis and takes place in young people's homes and placements. However, the weekly social group is informal and open to all care leavers and to those about to leave. Although there is no formal drop in service, some young people did drop in to see staff at the semi-independence unit or simply to spend the evening watching television in the unit's living room rather than alone in their flat or bedsit. The importance for some young people of easy access is amplified by one quite isolated young man. He had been visiting the team two or three times weekly for social contact and support but, once the project moved, it was too far to travel and he was reduced to seeing his leaving care worker "every now and again", thus compounding his isolation. Once the main project base moved most young people relied on home visits from staff.

For those not referred prior to or at the time of leaving care, later access to the scheme was unusual. The importance of linking young people in to schemes prior to moving is reinforced by looking at the comparison group. Only one out of the eleven in the comparison group had any subsequent contact with a leaving care scheme during the research period. Six of these young people, mostly from fostering backgrounds, had not heard of the scheme and did not know what it offered. Not all of these young people needed additional support, as they felt they were managing. This was particularly true of two leaving stable foster placements which they viewed as their family home. Two other young people were offered an opportunity to explore what both the City schemes offered, usually for semi-independence placements, and rejected them; deciding they didn't want to share, objected to the rules and controls or wanted accommodation in their own localities where they had links.

Some, though, were in difficult circumstances – for example, without permanent accommodation or with little money – and lacking support. One young man was living at his girlfriend's father's flat, had no income, had just become a father and, in addition, his social worker had just left. Although he battled through these problems admirably, a referral might have eased his load. Another young man still with foster parents and without any social services contact was unaware of his entitlement to any financial support should he decide to move on. Whilst schemes cannot cater for all needs, it is of concern that the majority of our comparison group had not been signposted to a possible future source of support. However, it is to be hoped that the later introduction of more formal procedures may have overcome some of the access problems to this scheme (see Appendix Figure 4).

Developing options

Accommodation

The lack of a clear framework for the scheme to operate within from its outset had implications for its ability to develop accommodation options for care leavers in this authority. During the period of our research the two main options were the four bedded semi-independence unit and the arrangement of accommodation in independent tenancies – the latter always being in short supply. For a time the scheme also rented two private houses which it sub-let to care leavers. Despite good informal links with the housing department's single strategy unit, the lack of formal procedures agreed with local housing providers often meant that recourse had to be made to the private sector. Young people using this scheme appeared to have limited access to supported transitional accommodation in hostels or supported lodgings. Without formal links with hostels for young people in the city and in the absence of supported lodgings, the scheme had a narrow range of options to offer young people at this stage of its development. As a result, most scheme users moved straight to independent accommodation regardless of their ability to manage. Perhaps not surprisingly, the experiences of those young people who were ill-equipped to cope with a direct move from care to independence were more likely to include loneliness and isolation:

"I couldn't get used to being by myself".

This young man, who was unable to manage in his flat, said he would still like to return to his children's home if he could. Another young person wished he had moved into a preparation hostel before moving into his own tenancy. Breakdown situations were linked mainly to relationship problems and only two of our young people were still in their original tenancies by our final interviews.

By the completion of our research the scheme had expanded its accommodation resources, which now included supported lodgings arranged through the Social Services Response Team and six 'guaranteed' local authority tenancies managed by the scheme which allowed the transfer of the tenancy to the young person after one year (see Appendix Figure 3).

Financial assistance

City offers up to £1000 (July 1994) in leaving care grants, although it remains discretionary and is applied for by social workers through neighbourhood offices. The first £500 is fairly automatic and can be approved by office managers, the remainder has to go to Assistant Director level. Leaving care scheme workers were critical of the delays caused by the approval system. A range of discretionary top ups are available for young people unemployed and unable to claim, in youth training, full time college or on low incomes.

In relation to our sample, five young people were receiving top ups at our first interviews and all those in independent accommodation had received leaving care grants. One social worker supporting a young woman at college highlighted the problems of achieving an integrated service. Although young people are in the care of the local authority *as a whole*, the local education authority repeatedly refused to provide a discretionary grant on the grounds that she was in social services care. They said:

"that because she's in the care of the local authority she's not eligible for a grant, which I feel is a case of buck passing myself. She's in the care of the city council, the local

authority, and under that banner comes education, social services and all the other stuff".

In consequence, her social worker had to arrange social services funding to enable her to pursue her college course.

Careers

Most of the young people received some assistance with work, training or education. This included advice and assistance with training, college or job applications, liaison with colleges and YT schemes when problems arose, working with young people to sustain their motivation and organising financial support for post 16 education. Although the primary focus of this scheme's work was on helping young people move into independent accommodation and sustain their tenancies, career development was also discussed, although the degree of attention paid to this area was variable.

Careers help was offered on an individual basis rather than through the development of formal links with colleges, employers or training agencies. Assistance with career development was more likely to be successful for those young people who made planned transitions to independence than for those referred in crisis situations. The only two young people on this scheme who continued their education post 16 had made well planned, smooth transitions to council tenancies and had been well supported both by the scheme and by their social workers as they settled in to their independent accommodation. Where professional support included a clear focus on career development as part of a co-ordinated package of support, the benefits were clear.

> Pat moved into a council flat and, once established there, resumed a college course. She was financially supported in this by a top up from the social services department and, equally important, received help with college applications and steady encouragement from her leaving care worker and social worker. Her leaving care worker took care not to be over intrusive, helping Pat sustain her motivation and making herself available to help her resolve any problems that arose at college while respecting her need for autonomy to run her own life. This worker felt that success at college was an essential ingredient in Pat's successful transition to independence, describing her college attendance as "the backbone of her rehabilitation from care to the community."

Scheme support

The team have evolved a way of working that has a primary focus on practical assistance to young people through transition – assisting young people with preparation prior to moving; finding and helping young people set up accommodation including furnishing, decorating, arranging payment of bills and help with life skills, in particular cooking, shopping and budgeting. This activity appears helpful and productive for young people. There is also evidence of broader help but less of it – with employment/further education; dealing with family relationships and developing community links. Clearly success in some of these areas can have a knock on effect for personal and social development as young people become more confident in their ability to cope and their image of themselves improves.

The service is mostly delivered through individual work, but there is also the weekly social group and an occasional series of cookery classes. In addition, one young woman had attended a fortnightly mother and toddler group at the project base which she enjoyed for company and conversation.

Key workers' role in preparation

Eight of the eleven young people were referred by social workers or residential social workers for assistance with preparation while still in children's homes, the time scale ranging from a few months to one and a half years prior to their move. Either social workers felt that the children's home was not providing sufficient support in this area or residential social workers themselves felt that the team had additional expertise. The team itself is gradually trying to move away from this area feeling it should be the province of residential social workers and as pressure of work with young people in the community has grown.

Broadly the team's role in this area was positive. The young people found their inputs helpful and social workers appreciated being able to liaise with a specialist worker in planning transitions. The focus of work included: building relationships with young people, assessing their needs and abilities, getting them to focus on the move to come and confidence building. More practical help was given with cooking, shopping, budgeting and housing applications. Much of this work appeared to take place informally, that is without drawing up individual preparation plans with young people and social workers.

The two most positive assessments came from young people who spent several months at the semi-independence unit managed by the leaving care scheme themselves. They valued the practical and emotional support they received on a daily basis. One young man speaks with pride of the responsibilities he had there:

"You did your own shopping, your own cooking, washing up, washing of clothes, ironing, tidying up and cleaning . . . It was better than all the other places I've been to".

Another says more succinctly, "It made me see meself differently".

Also available to young people was a weekly social group run at the project base for those preparing to leave care and for those already in the community. The aims of the group were mainly social, to encourage young people to make contacts, relieve isolation and develop leisure interests. Only two of our young people used the group prior to leaving care, both of whom were quite isolated and had difficulty making friends. They enjoyed the social aspects of the group and found them fun. One said it was mainly about visiting "sports centres and having tea"; the other that "she showed me how to make shepherd's pie, play squash and tennis". The latter young person, however, expressed concern that she would have liked more individual time with her leaving care worker at these sessions, finding it hard to take the initiative to get her attention in that context and that she had been expecting a more serious preparatory focus. For this she had to depend on visits to her children's home which she felt were too infrequent and seemed to centre on shopping trips. Another young man who opted for a different scheme also found the group not directive enough – "it seemed more like fun and games than (about) moving into your own place" – and that the staff "hardly spent any time with you" individually. These comments point to the diversity of young people's needs and expectations. Perhaps a weekly social group that attempts to cater for all in a generic manner is unlikely to meet with universal approval. Some simply enjoy meeting for fun and relaxation, or to escape isolation, while others expect a more serious focus. These mixed responses to the group point to the need for a group's aims to be clearly explained to those who are considering joining it.

Key workers' role in transition

Although support available to these young people at the preparatory stage had been broadly positive, as our earlier profile indicates, many still lacked some of the practical and emotional resources needed for a smooth and successful transition. Although most young people were positive and optimistic about their new circumstances, social workers and leaving care workers felt that at least five of these young people had been propelled into a move before they were ready and were frustrated at the systemic 'push' factors that require young people to move to independence at a given age rather than according to need and ability.

Six made well planned moves to independence, and four of these had had a period of preparation in a semi-independence unit (either attached to their children's homes or provided by the scheme). As a result of extended planning these young people received preparation in practical skills and made smooth initial transitions to independent tenancies. Of the remaining five, four left care abruptly in crisis situations, while one young woman (already known to the scheme) walked out of her children's home and disappeared for a few weeks before requesting help with accommodation. For these five young people the scheme provided emergency help with finding accommodation as well as follow up support.

Clearly this period of helping young people to set up their homes is one of intense activity for social workers and leaving care workers and the focus of leaving care scheme work was solidly practical, involving regular visits (weekly or more frequently to those considered vulnerable) and quite close links with social workers to co-ordinate tasks. Help focused on organising leaving care grants, helping young people to furnish and decorate their flats, setting up systems for paying bills, advice with budgeting and other practical skills. The practical help offered at this stage was valued both by young people and social workers. As one young woman explained:

> *"Well, first of all she helped me get the money, me leaving care grant . . . and when we (got) it we'd . . . make a list of what we needed for the flat and then go out buying it. She helped me decorate, . . . helped me to go shopping for the things that I needed. Quite a lot actually."*

What was valued at this time of uncertainty was not just practical assistance but also the reassurance, company and positive reinforcement that contact could offer as young people were trying to stabilise their lives; the importance of knowing someone was backing them up. A number of statements from young people hint at these broader needs:

> *"She was someone I could talk to as well"*

> *"They're there when you need 'em."*

> *"He's always there."*

> *"She's just like a mate."*

The social workers of these young people also felt positive about the role played by the leaving care scheme at this stage. They all appeciated being able to share the burden of planning these transitions into the community, particularly where young people were felt to be too young, immature or vulnerable for such a move. In most cases liaison remained informal but in two cases, where the young people were felt to be especially vulnerable and unlikely to manage, intensive written support plans were drawn up in planning meetings. One social worker pointed to both the importance of the scheme's practical role at this time and also of the additional insights that can be offered by a specialist service:

> *"(The scheme's role) seems mainly practical, but I think that's what (young person) need at that stage. You can't really concentrate on their spiritual and emotional side if you've no roof and no food in your cupboard . . . I think that's crucial, because a lot of social workers wouldn't know where to start with those sort of things. I mean the social workers can work with the counselling and so on, but . . . finding a doctor and registering themselves at the library, a lot of social workers wouldn't even think about it".*

Of those who made planned, well prepared transitions most were able to settle into their 'homes' and were managing well at the outset with varying degrees of support. All were living alone in council, housing association or private tenancies. Two, however, were struggling to cope in independent accommodation despite intensive support from the scheme. Both were extremely vulnerable young people who were ill-equipped to cope with independent living at this stage in their lives and who may have benefited from an intermediate stage in supported accommodation had this been available.

However, the experiences of the four young men who made crisis moves from care placements highlight some of the scheme's problems with focus and co-ordination. All four of these referrals were emergencies arising from placement breakdowns, in one young man's case due to eviction from the scheme's own semi-independence unit following his attempted arson on the building. The scheme responded positively to these emergencies and was actively involved in finding accommodation and helping the young people to settle in but in such circumstances choices are inevitably constrained. Three were found bedsits and the fourth, who had been evicted by the scheme itself, was placed in a bed and breakfast hotel because no other accommodation was available. All but one were unhappy in their accommodation, felt isolated from friends and felt they had had little choice about where they lived due to the circumstances in which they had left care. Nevertheless, despite these problems it should be borne in mind that the scheme did succeed in finding emergency accommodation for a group of young people who were at serious risk of homelessness.

The three young men living in bedsits all felt some confusion about what the scheme could offer them and what further entitlements they had. One felt that the scheme's role was over now that he was accommodated; another that its help was primarily for young people still in care and that, in consequence, he was not expecting much further assistance. Lacking a clear understanding of the scheme's services, the choices available to these young people about how they might use scheme help were necessarily limited.

Joint working with social workers

This confusion about scheme services was shared by four of the social workers interviewed, including the workers of the three young men accommodated in bedsits. These social workers were unclear about the role of the scheme and about the boundaries between their work and that of the leaving care workers. All had experienced communication difficulties with the scheme and some were not sure precisely which team member was responsible for their young person or if, in two cases, anyone was still in touch at all. Indeed, some of the leaving care workers themselves seemed somewhat vague about the focus of their work with these young people and in some cases there was little evidence of planned and focused intervention – "to know that I'm here" or providing a "crutch to lean on" were typical statements of aims. These comments point to some serious difficulties in communication, liaison and co-ordination of the service in these cases. While crisis referrals are unavoidable in this area of work it is perhaps at these times that clear procedures and clarity about professional roles and objectives are most valuable.

However, there was greater clarity about the division of roles and responsibilities when young people were referred early to the scheme and made planned transitions from care. Liaison and joint-working with social workers was generally good for all of the young people referred for preparation. Mostly this took place through informal phone contacts but two social workers mentioned the use of regular planning meetings with circulated minutes to reinforce decisions taken and the division of responsibilities. In these cases the leaving care worker had responsibility for developing practical skills whilst the social worker focused on family issues, counselling and wider emotional support. One social worker expressed a fairly typical relief at having someone else to share the load:

"They take the heat off you a bit if they can take some of the tasks on board, . . . then that's less for you to do . . . It's a big job for one person . . . supervising the support of somebody leaving care . . . It's much better spread out (between) two people"

Joint working arrangements established with social workers at the preparation stage and the opportunity to build a relationship with young people in advance of the move, seemed to provide a platform that enabled these young people to make a smooth transition to their initial accommodation. It also led to greater young person and social worker satisfaction in the service offered.

Key worker support – continuity and closure

Within two years of leaving care half (6) of the young people had lost touch both with the scheme and with their social workers and had effectively disappeared. Only four were still in touch with the scheme by this stage, of whom three were in occasional contact and only one had regular key worker support.

Although the early transition phase was one of intense activity, in some cases there appeared to be a lack of focus and longer term planning for the support needs of the young people. One result of this was that the level of support offered did not always appear to be explicitly related to the needs of each individual. Across the whole group of eleven scheme users the young people who initially received the most active and directed support were among those who had made planned rather than crisis moves to independent accommodation and, in some cases, these young people had more family support. In particular, for the four young men who left care in crisis situations there was little evidence of long term planning, with attention focused primarily on meeting their immediate need for accommodation. The nature and extent of support offered to young people with varying needs did not appear to be planned by the scheme but appeared, rather, to depend on which particular key worker was allocated to each young person. Rationing of the level and duration of scheme support thus appeared to occur in an ad hoc rather than in a planned manner.

The pressure of crisis work on staff time meant that in three cases key worker support was withdrawn within a few months of young people moving to their first independent accommodation. For one young person this was the result of a clear decision not to allocate another key worker when her worker left, as she was a capable young woman who, in any case, was in continuing contact with her social worker. For two young men, however, key worker support gradually tailed off, apparently without a clear decision being made. Both appeared settled in their accommodation and, as one of their social worker's put it, contact by the leaving care worker "sort of fizzled out."

One of these young men, isolated and severely depressed, had a serious breakdown some months later and at this stage his key worker offered intensive help once again, closely co-ordinating her work with his social worker. He was assisted in rebuilding the interior of his house, which he had partly destroyed during his breakdown, in looking for work and in attempting to trace his mother. His key worker also tried to involve him with groups of other young people and encouraged him to drop in to see staff at the semi-independence unit whenever he needed company. Although his social worker was critical of the lack of training and experience among scheme staff, she felt that the scheme's help was crucial: "he wouldn't have survived without them." However, within a few months this young man had disappeared.

In four other cases key worker support ceased when the young people disappeared. Among these were the vulnerable young man in bed and breakfast accommodation and two of the young men in bedsits. The latter reappeared a few months later and, both homeless by this stage, requested help with finding accommodation. Having already established relationships with scheme staff, they felt able to contact them again when they needed help and the scheme responded promptly to their needs. Despite working on a range of issues with them in order to help establish them in more stable circumstances, these young men disappeared once again after a few months.

Among the six young people with whom the scheme had lost contact by the end of the study were the four young men referred initially following placement breakdowns and placed in unsupported accommodation, in bedsits or bed and breakfast. These four young men had left care in crisis situations and had found it hard to settle in the community despite scheme support. However, despite the continuing lack of stability in their lives they had felt able to turn to the scheme for support when they needed it and, in at least two cases, the scheme had prevented their continuing homelessness.

By the end of the study the scheme had remained in continuous contact with four of the young people, although by this stage only one young woman was receiving regular key worker support. The other three were only in occasional contact, but appreciated the support the scheme had given them, which in all cases had been planned and comprehensive, including attention to practical life skills, career development, personal relationships and social networks. One young woman, who had been able to move into the scheme's semi-independence unit when her landlord suddenly decided to sell her house, commented appreciatively:

"Cos if I didn't have (the scheme) I would have been out on the street, I wouldn't know what to do, who to go to and it has been helpful, you know . . . I think they've

given everything that they need to give, they've bent over backwards for me, that's the way I see it anyway."

The only young person still receiving regular key worker support was Ellen.

Ellen had moved to a council tenancy at 17 following a period in an independence unit at her children's home. Both her social worker and leaving care worker had felt she was far too immature to cope alone. The pressure for young people to move on from care placements at a given age rather than according to needs and abilities, and the scheme's failure to develop a range of accommodation options to meet varying needs for support, meant that this vulnerable young woman moved into independent accommodation before she was able to cope with living independently. Her early attempts at independence broke down and, after disappearing for several months, she approached the scheme once again, heavily pregnant and homeless. Continuity in her link with her key worker, who had previously worked in her children's home, was crucial in enabling her to approach the scheme once more for help after a break in contact. The scheme assisted her move to a supported hostel for mothers and babies and continued to work with her on developing the skills and resources she would need for a future move to independent accommodation.

The scheme's informal approach in working with young people therefore had many strengths, as young people who had had some initial contact with key workers felt able to contact them for further support when necessary. Also, isolated young people were encouraged to attend the weekly social group and in some cases to drop in to see staff in the independence unit on evenings when they felt lonely. Young people appreciated feeling that their key worker was "like a mate", complementing their social workers' more parental role.

However, this informality in approach was accompanied by a lack of formal assessment and rationing procedures, which meant that in some cases the scheme was predominantly reactive to crises in young people's lives and paid less attention to clear, focused planning for their longer term needs. Sometimes associated with this was a lack of clarity about aims and how objectives were to be achieved, which led to confusion among young people and social workers. The scheme's particular balance between informality and flexibility and more focused and directed work sometimes led to inadequate assessments and a lack of planning, particularly where referrals were made in crisis situations.

The scheme's focus on training in practical skills and in assisting young people in finding and settling into independent accommodation meant that it was a valuable resource both to young people and social workers, and was particularly helpful to young people at risk of homelessness. However, it was able to mobilise only a very narrow range of housing options, in most cases helping young people move into independent tenancies. Without formal links or nomination rights to facilitate access to council or housing association properties, it was often forced to rely on placing young people in private tenancies, which are both more expensive and more insecure. In addition to focusing its energies on finding individual tenancies, the adoption of a wider developmental role might have improved access to secure tenancies. Equally importantly, it might have expanded the range of supported accommodation available to care leavers, such as supported lodgings or hostels. This would offer care leavers in City a wider range of accommodation options to meet different needs and indeed, after this study ended the scheme was beginning to develop in this direction.

Many of these difficulties have arisen from the scheme's rapid and ad hoc development in the absence of a clear policy framework within the social services department to clarify the role and objectives of the scheme within the child care service as a whole. In addition, the lack of guidance, support and training from the department has been detrimental to the scheme's development. The introduction of clear policies for referral, assessment and review at the time this study came to an end may well resolve some of these issues.

CHAPTER 17

CITY LEAVING CARE SCHEME (VOLUNTARY)

Background

Our third scheme, also operating within the City authority, was launched in 1986. It is based in a terraced house in a residential area which provides office accommodation plus a large sitting room and kitchen, enabling the project to use these premises both as a working base and as a group centre for young people. In addition, the project manages nine small trainer houses scattered around neighbouring districts of the city. It has remained a small scheme with a project leader and four social work staff supplemented by the use of students and some volunteer befrienders. This factor, combined with its distinctive project base near the city centre, has helped the scheme to develop a strong project identity for young people who use it.

The scheme is directly managed by a voluntary agency working in partnership with the local social services department. It is jointly funded (50% social services department, 50% voluntary) on a purchaser/provider basis clarified in a service agency agreement. The voluntary agency has responsibility for policy development within the scheme and for the direct management, support and training of staff (see Appendix Figure 1). It also undertakes regular monitoring of the scheme's progress.

This arrangement has offered scheme staff a clear structure to operate within and an opportunity to develop coherent foci and boundaries to their work. Policies developed at the national and regional level by the voluntary agency in relation to work with troubled young people, though not specifically care leavers, provide a framework for the team, although projects develop their own identity in response to local needs and conditions.

However, while this study was in progress, the local authority did not involve the scheme in local forums for policy or service development in the field of leaving care and did not encourage the co-ordination of the scheme's work with the authority's own leaving care system (City ssd). This led to a somewhat fragmented leaving care service across the city as a whole. It was not until the end of 1993 that the introduction of local authority policy and procedures formally integrated the work of this scheme with City (ssd)'s leaving care provision and introduced referral, planning and review processes for City as a whole. Prior to their introduction the scheme had developed its own procedures and information, including a leaflet for young people and information for social workers. Young people using the scheme have access to both the local authority and the agency's complaints procedures.

Approach

The scheme's work is underpinned by a 'psycho-dynamic' or therapeutic approach. Recognising the inter-dependent nature of our lives (as most schemes do), this scheme emphasises the need for bonding and trust between young people and key workers as a basis for learning about interpersonal relationships in the adult world. It stresses this area of personal and social development, believing that more practical skills will grow from an emerging sense of inner security. It also tries to balance nurturing, empowering through negotiation and, where necessary, challenging and controlling young people, seeing adolescence as a phase in which the struggle between adult and child identities are at their most acute. Whilst inevitably involving a mix of planned and crisis based work, their approach attempts to be highly structured, pro-active and primarily worker-led with the degree of joint negotiating with young people increasing as they gradually develop a greater sense of purpose and control over their lives.

The scheme offers a specialist accommodation based service to the local authority for limited numbers of young people. It centres its service on the provision of shared trainer flats for up to 20 young people referred by social services. These young people are offered an intensive and wide-ranging package of support for 12–18 months aimed at preparing them for moving on into independent accommodation in the community. Their move on accommodation is arranged and continuing support is available, although usually at a less intense level (see Appendix Figure 3). Occasionally the scheme will work with young people living independently who are unable or unwilling to buy into this complete package. However the priority given to those undergoing training is quite explicit. The support offered involves a mix of individual and group work.

Profile of scheme users

Five young people included in our research were receiving support from City (vol)'s scheme. Two were male and all were 16–18 years of age. One had been in a stable foster placement for ten years but came under pressure to leave once pregnant. Another had a stable placement in a children's home for two and a half years. The third 'looked after' for three years, experienced three placements of both types. The fourth had been with an adoptive family but, following disclosure of sexual abuse, returned to care for three years and, finally, one young man who had been 'looked after' all his life had experienced *nineteen* different placements! Perhaps not surprisingly given his sense of instability, an earlier attempt at transition through a supported lodgings placement had broken down prior to his referral to the scheme.

Four entered the scheme's trainer accommodation. The fifth, a young man in unstable circumstances who had made five moves since leaving care some months earlier, was considered unsuitable for a trainer flat. After lengthy discussions with the team and with him and his social worker, it was agreed that his lifestyle, which included some offending and drug use which he felt unable to give up at that time, was inappropriate. He was offered key worker support in his own accommodation, a private bedsit.

All five of these young people had experienced rejection, had low self esteem and little confidence and, in consequence, were insecure about themselves and their abilities. All had minimal or unsatisfactory contact with their families and had problems making relationships to varying degrees. Not surprisingly, the young woman who had been abused was angry, found it hard to trust and her feelings were compounded by rejection, the family having reintegrated the father and thereby excluded her. None had managed to sustain employment or training, all were unemployed, and one was about to have a child when first referred. Two had quite good practical life skills at this stage, two were fair and one poor, although all needed intensive help in some areas, particularly budgeting.

Access and rationing

The City (vol) scheme is well established in the authority and referral procedures are clear. Referrals are normally made by social workers for young people who are still being 'looked after' when initially accepted onto the scheme. The vast majority of referrals are for a period of supported preparation in the trainer houses. Initial referral is followed by the young person and social worker visiting the project to meet the project leader and the project worker who will become the key worker (see Appendix Figure 4). Although informal, this meeting enables the scheme to explain the support package available, make an initial assessment and begin to test out the young person's commitment to working with the scheme. Although the scheme is formally open to any care leaver, subject to social worker approval, the assessment process filters out young people who appear unlikely to benefit from the scheme's structured approach or who feel unable to accept the clear terms on which support is offered. The ethos of this voluntary scheme, with its arms length relationship with social services, can sometimes enable them to be more successful at engaging the enthusiasm of youngsters disaffected with the care system and with social work. As one scheme worker explained:

> *"I was able to come in fresh and say, 'look this is what we can offer you . . . We can offer you a shared house with someone else, weekly meetings around managing the house, help with budgeting, emotional support, help with your career . . . We'll fight, we'll argue, we'll laugh, we'll do whatever but it'll all be for you' . . . We hope that (the young person) might find that we're more open, more accessible and different".*

When there are no immediate vacancies, the young person is placed on a waiting list and encouraged to attend the weekly group run at the project. If the young person feels too uncomfortable in a group setting, arrangements are made for preparatory work to take place solely on an individual basis. Although primarily social, the weekly group offers an opportunity to build relationships and assess skills and regular attendance is seen as demonstrating a 'measure of commitment'. As such, project staff view regular attendance at the group as being like a process of 'self referral'. As one leaving care worker reported saying to a young woman whose attendance at the group was erratic:

> *"It's about you wanting it and by you not coming to us it feels like you don't really want us".*

The only requirement is for the young person to show commitment to the scheme and the support it can offer. Without this the core relationships, which the scheme sees as fundamental to its work with young people, cannot be built. Young people are made very aware of the commitment they are making and this is crystallised at a meeting with them and their social workers prior to moving in. A licence agreement for trainer accommodation is signed which clarifies the rules and responsibilities attached to scheme membership on both sides.

City (vol)'s assessment process therefore has both formal and informal elements, taking place not only through meetings with the young people and their social workers but also during the period when young people attend the weekly social groups while awaiting the offer of a tenancy in a trainer house. It is during this period that project staff make a more complete assessment of the young people's needs and abilities. Given that the relationship envisaged is long-term, lasting two to three years, there is early emphasis on creating a bond and sufficient trust between young person and worker to enable work to proceed according to their individual needs and at their pace. The aim is to develop an overview of the young person's needs and an overall plan that can be followed, despite the periodic crises that surround young people's lives. One social worker of a young woman whose life was crisis laden, working in partnership with the scheme, valued this planned approach highly:

> *"I think . . . despite responding to events (that) we try to keep some sort of overall plan in mind".*

While the scheme was well known to social workers in City, young people's direct access to the project was limited by a lack of information available directly to them. Over half of the comparison group in City had never been signposted to the scheme by social workers and did not know of its existence. Access is normally formal, via the young person's social worker, with young people going through a process of 'joining' the scheme. Young people who hear of the project may refer themselves directly but their social workers must be involved from the outset. Given that the scheme offers a small scale specialist service rather than a universal service to all care leavers in its geographical area, direct access for young people may be less important than for our other schemes. However, those young people who were unaware of the scheme's existence clearly did not have the option of considering the full range of leaving care services that were locally available. With the formal coordination of the scheme's work with City (ssd)'s provision for care leavers, which occurred after this study was completed, some of these problems of access may have been resolved.

For those who do join the scheme, its inclusive nature and mix of individual and group work at the project base give it a strong project identity. Staff contact is usually by appointment and, whilst there is no official drop-in facility, some young people do use it in this way. The team also offer a seven day a week on call service for young people. It may be that for the few young people that are worked with who do not use the trainer flats identification with the scheme is more problematic. The young man being supported in his bedsit, whilst receiving positive individual support, stopped attending the group after a while. Although made welcome he felt more marginal, as if he were outside the main system.

With its formal access procedures, the scheme is able to ration its resources in an explicit way and this is crucial if the intensive package of support envisaged is to be operable. Primarily numbers are restricted by the trainer accommodation available and, if all works according to plan, the numbers needing less intensive help once they have moved on compensate, at least to some extent, for the more structured needs of new entrants.

Developing options

Accommodation

For most young people using the scheme, assistance with accommodation is organised in two phases. First, the scheme provides intensively supported accommodation in trainer flats. Second, it facilitates access for young people to move on accommodation through links it has developed with local housing providers. The provision of accommodation in trainer flats is the core service offered by the scheme, through which it develops its wide ranging and intensive programme of support to young people making a phased transition from care placements to independent accommodation.

The scheme's trainer flats are organised as a dispersed hostel. They are rented from the local authority and from housing associations and issued to young people under licence. The usual stay is 12–18 months, although none of our sample completed their time there and most moved on after a few months. The scheme's 20 bed spaces are situated in eight two bedroom houses and one four bedroom house. The licence agreement signed before young people move into the properties clarifies the rules and expectations the scheme has of residents and the support package young people have a right to expect. It also serves as a means of clarifying roles and responsibilities with social workers. The agreement covers use of drugs and drunkenness, informing workers of nights away or overnight guests, attendance at weekly house meetings and an expectation to attend the weekly group at the project base. The workers retain keys to the properties for use in emergencies, which they feel is crucial to their protective role if crises occur.

The weekly house meetings held in each trainer house deal with issues regarding the care of properties, problems with neighbours or other young people and any problems arising between young people sharing the property. In order to approximate to the real world and to avoid role ambiguity for a scheme which has both a landlord and a social work relationship with young people, the worker attending the weekly house meeting is not normally the individual key worker of any of the young people living in a particular house. Young people therefore have a relationship with one worker in a landlord capacity and another as their individual key worker and befriender.

Links the team have built with housing providers, both housing association and local authority, enable move-on accommodation to be organised through the allocation system. For those young people who do not use the trainer flats, the team assists social workers to find appropriate accommodation. Once our research was completed the scheme also began to offer a small number of supported lodgings.

Although this system of transitional accommodation involves more built-in movement for young people, this drawback may be outweighed by the opportunity the scheme affords young people to learn and make mistakes in an intensively supported environment.

Financial assistance

The scheme works to the same social services policies for financial assistance that cover the whole local authority. The first £500 of leaving care grants is administered directly by the scheme, the balance up to a further £500 has to be approved by the social services department's Assistant Director. The social services department provides money for the scheme to administer top ups in line with social services policy. Income top ups usually end at the eighteenth birthday as young people become eligible for income support, the exception being where young people are in full-time education. In this situation funding continues until the course is completed.

In our sample, four out of five young people were receiving income top ups at the time of the first interview: three were unemployed and one about to have a baby. By the final interview some eighteen months later, only this young woman was still receiving financial help, which paid for her place in supported accommodation and topped up her social security benefits. Her attempts at independent living had broken down, there were concerns about her parenting abilities and at this stage she was staying temporarily in supported lodgings with her second baby. Four out of the five had also received leaving care grants as they moved to their own accommodation during the research.

Careers

The scheme offered occasional group based services to assist young people in developing career options, such as running an employment skills group or, towards the end of the research, arranging for a careers officer to run regular sessions at the project base. However, most support with career development was offered on an individual basis. A focus on education, training or employment was an important component of individual support to young people establishing themselves in the community. The informal access available to young people who had joined the scheme meant that they could drop in for advice about college or job applications as well as discussing these with staff at the weekly group sessions or during individual appointments with their key workers.

Links with local colleges and training agencies had been developed by staff on an individual basis but by the end of the research the scheme was beginning to develop more formal links with colleges, TEC's and employers. As well as offering practical help with applications and liaising with agencies and employers on behalf of young people, scheme workers also worked on questions of motivation and the establishment of work routines.

> Peter's emotional difficulties arising from parental rejection, and the numerous moves he had made during his time in care which had led to many changes of school, made it difficult for him to sustain work or training. Although on a youth training scheme prior to our first interview, he was struggling to maintain commitment to it. His leaving care worker saw this as one priority and worked closely with him, providing an alarm clock, discussing the need for routines and self-discipline. When this failed she tried to explore other career options. After leaving his trainer house, which was enforced through drug related threats, a brief period of stability in his own flat enabled her to help him start a college course, but he was unable to sustain it when, once again, his life became submerged in a maelstrom of instability and movement.

As already noted, all the young people using this scheme had experienced rejection, had low self esteem and lacked confidence in themselves and their abilities. Their inability to sustain education, training or employment was, at least to some extent, associated with these emotional difficulties and with their problems in maintaining relationships. For example, Catherine's difficulties in sustaining work discipline and working relationships resulted in her drifting through a succession of jobs from which she either walked out or was sacked. For all four of the scheme users available for work or training, difficulties with motivation, self discipline and relationships at work or college were part of a wider problem of instability and lack of direction in their lives. Scheme staff were attempting to assist both with these underlying problems and with the day to day difficulties the young people encountered in relation to careers. However, where these underlying problems have not been resolved at an earlier stage or have been compounded by instability in care careers, the challenge to schemes in assisting young people with career development can prove particularly difficult.

Scheme support

Whilst the individual relationship with the key worker is seen as the core relationship, it is also reinforced with a range of group activities. There is a weekly social group both for those waiting to join and for those using the scheme. In addition, a number of other groups have run according to demand. During our research these included seven week preparatory groups run twice yearly; group work with a focus on health and personal development (using a specialist worker from the agency) and, in the past, mother and toddler groups and groups focusing on employment issues.

Key working and the trainer flat experience

All five of the young people were referred by social workers for a period of preparation in the trainer flats. As mentioned earlier, four were accepted on to the scheme and the fifth, who felt unable to change his lifestyle, was offered individual support in his bedsit and attendance at the group. In all cases the help offered was intensive, at least twice weekly contact, covered most dimensions of young people's lives and focused on areas young people were finding most difficult.

For Peter, the young man referred to earlier, although his deep seated insecurities limited his ability to sustain work or find a stable platform for himself, either within the project or later in the community, scheme support was both wide ranging and holistic in approach. In keeping with the scheme's philosophy, his key worker was attempting to strengthen his self image and his ability to make and manage relationships.

Abandoned at birth and having suffered 19 moves during his care career, a consequence of this instability had been to leave Peter with a very insecure sense of himself, lacking in confidence and in motivation to take control of his life. Troubled by rejection, isolated and lacking knowledge of his personal history, his leaving care worker was trying to negotiate access to his files for life story work, to encourage him to make friends outside the project and to renew links with his last foster parents, unfortunately unsuccessful. In response to him letting strangers in to the house, she was trying to explore the need to protect oneself and control one's personal space, crucial issues for vulnerable young people and one of the factors that led to later breakdown for him. Her approach was proactive and challenging, trying to offer him an overview and to limit every day distractions from the path he had agreed with her. As she said at this stage, "I think he wants me to push him to do things". All was not gloomy, he was positive about his time there, although finding it "scary at first". Compared to workers he had known previously, he found the staff "easier to talk to, much more open, they can all have a good laugh". The quality of relationships he established also enabled continuity of support to be offered through subsequent crises.

This case illustration is not untypical. Two of the other young people also felt their experience in trainer flats had been positive, even though their lives remained problematic.

Jackie said ". . . you were allowed to be independent and learn to live on your own". She valued the practical help she received with housing, benefits and budgeting, but also the personal and emotional support; having someone to talk to and "to know they're there if anything goes wrong". However, this young woman was also insecure, lacking self esteem, had few links and found it hard to trust others. Her vulnerability to exploitation also led to her having to leave the flat in response to difficulties with local youths and she was found a place in a supported hostel. Unfortunately we were unable to interview her again to see how she progressed.

Reflecting back positively on her experience in the trainer flat at the final interview, Denise, a young mother said:

"I mean (the scheme) set me up in one of their houses, they learnt me how to look after meself and basics. I mean that's where it all first started off, from learning how to do everything and cope on me own . . . That was useful, yes".

Pressured to leave her long-term foster home once pregnant, work at the project centred on: preparing for a planned move on to a council flat; developing life skills; assertiveness and managing relationships (particularly in relation to her boyfriend who tended to dominate her); and preparing for parenthood. A student worked on parenting skills and the leaving care worker was exploring networks of support in the community for when she moved on, since there were concerns about her ability to manage (health visitor, Homestart, nursery places). At the second interview she was living in her council flat but, despite regular weekly visits from her leaving care worker (and support from her social worker), she was finding it hard to cope and was pregnant again.

Whilst these young people accepted the need for the rules and controls attached to shared living at the project, even if they were not always able to live up to them, one young woman felt negative about her experience there. She found sharing stressful and conflicts developed with other young people at the project over cleaning, thefts and loss of food. She experienced the scheme as too intense, interpreting the care and concern offered as intrusive and over-controlling. Ultimately rejecting help and refusing to compromise, she walked out and, after periods in a caravan and small flat with her boyfriend had, by the final interview, moved into a council house with some help from the scheme. Her anger and frustration at her life, linked to sexual abuse and her loss of family, also remained fiercely directed at the scheme.

This scheme's comprehensive package of structured, intensive support is unlikely to suit all needs. Three young people from our comparison group were introduced to the scheme by their social workers and rejected it. Reasons ranged from not wanting to share, to finding the rules and controls attached to participation too restrictive and, in the case of one young black woman, preferring to remain in her part of the city where she had good links.

It is difficult to know how representative such a small sample of young people is of the careers of young people passing through this scheme, but it does raise some possible pointers to the strengths and difficulties associated with this type of provision. First, young people do need to commit themselves to shared living with all the pressures and strains that this can involve. If they cannot, as in the case above, then it can also destabilise the lives of those around them. If they can, then the benefits of group living, mutual support and intensive worker support can bear fruit. For many young people in care, whose own lives have been destabilised, the mature skills of negotiation and compromise that are needed to share are not easy to learn. Second, two of these young people appear to have been forced to leave through threats made to their personal safety. One of the difficulties of protecting young people in shared housing, particularly where the houses become known locally, is their vulnerability to exploitation if they lack the skills to control their space, however much they may willingly contribute to their own downfall.

Joint working with social workers

The structured framework and philosophy within which the scheme operates, allied to definite procedural steps prior to joining, laid a solid foundation for close co-operation with social workers. In all cases social workers were clear about the work the scheme was trying to undertake and role clarity and task sharing were usually reinforced through regular planning meetings with the young people. Communication was good and ambiguity and possible duplication of roles thereby kept to a minimum. For young people entering the trainer flats the scheme would usually take the lead role with a young person, expecting the social worker to reinforce that progress and perhaps focus on wider family issues. As one leaving care worker said, it was agreed that:

"I would do the day to day groundwork but that the social worker would (be) there to reinforce certain issues that came up".

Once the young person moved on from the project, respective roles and degrees of involvement would be negotiated according to circumstances. For example, in the case of the young mother, Denise, the scheme had taken the central support role during her stay at the project and her time in her council flat. By the final interview, her inability to control her flat and the arrival of a second baby meant that she had moved into temporary supported lodgings. Her social worker was now intensively involved due to concerns about her parenting skills. In consequence, her leaving care worker had reduced her contact to monthly visits, planning to step this up again when she once again moved to independence.

All the social workers were positive about their experience of working in partnership with the scheme. They valued the scheme's specialist expertise and knowledge of local resources, some feeling that they had learnt through their involvement. As a small voluntary scheme, it offered flexibility and support tailored to meet individual needs. They appreciated that specialist workers could be more young person centred and less authoritarian in their work than could social workers, being constrained by their statutory and 'parental' responsibilities and the need for a family focus to their work. One also mentioned the importance of the project base and group work in encouraging young people to socialise, develop social networks and relieve isolation. However, one social worker, whilst appreciating these strengths, raised a thorny and recurring theme about the perceived difference between statutory and voluntary agencies. Based on her experience with the disaffected young woman who left the scheme, she felt that voluntary agencies had more autonomy to be selective about who they worked with, particularly where young people were difficult or disruptive:

"They do have certain boundaries which I think is fine . . . If the young person oversteps those, they'll try and sort it out, but ultimately they'll say, well . . . maybe the scheme isn't appropriate for them".

Whilst the scheme clearly did work hard to engage this young woman's co-operation, once she left, further contact depended upon her approaching the scheme. Whilst the door was open for further support, the scheme felt they needed this measure of commitment from her.

Post scheme support – continuity and closure

Like most schemes, this one makes an open-ended commitment to young people. Support can last for as long as young people want to receive it, although, given the scheme's commitment to young people in the trainer flats, it may not continue at the same level of intensity. Even where a young person appears to be stable in the community and a negotiated decision is reached to end regular visiting, the door remains open. It is hoped that the quality of relationship established will enable young people to return for help without fear of stigma. One worker expressed this belief in the following way:

"*. . . the other side is that there is somebody that, should the crunch come, she would call on and, in the future, . . . that will remain. Even if we agree that . . . my actual contact stops we as a project will say to her, if ever you've got a problem, if you ever need help, . . . you know you can always ring and we'll help*".

The open-ended nature of support was also valued by concerned social workers:

"*(The scheme) has said they'll stay with a person for as long as they need them. So even if she's off the care order, it don't matter, they'll stay with her, which is good because I think she's going to need help*".

By the final interview two of these young people were still receiving regular support from the scheme, some 18 months later. Of those who were not, one was lost to the study and the other, the young woman who had rejected their help in the past, still felt she could contact them "when I want sumeat". She had in fact approached them on several occasions for help with obtaining her council house, her leaving care grant and with buying furniture, although remaining dismissive in overall terms. The young man receiving support in his bedsit, already quite heavily involved in the local drug scene, felt his best chance of escape was to leave the area. By the second interview he was living in a supported hostel in the Midlands and appeared to have gained a measure of stability in his life, coming off drugs and joining a YT scheme.

For the remaining two, Denise and Peter, continuity and consistency of support had proved crucial.

Both valued highly the support they had received and appreciated the way prompt and practical solutions were found to his problems:

"*If I didn't know what to do I'd just talk to them about what was wrong and they'd take it from there*".

Peter compared this approach favourably to that of an earlier social worker:

"*I mean I went down to talk to her sometimes. She'd just sit there looking sad, saying I had some problems . . . Looking sad, you know, like they're trained to do it . . . I'd like her to say, well, how about doing this and how about doing that*".

Denise valued consistency of support and the quality of relationship she had with her key worker.

"*I mean (she's) always cheerful, she's helped me out, . . . she's always talked to me, you know, if we've had any trouble, she's always been there*".

On the face of it, the outcomes for these young people of their involvement with the scheme appeared patchy. All, in differing ways, were struggling to find a place for themselves in the adult world. None had found a stable home nor career nor positive network of support that could sustain them through this transition. But for those above, the continuity in support offered meant that they still had options, choices that they could make and the support to enable them to try again. For local authorities that take their responsibilities as 'good parents' seriously, it is perhaps this open-ended commitment to support that is most crucial for care leavers.

The emotional insecurities of these young people reached back to their experiences prior to care and, for some, had been compounded by disturbance and disruption during their care careers. Throughout this text we have suggested the need for a through care experience for young people that offers them the opportunity to experience stability, continuity of support and encouragement and the chance to repair fundamental insecurities. In this light preparation to leave care, involving the active participation of young people, needs to form part of an individually structured care plan from the point at which young people are accommodated, with arrangements for the regular review and monitoring of progress. Prior to young people leaving, this process should culminate in a leaving care plan that includes a formal assessment of young people's practical and social skills, the networks of support available to them in the community and include arrangements for monitoring their later progress. Whilst this would help to structure social work thinking about support needs, it may also help to place the need for a flexible leaving age that is needs-led more firmly on the agenda. What seems clear from this evaluation is that it is unrealistic to expect young people with fundamental insecurities about themselves, with few links and difficulties in making and managing relationships, to make a smooth transition to the adult world. It also points to the need for a holistic approach to the development of practical life skills. These can only grow and be deployed if young people have a fairly secure emotional base within which to operate. If these more deep seated problems are not tackled earlier, it may even be beyond the resources of highly structured and intensive schemes to repair the damage.

CHAPTER 18

COUNTY LEAVING CARE SCHEME

Background

Our fourth scheme aims to provide a service to all care leavers and those already living independently spread across a large county authority containing a city and several district councils. Throughout the research period the scheme has not had its own premises. Initially it was located, along with other social work teams, in a converted children's home on the outskirts of the city to which young people were not allowed direct access. The scheme was then given office space in a large social services divisional building in the city centre. With insufficient space for group and drop-in activities, direct access for young people remains mostly limited to a formal duty system managed by the scheme. These restrictions allied to the complexities of delivering a service across such a disparate authority have, as we shall see, significantly influenced the shape of scheme services.

It is the oldest of our participating schemes. Originating from a supported accommodation initiative with a housing association in the late 1970's, a specialist leaving care team was created in 1985. It is directly funded and managed by Social Services. The team leader is responsible for managing, supervising and supporting the work of the team and is herself responsible to a principal officer. The scheme has responsibility for developing and co-ordinating leaving care services for the county as a whole.

In addition to the provision of direct services, through the team leader, the scheme has a central role in advising and assisting the authority to meet its responsibilities under The Children Act 1989 and in monitoring county-wide provision. Work has progressed in a number of areas: systems for appoval and monitoring of all leaving care grants and issuing guidance to social workers on financial assistance; co-ordinating services for teenagers 'in need' (Section 20); and assisting with a review of the appropriateness of services for young people with disabilities and for young people from minority ethnic groups. There is a complaints procedure booklet for children's services and assistance in drawing up complaints is available from a children's rights officer. The team works to a simple policy and procedures document issued to social workers in 1990 that outlines referral procedures and services offered (see Appendix Figure 3).

The scheme has focused on providing and co-ordinating access to a range of accommodation options for young people throughout the county to meet differing needs (individual tenancies, supported lodgings and hostels, the latter including a 'floating support' scheme). It has also focused on ensuring access to financial assistance. In this sense it attempts to ensure that young people's most basic needs for good quality accommodation and the means to make a home are met.

In response to these initiatives, a complex and specialised staff structure has evolved, although roles do overlap. Having twelve social work staff in all (including the team leader), four are 'generic' workers offering key worker support to young people in care and in their own accommodation, managing referrals, the duty system and linking with children's homes and hostels; two are 'accommodation' workers, their primary role being to manage a supported lodgings scheme; five are 'project' workers running the scheme's two directly managed hostels and the 'floating support' scheme and offering key worker support to young people passing through them (see Appendix Figure 1).

Approach

County has developed a structured social worker-led approach with quite explicit mechanisms for rationing resources, primarily at the point of referral and allocation. The scheme acknowledges that with present resources it has to offer differing levels of service to young people. All those leaving residential care are offered key worker support if they want it, reflecting the links between the team and children's homes, and those entering the scheme's own supported accommodation receive a comprehensive package of support. For others, key worker support is allocated according to circumstances and rarely at the same level of intensity. Although the duration and nature of support is flexible and negotiated with young people, the terms of involvement are primarily shaped by staff, work tends to be task oriented and decisions will be made to close cases if young people return home, are rejecting support or not making themselves available. Contact also tends to be reduced if young people enter other supported hostels where hostel staff, perhaps understandably, are expected to take the key role. Equally for young people in their own accommodation visiting quite quickly becomes less frequent if they are seen to be coping, although contact can remain open-ended. Decisions are therefore made about the level of active involvement according to the other supports that are perceived to be available to young people – from field social workers, hostel staff or their family. Given that the 'generic' workers have caseloads of 25 plus, difficult decisions about relative priorities for contact continually have to be made.

In this context, the scheme places a strong emphasis on the duty system, the cornerstone of an advice and information service to social workers and young people, to ensure that they are seen at least once and have access to information and financial help. All work with young people is on an individual basis; there are no groups or drop-in facilities. Apart from the duty system all contact is in young people's homes or placements. The limited informal access available to young people has tended to give the scheme a weak project identity.

Profile of scheme users

In total we selected 30 young people from County for inclusion in our research. Of these, 15 were using the scheme and had key workers at the outset. However the pattern of usage of this scheme was varied, with some young people gaining later access to help and others moving away. Of the original participating sample, four were still receiving key worker support at varying levels of intensity at the end of the research. Two others had completed stays in a supported hostel and moved on to stable accommodation. Four had received more intermittent support, although three of these had key workers again at the end. Two young men who had been in 'floating support' accommodation lost contact with the scheme once their situations broke down. Finally, for three young people, involvement was short-term; one returned home to family after a hostel break down, one was persistently hard to contact and the other was felt to have sufficient networks of support.

For the comparison group patterns of involvement were equally complex. Three were referred by social workers for key worker support after the first interview and a further two shortly before the end of the research. Two used the duty service for housing and financial assistance when moving to their own accommodation. For a further three the scheme acted in a consultancy role at reviews and planning meetings prior to transition but did not become actively involved once they hd moved. These patterns suggest that the well established nature of the scheme and sound referral procedures enabled the scheme to reach most of these young people in some way.

Returning to our original participating sample, it is noticeable that the practical and emotional resources available to most of these young people to help them negotiate transition were higher than for those using some of our other schemes. Two thirds of this sample were female; three of these young women were black or of mixed heritage; and three were already parents at the point of leaving care. The split between backgrounds in residential and foster care was even. Most had been in care long-term, two thirds having been accommodated for four or more years and one half for over ten years. Most had experienced movement, with two thirds making one to three moves and only two remaining in one placement throughout. Almost all left their care placements to move into transitional or permanent accommodation early, just under one half at sixteen and only two were eighteen when moving on.

However, and despite a majority (nine) not having parents upon whom they could rely for support during transition, two thirds were quite confident and secure in themselves and had fairly positive networks of support. These included in some cases parents, in others older siblings, extended family members, ex-foster carers and friends. Two thirds also had quite good practical life skills, although most needed support in some areas, particularly budgeting and negotiating skills. Only three had very poor life skills (two male) and only two were very insecure, uncertain of themselves and found difficulty making relationships – one a young man who had been with the same foster carers throughout his life, viewed them as his family but descended into insecurity and instability when the placement broke down; the other a young woman recovering from parental sexual abuse. Two brothers, although quite able, were also uncertain and quite isolated having returned to the county after several years placed out of authority in order to build links with their family (which remained difficult) and return to their roots.

Access and rationing

For the majority of young people, referral to the scheme is made by their social workers, although the team accept referrals from young people directly and from housing agencies in the area. For young people in residential care referral is automatic and a team member attends post-16 reviews in an advisory capacity. More informally, given the link role 'generic' staff have with children's homes, most young people get to know of the scheme and its link worker well before moving on. For those in foster care referral is less certain and, concerned about under-representation, the team has been building links with fostering workers and carers to try and ensure early referral. All initial referrals are taken to weekly allocation meetings where a preliminary decision is taken about the action required. Early referral, whilst important for planning effective transitions, does not necessarily mean that the team will engage in active work with the young person, but it does mean that at a minimum it will act in an advisory capacity to social workers and carers.

All referrals of young people in care for the scheme's supported accommodation (two hostels and dispersed scheme) are made through this system; referrals are not accepted directly. Initial referral is followed by a visit to the projects and a series of meetings with young people and their social workers to explain the support package available, gauge the young person's commitment to joining and to clarify roles and expectations.

As a relatively small team attempting to offer a universal service across a large county clear mechanisms for rationing the resource are required. In 1990 the team received 627 enquiries (not all initial referrals) of which 12% were allocated key workers, 46% were dealt with on a duty basis and 42% were deemed to require no further action. The action decided upon at allocation meetings depends on a number of factors: the nature of the request; existing case load pressure; the degree of support young people have from other workers – a concern here is to avoid duplication and not to release social workers from their responsibilities; and the quality of relationship between leaving care workers and young people which may make them well placed to undertake a particular piece of work. However, there is flexibility and if further support needs are identified at a duty session these can be accommodated and young people dealt with on a duty basis are welcome to re-contact the scheme again for further help although, in this sense, the onus rests with them.

As we have suggested, informal access to the scheme for young people is limited. In addition, the duty service is city centre based and for those young people living in outlying towns and villages access is further reduced. They can either phone up or negotiate access to help through the duty system at their local social services office. For young people with key worker support and an established relationship with a staff member the hurdles that this can involve are likely to be less of a problem, for others they are likely to need a discrete problem and an ability to admit to difficulties before contacting.

The need for social workers to link young people in early, to enable an informal and trusting relationship to develop, is therefore crucial and, for most of our participating sample, especially those from residential care, this was the case. For one young woman who remained quite unstable and moved to a different part of the country for a time, these links were quite important in her being able to return for help:

". . . 'cos it's easier going to someone you know than a total stranger".

Although wary of adult advice, she trusted them. However, another young woman who was staying temporarily with her father when social work support ended, and not linked in with the scheme at that point, had to negotiate her own way through the homeless route to obtain permanent accommodation, although she did approach them later for a leaving care grant. Although skilled enough to do this and strongly independent, she expressed confusion about how to ask for help:

"I didn't know whether they'd be able to help me. I didn't ask them 'cos I didn't know how to ask them. I didn't know in what areas they'd be able to help me".

Another young woman, stable in a foster home throughout her life and remaining there through the study, had no contact with the scheme and had never heard of them. She appears to have been simply forgotten by social services with no recognition of leaving care nor of her entitlements to future help. Although very able she felt neglected:

"I would have liked them to come and speak to me about what I could and couldn't have . . . They could have said you're entitled to this or you're entitled to that, or what are you going to do now . . I didn't expect a big medal saying congratulations you've come through this successfully, but I suppose it would have been nice to have a chat with somebody".

Finally one social worker closing the case of a young parent not linked in with the scheme reflects upon the hurdles of negotiating duty systems, aware that this is less than adequate:

"I suppose in some ways it's . . . placating. I mean what we're saying (is you) can go to the duty officer in reality . . . To get beyond that, or if she was to say look, I was formerly in care, the duty officer might say, here's the telephone number, ring the leaving care team. The services, they're not easily accessible beyond eighteen. You've actually got to be fairly determined to get through".

Although the access issues raised here go beyond the particularities of this scheme and in a real sense are pertinent to all care leavers, it may present more problems to a scheme that lacks an informal social base. In fact, as we have seen, access to this scheme was quite good. Only five out of thirty, including the two young women above, had no involvement with the scheme at any point, although contact for a further seven was quite minimal.

Developing options

Accommodation

The complexities of attempting to provide a flexible range of accommodation options for young people in a large county authority have required a major investment in this area of work. Positive links have been built with the city council, housing associations and, to a lesser extent, with district councils to obtain priority to individual tenancies for care leavers. In addition, through a variety of partnership arrangements a range of transitional accommodation options have been developed. Crucial to the success of these developments has been the willingness of social services to make imaginative use of Section 24 funds to help promote joint ventures and in-house initiatives.

Individual tenancies: Positive links have been developed with the city council and housing associations. The former offers priority access to care leavers and for the latter access can be negotiated through the council's nomination rights. The problem for the team during most of our research has been gaining access to accommodation from the district councils. Often young people are only eligible to put their names on the waiting list at 18 years of age with no guarantee of when an offer will be made. The choices have tended to be to remain in foster placements on a lodgings basis; to venture into the private market or move to the city away from their supports. Equally for young people in residential care (all city based) moving back to their own areas has been problematic. Towards the end of our research negotiations with these district councils, stressing the inter-agency requirements of The Children Act, has resulted in more success, including an agreed protocol and nomination rights. Some access is available through hostels and the scheme is trying to develop dispersed flats and supported lodgings in these areas.

Supported lodgings scheme: Two 'accommodation' social workers have been employed with primary responsibility for developing and managing this scheme. A panel system of approval is in existence and includes police checks and references. At present there are 20 plus places (mostly city based), they are not time limited and are funded through a combination of the young person's income, housing benefit and top ups from social services. Whilst these workers primarily support providers, young people also have a key worker from the 'generic' staff. However the 'accommodation' social workers do provide key work support in some cases. In addition, supported lodgings are also provided directly through divisional offices. Six of our sample experienced supported lodgings at some point. Two were able to remain in their foster homes throughout the study (one unfunded) and one remained stable with ex-residential carers on this basis. A further two used divisional lodgings; one, a young woman with learning difficulties, had a very successful stay for 12 months before moving on to her own accommodation. Only one used the scheme's lodgings, an insecure young man whose foster home had just broken down, but despite intensive support plans being drawn up his situation broke down within a matter of weeks.

Directly managed supported projects: Three supported projects are managed directly by the scheme in partnership with housing associations, the council and, in one case, jointly operated with a voluntary agency.

The first is a five bed supported hostel for young women leaving care staffed by one of the scheme's project workers. It offers a flexible 12 month stay with move on accommodation provided by the council and the housing association that provides and manages the building. Two young women from our sample had successful stays here.

Second is the dispersed hostel, a 'floating support' scheme in which individual units of accommodation are provided by the city council and housing associations. Flats are initially issued to young people under licence and peripatetic support is provided by two project workers for as long as young people require it (usually about 12 months). Once young people are able to manage, the support can be withdrawn, the young person is issued a standard tenancy agreement, the property is handed back to the housing agency and a new property offered to begin the process again. As we have seen, three of our sample moved into this scheme. Two young men lost control of their flats after a few months but the third, a young woman, remained stable throughout.

Finally, for young people with learning difficulties, the scheme, in partnership with a housing association and voluntary agency, has developed a six bed hostel offering intensive support and a three bed house for those able to manage more independently. Referrals come from a variety of sources and it is staffed by two of the scheme's project workers and a third worker employed through hostel deficit funding. It offers a flexible two year stay with guaranteed move-on accommodation. Unfortunately none of our sample used this project.

Financially supported projects: In addition to the above, the scheme has negotiated nomination rights at three other hostels throughout the county in return for social services department funding to help managing agents run the properties, thereby guaranteeing access for care leavers. In overall terms this represents part of a rolling programme and the level of contact between the team and accommodation providers is such that any new initiative in the county is discovered at a sufficiently early stage to enable negotiations for access. As we have already indicated, the 'generic' staff have responsibility for linking with hostels and a third of our entire sample stayed in a hostel at some point in their early post-care careers, although not always successfully.

Two thirds (20) of our entire sample received help from the scheme in planning the move to their initial accommodation, either directly through assistance with applications, liaison and finances or indirectly through advice to their social workers. Of those who did not, the majority (6) had remained in lodgings, with foster carers or relatives. One half (14) of the sample remained stable throughout the research period, nine staying where they were and five making a further planned move to their own accommodation or a second hostel; and of those whose early post-care careers were more disrupted, three quarters (12) seemed to have been stabilised by the final interview in homes of their own. Only four young people continued a pattern of instability throughout and two of these were being offered ongoing help from the scheme.

Our data therefore suggests that the investment made by the scheme in accommodation and its core role as a specialist resource in co-ordinating moves and applications appears to work effectively and has facilitated access for the vast majority of our sample. At a minimum it enables the scheme to be aware of most care leavers, to have some contact with most and to monitor their early post care careers.

Financial assistance

All leaving care grants (£775, July 1994) are administered by the scheme. This enables the team to offer some direct or indirect assistance through social workers to virtually all young people who move to independent living, provided that young people still have social work support at that stage or have been made aware of their entitlements. Where young people are eligible for a community care grant from the Social Fund this is usually deducted from the leaving care grant. All the young people in our sample who moved to independent living received a grant.

Individual income top ups for young people are administered by the divisional offices and are available if young people are unemployed, at college, on training courses or in low paid work. Most top ups end at eighteen unless a place at college or in supported accommodation depends upon it. Exactly half of our entire sample (fifteen) received top ups at some stage; nine of these were in the participating and six in the comparison groups. Five of these young people were still receiving them at the final interview. Those who did not receive them were either able to claim income support or were waged. Entitlement to financial assistance ceases if young people return to their family home, although some help can still be offered to maintain the placement at the discretion of the divisional office.

The team has responsibility for ensuring that social workers are aware of amounts available and application procedures. In an attempt to limit the operation of discretion and to develop a more 'rights' based approach to assistance the team, in collaboration with the Children's Rights Officer, have issued guidance to offices on payments. The principle underpinning this is that no young person should have less than an agreed amount to live on after housing and training costs are met. Our data suggests that one key objective for the scheme, that young people should have the basic financial means to make and maintain a home, is broadly being met.

Careers

As with our other schemes help in the area of education and employment has been individually based. For those in the scheme's directly managed supported accommodation careers help formed part of a comprehensive package of support. For those living independently assistance was more likely to be restricted to advice about college and employment options. Young people were often then expected to take the initiative based on that advice. Some were able to do so but others, lacking confidence, motivation, confused about their abilities or the direction they wanted their lives to take, found it more difficult. Perhaps for these young people more structured support was required. For example, a young man returned to County after several years placed out of authority with the aim of re-establishing links with his family and community. Although he started college the stress of his transition and of the course work was too great and he dropped out. Despite careers advice from both his social worker and the scheme, he lacked confidence to act upon it and remained unemployed throughout the research. In contrast, detailed advice given to three young parents about the possibilities for a return to learn, including information about social services funding and child care, was crucial in enabling them to expand their horizons. Although not wanting an immediate return, it enabled them to feel that their future aspirations were realistic and that support would be on hand to assist them.

The scheme had not yet developed any formal links with employers, careers, colleges or training agencies to promote wider career opportunities for young people and relied upon informal connections made by individual staff members. This area was recognised as a priority for future development. Opportunities to offer careers help in an informal and collective setting were inhibited by the absence of drop-in or group facilities. In this sense the chance for young people to offer mutual support to each other and share their concerns were limited.

Scheme support

As we have indicated, the size and complexity of this authority has led to the development of a more complex scheme staffing structure and of explicit rationing procedures to enable the scheme to manage its resources effectively. In consequence, differing levels of service are available to young people; for example, between those entering the scheme's directly managed supported accommodation, those reliant on key work support from the 'generic' staff in their own independent accommodation and those dealt with on a duty basis.

Key worker support – supported accommodation

Five young people from the participating sample left care placements to enter the scheme's directly managed accommodation with key worker support offered by project workers. Two young women left foster placements for the scheme's semi-independence hostel and three (two male and one female) moved into dispersed flats ('floating support' scheme).

The procedures for gaining entry are well structured. Once referred by the central team for either form of provision the young person and their social worker make several visits to the project (usually three). These enable project staff to make an initial assessment of the young person's skills and support needs, to gauge their commitment to joining, to clarify rules and expectations and to explain the support package on offer. Selection is based on the young person's willingness to abide by the terms of membership and to accept the support on offer and not on their current skills and attributes. These meetings culminate in the signing of a licence agreement which forms a contract between the young person and the scheme and also serves to clarify the expectations the scheme has of social workers. All young people are expected to have social work support for the duration of their involvement with either project. It clarifies roles and forms a basis for joint-working. The projects tend to focus on the day to day practical and emotional support of young people and social workers are expected to reinforce that progress and offer wider counselling on care background and family relationships.

In all cases moves were well planned and co-ordinated over several months and the support available to young people was wide ranging and needs-led. Although practical help with preparation is not a major focus of scheme work, one project worker, unhappy with the lack of preparation being offered to the two young men in their children's homes, spent several months preparing them for the move to their dispersed flats. Work focused on life skills, work issues (including interview techniques), confidence building and planning the move. Once young people moved in the support offered was intensive.

For the two young women in the hostel it offered an opportunity to test their skills for independent living in a closely supportive environment, to build their confidence and to think through the direction they wanted their lives to follow. Both were unemployed and uncertain about their futures. As part of a comprehensive package of support, one was linked – via a specialist careers advisor – to a YT scheme in child care and, despite moving to her own flat, she was continuing successfully on this scheme at the close of the research. The other young woman became pregnant and, with scheme support, moved into a specialist hostel for young mothers where she was encouraged to resume a college career. Once they had moved on formal support from their project worker ceased, although both retained some informal contact. The structure of this scheme meant that for more formal help they would need to refer themselves back to the central team for support by the 'generic' staff, the primary responsibility of the project worker being for hostel residents.

Reflecting back, both young women were very positive about the help they had received. Both felt the hostel had struck a positive balance between support and autonomy, company and privacy:

"Well you're not really on your own in a way 'cos there's . . . always someone in the house. I mean, they respect you when you want to be on your own, they'll go."

Support with practical skills, the chance to build confidence and talk through problems was also important. As the one in her own flat summed up succinctly, "I wouldn't have been able to manage if I'd just moved straight into here."

For those moving into the dispersed scheme a similarly intensive package of help was available, although outcomes were not quite so succesful. For the young woman, structured and continuous support from her leaving care worker and social worker, whom she had known long-term and felt very close to, enabled her to stabilise herself in the community. Her confidence, skills and maturity were growing and support was continuing at the final interview, although at a less intense level. She felt this support and the reassurance it gave her had been invaluable in enabling her to build her life:

"It's helped me settle down a lot quicker . . . than what I would have. I think any other person they'd be struggling (but) I've got so many people I can turn to if I've got any trouble . . . so I'm lucky."

For the two young men outcomes were different, both found freedom difficult to cope with, lost control of their flats to friends and began to offend. For one this was a resumption of a pre-care pattern. Both disappeared from their flats shortly after the first interview and, whilst one was lost to our study, neither received help from the scheme again. The other, sought by the police for a serious car offence, stayed with his sister and, after a period in custody on remand, was lodging with an older friend at the final interview. Although support offered by the scheme during their stay at the flat was positive, the possibility for joint-working was eroded as both experienced changes in social worker at a time of difficult transition (both cases were closed soon after leaving the flats) and visits planned by their residential workers did not materialise. For the second young man his new found freedom went to his head and, feeling he did not need support, he began missing appointments with his project worker. He reflected on this clearly at a later interview:

"I think I just messed up, . . . friends took over my life and I thought it was just great. I can live on me own, do what I want, when I want, nobody to tell me what to do."

A potential problem for schemes with specialised staff structures and clear boundaries of responsibility between its different sections is that it can be hard for young people who have 'messed up' to return for help. Once he left the flat the project worker's formal role ceased and the main route back for help would have been through referral to the central team. Having 'failed' this was hard for him to do when he did realise he needed support. Without scheme or social worker he was on his own:

"At first I thought I don't need help and then I did but there was no one there to help me."

At the final interview, after his release from custody, he was receiving practical help from a probation officer but remained unemployed.

Key worker support – 'generic'

The four 'generic' staff have responsibility for accepting all enquiries and referrals to the scheme; managing the duty and advice service; offering key worker support to young people through transition; and maintaining links with children's homes and hostels. Where key worker allocation is required negotiations take place with the young person and their social worker to establish the nature of that involvement, whether it will be primarily in an 'active' or 'consultancy' capacity, and forms the basis for an informal contract, although this is rarely written. Direct work with young people is negotiated and subject to review, but the terms of involvement are primarily shaped by staff. The need to marshall scarce resources means that where work is not seen as productive, where young people are resisting help or where they return home, cases are likely to be closed. In addition, where they are seen to have other supports, involvement is likely to ease back. In this sense work is task focused.

The philosophy which underpins work with young people represents a balance between support and self-responsibility – "cushioning young people to enable them to do things for themselves". Concerns about the dangers of dependency mean it is not a 'do for' approach. Only in exceptional circumstances will the load be taken from young people's shoulders. Emphasis is placed on offering advice and support to explore options but responsibility for decision making and their consequences remain with the young person. Recognition that care tends to damage self image leads to a strong emphasis on confidence building – "giving them the tools to feel good about themselves" – to enable them to find a place in the adult world, to build networks, find employment and deal with agencies.

When workers feel a young person is coping they will try to ease them away from the scheme, to limit reliance upon staff. However there is flexibility, even if young people are not experiencing definite problems contact can be ongoing if young people want this, but at a lower level of priority:

"It's because our role is seen as a more supportive (one) and if the young person is explicitly saying they want to continue then it will . . . Then that case (may not) have high priority, the visiting may go down to every two months".

So whilst most work is task focused it can also be open-ended.

Of the remaining ten in our original participating sample, three recieved **'continuous'** key worker support throughout the study, for a further four contact was more **'intermittent'**, although three of these had key workers again at the end, and for three involvement was **'short term'**. In addition three were referred by social workers for key worker support after the first interview and a further two just before the close of the study. Of the ten, four were from residential backgrounds and six from foster care.

Long-term continuous support

Six of these young people received this form of support during the course of the research. Although described as 'continuous', the scheme's rationed and problem focused approach points, for some, to a pattern of contact involving periods of scheme activity where circumstances demand it, with support easing back or being withdrawn at other times. However for all these young people links were maintained and the cases remained allocated. Four were very positive about the help they had received while, for two brothers, their appraisal of the scheme's involvement in their lives was more qualified.

Julie, after an unstable care career, had walked out of her children's home and was staying with friends. Wanting accommodation she was advised at a duty session to approach the council as homeless. Already pregnant, after a brief stay in a homeless hostel, she was offered a flat. Her situation broke down after violence from her partner and she was re-referred to the scheme by her social worker who was closing the case. A return to care was organised for her and her baby until a new flat was allocated near her family. Her leaving care grant was organised, help offered to settle in and to "wade through the bureaucracy" (housing benefit, council housing department and DSS). Both able and independent, links were being maintained that balanced this with making further support available should she need it. She summed up the help she had received:

"Well if it hadn't been for the leaving care I wouldn't have been able to get where I was now. When it comes to going places and that I'd put them off because I don't know what to say and . . . (my worker) was there to support me".

Similarly Mary, whom the scheme had assisted in moving first to a supported hostel and later into her own tenancy, really valued the support she had received. For her it was important:

"just to know that there's someone actually interested in me, in what I'm doing and what I'm achieving".

The careers of the two brothers through the scheme were more complex. Having been happily placed out of authority for several years their planned return to the city represented a huge and risky step, involving as it did a need to rebuild family links, to make sense of their pasts and to construct new lives. Several planning meetings took place prior to the move involving them, the scheme and social workers. Plans for supported lodgings meant they were allocated an 'accommodation' social worker from the scheme. However shortly before arrival they had changed their minds, wanting a hostel, dispersed flat or independent accommodation they could share. Both arrived insecure and uncertain and temporarily went to stay with family members – one with their father and another with a sister.

Jim, still 17 and having a social worker, was quite quickly found an approved foster placement with a friend of his father. For him, with social work support, the scheme's role was reduced and centred on future accommodation options. The scheme structure meant that he was reallocated to a worker from the 'generic' team as he no longer wanted lodgings. Contact remained limited until his placement broke down some five months later. After temporary stays with family the scheme found him an hostel place. His older brother Jack was also realloctated within the team, but when his relationship with his sister disintegrated after a few weeks his new key worker was on leave. He approached the duty service for help but, unsure of the advice being given, he went away and lodged informally with a friend of his sister. Unemployed (after plans for college had fallen through), isolated and demoralised, he felt unhappy with the support on offer. From these lodgings he spent several months with family members before a hostel place was found. It appears that whilst living with family his priority for scheme involvement had been reduced. Both moved from their hostels to neighbouring flats in a housing association managed tower block but, being shy and lacking street wisdom, they found the pressures from other young people there intolerable. In fairness to the scheme, whilst they had helped organise the move they advised strongly against it, aware that they might be unhappy and also that they would lose their priority for future housing. It was only at the final interview that they appeared to be settling together in a private shared house with scheme help.

Clearly for these two, the scheme's structure (having to change workers mid stream) and relative priorities for involvement had not helped them through a very difficult set of transitions. Uncertain of themselves, lacking friends and finding their family an unreliable source of support, they had needed a more intensive and structured programme of support than the scheme seemed able to offer. Its primary focus on their accommodation needs, whilst obviously important, had limited help in other areas (careers, networks, family) and they became demoralised and unmotivated. Pressure on scheme time also meant that they felt there was insufficient space for them to get the counselling they needed. Both felt the onus had been on them to obtain a service:

"If I want something I've got to come and sometimes it's an effort to get what you want."

But by the final interview their opinion had become more reflective. One, aware that he had not always heeded advice nor been able to take the initiative, perceptively commented:

"Sometimes if they give you advice you can take it or not take it, they don't know your personal situation as well as you. But sometimes you've just got to do what you think is right. If it's wrong, well it's tough, you've just got to live with that. I've made a fair few mistakes while I've been down and I wish that I'd listened a bit more, but that's all part and parcel of life. My opinion of them's changed a lot, they got me a grant, got me somewhere to live, they will help".

Support was continuing and their hope was that finding a stable base together would enable them to build more community links and re-examine their career options.

Intermittent support

Several young people received more intermittent support from the scheme for different reasons. For example, for two young mothers in unstable circumstances, contact was lost when they left their flats.

Jane was escaping violence from her partner and moved to a different part of the country; the other, Alison, could not cope with living on her own and moved between family and friends. Jane, disillusioned with the instability of life for her and her two children (she had never found permanent accommodation and used a succession of hostels), returned to the city to try again with her partner. By the final interview, her situation had broken down again and, fearful of further violence, she had contacted her key worker. Help was offered to leave and, staying temporarily with her mother, plans were being drawn up to re-stabilise her once more. For Alison, intensive and consistent help from her social worker enabled her to come through several months of instability. Although the move to her first flat had been well planned and co-ordinated, she had never been able to settle, remaining insecure and fearful. Post move contact from the scheme had been limited due to pressures at the base and her social worker had had to take the lead support role. From the scheme point of view, her case was closed when she disappeared and was no longer making herself available for contact. Eventually her social worker managed to obtain a new flat for her and helped settle her in and, shortly before the last interview, the young person herself had contacted the scheme for advice about college. Her social worker was having to close her case as she was already 19 and key worker support therefore resumed. Plans at this stage were to explore college options, funding and child care arrangements and to help her manage her flat.

Alison's social worker was unhappy with what he perceived as the limitations of the scheme, feeling that he had had to carry the main burden of transition. Although valuing the scheme as a specialist resource for accommodation and finances, he felt it should have offered more active and wide ranging support – as we shall see this is not an uncommon perception amongst social workers in this authority. Whilst liaison was maintained and terms of involvement made clear to social workers, this kind of disatisfaction is likely to be a problem for schemes that structure and prioritise their work in this way. However, what is perhaps most crucial is that links made with these young people at an early stage, for two whilst in residential care, enabled them to return when they needed help; contact could be restored and further help given.

Short-term/duty access

Three young people received shorter-term post care support from the scheme.

For Cathy, a young woman in a long term foster placement in an outlying town, referral had been made one year before a planned move. Plans for a move to a supported hostel in the town were undermined when her foster parents demanded she should leave early, at a time when she was preparing for her school exams. Her transition to the hostel was therefore accelerated. Having had a sheltered upbringing she was still both immature and lacking in skills and the placement proved a disaster, as she quickly lost control to friends and was evicted. Once she moved into the hostel, a combination of the distance from the scheme allied to the support she had from social worker and hostel staff, led her leaving care worker to negotiate a reduced role. Whilst not offering active support, liaison and consultancy were to continue. Unfortunately this broke down when problems rapidly began to accumulate, the scheme was unaware of what was happening until it was too late to intervene.

Cathy returned to live with her family nearby. The scheme therefore terminated its involvement and support continued from her social worker. The latter offered continuity; negotiating her return, helping to resolve tensions and encouraging her to resume college. By the final interview, wanting more autonomy and growing in confidence and maturity, Cathy had negotiated entry to a supported homeless hostel for young people in the town. She had settled and was continuing at college. Whilst no longer receiving active help from the scheme, they were aware of her circumstances through a link role they maintain with the hostel. Her move had been a shrewd one. Approaching 18 she had not yet been able to apply for permanent accommodation in her own right in this town and the hostel, whilst offering a supportive environment, would attempt to broker this for her.

Whilst this case illustration points to the dangers of accelerated transitions for young people, it also demonstrates the mechanisms through which the scheme feels it has to ration its resource and negotiate its involvement with other professionals. For this to work effectively liaison has to be close and constructive. In this case her leaving care worker felt that the 'lapse' had been untypical:

"*. . . it seemed to be . . . an untypical lapse and hopefully lessons will have been learned, 'cos it seems to be that (she) has paid the price for a lot of departmental and other mismanagement here*".

Our final illustration points to some problems associated with later access for young people where schemes lack informal/social access points and have to rely upon a duty system that, in this authority, is city based. It highlights the difficulties for a young mother, Jenny, living in a town some distance from the city who felt quite unsupported during and after transition.

Living in a stable foster placement, Jenny had been referred to the scheme 18 months before her move to help organise accommodation. Scheme involvement at this point was restricted to reviews and housing liaison. Already a parent at the time of her move, contact increased to organise her leaving care grant and a leaving care worker spent half a day with her discussing the scheme's services. At this point positive about parenthood, well skilled and with support from her foster mother, no further help appeared necessary, although Jenny was welcome to contact the scheme in the future. Shortly afterwards, at 18, her social worker closed her case and the scheme wrote inviting contact. Unfortunately, she misinterpreted the letter, thinking it was the end of all support, failed to respond and a further letter was sent closing her case. Although finding transition hard, and despite running up some debts, she was coping. However, by the final interview Jenny had a second child and was pregnant with a third. Having lost the support of her ex-foster mother she just had her partner to rely on. Despite managing quite heroically, the stresses upon her were immense. They had little money, her council house was poorly heated and damp, she got no break from child care and felt that her identity as a young woman was being subsumed in motherhood (her pregnancies had not been planned). For the first time she was really fearful about how she would manage in the future.

Proud and self-reliant, in spite of these problems, Jenny had not felt able to approach the scheme for help. She had been attempting to negotiate a transfer herself and had been to the duty service at the local social work office for advice about debts. She was very keen to find a play group for her two children, principally to give herself a break but also to help their socialisation. She was disparaging about support she had received from past social workers and, indeed, from the scheme.

"They're useless, and I thought they were meant to help you when you leave care, but they never."

Despite feeling the need for practical help, Jenny's past experience and the stress of 'cold phoning' the duty service were likely to prove to much. She would only do this if she could be sure it would lead to **action** and not just **talking**. The lack of an informal point of contact where young people could drop in without having to present a specific problem makes this step more difficult. Equally it is harder when there is no established relationship with a staff member. Her feelings echo those of the young woman discussed earlier who did not know 'how' or 'who' to ask for help. The logistics of running a centrally co-ordinated service across a shire county also contribute. Given that the duty system is city based, direct access for those in outlying areas is severely curtailed. Although more user friendly alternatives all have time and resource implications, a number of strategies could be considered: low key befriending visits from the scheme might have made it easier to seek help when she needed it, perhaps using volunteer befrienders if the scheme could not provide this directly; more decentralised access points through a duty service, drop-in or groups would make approaching the scheme easier or, finally, the possibility of exploring a partnership with a voluntary agency that could provide some of these direct services on a smaller scale.

Whilst our study can highlight some difficulties associated with access, it cannot point to the scale of these problems. Indeed, as we have suggested, for most young people in our sample access to the direct and indirect services of the scheme was positive. Only five had no contact throughout, although most of our young people who gained later access to the scheme did so through social worker referral. Only two self referred at a later point for help with leaving care grants.

Joint working with social workers

In its relationship with social workers the scheme attempts to establish a structured and negotiated *modus operandi*. It tries to clarify at the outset the nature and limits of its involvement in definite cases. Allocation meetings represent the initial forum for determining whether enquiries from social workers can be met through offering advice and information (either directly or through reviews/planning meetings), through a duty contact or require key worker allocation. There is a clear expectation that where young people have social workers they should retain a lead role in offering direct support; the service offered is specialist and supplementary. For a scheme with limited resources and a commitment to assisting 18–21 year olds and, indeed, to helping young people 'in need' who have not been in care (about 16% of referrals from housing agencies), this expectation seems realistic. It would seem that once work is undertaken, subsequent movement between its 'active' and 'consultancy' roles (i.e. where support is eased back) is usually negotiated. Our data suggests that it rarely happened by default. In these cases liaison usually continues so that support can be picked up again later if necessary.

For those entering the scheme's supported accommodation, as we have seen, definite procedural steps prior to joining lay a firm basis for joint-working. Social workers are clear about what the scheme is offering and the expectations it has of them. Task sharing and role clarity are reinforced through regular planning meetings which are usually chaired by the scheme's team leader. Unfortunately for our sample, joint working arrangements were inhibited by changes of social worker for three of the five young people at this point of transition. These young people were not only having to adjust to major changes in their lives but also to build a relationship with a new social worker. One young woman, after three changes in several months, never had stable social work support again. She relied on the scheme for all her help. The remaining two social workers were very positive about the role the scheme had played in the lives of their young people. They felt it had offered them time to build their skills and confidence, to mature and find more direction to and control over their lives.

As we have indicated, where young people were receiving key worker support from the 'generic' team, responses (from both social workers and young people) were more mixed. All social workers valued the specialist role of the scheme, particularly in relation to the development of and structured access to accommodation and financial resources. The advice and information service, being able to obtain up to date and accurate information, was also universally considered important. Where the team had been able to offer continuity of support through transition this was valued not only by young people but also their social workers. In relation to one young woman who had experienced two social worker changes and a period unallocated, at the final interview, her current social worker summed up the significance of the scheme's role:

> *"She's gone from being in a home to being semi-independent, in a hostel . . . (and has now) become independent, and throughout she's had leaving care team support".*

However a substantial minority felt that the scheme's role was too restricted – emphasising advice, consultancy and the provision of accommodation resources – and failed adequately to share the burden of supporting young people through transition. For them a much more hands on approach was needed. The following comments illustrate this perspective:

> *"I think that their role has been very minimal and I think that because the divisional social worker is involved, and involved quite intensively, then they do tend really to opt out of their responsibility".*

> *"I think they should take a much more forward role".*

One social worker, heavily involved in supporting a young parent struggling in her own flat and in relation to whom there were serious parenting concerns, was not considering referral to the scheme. She felt their support could not be intensive enough for her needs:

> *"The Leaving Care Team are quite rigid in what they do and deal with housing and financial affairs really . . . (Her) housing has been very settled and the financial side*

of things I've been dealing with . . . (They) will only see people . . . once every couple of months."

However realistic this social worker's assumptions may have been, and the implication could be that she was thinking about **transferring** responsibility rather than **joint working**, it points to a prevailing perception amongst some social workers. What seems to be at issue here is that, as a small team operating in a large county authority, the scheme is unable to deliver what hard pressed social workers most need, a pair of hands to take on or take over the time consuming practical tasks of transition. It also suggests that the scheme's wider role in developing policies, co-ordinating services and developing accommodation and financial packages is less visible to social workers faced with competing demands on their time. The expectation that social workers should retain primary responsibility for practical support met with some disapproval. Several mentioned the pressures of child protection work at their offices and pressure from managers to reduce their involvement, to give care leavers a lower priority. Some concerned social workers did struggle with office managers to continue support beyond 18 where young people seemed vulnerable and, with some exceptions, most in this authority received social work help until eighteen. If social workers represent an important source of continuity to young people through a difficult transition to adulthood, perhaps the pressure to reduce involvement would come sooner if the scheme **were** able to play this active role.

CHAPTER 19

LEAVING CARE SCHEMES: THEMES AND ISSUES

This chapter will explore a range of themes and issues that arise from our discussion of leaving care schemes. Our discussion will be structured around three broad areas: issues that relate to the distinctive features of schemes; to access and equal opportunities and to the services schemes offer.

Introduction

Schemes and projects carrying the label 'leaving care' are of recent origin. Maureen Stone, in her 1989 survey of 33 specialist schemes, found that only one was in existence in 1978 and the majority, 82 per cent, started in 1985 or later (Stone 1990). But this new designation does not mark the beginning of leaving care practice any more than say the introduction of 'community homes' by the Children and Young Persons Act 1969 marked the start of residential child care. Schemes, projects and programmes to assist young people leaving care are as old as the child care services themselves, whether they were unrecognised as part of the ordinary socialisation process taking place in foster families or more organised such as 'in service' placements for young women, the 'services' for young men, 'working boys hostels', 'lodgings houses' and designated after-care children's officers, just to mention a few.

In our introductory chapter we have already outlined the background to the 'awakening of leaving care' including the development of specialist schemes. All our schemes were well established before the introduction of the Children Act 1989, in October 1991, but as our research has shown, our four schemes have made a substantial contribution to the implementation of the new duties and wider discretionary 'leaving care' powers contained within the Act in their local areas. Indeed, senior managers and scheme leaders all agreed that the Act has increased the profile and awareness of 'leaving care' within their local authorities and that this has influenced changes in policy and practice. And in one of our four areas, County, the Act is acknowledged as directly contributing to an increase in both revenue and capital resources for care leavers.

To date, our research represents the most detailed investigation of leaving care schemes – taking place during the first three years of the new Children Act – and in this chapter we will be drawing upon our material, as well as completed research and related literature, to explore key themes and issues. These will be considered in three main parts: the distinctive features of schemes; access and equal opportunity issues; and the services schemes provide within the overall context of child care services.

Scheme features

The different geographical and organisational contexts of our four schemes influenced the development of differing approaches to organising and delivering services. Different scheme models have been identified in the literature including by service delivery (Stein 1991, Bonnerjea 1990, Stone 1990), process (Smith 1994) and philosophy (Stein 1991). Our research suggests that although we could classify our four schemes by reference to these different models, any single model classification would by itself be an oversimplification. We have suggested three dimensions as a basis for identifying the distinctive features of schemes: approaches to service delivery; the service provider and the policy role of schemes. We will explore each of these in turn.

Approaches

'Approach' is made up of three related components: perspective; methods of work; and the degree to which scheme services are 'young person demand led' or 'social worker planned and led'. The last of these represents a continuum in that all schemes have a mix of both types of service. These related elements have a significant influence on the culture of a scheme, the way services are structured and the relationship between young people and staff.

All four schemes, to varying degrees, recognised the importance of adopting an holistic approach to supporting young people leaving care. They were aware that an intensive programme of practical life skills training, in itself, would prove inadequate unless young people could gain a sense of emotional security and the skills to develop a range of social supports capable of reinforcing it. Our data strongly reinforces this approach. For a number of our sample with quite well developed practical skills, their ability to deploy them deteriorated when wider life crises created a sense of instability in their lives.

However, for each of our schemes there were discrete differences in the way these common aims were delivered (see Appendix Figure 5). As our research has shown, our schemes struck different balances between 'planned worker led' and 'young person demand led' interventions. An issue for all schemes is the need to balance the time spent responding to the demands made by young people, which can be accentuated where services include open access or drop-in provision, and the need to develop longer term planned work with individuals. In addition, whilst crisis response is inevitably a part of scheme work, it needs to be managed as an overall proportion of worker time if a proactive and planned approach is not to be displaced by one that is primarily reactive.

Differences were most marked between County and District, the former being our largest authority and the latter our smallest (and indeed one of the smallest local authorities in England). County was offering services – including accommodation, financial assistance and advice/support – to the whole local authority and thus, as a scarce resource, felt it needed to prioritise and target its key worker support to those young people in greatest need. Differing levels of service were available to young people. Those entering the scheme's supported accommodation were offered a comprehensive package whereas those in independent accommodation tended to be offered support according to their needs and the other supports available to them. A priority was therefore placed upon the duty system, the cornerstone of its advice and information service. Field social workers were expected to maintain a primary support role and the scheme's direct work was subject to regular reviews and case closure so that their resources could continue to be used to the best effect. With little direct access to the project base for young people, the planning of individual work with young people off site and explicit rationing was made easier. Although all work was negotiated with social workers and young people and, for the latter, could be open ended, the scheme tended to adopt a task oriented approach and the terms of its involvement was structured and primarily worker led. As we have seen, this structured approach enabled the scheme to deliver an effective universal service, despite the size and complexity of the authority. However this model did lead to some social workers and young people feeling less satisfied with the service and also to the scheme having a weaker project identity for young people.

District was also the main provider of leaving care services for its local authority but, in contrast to County, it was able to offer direct services to all care leavers – whose numbers were relatively small. As we have seen, its community based approach included a range of centre based 'open access' services including groups, a daily 'drop in' and other social activities. In addition, structured individual support was available from staff. It offered flexibility and informality and young people were able, within limits, to choose the nature and intensity of their involvement with the scheme. However, as we have seen, the tendency for 'open access' services to be demand led, meant that this scheme introduced some rationing mechanisms in order to protect the proactive planned work being undertaken by staff. Once young people appeared to be coping in the community a negotiated withdrawal of key worker support took place, leaving them free to use the 'open access' services. Also, during the course of our research, the length of the daily drop-in was reduced and a waiting list introduced. The tensions involved in trying to maintain a balance between demand-led and worker-led services are likely to increase as pressures upon the service intensify. Equally, it remains an open question how well this model would translate to a large urban or county authority with far larger numbers of leavers and greater distances to cover. Perhaps schemes might run the risk of being overburdened with crisis work.

The City (vol) scheme was the only one that was not attempting to provide universal coverage across its authority. It was more of a closed scheme, rationed by the number of trainer flat places available and it therefore offered an intensive and comprehensive service to a restricted number of young people. Its therapeutic approach involved structured individual support reinforced by group work activities at the project base. For those using the scheme it therefore had a strong project identity. The scheme gave explicit priority to those undergoing training, and support for young people who had moved on was usually at a less intense level. However, the quality of relationships established usually presented few barriers to a later return for help. Its approach was primarily worker-led but allowed for increasing negotiation as young people appeared able to take greater responsibility for their lives. For those young people able and willing to buy into this complete package, it offered intensive and wide ranging preparatory support. This model may therefore be particularly suited to those from more institutionalised backgrounds and to those who lack the skills and confidence for greater initial independence.

For most of our research, City (ssd) lacked a clear policy, procedural and managerial framework within which the scheme could operate. This, plus the lack of clear rationing procedures at the point of referral and assessment of needs, inhibited the possibilities for planned work, increased the tendency for crisis response work to take a greater proportion of scheme time and made effective liaison and co-ordination with social workers more difficult. Without this framework the balance between direct and indirect developmental services suffered (most notably the development of accommodation resources). The lack of clarity about the services it was to offer resulted in some confusion for leaving care workers, social workers and young people. As we have seen, some of the latter were unaware of the precise role of the scheme. Where young people (especially those in children's homes) were referred early, enabling an informal relationship between leaving care worker, social worker and young person to develop, the scheme appeared to work effectively. The effect of the lack of formal procedures to establish a *modus vivendi* with young people and social workers appeared to be felt most acutely where referrals were made on an emergency basis, where placements had broken down and where, in consequence, an informal approach was less adequate. In consequence, some young people identified closely with the scheme while, for others, the relationship was more distant and less certain.

Recent research from the United States has suggested that services for care leavers have to be both 'categorical' – capable of reaching out to all young people in an authority – and 'intensive' – being able to respond to individual needs (Waldinger and Furman 1993). Our research would suggest that in order to respond to the diverse needs of care leavers, direct services need to be flexible and offer different responses along our continuum to meet differing needs; to find a balance that is appropriate to local conditions, to the aims of the project and to the needs of young people who will be using the scheme.

A highly structured social worker led model may facilitate comprehensiveness, planning and the allocation of scarce resources but, on the other hand, may limit access to help for young people in crisis situations or just when lonely and wanting to drop in for a chat. It may also reduce opportunities for young people to socialise and gain support from other young people. Overly worker led approaches may also reduce the opportunities for young people to gain more control over the way they use services (Frost and Stein 1989) and weaken their identification with the scheme, a factor that may assist longer term 'returners' to obtain help (Dobson 1994).

At the other end of the continuum a pure demand led model will increase demand pressures on scheme time. It may therefore fail to offer intensive support to young people who are experiencing particular difficulties or enable staff to engage in planned longer term work to help with assessed needs. In this context, a greater proportion of scheme work is likely to become crisis based and reactive, thereby inhibiting the comprehensive coverage of the scheme. We have highlighted the distinctive ways in which our schemes were attempting to grapple with these problems and the influence they had upon scheme culture, the shaping of services and the relationship of young people to the schemes.

Service Providers

The nature of the providing agency – including its ethos and its organisational, management and staffing structures – may also give a distinctive flavour to schemes. The services of two of our schemes, District and City (vol), were 'provided' by voluntary agencies in partnership with their local authorities. Our other two schemes were directly managed by social services.

The different cultures between 'voluntary' and 'statutory' leaving care providers have received attention in the literature (Bonnerjea 1990; Stone 1990). Bonnerjea, for example, has discussed the advantages local authorities perceive by entering partnerships with the voluntary sector. This, in summary, includes: increased choice of services; informality, flexibility and specialist expertise; and more empowering less stigmatising relationships with 'older' teenagers. Stone also stresses the key role of the voluntary sector – in terms of independence, advocacy and as a check on social services power over the lives of young people. And more recently voluntary agencies providing leaving care schemes have been characterised as tending to have a young person centred 'open door' approach and local authorities a more controlling and crisis intervention approach (Mitchell 1994).

The picture that is generated from our research is, however, more complex. First, there were distinctive features or differences between both our voluntary providers. As we have seen, these schemes were at different points on our continuum and had slightly differing perspectives that underpinned their working relationships with young people. These differences were also apparent between them and our statutory providers and between the latter themselves. Second, young people and social workers engaged with all these schemes valued their specialist expertise – particularly in relation to accommodation and financial resources. Third, most felt that schemes were able to work in a young person centred way and contrasted this with the family and parental orientation of social workers. Whether statutory or voluntary, scheme staff attempted to advocate for young people's rights and, even in the most structured schemes such as County, work with young people was negotiated. Finally, most young people themselves felt that the quality of their relationship with their key worker was more informal and adult oriented – "she's more like a mate" or "they treat you like an adult" were typical comments. As we have seen, some young people therefore experienced joining a scheme as being akin to a *rite de passage*. Moving on was not necessarily a denial of their past or a rejection of past carers but an opportunity to move forward.

Undoubtedly there are advantages to local authorities in being able to purchase services from voluntary agencies and, for the latter, their greater autonomy may offer more room for manoeuvre. As one of our leaving care workers commented, it may be that the arms length relationship of voluntary agencies may make them better placed to engage young people who are totally disaffected with social services. However, it is perhaps less important whether a scheme is located in the statutory or voluntary sector than it is for it to have a clear sense of direction and an appropriate managerial and resource framework within which to operate.

Policy Role

Two of our schemes, District and County, had a major impact upon leaving care policy within their local areas. District's policy role was derived from its position as a direct 'provider' for all care leavers within the authority. As a team they handled all the leaving care work including the links with key agencies such as housing and social security. Their work and specialist expertise were perceived as very positive by the authority. Managerial arrangements with the authority were simple and effective and clarified through a service agreement between 'purchaser' and 'provider'.

County's policy and development role was derived from its remit to provide a County wide service supported by clear managerial, policy and structural arrangements (see Appendix Figure 2). As we have seen, this scheme had the most wide ranging policy brief and this included developing and coordinating access to accommodation; setting up and administering all leaving care grants; issuing advice to social workers on financial assistance; coordinating services for homeless teenagers (Section 20) and helping to monitor and review leaving care services. The clarity of these structures in a geographically disparate authority was influential in enabling the scheme to deliver its core services effectively.

In contrast, for most of our research, both schemes in the City authority were not part of an agreed local authority policy framework. This meant that City (vol) as a direct 'provider' of services to referred young people from the authority remained completely outside of its policy structure, even at a consultative level. We have also highlighted how the lack of a coherent framework inhibited the development of both direct and indirect services within the City (ssd) scheme. Effectively the work of the two schemes was uncoordinated, there was no official forum for communication and problem sharing and attempts to provide a comprehensive service across the authority were impeded.

However towards the end of our research a new service agreement between the voluntary agency and the local authority was drawn up. In addition, the introduction of formal authority wide policies and procedures and the appointment of a new senior manager with responsibility for leaving care were perceived by both schemes as a positive step. Arrangements are also being made to establish a city wide forum that will bring together all the different agencies involved in leaving care policy.

A number of issues arise from this brief discussion. First, where voluntary agencies enter into partnership with local authorities the service agency agreement needs to provide a framework for joint working. It should clarify the services which the agency is expected to deliver but these should be placed within the context of leaving care services as a whole. In other words, it would be helpful to include arrangements for incorporating the agency into policy and service development. Second, there needs to be a senior manager within social services with responsibility for the provision or purchasing of leaving care services to whom schemes can then relate. Third, none of our schemes or authorities had attempted to involve young people directly in the development of leaving care services or policies, a strategy that could help to ensure their appropriateness. Fourth, the corporate approach that leaving care services require suggests the need for a broad forum incorporating all agencies (statutory and voluntary) that are involved with care leavers. Discussions at this level can raise awareness, resolve problems and feed into the policy process.

Finally, although two of our schemes had a significant role in relation to leaving care policies, all our schemes had difficulty in influencing 'in care' policies and practice – in particular the quality and nature of preparation, the assessment of needs and abilities prior to leaving and, crucially, the timing of leaving care. The expertise that schemes derive from supporting young people in the community suggest that they could make a valuable input to policies in these areas. In this sense 'leaving care' needs to form an integral part of a wider child care strategy in which preparation for adult life and the supports young people will need to sustain it are continuously in mind from the point of entry to care. We will return to the elements of this through care approach in chapter 23.

Access and equal opportunities

At the risk of stating the obvious, it is of fundamental importance to schemes that young people, carers and social workers likely to benefit from their services are offered clear and ready means to access them. When designing a service, consideration needs to be given to the nature of the target group – for example, whether the service is designed to reach all leavers within an authority or a more restricted group – and to the best means of reaching out to them. First, at a formal level, establishing a sound managerial/organisational structure and clear scheme objectives at an early stage will help schemes to provide comprehensive information about services and referral procedures to potential users. Second, schemes also need to consider arrangements for enabling young people to gain informal direct access, both at the point of leaving care and at later stages of their post care careers. Finally, they need to ensure that all young people have an equal opportunity to access services and to consider the particular needs of black young people, young parents, young people with disabilities and others with special support needs. We will look briefly at each of these areas in turn.

For all our schemes, despite an acceptance of self referrals from young people and other sources, the vast majority of formal referrals came from social workers. Two of our schemes (District and County) were well known within their areas. This was a consequence of having clear policy statements, referrer and user information, formal procedures and through having a clear managerial and organisational context to work within. In consequence, as we have seen, all but one young person in District and all bar five in County gained access to the direct or indirect services provided by these schemes at some point.

The difficulties that can arise in these areas are best illustrated in our research by City (ssd). This scheme was operating against a background of organsational change, policy review and confusion and lacked agreed procedures. As a result many young people and social workers in the authority lacked knowledge of the scheme, its services and the help it could offer. Unless young people in this authority were referred to the scheme prior to leaving care, they were very unlikely to gain later access. A majority of the comparison group had never heard of the scheme nor been signposted to it as a potential source of future support.

The lack of an overall policy framework for leaving care services in City also affected the City (vol) scheme. However, given that it was offering a specialist accommodation based service to a limited number of young people and had been in existence for a longer period, problems of formal access were reduced. The introduction of a policy and procedures document towards the end of our research in City authority is already leading to greater awareness. Raising the profile of schemes, establishing clear authority wide procedures for leaving care that include schemes and the production of leaving care guides accessible to young people and social workers are therefore important issues for scheme access. They influence the degree to which **all** care leavers have an opportunity to access services.

On a similar theme, three of our project leaders expressed concern that young people in foster care and their foster carers may be unaware of their schemes, or regard them as an inappropriate resource. Residential care was regarded as being prioritised by three of our schemes in both policy and practice. However, evidence from our survey, our qualitative sample and other completed research (NFCA 1992) indicates that young people leaving foster care have a pattern of accelerated transitions similar to those leaving residential care. It also suggests that only about one third of those leaving foster care have ongoing contact with their carers and that informal support offered by carers continues to go unrecognised. Our schemes were aware of the need to build links with fostering social workers and carers in order to ensure a more universal service. However, links with children's homes by scheme staff enabled more informal contact with young people and led to a greater certainty of referral. For example, invitations to in-care reviews were automatic. Procedures in relation to those in foster care were less certain and dependent on social workers contacting the scheme.

Even if a majority of initial referrals formally derive from social workers, schemes also need to consider creating an environment that encourages direct access to help for young people and minimises the barriers to gaining a service. The discussion of our schemes has raised a number of issues. First, and perhaps most important, is the need to link young people into schemes at an early point before leaving. A number of our sample struggled without support, were unsure 'who' or 'how' to ask for help or what services were available. Early information about schemes and an informal introduction might have helped. In our discussion of County, we have looked at the barriers that young people can face if they need to access formal help through a duty system. In contrast, some young people who disappeared for a time were able to return for help at a later point because they had a relationship with a leaving care worker. They had established trust and the pressures of 'cold calling' were reduced. If young people are likely to require scheme help once they have moved on, our data suggests that links made prior to leaving will prove valuable.

Second, the informal atmosphere of schemes that have an active social centre are helpful here. For example, the 'open access' services provided by District offered young people flexibility in the way they could use the scheme. They could attend groups, pop in to socialise or have immediate access to help through the drop in. The barriers to involvement were minimal and young people did not need to have a specific problem to call in. However, as we have seen, the need to balance these demand-led services with sufficient space for staff to undertake planned proactive work is a potential problem for schemes of this type. For County, the size of the authority and limited direct access made the relationship of young people to the scheme appear more formal and distant. Contact was only available either off-site or through an appointment based duty system at the city centre office. For those living in outlying areas of the county, direct access was therefore curtailed. For schemes of this type, structured and planned work with individuals is facilitated but, for young people, early referral and an established relationship with a keyworker are more crucial for later help.

As regards 'equality of opportunity' all our schemes have formal policy statements derived from their employing authority or voluntary agency and such data is requested as part of our schemes' referral processes. In response to concern about the possible under-representation of black and mixed heritage young people being referred to the scheme, County introduced a separate 'race and ethnic monitoring' form in 1993. Information requested by our schemes provides the potential for systematic equal opportunity service monitoring although there was little evidence that this was regularly available or utilised. All our schemes have some form of anti-discriminatory practice statement and analysis of our qualitative data indicates that our schemes were working with diverse groups of young people. During the period of our research, however, there was a lack of specialist provision, particularly for young people from ethnic minority groups. County scheme's accommodation strategy included project support for black young people, young parents and young people with learning difficulties. City (vol) had run an 'out of centre' community based parents group and, at some stage, District had operated an ante-natal group and an exchange for second hand baby items. However, there appeared little else. It is difficult to assess the impact of 'non provision' on scheme usage but City (vol)'s project leader was in no doubt that their referrals and therefore their work with black young people had increased when they had more black workers. Recent literature has also suggested the importance of black role models, specialist projects and the need to address identity issues before black young people leave care (Francis 1994b). In both County and City links with hostels catering primarily for black young people did provide important additional options.

In addition, there is evidence from our research that the location of some 'move on' accommodation in predominantly white areas and the lack of scheme accessibility for young parents and people with disabilities may be restrictive and thus deter referrals or regular usage of schemes. For example, social workers in City mentioned two young black people who rejected places in trainer flats provided by City (vol) scheme because of its location, preferring to choose hostels in their own part of the city where they had informal supports. Access to the project building in District was an issue for young mothers and those with disabilities and, as we have seen, County's location in a large central social work office meant that there was no informal access for young people. The issues raised here need to be carefully considered and schemes have an important role in assessing the particular needs of these groups of young people and developing services appropriate to them. These may either be provided directly or through linking young people in with existing community provision.

Scheme services

It should be clear from the scheme profiles that each of our schemes, to varying degrees, were providing services at a number of different levels. At the broadest level they had responsibilities associated with developing and coordinating access to leaving care services. In more specific terms this involved: developing resource options and building inter-agency links to facilitate this – for example, accommodation, careers, finances; providing advice, information and consultancy services to young people, social workers and carers both prior to and after leaving care; providing direct support to young people and establishing arrangements for joint working with other professionals. In this section we will explore some of the issues that arise from our research in relation to these areas.

Accommodation Resources

Throughout the 1980's accumulated evidence of the over-representation of care leavers amongst the homeless fuelled concerns about their vulnerability upon leaving care (Strathdee and Johnson 1994; Randall 1987). In part, the rationale for specialist schemes stemmed from a recognition of the need to improve the access of care leavers to forms of accommodation that could improve their life chances. As we have seen, our schemes were making a major contribution to this area of development. The approaches taken by our schemes were subtly different. County, for example, had invested more heavily in a range of directly managed supported accommodation options and had evolved a more specialised staff structure to cope with them. District, on the other hand, had concentrated more of its energy on facilitating access to good quality mainstream housing through its links with housing providers. The more restricted options available to young people using the City (ssd) scheme – where young people often had little choice but to move directly to independence – highlights the importance of this area of development. Might there be an association between the numbers who disappeared from their flats and from the study during our research period and the more restricted choices available to these young people? Looking across the schemes as a whole, initiatives included ensuring access to good quality tenancies through links with statutory and voluntary housing providers and developing a range of supported options – hostels, supported lodgings, trainer flats and, in County, a 'floating support' scheme. A number of issues require further consideration.

First, our study confirms the need for a wide range of accommodation resources to meet the diverse needs and choices of care leavers. However local authorities organise their leaving care services, this represents a time consuming and specialist function that needs to be performed. Requiring an authority wide overview of resources, it is likely to be best met by a centrally organised specialist team.

The advantages that choices offer young people were apparent from our sample. Despite the built in movement that transitional forms of accommodation can imply, as we have seen, many young people found periods of time spent in supported accommodation helpful as they were attempting to find their feet in the adult world. For those with limited abilities, deep seated insecurities or who had missed aspects of preparation in care, the intensive support available in trainer flats, hostels and supported lodgings was particularly valuable. Some felt they would not have survived in their own flats and, indeed, a few were unable to manage when they did move on. For those more able but still wanting a supported environment, the development in County of a 'floating support' scheme offered benefits. Smith (1994) points to some of the advantages of this type of provision over more traditional special needs housing based on the hostel model. It avoids problems of behaviour 'contamination' and built-in movement for young people; there is neither a requirement to share nor move-on blockages since the tenancies are permanent; support can be flexible and needs-led and finally, for the housing provider, it should mean that potentially difficult tenants are only handed back when ready for independent living. Our study did point to some problems where young people were gathered together in hostels and houses that became locally known.

For others in our sample, ready to try their own flats, a supply of good quality permanent tenancies was needed. However, while the development of accommodation options is necessary, it should not be at the expense of policies that recognise the importance of a flexible, needs-led approach to leaving care. The minority of young people in our sample who were able to remain with carers until they felt ready to leave 'home' were, perhaps, the most privileged of all.

Second, our research highlights the importance of ongoing support until young people feel they no longer want or need it or they develop alternative networks. For many of our young people the provision of housing alone would, in itself, have proved insufficient, as many lacked the skills and confidence to manage their homes without support. The 'housing plus support' approach developed by our schemes was also a major factor in increasing tenancy allocations. Housing providers were more likely to take a risk on a young person if support plans were in place and negotiated with them.

However, there were variations in the level of support available to young people. In County, for example, support varied between those in supported accommodation and those in their own tenancies and in City (vol) between those in the trainer flats and those who had moved on. In City (ssd) there was a tendency for planned scheme support to fall away soon after transition. In addition, a number of field social workers, under the pressures of child protection work, also reduced the priority given to young people who had moved on. In some cases, notably in District, they often attempted to pass full responsibility to the scheme. While resources obviously need to be rationed, if young people are to be offered the best chance of a successful transition and, indeed, to minimise later crisis demands on social services, a careful assessment of their skills and social supports needs to be undertaken before support levels are reduced. Part of the ongoing support available to young people needs also to include the provision of respite accommodation for those in crisis. In our study this appeared to be restricted to young parents where there were child care concerns and to those with learning difficulties. However, a number of others also experienced crisis and would have benefited from a period in more sheltered accommodation.

Third, our study points to the importance of formal agreements and joint planning with housing providers. The development and involvement of our schemes in these formal structures combined with more informal networking contributed greatly to the success of our schemes in developing their accommodation resources. During the period of our research this included formal agreements with housing associations and both local and district housing authorities. The extent to which schemes should become direct 'providers' and managers of accommodation is a matter for some debate. On the one hand being a 'provider' solves a resource problem, gives greater control and provides a greater measure of protection for young people and opportunities for risk taking. It offers a chance for more intensive help to be given to those in supported accommodation. On the other, it can involve some duplication of mainstream housing resources and lead to an ambivalent role for scheme staff as both housing manager and support worker. 'Facilitating' the provision of appropriate accommodation by housing agencies may give schemes more freedom to focus on their support role and also enable them to spread their resources more thinly. These are issues that schemes will need to carefully consider when attempting to find a balance appropriate to their local conditions.

Financial assistance

Developing arrangements to meet the financial needs of care leavers was a central part of our schemes' work. As our research has shown our schemes implemented their local authorities' discretionary powers to provide leaving care grants, 'top up' payments and education grants and also advise young people in respect of community care grants, social fund loans, housing benefit and income support (including severe hardship payments, bridging allowances and maternity grants). In addition both our voluntary schemes, District and City (vol), being centre based were able to provide 'hidden' support: a warm place to go, a cup of coffee, an occasional meal, help with transport – which for many young people on limited incomes could be a considerable boost.

Our research does raise a number of issues which require further discussion. First, and consistent with the findings from other studies, there was a significant difference in the maximum leaving care grants available (First Key 1992; Rickford 1992). By July 1994 County's maximum grant was £775 (index linked) and District's £1245 (index linked). There were also differences in the amounts of topping up payments available. In relation to these financial areas, the kinds and amounts of financial help young people can expect to receive will depend on where they happen to be 'looked after' – which raises important issues of 'territorial justice' for care leavers. Given the commitment of our participating authorities to providing financial assistance, it is likely that these variations are in fact much less marked than they are nationally (see, for example, Sone 1994b). Second, because control of topping up payments rested with local social work offices, problems and inconsistencies in relation to discretionary decision making occured. All three authorities had issued guidance to social workers covering assessment of financial needs and, in County, the scheme's policy role included attempts, in conjunction with the Children's Rights office, to steer the principles underpinning financial assistance towards a more rights based approach.

A final, and perhaps more complex area, concerns the division of financial provision, particularly between local authorities (as empowered by the Children Act 1989) and the Department of Social Security. Both our survey and follow up research have shown that local authorities, mainly through our schemes, are increasingly obliged to accept a major responsibility for ensuring that young people who 'cease to be looked after' have a basic minimum income to enable them to manage to live independently (see Chapter 7 – 'incomes'). In all of our local authority areas 'topping up' payments were used to substitute for refused income support claims and, in two, to raise income levels above those of income support and this was stated in formal procedures:

"The benefit system discriminates against single young people in such a way as to prejudice the welfare of those who live independently or semi-independently. It is a commitment of this Department to ensure that young people leaving their care receive

*an adequate income to live on, which is above the current level of income support
allowed to 16 and 17 year olds".*

(DISTRICT'S LOCAL AUTHORITY PROCEDURES, 10.1)

We have pointed to the implications for young people of inconsistent decision
making at the local level (Chapter 7 – 'incomes'). Decisions to accept or reject
income support claims for those under 18 appeared to be based more on the status
of young people living independently (whether they were subject to a care order)
than upon their current needs. In some cases, if social services then funded the
young person, they would have to bear the full cost as housing benefit subsequently
refused claims. Recent evidence points to a continuing deterioration in this situation
and its extention to social fund grants where authorities provide leaving care grants
(Downey 1995). We have also pointed to the need for a corporate strategy at both
national and local level in order to provide consistency and an inter-agency approach
to meeting the financial needs of care leavers. If Section 24 funds are intended to
meet the additional needs that young people have as a result of being in care, then the
need to use these funds to provide basic income support should be avoided. The role
of social security, housing benefit and of educational authorities therefore requires
review. As one of our social workers commented, at a time of financial constraint, the
need to avoid 'buck passing' is paramount.

As our research has indicated our local authorities are doing their best to
financially support our young people but, by definition, they cannot offer a
universalist service – so there will be variations and inconsistencies. Neither are they
empowered to financially provide for all young people who, for whatever reasons,
become estranged from their families – but whose 'objective' needs may be the same
as care leavers. We would argue that there is a strong case for reviewing the
relationship between local authority discretionary empowerments and Department
of Social Security universal entitlements in relation to **all** young people under twenty
one living independently.

Education, Employment and Training

We have already identified the low educational attainment of most of our young
people and explored some of the underlying reasons. Our four schemes were
assisting many young people with few if any qualifications, in a highly competitive
job market, and thus with limited employment opportunities and choices. During
most of our research, work in this area was mainly at an individual level. However
both District and City (vol) were developing more structured arrangements. By the
end of our research this included: careers' officers visiting the schemes on a regular
basis; an employment skills group; education and employment assessment; and more
formal links with colleges, TEC's and employers. There was a recognition by all four
schemes of the importance of developing future initiatives in this area. Smith (1994)
has outlined the positive contribution of an employment worker based in a leaving

care scheme in relation both to a developmental and networking role in the local area and to direct work with young people. She suggests the following principles need to be incorporated in any scheme which aims to work on employment issues with young people:

- "gather detailed information about a young person's achievement and potential:
- carefully assess each young person's capabilities so far as employment is concerned;
- work with each young person in a creative way to increase their 'employability' before taking on the demands of education, training or employment;
- ensure that employment initiatives are flexible;
- look at creative ways of opening up employment opportunities for young people;
- forge links with local community services;
- provide adequate emotional and financial support for young people who take part in education, training or employment;
- raise the awareness of social service departments regarding the needs of young people in the employment field." (Smith 1994 p 87)

We would support these principles but would also wish to stress the importance of the 'in care' experience to education, thus laying the foundations for employability. Overall, education should be given a far higher priority in relation to pre-care, care and post-care careers:

"At the pre-care stage educational links and performance should be a key part of supervision plans, preventative work and any assessment process including the decision as to whether a young person should be 'looked after' by social services".
(STEIN 1994 p 358).

In relation to young peoples' 'in-care' experience we have highlighted the need for a proper balance to be established between the traditional welfare concerns of social work and the prioritisation of educational progress, the latter being, as we have seen, a key determinant of future life chances in the employment field (see chapter 6). Education needs to be a central part of the child care planning and review process. Placement stability represents a pre-requisite for educational development, reinforced by active support from carers and social workers and the maintenance of close school links. Expectations of young people need to be raised and intensive compensatory help made available. This will represent a challenge to the 'non-achieving welfare culture' of some children's homes.

Ideally, the post-care stage should build upon progress already made. However, as we have shown, one half of those leaving care were unemployed and two thirds entered the insecure route (see chapter 7). Along the lines suggested by Smith, active compensatory inputs are needed at this stage to help young people identify their strengths and weaknesses, prepare them for work and training and to assist them with opportunities for a return to learn. Continuing support is essential both to offer encouragement and motivation and to make available financial assistance from Section 24 funds to those entering employment, training and education. A structured and pro-active approach to careers planning needs to be an integral part of a well planned transition from care.

As with housing, however, the degree to which schemes invest in a direct role as 'providers' and managers of careers resources will continue to be the subject of further debate. It can offer more control and help to ensure services are appropriate to the needs of care leavers. However, it also carries a danger of separating these young people from their peers, of maintaining a continuing institutional link and of duplicating services in the mainstream. Networking to promote opportunities is obviously crucial and schemes will need to decide whether 'facilitating' appropriate opportunities/courses in mainstream sectors can adequately meet their needs.

Developing self esteem and social networks

The recognition by our schemes of the inter-dependent nature of adult life meant that enabling young people to develop a positive sense of self and a range of social supports that could sustain it was an important focus of their work. Helping young people to establish and maintain a home, find employment or return to learn can have a positive impact on their perception of themselves. Of equal importance to these young people was the quality of their contact with family members and their need to establish a positive circle of friends.

In chapter 8 we saw that, whilst the level of contact with families was very high, the quality of those relationships was considerably more variable. Even some time after leaving care, many young people who had been rejected or had poor family relationships were still attempting to renegotiate with their families. For some, links with extended family members or older siblings were crucial. For others, more profoundly rejected, limited contact offered a symbolic reassurance; a sense of belonging crucial for self-identity. Parenthood often induced the need for a reappraisal of family relationships and, for some with few links, an investment in partners and their families or other friendships offered compensations. Clearly then, this represents an area in which young people are likely to need continuing support.

In relation to families our schemes were, in broad terms, playing only a minimal role. With limited resources, boundaries needed to be drawn and their focus tended to be on the young person as an individual. Family work was primarily viewed, perhaps rightly, as the province of social workers. Where young people moved into supported accommodation, an expectation of continuing social worker support and formal agreements and arrangements for the regular planning and review of work provided a basis for a clear division of responsibilities. Usually the scheme took on the daily support of the young person and the social worker focused on wider family issues. However, for those in their own accommodation their were gaps. As we have seen, the support role of social workers tended to decline as other statutory requirements took over and fewer than one third were actively engaged on family issues once young people had moved on. Given the continuing need for advice, support and mediation and its importance to success in other areas of young people's lives, joint working arrangements to include family support need to be established. Our findings also suggest that a focus solely on parents is insufficient and that possible links with grandparents, aunts, uncles and siblings could be explored.

In relation to friendship networks our schemes were much more active. Aware both of the need for positive friendships and of the vulnerability of some young people to exploitation by others, they were trying, not always successfully, to help young people establish social contacts and develop the skills to manage relationships appropriately. Many young people were socially isolated and, in relation to our sample, this was especially true of those with learning difficulties and some young single parents. Most young people, managing on very low incomes, lacked the resources to regularly frequent pubs, clubs and discos. The specialist knowledge our schemes had accrued of local youth, leisure and community provision enabled them to help young people find low cost ways of making local contacts. In addition those schemes that offered groups and a social centre were valued by young people living independently. They offered a chance to develop social skills, to socialise and to arrange social activities. This represents an important area of work for schemes as few social workers appeared to have much knowledge of young people's social networks or of the strategies that could be tried to improve them.

Link with prime carers and social workers

We have suggested throughout that perhaps the greatest challenge facing the care system is to find ways to offer young people a compensatory experience that maximises stability and continuity in support and minimises further disruption and discontinuity in their lives. In addition it needs to build in choice for young people and opportunities to participate in their key life decisions. 'Leaving care' is a pivotal moment in their careers and, if continuity is a desirable aim, then the working relationships established between schemes, prime carers (foster and residential) and social workers are of crucial significance. In this context schemes, as a specialist resource, should be able to build upon the practical and social supports available to young people when they move on, including their carers and social workers, and not replace them. Completed research has highlighted the dangers of discontinuity for young people inherent in this tendency (Stein 1990). To achive this, arrangements that facilitate close joint working are required.

Our study, like others, has confirmed that movement and disruption remains a likely feature of young people's care careers (Biehal et al 1992; Rowe et al 1989; DHSS 1985). For some, continuity was further hampered through the nature of moving on. Although some young people felt ready to move, as we have seen, others did so when placements broke down or they were pressured to leave and move into scheme accommodation. Inbuilt expectations of moving on at 16 or 17 also influenced transitions, especially but not exclusively for those in residential care. Our schemes were, therefore, working with the 'realities' of the care system and offering support to a range of young people, only some of whom felt able and willing to move.

In relation to residential care, three of our schemes had historical and formal links with children's homes and assisted with preparation plans; either through an advice and consultancy role at reviews or through direct work with young people. As we have seen, links made with residential and social workers at this stage helped young people to make well planned transitions. However, few residential staff appeared able to offer young people continuity once they had moved on. Our survey also pointed to a low level of follow up support, with fewer than one tenth (7.5%) of young people still in touch with their residential carers 6–9 months after leaving care (Biehal et al 1992). For most young people the onus is on them to return to their former homes if they need support but, given the changing nature of regimes and pressures on staff, the environment is not always welcoming to returners. Continuity for young people requires recognition to be given to an aftercare role for residential staff. Rather than concerned staff visiting in their spare time, as sometimes happens currently, aftercare work needs to be properly recognised, funded and given space on staff rotas. The few young people in our sample who retained links valued them highly, greater continuity was ensured and, through joint working arrangements, the scheme was then able to offer additional specialist services.

We have highlighted similar issues in relation to the informal and unrecongised continuing support provided by foster carers. We have suggested that greater use could be made of their expertise to offer continuing support and of funding to create supported lodgings placements, thereby enabling young people to leave 'home' when they feel ready. Links between our schemes and foster carers were less certain and, at the preparatory stage, more likely to be restricted to advice and consultancy at reviews. During our research none of our schemes had formal links with foster carers or carers' groups and several scheme staff felt that the advice offered was, in some cases, treated with suspicion by carers who perceived a threat to their role and abilities. We have already stressed the need for authorities to develop comprehensive policies and guidance to govern the preparation process (chapter 9), for it not to be left to chance. In addition, schemes should be able to feed into policy development the expertise they gain from supporting young people in the community. There is clearly also an educative role for authorities and schemes to play in convincing carers of the benefits that might accrue to them (and the schemes) from a cooperative consultancy approach – some of our carers had, after all, been largely left to cope alone. Policies designed to promote continuity of care combined with the development of closer working relationships between schemes and prime carers would, in our view, offer young people more choices on leaving care, reduce disruption and discontinuity and lessen the dangers of schemes having to take on a primary care role, for which they are not effectively resourced.

Another important source of continuity for young people during and after transition is the relationship they have with their social worker. For some of our sample this had been built up over several years. The links between our schemes and social workers have been dealt with in some depth in our scheme profiles, but a number of issues require further discussion.

First, a 'good parenting' model of practice would suggest that those who have been involved in parenting young people, such as social workers, should be able to continue supporting them until they feel established in the community. Given that most of our sample moved on before 18 years of age, three quarters were still receiving support from social workers at the first interview. However, by the final interview some 18–24 months later, while two fifths were still in contact the nature and frequency of that contact varied considerably. A minority were still receiving regular planned visits, especially where there were real concerns about their ability to cope but, for the majority, contact depended on young people approaching their worker if they needed help. This tendency for planned support from social workers to fall away soon after legal discharge has also been highlighted elsewhere (Biehal et al 1992; Garnett 1992). In addition, a minority of our sample experienced social worker changes at the point of transition which added considerably to the stress and confusion of moving on. A number of social workers spoke of departmental pressure to reduce their involvement with young people arising from staff shortages and a prioritisation of child protection work. Although some social workers attempted to resist these pressures, where support was reduced further discontinuity was created for young people at a vulnerable period in their lives.

Second, these patterns also had implications for our schemes. We have noted variations between the schemes in their expectations of a continuing social work role. County's rationed approach to the allocation of its resources carried an explicit expectation that social workers would continue to support young people through transition. Negotiations with young people and social workers provided a contractual basis for further work. However, as we have seen, this approach can lead to dissatisfaction from hard pressed social workers wanting schemes to adopt a more hands on approach. By contrast, in District, we noted a tendency for social work support to fall away and responsibility to be placed upon the scheme for primary support. Some young people chose to transfer to the scheme and, while this option should be available to them, this tendency does carry with it an inherent danger of displacing important future sources of support for young people and of breaking links with their pasts.

Finally, clarity is required if joint working arrangements between schemes and social workers are to prove effective. Where young people entered our schemes' supported accommodation, the negotiated process of joining laid a framework for a clear division of responsibilities. Social workers were aware of the services offered by the scheme and the limits of its involvement. Expectations of their continuing role were enshrined in a formal agreement which included arrangements for the regular planning, review and monitoring of joint work. It also provided a basis for social workers to defend their continuing involvement with young people. Perhaps most importantly of all it meant that young people were aware of the support they could expect and from where it would come. To offer this kind of framework, schemes need to have a clear organisational, managerial and policy context within which to work; an awareness of the direction and limitations of their work. We have seen that, in the case of City (ssd), limitations in this context resulted in confusion for some young people and social workers; joint working and communication were made more difficult.

However schemes organise their services it would seem that, at the outset of their involvement with a young person, formal arrangements of this type would facilitate a process of close collaboration. Indeed, in the context of a through care approach aimed at offering young people continuity in support, the involvement of carers and, where appropriate, significant family members would be helpful at the planning stage. Discussions about strategies to support young people could then take place holistically, in the context of all the social supports available to them.

• Summary points •

Our leaving care schemes have all made a significant contribution to assisting their local authorities meet their new duties and powers under the leaving care sections of the Children Act 1989. Our discussion, organised around three broad areas – scheme features, access and equal opportunities and scheme services – has highlighted a number of issues that merit further attention:

Scheme features

- Distinctive differences in the 'approaches' of our schemes have been identified. These centred around differences in perspective, methods of working and around each scheme's search to find an appropriate balance between 'young person demand led' and 'planned worker led' services; between more reactive open access services and the need for planned pro-active work with individuals. Each scheme needs to find a balance on this continuum appropriate to local conditions, the aims of the project and the needs of the young people they are serving.

- Despite a prevailing perception that tends to polarise voluntary and statutory sector provision, our research identified distinctive differences in approach between our voluntary schemes, between our voluntary and statutory schemes and between our statutory schemes. It appears less important whether a scheme is located in the voluntary or statutory sector than it is for it to have a clear sense of direction and a sound managerial and resource framework within which to operate.

- Our schemes also had differing degrees of input in helping to guide the leaving care policies of their authorities. A designated senior manager within social services with responsibility for the provision/purchasing of leaving care services is desirable. Both schemes and young people need to be involved in defining needs and in the development of services. An authority wide forum incorporating all agencies involved with care leavers may be helpful. Finally, leaving care policies need to form part of a wider child care strategy that links prevention, substitute care and accommodation and leaving care; it cannot remain tacked on to the end of the care process.

Access and equal opportunities

- For young people to have an equal chance of accessing scheme services, schemes need a positive profile in their areas, clear policies and referral procedures, a well organised managerial framework and widely circulated referrer/user information.

- Accessible guides and information about services should be made available to young people and other scheme users.

- Formal and informal links with children's homes helped young people to be aware of services. Links with foster care were less certain and more dependent on social workers contacting the scheme. The development of links with foster care requires attention.

- Schemes also need to consider ways of encouraging informal direct access to scheme support for young people. If young people are likely to need scheme help after they move on, early referral and a chance to make links with scheme staff is likely to prove helpful. Schemes that have an active social centre (groups, drop ins and social events) tend to create a stronger project identity and may improve later access for young people.

- All our schemes had 'equal opportunity' and anti-discriminatory policy statements and one had developed ethnic monitoring forms. However, not all scheme buildings were fully accessible and specialist provision to meet the particular needs of black and mixed heritage young people, young parents, young people with learning/physical disabilities and others with special needs should be a focus of attention. There were examples of enterprising practice, including scheme based ante natal groups, young mothers' groups and a scheme managed hostel for young people with learning difficulties.

Scheme services

Our schemes were providing services at a number of different levels: developing resource options based on an inter-agency approach (accommodation, careers, finances); providing advice and information services to young people, social workers and carers; offering direct support to young people and establishing arrangements for joint working with other professionals.

- The importance of developing a flexible range of accommodation options to meet differing needs has been highlighted throughout the book. To achieve this the involvement of schemes in joint planning and formal agreements with housing providers was crucial. Access to housing was facilitated through the continuing support to young people offered by schemes; it encouraged housing agencies to take greater risks. For young people, ongoing support to help them maintain their homes was valued as was the provision of respite accommodation when in crisis. A careful assessment of young people's skills and social supports is required before support is reduced. This did not always happen. The degree to which schemes become direct providers and managers of housing or restrict themselves to a facilitating role will be a matter of continuing debate.

• Our schemes were heavily involved in helping their authorities to discharge their discretionary powers to offer financial assistance to young people. Changes to young people's statutory entitlements have meant that authorities are increasingly obliged to use their discretionary powers to meet basic income needs. Decisions to refuse income support claims, often based on status rather than need, have created inconsistencies for young people. A corporate and inter-agency approach to meeting financial needs is required at both national and local level and the role of social security, housing benefit and educational authorities in relation to care leavers requires review. A review of entitlements to **all** young people under 21 is also required, since often their circumstances are little different to those of young people leaving care.

• The role of our schemes in promoting employment, training and educational opportunities was less well developed. Programmes in this area need to form part of a comprehensive strategy linking pre-care, care and post-care. The profile of education and career planning needs to be raised and made a central part of the child care planning and review cycle. Formal and informal networking to promote opportunities needs to be a core aspect of scheme work.

• Young people are likely to need continuing help to renegotiate relationships with family members. Schemes were not centrally involved in this area. However, joint working arrangements with social workers need to specify how that work will be undertaken. Our schemes were active in helping young people to widen their friendship networks and manage relationships successfully. Schemes with active social centres and group work activities are helpful for young people who are isolated. Knowledge of youth and leisure provision is also important.

Links with prime carers and social workers

If young people are to be offered a 'through care' experience that emphasises stability and continuity in support, then the working relationships established between schemes, prime carers and social workers are of crucial significance. As a specialist resource, schemes need to be able to build on the practical and social supports available to young people, not replace them.

• Although our schemes had assisted with in-care preparation to varying degrees, by the close of the research all felt this should be the province of prime carers. We have identified a need for clear policies and guidance to govern preparation, for it not to be left to chance. Schemes have a role to play in helping to develop a sound framework and in offering consultancy/advice to carers.

- Few residential staff were able to offer continuing support once young people had moved on and homes were not always welcoming to returners. Continuity requires recognition and funding to be given to enable residential staff to contribute to aftercare support. Links between schemes and foster carers seemed uncertain both prior to and after moving on. Continuing support from carers was also often unrecognised.

- Planned support from social workers tended to fall away after yong people left care. Although two fifths were still in touch 18–24 months later, in most cases the onus was on young people to contact if they needed help. If continuity is not offered by carers and social workers, then schemes have to take a primary support role. Replacing previous supports breaks young people's links with their pasts and displaces important future sources of support. Joint working with social workers requires clear procedures that facilitate an effective understanding of their different roles and responsibilities and provide a sound basis for collaboration.

PART 4

The section begins by discussing the ways in which outcomes for care leavers might be assessed and exploring how the nine outcome dimensions constructed for the study were defined. Outcomes for 53 of our sample are charted along the nine outcome dimensions. Finally, an holistic case analysis of outcomes is developed, which aims to assess outcomes in relations to the young people's individual 'starting points'. Comparisons are made between scheme users and a comparison group of young people who did not have scheme keyworkers. Some comparisons are also made with young people in the general population.

CHAPTER 20

ASSESSING OUTCOMES

This chapter discusses the ways in which the outcomes of interventions by leaving care schemes might be assessed. It explains how outcome dimensions were defined in this study and how decisions about comparing and grading outcomes were made.

So far we have charted the experiences of a group of care leavers and have considered the assistance given to them by four leaving care schemes. However, it is also important to look more closely at the connection between the service provided by schemes and the *effects* of receiving that service (or the outcomes) for the young people using them. The assessment of outcomes for young people may give some indication of how successfully the priorities of a scheme are being met in practice and serve as a guide to planning and prioritising work. If we assume that the purpose of leaving care schemes is to improve the well-being of young people leaving care, it is important to assess whether the outcomes they achieve in their work with care leavers meets their own, and the young people's, objectives. Despite the influence of many other factors on outcomes, we must nevertheless assume that the work of leaving care schemes does have an impact on what happens to care leavers. Information about outcomes can help schemes assess which aspects of their work are having a positive influence on young people's lives and how they might improve the service that they offer.

What are outcomes?

Outcomes have been defined as the effects or results of a process (for example, receiving a service) which can be attributed to that process (Knapp 1989). Two main typologies of outcomes have been developed to measure the effectiveness of social care in recent years. The production of welfare approach, which has informed recent work on assessing child care outcomes, suggests that there are two kinds of outcomes:

- *final outcomes* – changes in child welfare defined along the dimensions spanned by society's objectives for child care or child development generally, which are measures of the quality of life

- *intermediate outcomes* – measures of the quality of care, desirable in themselves and for the impact they have on final outcomes (Parker et al 1991; Knapp 1989).

For care leavers, final outcomes might include accommodation, employment, the presence of a network of family and friends, the ability to make and sustain relationships or a reasonable sense of self esteem. Intermediate outcomes might include the process of learning to sustain a tenancy, manage relationships or sustain employment or training. Cheetham et al make a similar distinction between *client-based outcomes*, which measure the effects of a service on service users, and *service-based outcomes*, which are concerned with the process of service delivery and hence the quality of care (Cheetham et al, 1992). Earlier chapters have assessed the *process* of service delivery by the four leaving care schemes. The following chapters consider the outcomes for the young people 18–24 months after they began to receive a service from the schemes. They ask the question: how effective were the schemes in bringing about positive changes in the young people's lives? And how can we measure success in achieving positive outcomes?

The outcome measures developed for this study are dynamic in that they seek to measure changes in young people's well being over time, subsequent to receiving a service from a leaving care scheme. Young people, scheme workers and social workers were interviewed shortly after the young people were assigned key workers at the leaving care schemes and were interviewed again on two subsequent occasions, the last being approximately eighteen months to two years after their first contact. In assessing outcomes, only data from the first and final interviews has been used for the sake of clarity. However, data from the second stage of interviews has been used in this study to give a fuller understanding of the young people's changing experiences and circumstances and of the work of the schemes. The choice of any time period poses problems. Assessing change too early may give insufficient time for the effects of receiving a service from schemes to work through, while too long a follow up period may make it hard to tease out the effects of scheme interventions from the influence of other factors as young people mature.

Outcomes of leaving care

In this study, we have looked at the outcomes for young people receiving a service from four different leaving care schemes. We attempt to tease out how far these outcomes can be attributed to receiving that service. This immediately raises enormous methodological problems. How can the effects of receiving a service from a leaving care scheme be measured when so many other factors may influence the outcomes for any young person? Outcomes for young people will be influenced by the personal histories and experiences they bring to the process of leaving care (their 'starting point'), which will have helped to shape their interpersonal and practical skills, their abilities and motivation. Outcomes will also be influenced by structural factors affecting all young people, such as labour markets, housing markets and social security policy. The intervention of a leaving care scheme is just one factor, although potentially a significant one, which helps to shape the outcomes for any young person.

Figure 20.1 Factors influencing outcomes

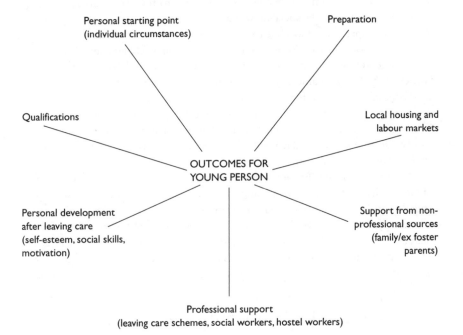

Personal starting point
(individual circumstances)

Preparation

Qualifications

Local housing and
labour markets

OUTCOMES FOR
YOUNG PERSON

Personal development
after leaving care
(self-esteem, social skills,
motivation)

Support from non-
professional sources
(family/ex foster
parents)

Professional support
(leaving care schemes, social workers, hostel workers)

This diagram indicates the complexity of factors which may have an impact on outcomes for any individual young person leaving care. However, leaving care schemes may be able to intervene to modify the effects of at least some of the factors influencing outcomes. As earlier chapters have shown, they may:

- help to develop policies and approaches to the preparation of young people for leaving care, and/or offer assistance with preparation to foster carers and residential workers

- encourage young people to continue their education and gain qualifications, and organise a package of financial and practical support to assist them in doing so

- develop links with local housing agencies, careers offices and employers, and offer individual assistance with finding accommodation and employment

- assist young people in developing practical and social skills, and help them to develop greater confidence and self-esteem

- help young people to develop and sustain social networks in the community (with families, ex-carers and friends).

Leaving care schemes may not be able to modify the effects of *all* these factors for any particular individual. For example, where a family persists in rejecting a young person or past experiences have made a young person adamant that they want no contact with the family, schemes will be obliged to focus on helping the young person develop alternative social networks. Equally, where a young person's personal history and experiences have left them seriously depressed, or with very poor self esteem or serious difficulties in building and sustaining relationships, it is unlikely that the interventions of scheme workers alone will be able to achieve major changes. However, they may be able to mobilise other sources of professional help in these areas. In evaluating the effectiveness of leaving care schemes, the enormous variety of young people's individual circumstances and hence their 'starting points' when they begin to receive a service must be therefore taken into account. This important *caveat* must be borne in mind when developing measures to evaluate the outcomes of interventions by leaving care schemes.

Any evaluation of scheme effectiveness must therefore recognise the full range of factors that may influence outcomes for scheme users and this recognition must underlie the development of any outcome measures. As Parker et al have observed, it is rarely possible to establish causal relationships for a child who is 'looked after' (Parker et al, 1991: 101). In the field of social care, outcomes are rarely clear cut. They depend on *degrees of probability*: how 'successful' is this young person likely to be in this particular set of circumstances? (see Coote, Harrison and Hunter 1994).

Defining outcome dimensions

Earlier research has suggested that a multi-dimensional view of outcomes is needed, to evaluate outcomes of child care along a range of dimensions (Parker et al, 1991: 78). A single outcome measure, such as obtaining accommodation or employment, cannot reflect the complexity of young people's lives and development. Success on one dimension may depend on achievement on another, for example achieving qualifications may have implications for success in the field of employment, or a lack of stable accommodation may make it hard for a young person to settle to work or training.

Following analysis of our survey a range of outcome dimensions was devised. Their development was informed by the youth transitions framework underpinning our approach to the study of young people (outlined in chapter 4) and guided by a review of the child care literature. In particular, drew on the work of Parker et al on assessing outcomes in child care (Parker et al, 1991). It was also informed by the research team's discussions with the local project groups which helped to guide the research in each authority. Outcome dimensions are not 'out there' waiting to be discovered and evaluated, they are socially constructed in this manner. The outcome dimensions devised for this study reflect current debates and priorities in sociology, social policy and social work. As theories and priorities change over time, those outcomes which are considered important to the well-being of young people may also change.

The following outcome dimensions were finally constructed, and will be discussed in more depth in the next chapter.

- Accommodation
- Life skills
- Education
- Career paths
- Social networks
- Relationships
- Identity
- Drug use
- Offending

Developing outcome measures

Some outcomes are easier to measure than others. Outcomes which measure hard facts such as whether young people using a scheme are employed or are pursuing further education or training, or have a reliable source of income or have accommodation may all be easily measured by means of the relatively straightforward collection and aggregation of quantitative data. Measurement of these outcomes, which can give an overall picture of scheme users' material circumstances, may give some indication of the effectiveness of a scheme. Although the impact of structural factors (such as local housing and labour markets) must be borne in mind, this quantitative measure of material outcomes will reflect work a scheme might undertake in developing accommodation options, either within social services or in partnership with other agencies; it will reflect the encouragement and practical and financial assistance given to young people undertaking post-16 education or training; and it will reflect the work of the scheme in ensuring that young people have a reliable source of income. All of this information will be of assistance when developing policies and planning services.

However, broad indicators of material circumstances can paint only a partial picture of a scheme's effectiveness, as these do not take account of the young people's individual circumstances (or 'starting points'). As Cheetham et al have argued, sometimes the presence of a caring person may be seen as more important than ends or outcomes (Cheetham et al, 1992). For young people whose history and experiences have left them ill-equipped to begin the process of moving into the community, a key worker who helps to bale them out as they initially lurch from crisis to crisis (while at the same time working with them in a more pro-active manner to meet their longer term needs for accommodation, income, daytime occupation and social networks) may be providing an invaluable service, but one which is much harder to measure in quantitative terms.

It is important, therefore, to be clear not only about overall service objectives but also about the expectations and goals of the young people and scheme workers. Outcomes must be considered in the light of these objectives. Outcomes therefore need to be assessed in the light of goals agreed (and regularly reviewed) by young people, scheme workers and social workers in each individual case as well as in terms of overall service objectives. Measuring outcomes involves analysis on a case by case basis as well as the collection of broad quantitative indicators of material outcomes.

It is clear from this that a range of outcome measures is needed in order to take account of the variety of young people's starting points as they leave care and of the variety of ways in which scheme workers can assist young people, in addition to giving broad indicators of scheme effectiveness in ensuring that young people have the basic requirements for living in the community: somewhere to live, something to do and an income. Adapting the typology suggested by Cheetham et al (Cheetham et al, 1992) two types of outcome have been assessed:

1. *Material circumstances* – accommodation, employment, further education/training, income.

2. *Quality of life* – self esteem, mental state (whether positive about the future or suffering from depression), social networks/social isolation, interpersonal skills, ability to maintain a tenancy, ability to sustain a job or place at college, self care and practical skills.

Comparing outcomes

The impact of receiving a service from leaving care schemes can only be evaluated if comparisons are made with other young people who have not received this service. As we cannot turn the clock back and start again to see what would have happened if a young person had *not* received a service from a leaving care scheme, outcomes for scheme users must be compared with outcomes for other young people. But who should young people using schemes be compared *with*?

Outcomes for scheme users might be compared with outcomes for other young people leaving care, or with young people in the wider population. As Knapp has pointed out, making comparisons with outcomes for others who are 'looked after' may encourage low aspirations, which may lead to a tendency to lower standards for 'looked after' young people, reinforcing attitudes of 'less eligibility' (Knapp, 1989: 14). He suggests that outcome measures should encourage comparisons with the wider population while being sufficiently sensitive to the needs of the 'looked after' population. This study attempts to address this problem by comparing outcomes for scheme users both with a sample of care leavers who did not have key workers at leaving care schemes and, where data is available, with young people in the wider population.

However, even by making both types of comparisons, we are not necessarily comparing like with like, as the individual circumstances or 'starting points' of young people when they first make contact with a scheme will vary enormously and will have implications for the outcomes that can be achieved. For example, the 'starting point' for a young person who has had a stable career with little or no movement between placements, has maintained good links with their family, has achieved some qualifications at school and has received wide ranging preparation for leaving care will be very different from the starting point for a young person whose care career has been frequently disrupted, whose relationship with their family is poor, who has left school with no qualifications and has received little preparation for leaving care. Taking these two extreme 'ideal types' to represent opposite ends of a continuum, we may find that a scheme needs to do very little in order to achieve very positive outcomes for the former, and may do a great deal of highly skilled work with the latter yet only succeed in achieving modest outcomes.

While the sample of scheme users and the comparison sample of care leavers not using schemes were stratified by gender, last placement and time 'looked after', this could offer only the broadest grounds for comparison. In addition, last placement was not a very precise guide to matching as many of the young people had experienced both residential and foster placements. Given the complex, multi-faceted nature of individual starting points it proved impossible to match precisely like with like across the group of scheme users and the comparison group before interviews began. Sample size is also a factor here. Matching two groups by care history, movement in care, patterns of family practical support, last placement, time in care, gender and ethnic origin would require a sample so large as to preclude the possibility of in-depth qualitative analysis. We have therefore sought to address this issue of linking 'starting points', interventions and outcomes by developing a holistic case analysis (see chapter 22).

A further obstacle to making precise comparisons is the fact that the existence of a leaving care scheme in a particular local authority could produce 'knock on' effects for other care leavers not using the scheme. For example, in working in partnership with housing agencies to develop options for care leavers, leaving care schemes may have an impact on the accommodation resources available to *all* care leavers and hence may influence the outcomes even for those not using the scheme. Similarly, a scheme's contribution to developing policy on leaving care in an authority may have implications for young people not using schemes as well as for those who do.

Finally, as the research progressed more and more young people in County and District moved from the comparison group into the participating group of scheme users as they began using the schemes and acquired key workers (heedless of the methodological problems they were creating for this study!). The numbers in the comparison group therefore shrank considerably in the course of the research.[1]

---

1. In County and District there were only six young people out of the whole sample who failed to gain access to scheme services in some capacity, although this did not include keyworker support for all (n=74). In City the division between those using and not using the scheme remained more rigid.

Also, some young people in the comparison group had a one-off or brief contact with a scheme at some stage, but were not allocated a key worker. For the purpose of this analysis, we have included all those who had key workers at leaving care schemes at any stage in the group of scheme users and those who had no contact with schemes or only a one-off contact in the comparison group.

Grading outcomes

Child care services have tended to concentrate their efforts on avoiding negative outcomes (for example, truancy) with less attention to positive issues (for example, gaining qualifications), and this has kept expectations low (Knapp, 1989: 20). The outcome measures in this study aimed to focus on measuring positive outcomes. In order to do so, clear criteria for achievement along each outcome dimension had to be specified. Of course, there is no universally accepted definition of 'good' outcomes along any of the dimensions studied, although there may be little disagreement in areas such as edducation or employment where positive outcomes are more clear cut. In most of the outcome areas, though, views about what constitutes 'good' or 'poor' outcomes depend on the values, expectations and aspirations of those who define them, and the views of care leavers, social workers, scheme workers, parents or researchers may differ. As there is no possibility of finding a value-free resolution to this methodological problem, the research team began by devising explicit criteria for the assessment of success. A schema for grading outcomes as 'good', 'fair', or 'poor' was drawn up for each of the outcome dimensions. This schema was informed by a review of the relevant literature for each outcome dimension and, where possible, by contextual information about young people in the general population (for example, in the fields of housing, education and employment).[2]

The research team then discussed the grading scheme with the project groups in the local authorities studied (which included care leavers, scheme workers, social workers, foster carers, managers and housing and education professionals) and a final schema for grading outcomes was developed. Ultimately, decisions about grading each outcome for each individual were taken by the research team as they analysed the interviews with the young people, scheme workers and social workers involved in each case. Grading was guided by the schema outlined above as the participants' accounts of their expectations and objectives, their experiences and interventions were analysed. Grading outcomes was therefore a complex evaluative process which was informed by the values of all involved in the research but was ultimately determined by the research team's assessment of outcomes for each young person as they analysed the qualitative data.

---

2. The literature reviewed for the various outcome dimensions is referred to in the appropriate chapters in Part 2.

It is important to remember that although outcomes in this study have been graded for the purpose of evaluation, according to the explicit criteria that were devised, most outcomes are difficult to grade precisely in terms of success or failure. As Parker et al have pointed out, outcomes are usually gradations along a continuum between success and failure, and failure in one area may be offset by success in another (Parker et al, 1991: 33). Equally, negative outcomes in one area may generate negative outcomes in another, for example a lack of family support or the loss of a job may make it hard for a young person to sustain a tenancy. It can also be difficult to arrive at an overall evaluation of the outcomes for a young person. Although for some young people most outcomes were unequivocally good or unquivocally poor, for many outcomes were good in some areas but poor in others.

If we return to the diagram at the beginning of this chapter, which charts the variety of factors which play a part in determining the outcomes for a young person leaving care, it is apparent that outcomes are the result of the *interaction* between these factors. There is an interplay between a young person's abilities and motivation, their self concept and sense of self esteem on the one hand, and factors in their environment, including their social networks, their access to accommodation, their financial circumstances and the support available to them, on the other. The implication of this interactionist perspective is that the interventions of professionals such as social workers or leaving care workers may give young people opportunities to develop their competence (their repertoire of skills and abilities) in dealing with their environment (see Parker et al, 1991: 59). In addition, they may intervene directly in the young people's environment to improve accommodation, training or employment opportunities for all care leavers through inter-agency work to develop housing or employment initiatives. Measuring outcomes for the young people provides a means of assessing the success of these interventions.

• Summary Points •

Outcomes for care leavers are influenced, in part, by their 'starting points' (their personal histories and experiences), which will have helped to shape their interpersonal and practical skills, their abilities and motivation. They are also influenced by structural factors affecting all young people, such as labour markets, local housing markets and social security policy. Leaving care scheme intervention is just one factor which helps to shape outcomes.

This study has constructed nine outcome dimensions as a framework for assessing outcomes for care leavers: accommodation, life skills, education, career paths, social networks, relationships, identity, drug/alcohol use and offending.

Outcomes for scheme users were compared with outcomes for a comparison group of care leavers who did not have keyworkers at the schemes and, in some instances, with data on the wider population of young people.

Decisions about grading outcomes were taken in consultation with project groups in the three local authorities and were underpinned by a review of the relevant literature for each outcome area.

CHAPTER 21

COMPARING OUTCOMES

This chapter discusses the outcomes for care leavers 18–24 months after leaving care. Outcomes are charted along the separate outcome dimensions identified in the previous chapter and comparisons are made between the group using leaving care schemes and the comparison group who did not have keyworkers at the schemes.

So far, we have explained how the different outcome dimensions were devised and how a schema for grading outcomes was developed. Using this schema, an assessment of outcomes for the young people along each outcome dimension was undertaken. This was based on a detailed analysis of interviews carried out on three occasions with the young people, their scheme workers and social workers, during a period of 18–24 months after the young people left care.[1] Some outcome areas, such as identity, relationships and drug/alcohol use were particularly difficult to assess and these findings must be seen as broadly indicative rather than precise.

By the time of our final interview 18–24 months after the young people left care, we were able to contact 53 of the original sample. Of these, 30 had a keyworker at a leaving care scheme, or had had a keyworker at some stage, and are referred to as the participating group. Another 23 had never had a keyworker, although a few had had a one off contact with a scheme at some stage. We refer to these young people as the comparison group. The following discussion of outcomes focuses on this group of 53 young people.

Although they did not have keyworkers at leaving care schemes, many of the comparison group did have some professional support. 78% had social workers in the early months after leaving care and 39% still had social workers 18–24 months later. The pattern was similar for scheme users, of whom 73% had social workers at

---

Table 21.1 Final sample (n=53)

	Participating group	Comparison group
City (statutory)	2	
City (voluntary)	3	11
County	16	8
District	9	4
Total	30	23

the beginning of the study and 43% had social workers at the end. Just under a third of the comparison group continued to see their former foster parents throughout the 18–24 months after they left care, a pattern similar to that for the scheme users, of whom a third continued to see former foster parents throughout this period.

Those in the comparison group were much more likely to have a positive, supportive relationship with a parent, a member of their extended family or with former foster carers. Nearly 70% of the comparison group could rely on some non-professional support of this kind, compared to only 43% of scheme users. In City, none of the participating group could rely on family members or foster carers for support in the early months after leaving care, although one of them did have a reconciliation with her mother within a year. In addition, the young people using schemes were far more likely to have experienced rejection by parents or long term foster carers. Nearly half (13) of the scheme users had experienced rejection by their families or substitute families, compared to only an eighth (3) of the comparison group.[2] The leaving care schemes were also more likely to be working with those who left care under the age of 18. 60% of those who were 16 and 63% of those who were 17 when they left care were in the participating group. In these respects, the participating group was significantly more disadvantaged than the comparison group. It is important to bear this in mind when comparing outcomes for scheme users with outcomes for those in the comparison group.

Accommodation

Two types of housing outcomes were assessed. First, the type of accommodation obtained by the young person and second, the young person's ability to sustain a

---

2. If we consider the initial sample of 74 young people, the pattern is similar. Nearly 43% (18) of the participating group had experienced rejection, compared to only 12.5% (4) of the comparison group. In City, nearly two thirds (10) of the young people using schemes had experienced rejection.

tenancy. The first outcome may give some indication of the work undertaken by schemes in helping individual young people find accommodation or in developing accommodation options for all care leavers, perhaps in partnership with other agencies. The second outcome may reflect the support given to young people with maintaining a tenancy. This might include direct help with budgeting, social skills (dealing with neighbours or friends), negotiating skills (dealing with landlords or benefit agencies) and practical domestic skills. It might also involve advocacy with housing providers and benefit agencies on the young person's behalf.

Grading the type of accommodation obtained was not always straightforward. For example, some private bedsits were of a high standard and offered reasonable transitional accommodation that the young person was satisfied with, whereas other bedsits were viewed as unsatisfactory by the young people. Similarly, some young people made a positive choice to live with relatives, whereas others were unhappy staying with relatives and had moved there only because they had nowhere else to stay. Grading housing outcomes was therefore based on an assessment of both the nature of the accommodation and the young peoples' and their workers' views as to its acceptability for their current needs.

a) Housing outcomes

Good Permanent tenancy; supported accommodation; other transitional accommodation considered acceptable by the young person (e.g. some bedsits); staying with relatives by choice.

Poor Homeless; insecure accommodation; bed and breakfast hotel; transitional accommodation unacceptable to the young person (e.g. some bedsits, homeless hostels); staying with friends; staying with relatives in emergencies solely due to lack of alternatives.

b) Sustaining a tenancy/supported accommodation

Good Young person coping (e.g. with neighbours and budgeting; or maintaining good relations with landlords/providers of supported accommodation and other residents)

Poor Young person has difficulty in sustaining tenancy (problems with budgeting; problems with neighbours, with landlords/providers of supported accommodation or with other residents; losing control of accommodation to other young people)

a) Housing outcomes

During the period of 18–24 months after the young people began using schemes there was an increase in the proportion of those whose accommodation was assessed as good. There was little difference in the quality of the accommodation for those in the participating and the comparison groups.

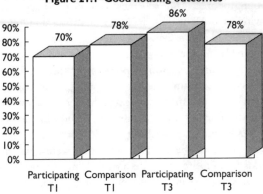

Figure 21.1 Good housing outcomes

There was an increase in the number of young people in good accommodation among those who had keyworkers at schemes during the first 18–24 months after leaving care, indicating that schemes were successful in helping young people find accommodation. Since improving access to accommodation is a key objective for schemes, the comparatively better outcomes for scheme users suggests that schemes were generally successful in this area of their work.

This picture of the increase in numbers in good accommodation must be seen in the context of the number of moves that many of the scheme users had made since first leaving care. As we saw in chapter 5, leaving care teams assisted the majority of those who had very unsettled early housing careers to find more acceptable or stable accommodation. Overall, over half (17) of those in the participating group at the end of the study had made three or more moves and a third (10) had made five or more moves since leaving care. None of the latter group had been able to rely on sustained family support, although some were in contact with their families and, for a few, family relationships had improved by the time they were last interviewed. These young people had to rely on leaving care schemes for support with establishing themselves in accommodation that other young people may receive from their families. Leaving care teams were therefore working with those young people who had the most unstable early housing careers, either because they initially left care in a crisis situation, lacked family support, moved initially to unstable accommodation with relatives or friends or because they experienced crises in their lives after leaving care. Schemes were able to assist them in dealing with this difficult period of transition and help the majority to find good accommodation within two years of leaving care.

Some of these young people were likely to move on again and require further assistance with finding accommodation, as nearly a quarter were staying in hostels or lodgings and a tenth were staying with friends at this stage. In some cases young people who had been unable to sustain tenancies of their own had moved back into supported accommodation for a while to prepare them for another attempt at independent living.

Only four young people using schemes were in poor accommodation 18–24 months after leaving care. All of these had poor networks and low self esteem, and most had been rejected by a parent or foster carer. Three had left better accommodation in order to flee violence, and all four had difficulty in sustaining a tenancy. Two were also suffering from depression. It appeared that all four would continue to need assistance from schemes for some time to come.

For both scheme users and those not using schemes, there was little difference in the proportion of those living in local authority or housing association tenancies 18–24 months after leaving care – about half in both cases. However, the early housing careers of those in the comparison group were generally more settled. Nearly half had made no more than one move during this period and a third had made no moves at all, although there were four (all from City) who had very unsettled early housing careers and had experienced numerous difficulties. Of the eight young people in the comparison group who still had social workers at this point, six had been assisted by their social workers who had discussed accommodation options with them or helped them with housing applications. The other two were living in settled situations, one with his mother and one with his long term foster carers. This highlights the importance of schemes undertaking a developmental role in the area of housing.

The proportion of those in the comparison group who were in good accommodation was high. It should be borne in mind, however, that some young people in the comparison group may have benefited from indirect development work on accommodation for all care leavers undertaken by the District and County schemes. In County all the young people in the comparison group and in District three quarters of those in the comparison group moved to good accommodation when they first left care, compared to just under two thirds in City where no such development work had been carried out at the time.

b) Sustaining a tenancy

The ability to sustain a tenancy was broadly similar between the participating and comparison groups.

Both groups showed a slight overall improvement within two years of leaving care. One element of success in this area involved care leavers' ability to control the use others made of their accommodation and prevent it being taken over by a stream of other young people dropping in or staying overnight, causing problems with neighbours and landlords and making it difficult for the young person to focus on education, work or training. There appeared to be no association between stability while 'looked after' and the ability to sustain a tenancy. Similarly, whether a young person's last placement was in foster or residential care appeared to make no difference to their success in maintaining a tenancy.

Gender did make a significant difference, however, as at all stages young women were twice as likely to be good at sustaining a tenancy than young men. A much greater proportion of young women than young men displayed an ability to budget and to maintain reasonable relationships with landlords, neighbours or other

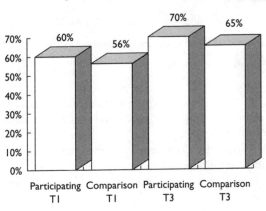

Figure 21.2 Sustaining a tenancy

residents. This raises the question of how far preparation for leaving care addresses gender-related differences in expectations, motivation and behaviour. Leaving care workers were generally well aware of the particular difficulties experienced by young men in sustaining accommodation.

Life skills

Life skills comprised budgeting skills, negotiating skills and practical skills, which included self-care skills and domestic skills such as cooking, laundry and cleaning. For the purpose of discussing outcomes, relationship skills are discussed separately (see below). An attempt was initially made to include an assessment of whether the young person had received adequate sex education and had adequate knowledge of contraception, HIV/Aids and safe sex. As little time could be given to this within interviews, it was not possible to overcome the problems inherent in self-reporting in this area, generated by embarrassment or by young people's need to portray themselves as knowledgeable. As a result, this important area had to be dropped from the study as an outcome measure.

a) Practical skills and b) budgeting skills

Good Consensus that most skills are good (young person does not need consistent help)

Fair Consensus that young person is just managing but needs support

Poor Young person lacks ability in budgeting or in all practical skills

c) **Negotiating skills**

Good Manages most encounters with officials/landlords/employers adequately

Fair Manages some of these encounters adequately

Poor Difficulty with these encounters

There was little difference in ability in practical self care and domestic skills between the scheme users and the comparison group, and only a slight improvement by the end of the study for either group. In the comparison group some improved their practical skills but some also deteriorated. On the other hand, in the participating group some with poor skills moved up into the 'fair' category, some with fair skills moved up into the 'good' category and none deteriorated, which may be due to scheme support.[3]

Figure 21.3 Practical skills

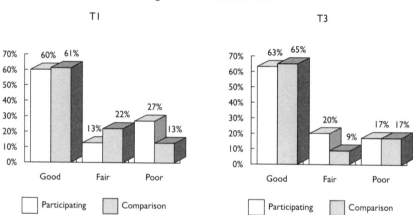

As for budgeting, less than half had good skills in the early months after leaving care in both groups, but the level of skills in the participating group was particularly poor. Within two years of leaving care, while both groups showed some improvement the group of scheme users showed a greater improvement in budgeting skills.

All care leavers may improve their budgeting and practical skills with time, as they have more practice once they leave care, but the fact that there was a greater improvement in both these skills for the group of scheme users suggests that schemes are having an impact in these areas.

---

3. Where percentages do not total 100% this is due to difficulty in making an assessment on the basis of the information available in certain cases.

Figure 21.4 Budgeting skills

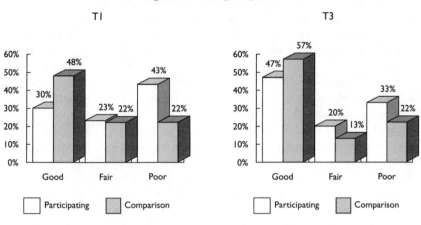

In the early months after leaving care, the comparison group were more likely to have good negotiating skills, but some had been unable to maintain these skills during a period of 18–24 months after leaving care. For the group of scheme users, the level of skills on first leaving care was lower, but none appeared to deteriorate. Their contact with leaving care schemes may have assisted them in maintaining their negotiating skills, if not in improving them.

Figure 21.5 Negotiating skills

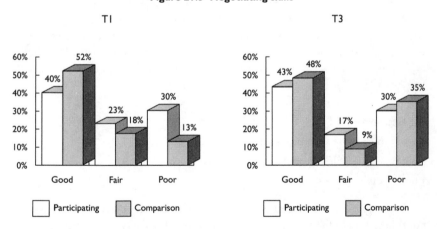

Most of the young people using schemes had some help with life skills, in either a group or an individual setting. Those young people who moved into staffed or dispersed hostels organised by the schemes all received help with these skills and many of the young people were very appreciative of this help.

The day to day support from schemes in dealing with budgeting, domestic tasks and self care may have been important in helping some of these young people maintain their skills they had learned. However, some needed more than keyworker support in order to maintain their practical skills. Those who moved into supported lodgings or hostels were more likely to receive intensive day to day support and it may be that for young people like these, skills learned are only effectively put into practice when they have a high degree of continuing and intensive support.

Last placement when 'looked after' made little difference to young people's abilities, but leaving care at an early age was significant. Of those who left at 16, only 46% had good practical skills within two years of leaving care, compared to 72% of those who left at 17 and 66% of those who left at 18. It appears that those leaving care younger found it harder to care for themselves even 18–24 months after they had moved on. Most significant of all was gender, as young women were twice as likely to possess good practical skills as young men, at all stages after leaving care. Similarly, on leaving care young women were twice as likely to have good negotiating skills as young men, but within two years the difference was much smaller as many young men improved while the negotiating skills of a few young women deteriorated. Stereotyped gender roles may play a part in determining both the motivation and expectations of young men and the nature of the preparation they receive before leaving care.

Education

Two aspects to educational success were considered. First, a simple measure of attainment was adopted from the schema used in Social Trends, as it was felt that this would simplify the process of making comparisons with the wider population of young people. In deciding how to grade attainment, both the levels of attainment in the general population and generally low levels of qualifications attained by 'looked after' young people were taken into account (Aldgate et al, 1993; Heath et al, 1989; Jackson 1988/89). With these considerations in mind, attainment was graded as follows:

a) Attainment

Good 5 or more GCSE's at grades A–C

Fair 1–4 GCSE's at grades A–C

Poor Low grades only/none

In recognition of the fact that attainment for 'looked after' young people is often poor, a measure of the progress they had made after leaving care was included as this might reflect encouragement and assistance given to them in pursuing their education. Progress was assessed qualitatively from the interviews with young people, scheme workers and social workers.

b) Educational progress since leaving care

Good Attendance at school/college (even if no qualifications obtained). Young person or professional perceives he/she has made progress in education.

Poor Young person attending school or college unable to sustain attendance. Young person or professional perceives that no progress has been made.

Educational attainment at the point of leaving care was poor for most of the young people in both groups. Both groups fared very much worse than young people in the general population, 54% of our initial sample had no qualifications whereas in 1990/91 only 8% of males and 6% of females had no graded results at GCSE (Social Trends 1994, Table 3.19). As already noted in chapter 6, school attainment tables for 1992 show that, of those 15–17 year olds enrolled that year, 38% obtained five or more GCSE passes at grades A–C, compared to only 7% in our sample (Department for Education, 1992).

As we have explained earlier in our discussion of schooling, a high level of disruption and movement in care had damaging implications for educational progress and attainment. Gender was another factor which had a significant impact on attainment, as the young women were more successful than young men in our study. Young women were three times more likely than young men to leave school with 1–4 GCSE's at grades A–C and 83% of the young men had no qualifications compared to 60% of the young women. There was very little improvement in patterns of attainment for either group by the end of the study, as very few continued their education after leaving care and, for those who did, the follow up period may have been too short for them to have obtained new qualifications. Only five young people gained further qualifications during the course of the research and of these, four were at a low level (GNVQ level 1).

A consideration of educational progress may offer more insights into the work of schemes in supporting young people in continuing their education. Only eight of the young people remaining in the sample by the end of the study had continued their education after leaving care. Five of these had keyworkers at schemes at some stage and three were in the comparison group. Across the whole group of 53 young people, educational progress while 'looked after' had been significantly better for young people whose last placement had been in foster care, who were three times as likely to have made progress as those whose last placement was in residential care. One and a half to two years after leaving care there was still some evidence that those from foster care were more likely to make good educational progress, as six of the eight young people continuing their education had this background. However, it must be noted that for at least one of the two young women who had left residential care, the new stability and encouragement she had experienced in her children's home had compensated for her poor edudcational progress prior to entering substitute care.

For all the young people a comprehensive approach to support was important, as it was difficult for young people to embark on or sustain their studies if their accommodation and financial circumstances were causing serious problems. Encouragement to continue their education from social workers, former carers and family members was also important in helping young people sustain their motivation.

Career paths

Analysis of the ESRC study of 5000 young people revealed that the three principal career paths of 16–19 year olds in the late 1980's were the academic route, the work route and the insecure route. We have therefore graded employment outcomes for young people on the first two routes as good and outcomes for those on the insecure route as poor (Roberts, 1993). Young women who were full time parents were not included in these gradings.

Good   Academic route (school; further or higher education)
            Work route (stable youth training; full time employment)

Poor   Insecure route (unemployment; unstable youth training; casual work)

Young people using the schemes were more likely to have embarked on insecure career paths when they first left care than those in the comparison group. Two thirds were either unemployed, dropping in and out of youth training or doing occasional casual work, whereas over half of those in the comparison group were on the work or academic routes at this stage.

Figure 21.6 Career paths (n=53)

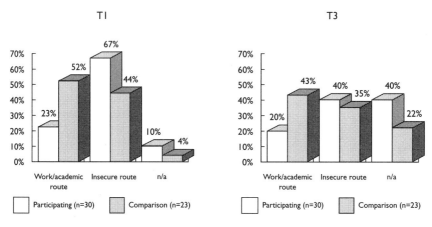

Across both groups, 52% were unemployed in the early months after leaving care.[4] These outcomes were significantly worse than those for the general population of 16–19 year olds, where in 1993 22% of 16–19 year old males and 16% of 16–19 year old females were unemployed (Social Trends 1994 Table 4.20).

Those who had made no moves during their care careers were more than twice as likely to be on the secure route at this stage as those who had made four or more

---

4.   In the initial sample of 74 young people, 50% were unemployed at this stage.

moves during their time in substitute care or accommodation. Similarly, those whose last placement had been in foster care were more than twice as likely to be on the secure route at this stage as those whose last placement had been in residential care, although within two years of leaving care there was no longer a significant difference in the career paths of these two groups.

Eighteen months to two years after leaving care, more young people in both groups had slipped to the insecure route, but a greater proportion of those in the comparison group had slipped from the secure route. All bar one of those on the insecure route at this stage were unemployed.

The most noticeable change was the sizeable increase in the proportion of young people who were no longer on either career path. In every case, this was because they now had full time parental responsibilities. All of these full time parents had previously been on the insecure route. Only nine of the young people using schemes were on the secure career route at any stage: seven of them were at college, two had stable attendance on youth training courses and none were in employment.

Where assistance with education or employment formed part of a comprehensive package of support, leaving care schemes appear to have been more successful in helping young people. However, the outcomes for young people in this area were poor for all the young people and generally worse for those using schemes than for those in the comparison group. This may be due in part to the young people's prior education attainment, to their lack of confidence or motivation, to other difficulties in their lives which made it hard for them to focus on career options or to the limited opportunities available to young people in the labour market. Nevertheless, there is clearly scope for schemes to develop initiatives to assist young people in establishing themselves on secure career paths.

Social networks, relationships and identity

The quality of social networks and the ability to make and sustain relationships are often closely inter-related. In addition, young people's self concept and self esteem may have been determined to some extent by the quality of their social networks and might be expected to have some impact on the nature of their relationship skills. It would be somewhat artificial to discuss these three aspects to young people's social and emotional lives in isolation from one another, so the following discussion seeks to evaluate outcomes in all three areas.

Social networks

Decisions about whether a young person had supportive social networks were based on the perspectives of young people and their scheme workers or social workers. Where their views differed, an assessment was made as to the nature of the young person's social networks, based on both the young people's and their workers' accounts of the nature and quality of their contact with families and friends. For example, earlier chapters have shown how some of the young people who had suffered parental rejection clung to fantasies of being accepted within their families although in effect parents continued to show little interest in them. In these circumstances, if a young person described his/her family as supportive but his/her account of the nature, frequency and quality of family contact suggested the opposite, and this lack of family support was confirmed by the social worker or scheme worker, a grading of 'poor' would be given. Both positive family relationships *and* a network of some friends were seen as a requirement for 'good' social networks.

Good Family (and/or ex-foster carers) perceived by young person and/or worker as supportive (offering emotional and/or practical support) AND has a network of a few friends

Fair Family (or ex-foster carers) perceived as supportive OR has a network of a few friends

Poor Young person feels (or is perceived by workers to be) lonely or isolated

The young people using schemes were less likely to have good social networks and more likely to have poor networks than those in the comparison group, although the proportions with fair networks was similar.

Over one quarter of the young people that leaving care schemes were working with had no close relationships with any family members (or former foster carers) or other young people, and two fifths either had no close relationships with their families *or* lacked a network of friends. Many were therefore socially isolated and entirely dependent on professionals for support. The picture for those in the comparison group was slightly better, but nevertheless less than half of these young people could be said to have good social networks and nearly a fifth lacked support from any non-professional sources.

Figure 21.7 Social networks (n=53)

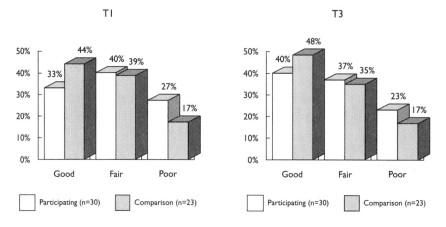

Within two years of leaving care the difference between the scheme users and the comparison groups was slightly smaller and there was a slight increase in the proportion of young people with good social networks.

There was not a straightforward increase in the numbers with good networks, however. Overall networks improved for eleven young people but diminished for nine others. Among the scheme users there was a positive change in the social networks of seven young people, but in only one case could this be directly attributed to the work of the scheme. In one other case a scheme worker was trying to help a lonely and shy man extend his social network by introducing him to clubs, while two of the young women were receiving help from their social workers in maintaining contact with their families. Scheme workers focused more on helping some of the young people to widen their friendship networks, but in some cases they also discussed strategies for dealing with family relationships. As we saw in chapter 8, there was an improvement in the quality of family relationships for some, as the proportion of those with positive family relationships rose from less than a third to a half during the course of the study.

Relationships

This area was also based entirely upon the perceptions of young people and their scheme workers and/or social workers and outcomes were graded according to the degree of ease or difficulty young people had in building and sustaining relationships. The aim was to assess the young people's ability to develop and maintain emotional ties. Again, in some cases young people's discussion of their experiences and relationships did not always include a clear personal evaluation of their relationship skills, but analysis of their accounts could give a broad indication of their abilities in this area, which was then cross-checked against the accounts given by their workers.

Good Reasonably confident in making and sustaining relationships

Poor Difficulty in building and sustaining relationships (indicators may be isolation; repeatedly disrupted relationships; poor social skills)

Overall, eleven young people improved their skills in building and maintaining relationships while for seven others these skills deteriorated. In only one case, however, was there evidence that an improvement in ability to manage relationships was associated with intervention by a leaving care scheme. However, scheme workers at all four schemes did try to help some of the young people improve their ability to develop relationships with others, encouraging some to become more assertive in dealing with other young people or their families, or in negotiating with their families to avoid a breakdown in relationships or in dealing with conflict.

For almost all of these eleven young people there was an associated improvement in social networks. Across the sample as a whole, all of those with good networks had good relationship skills, and most of those with good relationship skills had good networks. This was not surprising, as those with positive family relationships were more likely to have gained experience in sustaining relationships with others.

Identity

A wide ranging study of this kind clearly could not include a battery of psychometric tests to assess self concept and self esteem. The aim was to evaluate in broad terms whether young people had knowledge of their history, a reasonable sense of self-esteem and a sense of purpose. For black or dual heritage young people, an assessment was also made as to whether they felt comfortable with their sense of ethnic identity. This was defined entirely in terms of the black young peoples' own perspective and no attempt was made to base gradings on researchers' or workers' assumptions and how they *should* see their ethnic identity.

Secure   Reasonable self esteem; knowledge of background; some evidence of a general sense of purpose. For black/mixed heritage young people: also feels at ease with sense of ethnic identity.

Insecure   Lacking self esteem; lacking knowledge of background. For black/ mixed heritage young people: troubled by questions of ethnic identity.

There was little difference initially between the two groups of young people in the proportions with a secure sense of identity. A few young people in both groups had become more secure by the end of the study, and this improvement was more noticeable in the comparison group. There was also some variation between schemes, as young people on both the City schemes were more likely to have poor networks and an insecure sense of identity. As we saw in chapter 10, a number of young people gained in confidence and self esteem once they had lived in independent accommodation for a while, as they realised that they were more capable then they had previously assumed.

Figure 21.8 Identity

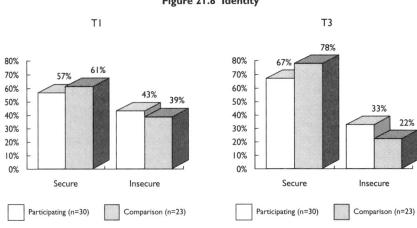

All of those with a broadly secure sense of identity had social networks that were either good or fair and had good relationship skills, whereas most of those with an insecure sense of identity had poor social networks and poor relationship skills.

All but a tenth of those with a secure sense of identity had positive, supportive relationships with family members (or in a small number of cases with former foster carers). This association of a secure sense of self identity with positive family relationships highlights the importance of helping 'looked after' children to maintain family links and assisting them in negotiating difficult relationships with parents or members of their extended family. As those with positive family relationships were more likely to have a secure sense of identity, and those with a secure sense of identity were more likely to have good relationship skills, they were generally better equipped to cope with living in the community.

Leaving care schemes had an important role to play in building young people's self-esteem and motivation indirectly, through assisting them to make a success of their lives in a range of areas, for example by sustaining a tenancy or sustaining a training placement or employment.

Drug/alcohol use (during past 12 months)

Problems of self reporting were likely to have occurred in this area. As workers were unlikely to be fully aware of drug/alcohol use in every case, these assessments can only be broadly indicative.

Good   No problem perceived by young person AND worker (perhaps some minor experimentation with soft drugs)

Poor   Perceived problem by young person OR worker with drug/alcohol use

None of the young people appeared to have a problem with alcohol abuse. At the outset of the study, 17.5% of the total initial sample of 74 reported that they had a drug problem, or were perceived by professionals to have a problem with drug use. A further 34% reported having experimented with drugs or having used them occasionally, but no problem was perceived by either the young people or their workers (although scheme workers and social workers were not always fully aware of drug use by the young people). The 53 young people we were able to contact at the end of the study included only six of the thirteen who had reported problems with drug use at the first interview, the other seven being lost to the study. Half of these young people were involved with schemes and half were in the comparison group. By the end of the study only two young people, both in City, reported continuing drug use. Both had experienced parental rejection and were leading very unsettled lives, repeatedly moving on to estcape threats of violence arising from their involvement in drug/criminal sub-cultures. Both were unemployed and were still finding it very hard to cope with living independently despite continuing support either from a social worker or scheme worker. The small numbers make it difficult to draw any firm conclusions about outcomes.

Offending (during past 12 months)

Problems of self-reporting arose here but an attempt was made to overcome this by basing assessment on both the young people's and their workers' accounts. Nonetheless, as workers may not always be fully aware of young people's involvement in criminal activities, these findings can only be broadly indicative.

Good   No offences

Fair   One or very few minor offences and no serious problem perceived by young person or worker

Poor   Persistent or serious offences

At the beginning of the study, three of the initial sample of 74 reported serious past offences, five reported either minor or serious offences since leaving care and a further six appeared to be developing an incipient criminal 'career' – a total of fourteen young people in all (see chapter 14). Four of these were lost to the study by the end of the research, leaving ten of them in the final sample.

Within 18–24 months of leaving care only six reported having committed offences in the previous year. Six of the original ten had committed no further offences during this period but two other young people had committed offences for the first time: one of them a young woman who set another woman's flat alight, driven by jealousy over her boyfriend's interest in her; the other a seriously depressed young man whose overwhelming despair lay behind his offending behaviour and repeated attempts at self harm. Three were young men with long standing criminal 'careers', but when interviewed two of these were living in stable situations following several months in custody, one with his mother and one with an older woman friend and her children, and at this stage both had firmly resolved to give up crime. Another, a young woman, also appeared to have settled down in recent months. Again, as numbers were so low it is not possible to draw any firm conclusions about outcomes.

Comparing outcomes

The proportion of young people in good accommodation when they first left care was slightly higher in the comparison group. This suggests that those scheme users not living in scheme-managed accommodation, such as leaving care hostels, dispersed hostels and supported lodgings, were more likely to be living in poor accommodation than those in the comparison group. One reason for this may be that the majority of those who left care in a crisis situation were scheme users, and some of these moved initially to unsatisfactory accommodation due to their emergency need for housing. This was a particular problem for City (ssd) scheme. However, those young people living in poor accommodation were more likely to move to good accommodation within two years of leaving care if they had scheme keyworkers, despite having early housing careers characterised by a high degree of instability. Also, young people in the comparison group in District and County may have benefited from these schemes' development of a range of housing options for all care leavers, not just for those with key workers at the schemes. Our findings suggest that leaving care schemes made an important contribution to improving housing outcomes either directly or indirectly for all care leavers.

Scheme users were also more likely to have improved their practical and budgeting skills during this period than young people in the comparison group. In some cases, schemes helped young people to develop these skills while they were living in children's homes or semi-independence units, as part of their general preparation work with young people about to leave care. However, those who developed these skills while living in supported settings sometimes lost them once they began living independently, which suggests that an ability to cope with practical aspects of living independently is closely related to other developments in young people's lives. Nevertheless, our findings indicate that schemes may be effective in helping young people to develop these skills before leaving care and to improve them once they have left.

Educational attainment was very poor in all three local authorities, which is consistent with the findings of previous studies of the education of 'looked after' children. Despite generally high levels of youth unemployment, the level of unemployment for this group of care leavers was also very much worse than for young people in the general population. As educational attainment by the age of 16 is the most powerful single predictor of later career paths, serious attention needs to be given by local authorities to developing more pro-active approaches in this area. The four schemes appeared to have little impact on educational progress and on employment patterns despite some work in these areas. These are areas that require further development.

Only a minority of young people in both groups had good social networks, including positive relationships with family members and with friends. In many cases scheme workers attempted to help young people improve their social networks, their relationship skills, their confidence and self-esteem, but it has been difficult to assess the impact of this work as so many other factors can affect developments in these areas. It is worth noting that the majority of those with a secure sense of identity had positive family relationships. This adds further weight to the findings of other studies which have pointed to the importance of maintaining family links for 'looked after' children and which underlie the Children Act's emphasis on maintaining these links wherever possible.

Comparisons with other care leavers are somewhat problematic, as the majority of those in the comparison group also had professional support, predominantly from social workers. Also, as already noted some may have benefited indirectly from scheme initiatives to develop accommodation options for care leavers in general. However, bearing in mind that the group of scheme users were significantly more disadvantaged than the comparison group in terms of non-professional support, schemes do appear to have helped young people achieve improved outcomes in key areas of their lives. Also, it is worth bearing in mind that many of the care leavers we interviewed appreciated the *process* of receiving help from schemes as much as the outcomes. Simply knowing that there was a caring adult who was interested in the developments in their lives, and who they could turn to for assistance as they made the transition from substitute care or accommodation and faced the difficulties that followed, was of great importance to many of the scheme users.

The leaving care schemes therefore appeared to be particularly effective in improving outcomes in the two core areas of scheme activity – facilitating access to good accommodation and developing life skills. In the context of the growing concern with homelessness among care leavers, which has been part of the rationale for the development of schemes, these schemes have been particularly successful. Few scheme users became homeless and, when they did, they were rapidly found accommodation with the schemes. The importance of a package involving housing *plus* support is highlighted, as young people's practical life skills often deteriorated when the level of support diminished. However, our findings also suggest that action is needed to improve education and employment outcomes, both during the time young people are in substitute care or accommodation and when they leave care.

• Summary Points •

This discussion of outcomes is based on interviews with the 53 young people who remained in the sample at the end of the study, together with their social workers and leaving care workers. Outcomes along nine outcome dimensions were graded as good, fair or poor and comparisons were made between the 30 scheme users in the participating group and the 23 young people in the comparison group. Some comparisons were also made with the general population of 16–19 year olds.

The level of support from social workers and foster carers was similar for both groups, but those in the participating group were far less likely to have positive, supportive relationships with a parent or other family member, and were far more likely to have experienced rejection by parents or long term foster carers. Young people using schemes were also more likely to have left care at the age of 16 or 17 than those in the comparison group. In these respects, the schemes were working with a group of young people who were significantly more disadvantaged than the care leavers in the comparison group.

There was an increase in the proportion of those in good accommodation among the group of scheme users but no change in this respect for the comparison group. Leaving care schemes were working with those who had the most unstable early housing careers and were able to help the vast majority find good accommodation within two years of leaving care. Leaving care schemes made an important contribution to improving outcomes, either directly or indirectly, for all care leavers. Scheme users were more likely to have improved their practical and budgeting skills than those in the comparison group. Neither group showed any real improvement in negotiating skills. Skills learned in supportive accommodation were sometimes lost when young people moved to independent accommodation.

Educational attainment for all care leavers was very poor compared to the general population. Poor attainment was associated with a high degree of movement while 'looked after'. Educational progress was generally better for those whose last placement was in foster care. A comprehensive approach to supporting young people in education is required, including assistance with finding stable accommodation, financial support and encouragement.

Early employment careers were generally poor and these care leavers were far more likely to be unemployed than other young people in the general population. Scheme users were more likely to have embarked on insecure career paths than those in the comparison group, but within two years of leaving care more young people from both groups had slipped from secure to insecure career paths. Outcomes were generally worse in this area for the young people using schemes.

The proportion of those with good social networks (comprising both family and friends) was poor in both groups, but significantly worse for those using schemes. The majority of those with a secure sense of identity had positive family relationships. This highlights the importance of helping 'looked after' children to maintain family links wherever feasible.

Over half of those who reported a serious problem with drug abuse were lost by the end of the study. Of the six who remained, only two reported a continuing problem with drugs 18–24 months after leaving care. Half of these six young people were in the participating group and half were in the comparison group.

By the end of the study only ten of the original fourteen who had reported offending behaviour remained in the sample. Of these, six reported having committed offences in the past 12 months, but by the time of the final interview three of these appeared to be living in stable situations and said that they had given up crime.

- The leaving care schemes appeared to be particularly effective in improving outcomes in the two core areas of scheme activity – facilitating access to good accommodation and developing life skills.

- Action is needed to improve education and employment outcomes, both while young people are in substitute care or accommodation and once they leave care.

CHAPTER 22

FROM STARTING POINTS TO OUTCOMES

This chapter develops a holistic case analysis of outcomes for young people using each scheme. This seeks to connect young people's 'starting points', their social environment after leaving care, professional interventions and outcomes. In order to do so, a broad grading of overall outcomes for each young person has been devised. Overall outcomes for scheme users and for young people in the comparison group are compared.

The previous chapter has shown the outcomes for the young people in separate areas of their lives – accommodation, employment, social networks and so on. However, while this approach may give some indication of the strengths or weaknesses of scheme intervention in particular areas of work, it presents only a partial picture. In measuring changes along single outcome dimensions, for example charting a deterioration in the quality of accommodation or the ability to sustain a tenancy, no account can be taken of other developments taking place concurrently in the young people's lives, or of wider underlying factors stemming from young people's care and pre-care histories. Parenthood, reconciliation with parents, or a relationship with a violent partner, for example, may all have consequences for outcomes along a range of dimensions – leading perhaps to better accommodation, an improved ability to sustain a tenancy or a more unstable housing career as a result of fleeing violence.

An evaluation of scheme support which takes account of the wider social environment and the varied 'starting points' of the young people, may provide a more realistic picture of the impact that schemes may have on their lives. For young people beginning their transition from care from a low baseline, for example, young people with no family support, poor relationship skills and few practical skills, schemes may intervene most effectively to achieve real, if modest, changes. Yet outcomes within two years may at first sight appear poor if the particular starting points of particular young people are not taken into account. Equally, services must be considered in the context of the young people's social environment – such as the actions of their family or partners, their involvement in a criminal sub-culture, or their experience of redundancy – which can also have an effect on wider outcomes. In order to set scheme intervention in the context of the young people's starting points and subsequent life experiences, a more holistic case analysis is needed. A holistic case analysis aims to evaluate the effectiveness of scheme interventions in the context of the particular starting points and subsequent life experiences of the young people.

At a case by case level, making links between *individual* young people's quality of life along each separate dimension and the quality of service they receive can illuminate the relationship between different aspects of a young person's life and indicate gaps in the service. In evaluating outcomes for a *group* of young people using a scheme rather than simply the outcome of professional intervention with a single person, it is difficult to work with a multiplicity of outcome measures and at the same time take account of individual histories and circumstances, without losing sight of indicators for policy and practice in a welter of detail. To put this more colloquially, there is a danger of not seeing the wood for the trees.

A measure of whether overall outcomes for a young person are broadly good or broadly poor would therefore be a useful tool in an analysis which seeks to link starting points, subsequent life experiences, professional intervention and outcomes. However, the problems of combining results along different outcome dimensions, leading to an *ad hoc* summation of gradings of different outcomes, have been well-rehearsed (Parker et al, 1991: 44–5). Overall outcome measures may obscure the relationship between different indicators and may hinder attempts to tease out causal chain effects. In addition, any summation of this kind involves putting a relative valuation on different outcomes, which in turn involves value judgements about the relative importance of different needs.

An assessment of whether overall outcomes are broadly good or broadly poor must therefore be founded on an explicit conception of needs. Maslow's hierarchy of needs, with five levels of need progressing from physical security to emotional fulfilment, suggests that basic needs must be satisfied before higher needs can be met (Maslow 1970). Doyal and Gough's conceptualisation of human needs as 'interwoven like a web' more accurately captures the complex interrelationship between different needs which is evident in our data (Doyal and Gough 1984: 11). They argue that autonomy and survival are basic human needs for all people in all circumstances, as people must have the mental ability to deliberate and to choose, and the physical ability to follow through their decisions, in order to achieve individual goals:

". . . in order to act succesfully, people . . . need physically to survive and need enough sense of their own identity or autonomy to initiate actions on the basis of their deliberations."

(DOYAL AND GOUGH 1984: 15).

In this formulation, autonomy is defined as a sense of agency, individuals' belief that their actions are "to be done *by* them and not *to* them" (Doyal and Gough 1984: 15). This corresponds broadly to the sense of purpose and control over their lives and the quality of self esteem that we have sought to capture in our qualitative assessment of identity. Survival would suggest shelter and a means of support, (as well as health, which we have not attempted to assess in this study). If we expect local authorities to act as a good parent, we would expect not simply a minimal degree of shelter but good accommodation, as defined in the previous chapter. In the discussion which follows, therefore, we have conceptualised the *minimum* requirement for broadly good outcomes as being when a young person:

- is in good accommodation

   and

- has a regular means of support (which may be a wage, benefit payment, or education grant and may include a subvention by the local authority)

   and

- has some degree of self esteem and some sense of control over their lives, *or* their self esteem and ability to take control of their lives has increased within two years of leaving care. This assessment also takes account of whether young people expressed unhappiness with their current situation or felt positive about their lives.

Outcomes of scheme intervention are also defined as positive in these terms when in work with young people whose 'starting points' involve a low baseline of skills, abilities and motivation and perhaps a lack of family (or substitute family) support, a noticeable improvement in the young person's circumstances can be observed.

In the analysis which follows, outcomes are considered in the light of the above objectives, which provide just one possible yardstick against which outcomes for care leavers can be measured. Whether an evaluation is being carried out by researchers or by schemes themselves in order to monitor practice, devising *any* objectives as a yardstick against which to measure outcomes is inherently problematic. If objectives are too limited, low expectations of a young person's ability to make a success of their life may be reinforced. If expectations are set too high, schemes will be set up to fail. As Parker et al have argued, outcomes chosen for evaluation should not be too ambitious, but neither should they reflect poor standards of service (Parker et al, 1991: 28). Outcomes therefore need to be assessed in the light of goals agreed (and regularly reviewed) by young people, scheme workers and social workers in each individual case as well as in terms of overall service objectives, which should also take account of the views of scheme users.

District

By the end of the study we were able to contact nine of the young people who had had key workers at the scheme. For eight of these young people, there was positive progress in most areas of their lives by this stage. For the first four, outcomes were not consistently good in all areas but there had been some improvement, whereas for the second four outcomes were broadly good.

The 'starting points' of the first four young people in this group set a very low baseline for development. Two young men had moderate learning difficulties and a third young man was very immature, naive and socially isolated, with poor communication skills. For all four, social networks and relationship skills were poor and their identities were insecure. Two of the young men had lost touch with their families many years earlier, and the third was exploited by his family, who stole his possessions, virtually destroyed his flat and used him to obtain drugs for them. The fourth, a young woman, had had minimal contact with her family while 'looked after' and said she chose not to see them. Three of them had been 'looked after' for most of their lives and three had had very unstable care careers with five or more moves between placements. One of the young men with learning difficulties had also experienced a traumatic transition from substitute care after the foster carers he had lived with all his life told him he had to leave as soon as he was 18 as they wanted to foster another child, even though he had always considered himself to be 'one of the family'.

All three received intensive help from the leaving care scheme. Accommodation in specialist supported hostels was found for the two young men with learning difficulties and the scheme worked closely with hostel staff to provide a comprehensive package of support. Their work was greatly facilitated by the fact that specialist housing provision and a specialist employment scheme for young people with learning difficulties existed in their area. For the third young man, scheme support was crucial when he was forced to leave his housing association flat due to harassment and extortion from other young people, which left him unable to sustain his tenancy and deeply in debt. Only scheme intervention to secure a rapid transfer to a council tenancy prevented him from becoming homeless at this stage. The scheme also addressed the issue of poor networks and relationship skills, helping one young man develop leisure activities through joining a football club and encouraging another to attend a group at the centre which helped him communicate a little better and become a little more assertive with other young people. Within two years of leaving care all were living in good accommodation and although their social networks, social skills and practical skills were still poor, there had been a noticeable improvement in all these areas.

The 'starting points' of the other four young people were quite different. Two had entered substitute care in their early teens and two in their late teens. One had had no placement moves and the others between one and three moves. All four had good social networks, good relationship skills and a secure sense of identity. Within two years of leaving care all four were living in secure council or housing association tenancies, having been assisted by the scheme in finding this accommodation and in establishing themselves in it. As one young woman explained:

"If you need them and you're on your own you can always call on them. And they give you a leaving care grant when you get your own place, to decorate and furnish your flat."

Although two were unemployed, one had been working but had been made redundant and the other was being assisted with college applications by the scheme. This group received help with improving their budgeting, practical skills and friendship networks. The scheme also addressed the issue of income, ensuring that the young people received any leaving care grants, subventions or education grants they were entitled to. Equally important to the young people was the knowledge that, should they run into difficulties, they would have someone to turn to:

"If I'm stuck for anything I can come down and ask 'em questions and they'll help me out if they can . . . it's good to know there's somebody around to help you, definitely."

Although these four young people had 'starting points' that were less problematic than the first four, all benefited from scheme intervention. Good outcomes in respect of obtaining and sustaining accommodation, budgeting, finding an occupation and extending networks were at least in part attributable to scheme intervention.

What of the young person for whom outcomes were less positive despite scheme intervention? Janet was a young woman with mild learning difficulties who had been sexually abused and had entered residential care in her early teens. Despite having had three placement moves, substitute care had provided more stability than she had experienced pre-care. She had had some contact with her grandmother while looked after, but had felt depressed during her time in substitute care. On leaving care her practical skills were good but her social networks and relationship skills were poor and she had little confidence and poor self-esteem. After spending time in a semi-independence unit attached to her children's home, she had moved out when a tenancy was offered although professionals had felt she was not yet ready. This situation rapidly broke down and, feeling unable to cope, she moved in with a friend and her friend's father. She soon became pregnant by her friend's father and later married him. Social work involvement continued once her baby was born because of allegations of sexual abuse made by her husband's daughters. Once she moved in with her future husband she became heavily dependent on him in every aspect of her life, with the effect that practical skills she had learned in the semi-independence unit deteriorated sharply because he took charge of everything, and she became even more socially isolated.

Her scheme keyworker reduced the level of support offered once her relationship with her future husband was established, feeling that she would now be able to turn to him for support. The keyworker felt unsure of his role, finding it difficult to discuss anything with the young woman due to the dominant influence of her future husband. In this difficult situation, the scheme had found it difficult to intervene and had withdrawn their involvement. The keyworker explained that his involvement had ceased because the young woman no longer wanted him to call, whereas she expressed disappointment that he no longer visited her.

Although she achieved greater emotional security through her relationship with her friend's father and was now settled in stable accommodation, Janet's limited practical abilities and social skills deteriorated sharply as a result of her dependence on him and her social isolation increased. The scheme remained concerned that if the relationship should break down, Janet would have few survivial skills and be completely isolated.

City (ssd)

Unfortunately, at the end of the study we were able to contact only two of the eleven scheme users we had initially interviewed. With both of these the scheme had achieved positive outcomes, although these were more limited in the case of the young woman who started from a lower baseline.

Hannah had entered residential care in her early teens as a result of physical abuse by her mother. She had remained in the same placement throughout, during which time she began to make progress at school as a result of her new found stability. When she first left care she had a few friends but minimal contact with her family, her relationship skills were good and she had a secure sense of identity. She also remained in regular contact with her children's home and her teachers during the early months after she left care and was still seeing her social worker occasionally.

The leaving care scheme had contacted her a year before she left care and saw her regularly during this period to help her prepare for moving out of her children's home. The scheme helped to plan and organise her move to a council flat and assisted her with decorating and furnishing the flat. This assistance with the whole process was well co-ordinated with Hannah's children's home and social worker and ensured a smooth, well-planned move out of substitute care. In the early months after leaving care she also received some help with budgeting and some counselling.

At this point her leaving care worker left and was replaced by another worker, and involvement tailed off. As the young person was well established in her flat and appeared to be coping, it was left to her to make contact with the scheme if she needed to. After this point her principal support was her social worker, who arranged funding to allow her to continue her education and helped her re-establish links with her younger brothers in foster care. Outcomes by the end of the study were very good, as Hannah was settled in her flat, making good progress at college, had had a reconciliation with her mother, had developed good budgeting and practical skills and had widened her friendship network through attendance at college. Hannah's smooth transition to independent accommodation was directly facilitated by the scheme's intervention, and although her good educational progress was not a direct result of scheme assistance it is unlikely that she would have been able to maintain her motivation and attendance at college if she had not been settled in stable accommodation.

Ellen started from a much lower baseline. She had entered residential care at 13 following physical abuse by her father. She had no contact with her father around the time she left care and although she began seeing her mother regularly at this stage, she appeared to offer little support. She had poor relationship skills, few friends and her sense of identity was insecure. Her life was chaotic and she appeared to have no sense of control over what happened to her, drifting from one crisis to another. Following a period in the semi-independence unit of her children's home she moved to her own flat at the age of 17. The timing of the move was dictated by the timing of the offer of a tenancy and by the local authority's practice of moving young people out of substitute care by this age, although her social worker and scheme worker felt she was far too immature to cope alone.

The leaving care scheme helped her plan the move to her flat and decorate and furnish it but the situation rapidly broke down, despite intensive support from the scheme. At this stage she disappeared for a few months, moving around staying with family and friends "here, there and everywhere . . . wherever I could get me head down." When she renewed contact with the scheme she was seven months pregnant, had given no thought to planning for the baby and was homeless. The scheme helped obtain another tenancy from the council and again helped her decorate and furnish it, but she never actually moved in. After staying for a while with her boyfriend she had to seek refuge in a mother and baby hostel in order to escape his violence. Only once she moved to this supported accommodation did she begin to cope better with independent living, as the hostel gave her stability, guidance and a routine. To the surprise of everyone her care of her baby appeared to be adequate, despite some problems. By the end of the study her confidence had increased, her practical and parenting skills had improved and her life was more stable, although she lived in fear of her boyfriend finding her.

In giving extensive practical support with both her moves and helping her deal with crises, the leaving care scheme had helped mitigate the effects of her early transition from care, her problematic 'starting point' and her continuing difficulties, contributing to an improvement along several outcome dimensions within two years of her leaving care. However, a fuller assessment when planning Ellen's transition from care might have considered whether an initial move to supported accommodation might have been more helpful to this young woman.

City (vol)

None of the young people we were able to interview 18–24 months after leaving care had very good outcomes by this stage. In all three cases, though, poor outcomes stemmed from the effects of their personal and family histories before leaving care rather than from failings in scheme support. Relative to many of the other care leavers we interviewed, the 'starting points' for these young people were particularly poor.

All three were deeply troubled by the rejection they had experienced. Catherine had been 'looked after' from birth, then adopted at the age of six but entered foster care at the age of 13 after disclosing that she had been sexually abused by her adoptive father, and later moved on to a children's home. At 18 she continued to feel hurt and angry that her adoptive mother had chosen to stand by her husband and had allowed Catherine to enter substitute care. These unresolved feelings of rejection and anger made her reject much of the support offered by the scheme. Peter had been abandoned at birth, had subsequently made 19 placement moves and was still preoccupied by his parents' rejection of him. Denise had been rejected by her family and later rejected by her foster parents when she became pregnant.

All three had very low self esteem, lacked confidence and were generally very insecure. Catherine was brittle and angry and found it hard to trust anyone. Denise and Peter lacked motivation and any sense of purpose, feeling unable to take control of any aspects of their lives, and were dominated, used and harassed by other young people. As Denise's scheme worker put it: "She has a very shaky sense of self." All three also had networks that were either fair or poor and recognised that they had no secure home base to turn to. As Catherine put it: "I'm stuck if I'm in trouble. I've had it."

All three moved to the scheme's trainer houses when they left care and received intensive and wide ranging support from their keyworkers, which was much appreciated by Denise and Peter. Denise later moved to a council tenancy with her child but found it hard to cope alone despite a high level of continuing support from her scheme worker and social worker, and left her accommodation when it was taken over by local youths. At the end of the study she was living in supported lodgings with her second child. There were serious concerns about her failure to bond with her children, her day to day care of the new baby, her new boyfriend's domination of her, her poor practical and budgeting skills and her very poor hygiene. She continued to receive support from her social worker but her scheme worker had withdrawn at this stage, although she was prepared to become involved again once Denise moved into a tenancy of her own.

Peter left the trainer house because of drug-related threats of violence from local youths and made six further moves between flats and hostels. At the end of the study he was living in a squat with his girlfriend. He was in poor health, which he ascribed to excessive drug use, and was still submerged in a maelstrom of instability and threats of violence. His keyworker was still involved, offering wide ranging support dealing with accommodation, work, motivation and taking control of his life, confidence, self-esteem and family issues. Peter very much appreciated having the scheme to turn to: "If I didn't know what to do I'd just talk to them and they'd take it from there."

Outcomes for Catherine were slightly better. After leaving her trainer house because of difficulties in sharing the accommodation, she made five further moves and two years after leaving care was living in a council house with her boyfriend. She had managed to find work during this period but either walked out of jobs or was sacked after a while. She was still fairly isolated and still had poor social skills. However, she had managed to sustain the relationship with her boyfriend for one and a half years. She also had reasonable practical skills, an ability to find work and seemed able to sustain her tenancy – all abilities the scheme assisted her to develop during her period in the trainer house.

For all three of these young people the scheme's structured, intensive and wide ranging support assisted them in their transition to independent accommodation.

The fact that outcomes were poor for two of them and only slightly better for the third appeared to be primarily the result of continuing problems arising from their past which had not yet been resolved. All three were consistently supported by the scheme through a very difficult period in their lives, and assisted in dealing with each crisis they encountered. In fact, for two of them, the scheme was the only source of support they had.

County

Of the sixteen scheme users we were able to contact at the end of the study, overall outcomes were good for twelve young people. Most of these young people began the process of leaving care from a fairly positive 'starting point'. Seven had had stable care careers, four having made no moves since early childhood, and the other three having made only one or two moves. Half had entered substitute care at eleven or over, three of these in their mid-teens. The majority (10) had good relationship skills and a secure sense of identity, and eight had social networks that were either good or fair. Three young women began their transition to independence from a low baseline, having suffered sexual or physical abuse and had unstable care careers. These three were rejected by their families, had poor networks and low self-esteem. One young woman with moderate learning difficulties also had a difficult 'starting point' due to her limited abilities and poor relationship skills.

Help from the scheme varied enormously, reflecting the County scheme's problems in providing a universal service for a large local authority and their consequent targeting of support. For seven of the young people scheme workers began attending reviews six to twelve months before they left care, discussing accommodation options, financial support and education, training or work, giving valuable assistance in planning for leaving care. Three received intensive support from a keyworker while another four received minimal support at the outset, but the level of support later increased. For five, however, the pattern was quite the opposite as they received skilled help with their transition from care but little follow up support.

Three young women received a comprehensive package of support. Two of the young women received a high level of support because they moved to a leaving care hostel managed by the scheme, which had a scheme worker on site. These two received help with practical skills, budgeting, relationship and negotiating skills and general confidence building. In addition, the keyworker took a pro-active, challenging approach with one of the young women regarding her drug use. Both benefited from this support and moved on successfully to other accommodation, but continued to receive some support from their keyworker. Both young women felt the hostel had struck a positive balance between support and autonomy, company and privacy. Within 18–24 months of leaving care they were settled in good accommodation and enjoying college. As one of them reflected once she had moved on to a flat of her own:

"I wouldn't have been able to manage if I'd just moved straight into here."

The third young woman, a young parent, moved directly into a flat and received consistent and wide ranging assistance from her keyworker. By the end of the study she was settled and coping well with independent living and parenthood, despite some financial problems.

For four young people keyworker involvement was low key at the outset but later became more intensive. Two young men with no stable accommodation, who had problems in arranging funding for further education and were socially isolated, complained that they had received minimal support from the scheme, although keyworkers had been allocated. This limited response appeared to derive in part from the fact that these young men stayed temporarily with members of their families, although family members were reluctant to help them and these arrangements proved to be unsatisfactory. However, providing only a limited service to those young people living with their families was one aspect of the County scheme's targeting of support. Within 18 months of leaving care the level of support had increased substantially and both were receiving advice about accommodation, education or employment, and widening their social networks. By this stage they had found satisfactory accommodation after making several moves and their social circles were beginning to widen, although both remained unemployed. They felt that the scheme's help had contributed to an improvement in their situation. As one of them put it:

"If I want something I've got to come and sometimes it's an effort to get what you want. But he (scheme worker) has done a lot of good things . . . My opinion of them's changed a lot. They got me a grant, got me somewhere to live, they will help."

For two young women support also increased. In both cases scheme workers became more involved once they moved out of supported accommodation – in one case from supported lodgings and in the other from a hostel. They received regular visits from their keyworkers who gave advice on practical skills, budgeting, social skills and parenthood plus general 'moral support' and encouragement. By the end of the study both were managing well in flats of their own, one continuing with her YT course and the other a full time parent. Both were enjoying independent living and feeling very positive about the future. These outcomes were a particular achievement for one of the young women, who had moderate learning difficulties yet had made a positive start to living in independent accommodation. The young parent felt that 'moral support' from her keyworker was particularly valuable:

"Just to know that there's someone actually interested in me, what I'm doing and what I'm achieving really."

However, for five other young people the pattern of support was quite the opposite. These five young women, (who included the three young women who began their transition to independence from a low baseline), were assisted with finding accommodation and were given assistance with claiming financial support, but once they had moved into independent accommodation support dropped off. Two were later evicted from their hostels but did not receive follow up support. Two of this group were critical of the limited support they had received from the scheme, while two only wanted minimal involvement.

In assisting these five young women in planning the move to their first independent accommodation, the scheme ensured a smooth transition to independence. However, three of these young people subsequently had very unstable early housing careers following this initial smooth transition from care, as one young woman made two further moves, two young women made four moves and one made seven moves within 18–24 months of leaving care. Yet contact with the scheme did not continue during this unsettled period. Nevertheless, by the end of the study outcomes were generally good for all five of these young women. Four of them had become parents and appeared to have settled in stable accommodation, in three cases with their boyfriend or husband. For all four of these young mothers, contact with their families and support from them had increased once they became parents. The fifth young woman was living in a hostel and attending college at the end of the study, and for her support from her social worker and from the hostel was crucial. Although the leaving care scheme provided a valuable service in assisting these young people with their transition from care, the broadly good outcomes for this group 18–24 months later were largely achieved as a result of the young people's own efforts in the intervening period, together with family or social worker support in some cases.

The 'starting points' of the four young people for whom outcomes were poor were apparently positive. Two had been in long term stable foster placements since early childhood and the other two had been 'looked after' for less than two years. Three had good relationship skills and a secure sense of identity, and two had good social networks. For all four, experiences around the point of transition from care or shortly afterwards appeared to lie at the root of their subsequent poor outcomes.

Ruth and Adam had spent most of their lives in stable long term foster placements, but Ruth had suffered physical abuse from her foster carers and Adam's placement had broken down when he was 16, although he had always seen himself as 'one of the family'. Ruth walked out of her foster placement when she was 18 and went to stay with her brother, who subsequently raped her. Adam became isolated and severely depressed once he left care, his depression exacerbated by unemployment. Both suffered breakdowns after leaving care and spent some time in psychiatric hospitals. One and a half to two years after leaving care, Ruth was living in a privately rented house and just coping despite financial difficulties, but Adam was staying in a homeless hostel. Both were still very depressed, and Ruth suffered from extreme anxiety. Both had made suicide attempts and leaving care workers feared further attempts at self harm. Adam's self esteem and confidence had declined sharply since he left care:

> "I'd love to go home but my (foster) mum won't have me because of the way I am now. I've gone much worse and I hate being like I am . . . I don't care about myself so why should I care about other people?"

Both Ruth and Adam had received consistent keyworker support from the scheme and by the end of the study were receiving counselling as well as more practical support. Ruth's keyworker was also helping her to re-establish herself in the community and giving assistance with budgeting and finding more affordable accommodation. Above all, Ruth valued having a supportive adult to turn to:

"If I ever need to speak to anybody, you know, she's always there. I think it's just the thought of having somebody there if you need them, which she is."

For both of these young people, traumatic life experiences meant that outcomes were poor in the first two years after leaving care. However, despite the poor outcomes at this stage, consistent keyworker involvement helped to support them through this difficult period of their lives.

Laura and Darren had been 'looked after' for less than two years and had good relationship skills and a secure sense of identity. However, Darren had embarked on a criminal 'career' well before he left care which was to cause further problems once he moved to independence and Laura's difficulties arose from her relationship with a violent boyfriend. Laura left the tenancy she had shared with her boyfriend, fleeing violence, and moved to another part of the country. She returned to County but did not make contact with the scheme for several months. By this time she and her two children had moved back with her boyfriend, but his renewed violence meant that by the end of the study she was anxious to leave her accommodation once again. Eighteen months after leaving care she was unsettled, fearful of further violence and anxious to move. Once she returned to County her keyworker attempted to support her, but found it difficult to intervene under the watchful eye of her boyfriend. Nevertheless, the keyworker was doing all she could to help her find alternative accommodation.

For Darren the pattern of support was very different. He received good preparation for leaving care from his scheme keyworker, with a strong focus on work (including interview techniques), life skills, and ensuring he had adequate financial support, and a good supply of clothes and material necessities before he left. He initially moved in to the leaving care scheme's dispersed hostel and received a comprehensive package of support from his scheme keyworker. However, his new found freedom went to his head, he allowed friends to take over his accommodation, ignored the hostel's attempts to set boundaries, began missing appointments with his keyworker and was eventually evicted. Once he was evicted it was left to him to contact the scheme for further assistance. He moved through a number of brief stays with friends and family, making seven moves within two years of leaving care. After several months in prison, he went to stay with an older woman friend and her children and appeared to find some stability and support in this situation. However, this accommodation was only temporary and he was unemployed. He no longer had a scheme worker or social worker, but did have a probation officer at this stage. Despite good preparation and comprehensive support in the dispersed hostel, outcomes were poor for Darren partly because he was not yet ready to cope with living alone and partly because of his involvement in crime. However, once he failed to make good use of the support that had been offered, the onus was on him to contact them if needed. This he felt unable to do.

In all four cases the scheme had offered comprehensive support to these young people, but for three of them traumatic experiences stemming from the breakdown in relationships with key people in their lives, and for the two young women violence inflicted by these people, led to poor outcomes at this stage. The fourth was simply not ready to cope alone when he first left care, despite receiving good preparation and intensive support when he first moved to independence, and once he 'messed up', as he put it, support fell away. A problem for a scheme like this, with a specialised staff structure linked to particular units of supported accommodation and clear boundaries of responsibility between its different sections, is that if young people 'fail' in the accommodation they may have to refer themselves back to the central team, rather than to a keyworker they know well.

Experiences, interventions and outcomes

Outcomes for young people are determined by a combination of factors. Their 'starting points' in terms of their social networks (and in particular the quality of family support available to them), their ability to make and sustain relationships, their self esteem, motivation and their care and pre-care histories all play a part in determining outcomes in the first two years after leaving care. Life events that occur once they leave care also play a part in shaping outcomes for the young people, as can local housing and employment markets and benefits policies that affect young people.

In this context, overall outcomes that were either broadly good, or at least represented positive progress relative to the young people's starting points, were achieved with three quarters (23) of the 30 scheme users who remained in the final sample. Unreservedly good outcomes across most outcome dimensions were achieved with over half of the young people (17). However, despite this positive progress they inevitably continued to experience difficulties and their future remained uncertain. Overall outcomes were poor for seven of the scheme users. Leaving care schemes intervene in the social environment of the young people and, alongside other influences, can play a part in achieving outcomes that are positive, or at least an improvement on the young people's 'starting points', for many of the young people. Bearing in mind that the 'starting points' for many of the scheme users set a low baseline for development, the broadly positive outcomes for a large majority of the young people indicates that schemes can make an effective contribution to help young people negotiate their transition from substitute care to living independently.

Past disadvantage, particularly rejection and abuse, continued to have consequences for a number of the young people, who experienced difficulties in making and sustaining relationships, sustaining motivation and often suffered from poor self esteem. The schemes' achievements lay in their ability to assist the young people in developing competence in a range of areas – in personal relationships, negotiating skills, practical skills and budgeting skills. Through helping young people develop these competencies and sustain motivation, and through helping to build their confidence, they helped many of the young people to make a success of moving to independent living. In many cases this transition was not smooth, but scheme workers were available to assist the majority of the young people in negotiating the difficulties they encountered and deal with crises. For many of the young people, particularly those with poor family relationships or no family support, the presence of a consistent, caring adult that they could turn to was valued more than any specific service.

Outcomes for the 23 young people in the comparison group were similar. For nearly three quarters (17) of the young people in the comparison group, overall outcomes were either good, in terms of the objectives specified above, or represented positive progress relative to their 'starting points'. Only three had consistently poor outcomes across most outcome dimensions. 'Starting points' were poor for all three of these young people. This group comprised a sixteen year old parent who had also had a baby at 13 (later adopted), as a result of incest by her brothers and had no family support; a young man with serious mental health problems with a history of extreme family violence; and a young mother who was extremely immature, described by her social worker as an 18 year old who was functioning as a 14 year old. Social workers continued their involvement with all three of these young people.

Outcomes were mixed for another three in the comparison group. Ryan had been rejected by his family and had been heavily involved in crime for several years. By the end of the study he was happy that relationships had begun to improve with his family, who were being far more supportive than in the past, and he had just moved into a council flat near his mother after making numerous moves since first leaving care. However, he had no visible means of support and his involvement in crime appeared to be continuing. Karen was a capable young woman who had managed extremely well in her own council maisonette and had been in stable employment for two years after leaving care, but once she was called as a witness in a prosecution of her former foster parents for sexually abusing other children in their care, she not only lost her only source of support but had to move to another area to avoid harassment by them. Two years after leaving care she was staying in temporary accommodation with a friend and was feeling isolated, but was continuing in stable employment and looking for alternative accommodation. Jenny was a very competent young woman who had two children and was pregnant with a third. She had lived with her partner in a council house ever since leaving care, but within two years her outlook on life was bleak as she struggled to bring up her children in cold, damp accommodation under considerable financial strain. She described her life as a struggle and was very worried about how she would get through the next few years. Neither of these two young women had support from any source at all, neither from their families or former foster carers, nor from professionals.

The similarity in overall outcomes for scheme users and for the comparison group should be seen in the context of the other forms of support available to the young people. As we saw in the previous chapter, young people in the comparison group were far more likely to have a positive, supportive relationship with a parent, other family member or former foster carer. This high level of family support, may help to explain why outcomes for those in the comparison group showed a similar pattern to those in the participating group. On the other hand, as already explained, the group of scheme users were far more likely to have experienced rejection by their parents or by long term foster carers. Also, as already noted, the level of social work support and foster parent support was similar for both groups. Around three quarters received social work support in the early months after leaving care, dropping to about two fifths 18–24 months later.

A central theme running through this study has been the importance of stability in young people's lives. However, it is important to consider the impact of stability carefully. Stability in substitute care was *not* necessarily a predictor of successful outcomes, as some young people were unhappy or abused in long term placements, or were rejected by carers once they reached their mid to late teens. These experiences had a continuing impact on their emotional security and their ability to make and sustain relationships once they left care. Continuity of relationships in itself is not sufficient, as it is both the continuity and the quality of those relationships which together have an effect on young people's future development. Similarly, a high degree of movement in care was not a predictor of poor outcomes overall, as only three of the sixteen young people in the final sample who had made four or more placement moves had poor outcomes along all or most outcome dimensions. However, as we saw in chapters 6 and 7, instability in care was associated with poor educational outcomes, which in turn hampered young people's chances of taking up post-16 education or finding employment. In addition, a lack of continuity made it more difficult for young people to make and sustain relationships after leaving care. One and a half to two years after leaving care, those who had made the highest number of placement moves were noticeably less successful at making and sustaining relationships. Of those who had made no placement moves, half were good at making and sustaining relationships, whereas only just over a third of those who made four or more moves had good relationship skills. However, caution must be exercised in drawing firm conclusions from this pattern as numbers were small[1].

A lack of family (or substitute family) support when leaving care was also associated with poor outcomes along most dimensions. Within two years of leaving care, outcomes were poor along most or all dimensions for half of those who had no family support when they first left care. Eight of the eleven young people for whom outcomes were poor had no family support at all when they first left care. Wherever feasible, helping young people to maintain relationships with parents and/or members of their extended family while they are 'looked after' may make an important contribution to the success with which young people subsequently make the transition to living out of care. Upon leaving care, young people who lack

---

1. Of the sample interviewed at the end of the study, 16 had made 4 or more moves (n = 53).

---

consistent and continuing support from parents, extended family or foster carers are especially likely to be in need of support from leaving care schemes.

In order to understand further the links between pre-care, in-care and post-care experiences for young people, the monitoring of outcomes for all care leavers would be a valuable tool in service planning both for 'looked after' young people and for those who have left care. As this study has shown, many care leavers have unstable housing careers and experience general instability in the first 18–24 months after leaving care. An assessment of outcomes solely at the point of leaving care can therefore provide only limited information to assist the planning of aftercare services. Following up care leavers in order to monitor outcomes in the early years after leaving care may also provide a mechanism for maintaining at least minimal contact with them. This may make it easier for those who have never used schemes or are no longer in contact with them to turn to the schemes for advice if they should run into difficulties at a later stage in their after care career.

In constructing measures for use in monitoring outcomes – both for scheme users and other care leavers – the question of who defines needs and who defines service objectives must be addressed. Professionals may impose definitions of need which correspond neatly with existing service boundaries, a phenomenon which has been widely documented in the literature on community care. Needs are not pre-existing attributes which await 'discovery' by professionals. Instead, assessments of need are socially constructed, influenced by formal social work theories, 'practice wisdom' and the pressure on workers to manage demand (see Biehal, 1993; Biehal, Fisher, Marsh and Sainsbury 1992). There is no reason why local care leavers should not also contribute to constructing a formulation of needs that local schemes should meet, and hence to setting service objectives. Outcome measures linked to these service objectives could also be developed in consultation with users.

The pitfalls of simple consumer satisfaction surveys are well known (see Pollitt 1988; Martin 1986). As we found during the course of this research, service users may not have a clearly formulated set of preferences. They may have low expectations of the service or be unaware of alternative types of provision. Involving young people in defining the needs of care leavers, the service objectives which aim to meet these needs and the outcome measures employed to monitor how successfully schemes are doing so, may address some of these pitfalls by helping young people develop a set of expectations against which they can evaluate the service. Developing outcome measures in consultation with users could therefore be part of a broader strategy to involve users in the evaluation of schemes and in planning for a service which is needs-led.

• Summary points •

An holistic case analysis is needed in order to evaluate outcomes in the context both of the young people's 'starting points', which provide a baseline for development, and their social environment. When outcomes for scheme users are evaluated in the context both of their individual 'starting points' and of their wider social and economic environment, the schemes' achievements – against the odds – are quite impressive.

Outcomes should be evaluated in terms of an explicit statement of service objectives, founded on an explicit statement of needs. Care leavers should be involved in defining needs and formulating objectives, both on an individual basis and in contributing to service planning for the scheme as a whole.

Outcomes were similar for both the group of scheme users and the comparison group. In both groups, for three quarters of the young people outcomes were broadly good (or represented positive progress in relation to their 'starting points') in that they met our three key objectives: good accommodation; a regular source of income; and a sense of purpose, together with a reasonable level of self esteem and a fairly positive view of their circumstances. However, despite this positive progress they inevitably continued to experience difficulties and their futures remained uncertain.

A lack of stability in care placements was associated with poor educational outcomes and poor relationship skills on leaving care, but was not a predictor of poor outcomes overall.

A lack of consistent and continuing family support was associated with poor outcomes. Over three quarters of those for whom outcomes were broadly poor lacked family support. Particular care should therefore be taken to help young people maintain family relationships where feasible, both while they are in substitute care or accommodation and after.

Monitoring of outcomes for care leavers would assist in planning services, both for 'looked after' children and for care leavers.

CHAPTER 23

DEVELOPING LEAVING CARE SERVICES

In the last two sections we have explored the distinctive approaches of our four schemes to organising and delivering their services, highlighted a range of issues in relation to scheme services and looked at how these schemes influenced the outcomes for young people involved with them. In our concluding remarks we want to highlight some points connected with the development of leaving care services in a wider sense.

Our discussion of the different approaches taken by our leaving care schemes suggests that there is no blueprint or ideal type model of provision. The evolution of our schemes was closely associated with the aims of the projects and the local conditions within which they were operating. While authorities therefore need to find an approach that is locally appropriate, our analysis of young peoples' experience of transition, our evaluation of schemes and of the outcomes achieved both for young people using and not using schemes, suggest that there are a number of broad areas that need to be addressed in relation to the development of leaving care services.

Developing an integrated through care approach

We have suggested that 'leaving care', although a pivotal point in young people's lives, needs to form an integral part of a wider child care strategy that links prevention, substitute care and after care. Helping to prepare young people for adult life and to develop the social supports that can sustain them, needs to be continuously in mind. Given the nature of shared parenting that the care system involves, the development of young people's practical, social and educational skills needs to be carefully planned, monitored and reviewed in consultation with them and at a pace they find appropriate. A precondition for this, and perhaps the greatest challenge facing the care system, is the need to offer young people a stable and positive care experience; a home base that offers emotional security, positive encouragement and a chance to recover from the stresses of their past lives. The relationships that young people are able to build at this stage with carers, social workers, family and friends will prove crucial to a successful transition.

In this context, leaving care services should not be an adjunct to care itself, a last stage entailing the rupturing of past links. Rather these specialist services should form part of a continuum, building upon a foundation of good practice and working in harmony with young people's existing social supports. Although, as we have seen, some young people will choose to transfer to schemes and, for them, that choice should be available, it should neither be required nor expected. Where young people have positive relationships with carers and/or social workers, authorities need to recognise and fund their continuing role until young people have established themselves in the community. Schemes would then be able to work alongside those taking a primary role in an advisory capacity and focus their direct support on those young people leaving care with few community supports and on the older age range living independently

However, as we have seen, our schemes were working within the present 'realities' of the care system. A reality where, for substantial numbers of young people, their care careers were marked by movement and disruption, their preparation was uneven, quite basic emotional insecurities remained unresolved and where a majority appeared to have limited employment possibilities. The difficulties this can present schemes was best exemplified by City (vol). Even for a highly structured and intensive scheme, the problems involved in attempting to support young people who lack the practical and emotional skills to sustain their lives and relationships with others can prove almost insurmountable. Without the continuity provided by the scheme, some of their young people would have spiralled into homelessness.

Developing a needs led service

Leaving care as an age related phenomenom is unrealistic. The expectation that quite vulnerable young people should move on between 16 and 18 years of age places an unfair burden upon them. Authorities need to explore ways of funding continuing care in foster and residential placements for those who need and want it, enabling them to move on when they feel ready. Some will choose to move on earlier and arrangements are needed to enable them to return if in crisis. For all young people, when 'independence' is first being considered, the drawing up of a detailed leaving care plan is essential. A recent survey by the Audit Commission found that two thirds of the local authorities studied still had no procedures to ensure that leaving care plans were prepared (Audit Commission 1994). Planning needs to take a holistic approach, include all significant adults in young people's lives, be young person centred and involve a careful assessment of their housing requirements, their skills, career possibilities and the social supports likely to be available to them in the community. This process needs to maximise choices for young people, ensure they are aware of their entitlements and of the future sources of support they can call upon. The onus should not be placed on young people to surmount the hurdles involved in accessing help from duty systems when crises occur at a later point.

The need for a clear authority wide policy and procedure framework

Authorities need to develop a structured policy and procedure framework capable of delivering a through care approach to leaving care services. It should include a leaving care policy statement reinforced by written procedures and practice guidance. It should be clearly written, comprehensive and accessible to those likely to benefit. It needs to identify the services available to young people (including those over 18), procedures for ensuring a corporate and inter-agency approach to meeting their needs and for monitoring and reviewing service development. Policy and procedures also need to take account of diversity and include strategies for meeting the particular needs of young parents, those with particular cultural and religious needs and those with learning and physical disabilities. A 'senior officer' with responsibility for the development of leaving care services needs to be clearly identified and arrangements for representation and complaints included. A separate guide to services should be developed for and with young people who are leaving care.

Where a specialist leaving care scheme is to be considered, its role needs to be specified within the totality of 'in care' and 'after care' services. As we have seen, schemes need a clear brief, adequate resources to develop direct and indirect developmental services and a structured policy, procedural and managerial framwork within which to operate. As with all those involved in leaving care services, opportunities for training and staff development are essential. In addition schemes, as a specialist service, need to be able to feed back problems and issues into policy and service development at all stages of young people's care careers. Finally, as part of all leaving care service provision, schemes need to have clear boundaries to their work, procedures to ensure access to and information about their services and arrangements that facilitate close cooperation with carers, social workers and other agencies.

Working together

Providing an integrated service for care leavers requires an inter-agency approach. The reluctance of departments to cooperate at a time of resource constraints, except where mandatory, has been identified (Audit Commission 1994). The existence of professional and departmental barriers were apparent in our study – for example, between social services, education and the benefits agency in meeting the financial needs of care leavers. As we have seen, our schemes were taking a lead role in developing inter-agency links at three levels: informal and formal scheme worker-agency worker links; formal scheme-agency links; and corporate departmental links (involving different departments within the local authority and departmental links with external agencies). Our findings would suggest that working together is greatly facilitated where there are jointly agreed formal arrangements, protocols and policies. These arrangements with housing providers were crucial in enabling our schemes to develop a flexible range of accommodation options. However, there is some way to go. Formal links were less evident in relation to social security and were only beginning to develop with colleges, employers and training agencies towards the close of our study.

Social service departments need to take a lead role in promoting strategies for inter-agency cooperation. The development of authority wide forums that bring together all agencies (statutory and voluntary) that are involved in meeting care leavers' needs are likely to be helpful. Discussions at this level can raise awareness, resolve problems and feed into the policy process.

Involving young people

We have stressed throughout that, as individuals, young people need to be involved in all key decisions affecting their lives. However, the experience they gain during their time in care and after make them well placed to participate in the development and monitoring of policies and services. Authorities need to explore ways of ensuring that the views of young people, as users of services, are directly represented in the process of formulating policies, procedures and services associated with leaving care.

By the close of our research, none of our schemes possessed formal collective structures in which young people could influence scheme development. In the past both District and City (vol) had run young people's forums but abandoned them when they became dominated by what the schemes' perceived to be a small 'unrepresentative' group of users. Apart from young person involvement in residents meetings for those in supported accommodation, user views were sought at an individual level; for example, through the planning and review process, newsletters and service evaluation forms.

Although there are undoubtedly practical problems attached to participation, with careful thought and preparation there are obvious advantages. Not only can young person involvement help to ensure the appropriateness of services but it can form part of an empowering process that helps to prepare young people to assume adult responsibilities. Although our schemes did involve young people in differing ways, perhaps more thought could be given to the development of a comprehensive strategy.

The importance of specialist schemes

We have suggested that leaving care services need to be both universalistic (capable of reaching all young people) and sufficiently flexible to meet differing needs. It should be apparent that the development of an integrated through care approach to delivering leaving care services requires a range of specialist functions to be performed. Our research suggests that the development and coordination of services and resources are likely to be best performed through a centrally organised team with an authority wide brief. However, consistent with a through care approach that promotes continuity, schemes would not provide all services directly but, wherever possible, work in partnership with carers, social workers and other agencies to offer flexible packages of support to meet individual needs. In this sense a comprehensive authority wide response to care leavers is likely to involve a patchwork of complementary services. For example, in our study City authority had two schemes, one with an authority wide brief and a second offering an intensive service to limited numbers of young people.

Our schemes, despite their differing approaches, were making a valuable contribution to helping their authorities meet their responsibilities as defined in the Children Act. Work was being undertaken at a number of discrete levels.

- contributing to policy development and the coordination of leaving care services;
- developing a flexible range of resource options for young people and, in some instances, coordinating access to them (especially housing and financial resources);
- developing inter-agency links to ensure an integrated approach;
- providing advice, information and consultancy services to young people, social workers and carers – including assistance with preparation and leaving care planning;
- offering direct individual and group based support to young people – including both those leaving care and, in an open ended manner, those living independently in the community.

Not all of our schemes had been able to make progress on all fronts and the strengths and limitations of their different approaches have been explored in earlier chapters. Nonetheless, these tasks are essential, complex and time consuming. Although a through care perspective stresses the need for young people to retain continuity in support from carers and social workers, it is unlikely that they, as individuals, could gain the necessary expertise. These tasks require an overview of the resources available, including: housing, welfare rights, career opportunities, advice and counselling services and youth and leisure provision. Indeed, as we have seen, the majority of young people and social workers who were working in partnership with our schemes valued highly the specialist knowledge base of scheme workers and the support they were able to offer. For many young people, the continuity offered by schemes, at a time when other supports were falling away, represented a lifeline as they struggled to find their feet in the adult world.

Monitoring

In the contract culture of today, concerns about quality and the use of resources have made pressing the need to monitor the effectiveness of services, especially for specialist services such as leaving care schemes. Monitoring outcomes for care leavers needs to take place at two levels. First, local authorities need to develop procedures for monitoring the progress of all care leavers. Monitoring young people over their early years of independence would enable at least minimal contact to be maintained with them, an important consideration given our evidence of instability in early post care careers. Awareness of the problems young people encounter would also provide a valuable tool to aid service planning both for those 'looked after' and for those who have left. Finally, data collected by all authorities would enable a national picture to be generated.

Second, schemes need procedures to evaluate the outcomes of their interventions in order to improve and develop their services. Our research suggests that these should include both quantitative and qualitative dimensions. The collection of quantative data is potentially straightforward assuming there is agreement on the categories. Qualitative data is more problematic – and hence its absence from most existing schemes – but it can make an essential contribution to improving the quality of services. The nine dimensions that we have researched may help to provide a structure (see Chapter 20).

In order to avoid unnecessary duplication of information, and thus the possibility of resistance, we would suggest the integration of monitoring data within a standardised leaving care 'Open Access Record'. This record would include data gathered from the referral form, the initial assessment of needs and from the regular planning and review process. Outcome data could then be gathered at agreed intervals. The record would have a multiple purpose. Young people and scheme staff could jointly monitor individual progress and the data provided, when aggregated, could contribute to the monitoring and review of leaving care services at both a local and, at least potentially, a national level.

Finally, discussions about monitoring outcomes raise questions about who should define needs and service objectives. Needs are socially constructed and, as users of services, young people need to be involved directly in defining the needs of care leavers, setting service objectives to meet them and arrangements for monitoring the outcomes of these services. The involvement of service users is vital to the development of a genuinely needs-led service.

REFERENCES

Advisory Council on the Misuse of Drugs (1993)
Drug Education in Schools, *London: HMSO*

Alaszewski, A. and Harrison, L. (1992)
'Alcohol and social work: A literature review',
British Journal of Social Work, 23 (3), pp 331–343

Aldate, J., Heath, A., Colton, M. and Simm, M. (1993)
'Social work and the education of children in foster care',
Adoption and Fostering, 17, No 3, pp 25–34

Allen, I. (1987)
Education in Sex and Personal Relationships, *London: Policy Studies Institute*

Audit Commission (1994)
Seen But Not Heard, *London HMSO*

Banks, M., Bates, I., Breakwell, G., Bynner, J., Emler, N., Jamieson, L. and Roberts, K. (1992)
Careers and Identities, *Buckingham: Open University Press*

Barnardo's (1989)
I Can't Go Back to Mum and Dad, *Ilford: Barnardo's*

Bebbington, A. and Miles, J. (1989)
'The background of children who enter local authority care',
British Journal of Social Work, Vol 19, No 5, pp 349–368

Berridge, D. and Cleaver, H. (1987)
Foster Home Breakdown, *Oxford: Blackwell*

Berridge, D. (1985)
Children's Homes, *Oxford: Blackwell*

Biehal, N., Clayden, J., Stein, M. and Wade, J. (1992)
Prepared for Living? A survey of young people leaving the care of three local authorities, *London: National Children's Bureau*

Biehal, N., Fisher, M., Marsh, P. and Sainsbury, E. (1992)
'A framework of rights for social work' in Coote, A. (ed)
The Welfare of Citizens, *London: Institute for Public Policy Research*

Biehal, N. (1993)
'Changing practice: Participation, rights and community care'.
British Journal of Social Work, 23, pp 443–458

Bilson, A. and Barker, R. (1992–93)
'Siblings of children in care or accommodation: A neglected area of practice'
Practice, Volume 6, Number 4, pp 307–318

Black and in Care (1984)
Black and in Care Conference Report, *London, Children's Legal Centre*

Bonnerjea, L. (1990)
Leaving Care in London, *London: London Borough's Children's Regional Planning Committee*

Broad, B. (1994)
Leaving Care in the 1990's, *Westerham: Royal Philanthropic Society*

Bullock, R., Little, M. and Millham, S. (1993)
Going Home, *Aldershot: Darmouth*

CEP (1994)
The Comparative Performance of the British Education and Training System, Working Paper No 644, *Centre for Economic Performance, London School of Economics*

Cheetham, J., Fuller, R., Petch, A. and McIvor, (1992)
Evaluating Social Work Effectiveness, *Buckingham: Open University Press*

Cliffe, D. and Berridge, D. (1991)
Closing Children's Homes: An End to Residential Care?, *London: National Children's Bureau*

Coleman, J., Hofler, T. and Kilgore, S. (1981)
Public and Private Schools, *Chicago: National Opinion Research Centre*

Coleman, J. (1993)
'Understanding adolescence today: A review', **Children and Society**, 7:2, pp 137–147

Coffield, F. and Gofton, L. (1994)
Drugs and Young People, *London: IPPR*

Cohen, P. (1986)
Rethinking the Youth Question, *London: Institute of Education*

Cohen, P. (1992)
Adoptive Identities, *Outline research proposal*

Community Care (1994)
'Lost from care', **Community Care**, 4 August

Cook, R. (1988)
'Trends and needs in programming independent living', **Child Welfare**, Vol LXVII, 6, November/December

Cook, R. and Sedlak, A. (1993)
Predictors of Outcomes for Youth Discharged from Foster Care, Unpublished paper presented at University of Illinois, September 1993

Coote, A., Harrison, S. and Hunter, D. (1994)
'When axes fall', **The Guardian**, 25 May

Craig, G. (1991)
Fit for Nothing: Young People, Benefits and Youth Training, *London: Coalition on Young People and Social Security*

Department for Education (1992)
School Performance Tables, Public Examination Results 1991, *London: Department of Education*

Department of Health and Social Security (1985a)
Social Work Decisions in Child Care, *London: HMSO*

Department of Health and Social Security (1985b)
Review of Child Care Law: Report to Ministers of an Inter-departmental Working Party, *London: HMSO*

Department of Health and Social Security (Northern Ireland) (1991)
In the Unknown, A Study of Young People Leaving Care, No 43, *Belfast: DHSS*

Department of Health (1991a)
Looking After Children: A Guide to the Action and Assessment Schedules, *London: HMSO*

Department of Health (1991b)
The Children Act 1989, Guidance and Regulations, Vol 4, Residential Care, *London: HMSO*

Department of Health (1991c)
The Children Act 1989, Guidance and Regulations, Vol 6, Children with Disabilities, *London: HMSO*

Department of Health (1991d)
Patterns and Outcomes in Child Placement, *London: HMSO*

Dobson, R. (1994)
'Rare breed', **Community Care**, 18–24 August

Downey, R. (1995)
'Care leavers caught in responsibility battle'.
Community Care, 26 January–1 February

Doyal, L. and Gough, I. (1984)
'A theory of human needs', **Critical Social Policy**, 10, pp 6–38

Fanshel, D. and Shinn, E.B. (1978)
Children in Foster Care: A Longitudinal Investigation, *New York: Columbia Press*

Finkelhor, D. (1986)
A Sourcebook on Child Sexual Abuse, *Newbury Park: Sage*

First Key (1987)
A Study of Black Young People Leaving Care, *Leeds: First Key*

First Key (1992)
A Survey of Local Authority Provisions for Young People Leaving Care, *Leeds: First Key*

Fletcher-Campbell, F. (1990)
'In care? In school?', **Children and Society**, 4, 4, 365–373

Francis, J. (1994a)
'In a drug fix', **Community Care**, 28 July–3 August

Francis, J. (1994b)
'Life lessons for freedom', **Community Care**, 29 September–5 October

Frost, N. and Stein, M. (1989)
The Politics of Child Welfare, *Hemel Hempstead: Harvester Wheatsheaf*

Fry, E. (1992)
'Lost in transit', **Social Work Today**, 29 October

Garnett, L. (1992)
Leaving Care and After, *London: National Children's Bureau*

Giddens, A. (1991)
Modernity and Self-Identity, *Cambridge: Polity Press*

Gilroy, P. (1987)
There Ain't no Black in the Union Jack, *London: Hutchinson*

Godek, S. (1976)
Leaving Care, *Ilford: Barnardo's*

Hall, S. (1992)
'The question of cultural identity' in Hall, S., Held, D. and McGrew, T. (eds)
Modernity and its Futures, *Cambridge: Polity Press*

Halsey, A., Heath A. and Ridge, J. (1980)
Origins and Destinations, *Oxford: Oxford University Press*

Hatfield, B., Huxley, P. and Mohamad, H. (1992)
'Accommodation and employment: A survey into the circumstances and expressed needs of users of mental health services in a northern town',
British Journal of Social Work, 22, pp 61–73

Heath, A., Colton, M. and Aldgate, J. (1994)
'Failure to escape: A longitudinal study of foster children's educational attainment',
British Journal of Social Work, 24, pp 241–260

Heath, A., Colton, M. and Aldgate, J. (1989)
'The educational progress of children in and out of foster care',
British Journal of Social Work, 19, pp 447–460

Hoinville, G. and Jowell, R. in association with Airey, C., Brook, L., Courtenay, C. et al (1987)
Survey Research Practice. *London: Heinemann*

Hubert, J. (1990)
'At home and alone: families and young adults with challenging behaviour' in Booth, T. (ed)
'Better Lives: changing services for people with learning difficulties'
Social Services Monograph, *University of Sheffield Unit for Social Services Research.*

Hudson, F. and Ineichen, B. (1991)
Taking It Lying Down: Sexuality and Teenage Motherhood, *Basingstoke: MacMillan*

Jackson, S. (1989/9)
'Residential care and education', **Children and Society**, 4, pp 335–350

Jones, G. (1987)
'Leaving the parental home: An analysis of early housing careers',
Journal of Social Policy, 16, 1, pp 49–74

Jones, G. (1993)
Young People in and out of the Housing Market, Working Paper 3, *Edinburgh: University of Edinburgh/Scottish Council for Single Homeless*

Jones, G. and Wallace, C. (1992)
Youth, Family and Citizenship, *Buckingham: Open University Press*

Jordan, L. (1992)
'Accommodation and aftercare: Provision for young people,
Journal of Child Law, 4, 4

Kahan, B. (1979)
Growing Up in Care, *Oxford: Blackwell*

Kiernan, K. and Wicks, M. (1990)
Family Change and Future Policy, *York: Joseph Rowntree Foundation/Family Policy Studies Centre*

Kirk, D., Nelson, S., Sinfield, A. and Sinfield, D. (1991)
Excluding Youth: Poverty Among Young People Living Away From Home,
Edinburgh: Bridges Project/University of Edinburgh

Klein, M. (1985)
Where am I Going to Stay?, *Edinburgh: Scottish Council for the Single Homeless*

Knapp, M. (1989)
Measuring Child Care Outcomes, PSSRU Discussion Paper 630, *Canterbury: University of Kent*

LMQR (1992a)
Labour Market Quarterly Report, February issue

LMQR (1992b)
Labour Market Quarterly Report, August issue

Lowe, K. (1990)
Teenagers in Foster Care, *London: National Foster Care Association*

Lupton, C. (1985)
Moving Out, *Portsmouth: Portsmouth Polytechnic*

Martin, E. (1986)
'Consumer evaluation of human services',
Social Policy and Administration, Vol 20, No 3, Autumn 1986

Maslow, A. (1970)
Motivation and Personality, *New York: Harper and Row*

Mason, J. (1994) 'Linking qualitative and quantitative data analysis' in Bryman, A. and Burgess, R. G. (Eds) **Analyzing Qualitative Data**. *London, Routledge*

May, T. (1993)
Social Research, *Buckingham: Open University Press*

McRobbie, A. (1991)
'Teenage Mothers: A New Social State?', in McRobbie, A. (ed)
Feminism and Youth Culture, *Basingstoke: MacMillan*

Millham, S., Bullock, R., Hosie, K. and Haak, M. (1986)
Lost in Care, *Aldershot: Gower*

Mitchell, D. (1994)
'Life after care', **Community Care**, 11–17 August

Mitchell, D. (1994)
'The forgotten few', **Community Care**, 18–24 August

Musick, J. (1993)
Young Poor and Pregnant: The Psychology of Teenage Motherhood,
London: Yale University Press

National Association of Citizens Advice Bureau (1992)
Severe Hardship – CAB Evidence on Young People and Benefits, *London: NACAB*

National Children's Bureau (1992)
Child Facts, 25 June, *London: NCB*

National Foster Care Association (1992)
After Care, Making the Most of Foster Care, (Fry, E.) *London: National Foster Care Association*

Oakley, A. (1990)
'Inviewing Women: A Contradiction in Terms'. In Roberts, H. (ed) **Doing Feminist Research**. *London: Routledge & Keegan Paul*

Office of Population Census and Surveys (1992)
1991 Census County Reports, *London: HMSO*

Office of Population Census and Surveys (1993a)
1991 Census Report for Great Britain, Part One, Volume 2, *London: HMSO*

Office of Population Census and Surveys (1993b)
1991 Census Household Composition, Great Britain (Topic Report Series), *London: HMSO*

Owusu-Bempah, J. (1994)
'Race, Self-Identity and Social Work',
British Journal of Social Work, Vol 24, pp 123–136

Page, R. and Clarke, G. (eds) (1977)
Who Cares, *London: Naitonal Children's Bureau*

Parker, R., Ward. H., Jackson, S., Aldgate, J. and Wedge, P. (eds) (1991)
Assessing Outcomes in Child Care, *London: HMSO*

Phoenix, A. (1991)
Young Mothers, *Cambridge: Polity Press*

Pollitt, C. (1988)
'Performance measurement: Concepts, consequences and constraints',
Policy and Politics, Vol 16, No 2, pp 77–87

Randall, G. (1988)
No Way Home, *London: Centrepoint*

Randall, G. (1989)
Homeless and Hungry, *London: Centrepoint*

Redpath, B. and Harvey, B. (1987)
Young People's Intentions to Enter Higher Education, OPCS Report, *London, HMSO*

Richard, F. (1992)
'Moving on', **Social Work Today**, 24 September

Richardson, A. and Ritchie, J. (1986)
Making the break: parent's views about adults with mental handicap leaving the parental home, *London, King's Fund*

Rickford, F. (1994)
'Baby boomers', **Community Care**, 8–14 September

Roberts, K. (1993)
'Career Trajectories and the Mirage of Social Mobility', in: Bates, I. and Riseborough, G. (1993),
Youth and Inequality, *Buckingham, Oxford University Press*

Rowe, J., Cain, H., Hundleby, M. and Keane, A. (1984)
Long Term Foster Care, *London: Batsford/British Agencies for Adoption and Fostering*

Rowe, J., Hundleby, M. and Garnett, L. (1989)
Child Care Now, *London: Batsford/British Agencies for Adoption and Fostering*

Russell, P. and Flyn, M. (1991)
Report by the National Development Team on a Workshop for Parents of Young People with Disabilities, held at Castle Priory College, 11–12 July, *London: National Children's Bureau/Voluntary Council for Handicapped Children*

Social Trends (1994)
Central Statistical Office, Number 24, *London: HMSO*

Sharpe, S. (1987)
Falling for Love: Teenage Mothers Talk, *London, Virago*

Smith, C. (ed) (1994)
Partnership in Action: Developing Effective Aftercare Projects, *Westerham: Royal Philanthropic Society*

Smith, C. and Nutbeam, D. (1992)
'Adolescent drug users in Wales'
British Journal of Addiction, 87, pp 227–233

Social Services Committee, House of Commons (1984)
Second Report, Session 1983–84, Children in Care (The Short Report),
London: HMSO

Social Services Inspectorate (1985)
Inspection of Community Homes, *London: HMSO*

Sone, K. (1994b)
'Home of their own', **Community Care**, 6–12 October

Sone, K. (1994)
'Pick up the pieces', **Community Care**, 15–21 September

Stein, M. and Carey, K. (1986)
Leaving Care, *Oxford: Blackwell*

Stein, M. and Ellis, S. (1983)
Gizza Say, *London: NAYPIC*

Stein, M. and Maynard, C. (1985)
I've Never Been So Lonely, *London: NAYPIC*

Stein, M. (1983)
'Protest in Care' in Jordan, B. and Parton, N. (eds)
The Political Dimensions of Social Work, *Oxford: Blackwell*

Stein, M. (1990)
Living Out of Care, *Ilford: Barnardo's*

Stein, M. (1991)
Leaving Care and the 1989 Children Act, The Agenda, *Leeds: First Key*

Stein, M. (1993)
Leaving Care, Research into Practice, *Leeds: First Key*

Stein, M. (1993a)
'The Abuses and Uses of Residential Care', in: Ferguson, H; Gilligan, R. and
Torode, R. (eds)
Surviving Childhood Adversity, *Dublin, Social Studies Press*

Stein, M. (1994)
'Leaving care, education and career trajectories',
Oxford Review of Education, 20, 3, pp 349–360

Stevenson, O. and Parsloe, P. (1993)
Community Care and Empowerment, *York: Joseph Rowntree Foundation*

Stockley, D.J. (1990)
**A Review of Literature and Statistics of Homelessness, Offending and
Young People in Local Authority Care** (unpublished paper), *Surrey: University
of Surrey, Department of Psychology*

Stone, M. (1990)
Young People Leaving Care, *Redhill: The Royal Philanthropic Society*

Strathdee, R. and Johnson, M. (1994)
Out of Care and on the Streets. Young People, Care Leavers and Homelessness, *London: Centrepoint.*

Taylor, C. (1989)
Sources of the Self, *Cambridge: Cambridge University Press*

Tizard, B. and Phoenix, A. (1993)
Black, White or Mixed Race? *London: Routledge*

Waldinger, G. and Furman, W. (1993)
Preparing Foster Youth for Emancipation, Unpublished paper presented at University of Illinois, September 1993

Wallace, C. and Cross, M. (1990)
The Sociology of Youth and Youth Policy, *London: Falmer Press*

Ward, M. (1983)
'Sibling ties in foster care and adoption planning',
Child Welfare, 63(4) pp 321–332

White Paper (1987)
The Law on Child Care and Family Services, Cmnd 62, *London: HMSO*

Who Cares? Trust (1993)
Not Just a Name: The Views of Young People in Foster and Residential Care, *London: National Consumer Council*

Wyatt, G.E. and Powell, G.J. (eds) (1987)
'The lasting effects of child sexual abuse',
Journal of Interpersonal Violence, 2(4)

Young Homelessness Group (1991)
Carefree and Homeless, *London: Young Homelessness Group*

APPENDIX

Figure 1 Background Information on schemes

Scheme	District (vol)	City (vol)	City (ssd)	County (ssd)
Started	1987	1986	1989	1985
Managed	By voluntary organisation (vol) in partnership with SSD	By voluntary organisations in partnership with SSD	By SSD	By SSD
Funding (July 1994)	Revenue costs met by SSD (100%). VOL provide building. Local fund raising and donations.	50% SSD 50% VOL	SSD core funding	SSD core funding
Staffing (July 1994)	Project manager 3¾ project workers ½ administrator	Project leader 4 project workers Administrator ½ secretary	Unit manager 2 senior care officers 7 care officers Secretarial support	Team Manager 4 social workers 2 social workers managing lodgings 3 project workers (SILP) 2 project workers (Rathbone project) Secretarial support
Background and experience of staff	Residential Social Work Teaching	Social Work Youth and Community Work	Residential Child Care Social Work	Social Work
Professional qualifications	Yes	Yes	Only Unit Manager	Yes (All Social Workers)

Figure 2   Managerial and organisational context (July 1994)

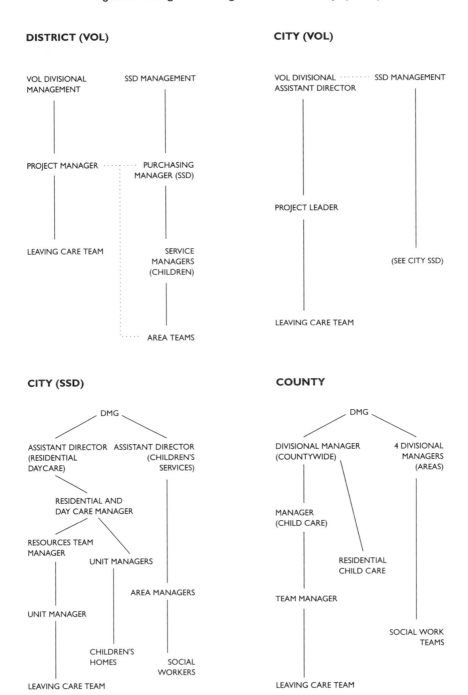

Figure 3 Leaving care scheme services

City (vol)	City (ssd)
1. INDIVIDUAL SOCIAL GROUPWORK SUPPORT AND TRAINING	
• individual project key worker	• individual key worker
• social evening once a week	• social evening once a week
• emergency 'on call' 24 hour service, seven days per week	
• volunteers	
• group work training	
2. ACCOMMODATION RESOURCES	
• trainer houses	• staffed semi-independent accommodation
• assistance in securing local authority housing, association and private rented tenancies	• 6 local authority tenancies
	• arrange supported lodgings (from 1994)
3. FINANCIAL ASSISTANCE	
• budgeting help	• budgeting help
• assistance in obtaining DSS, leaving care grants, topping up allowance	• assistance in obtaining DSS, leaving care grants, topping up allowance
• voluntary agencies in house trusts and grants	
4. EMPLOYMENT EDUCATION AND TRAINING	
From 1994:	
• careers officer attends project every two weeks	• no formal links, part of individual work
• both individual and formal links with colleges and youth training schemes	
5. SOCIAL OUTINGS AND HOLIDAYS	
• short holidays and trips out	
• summer activity programme	
6. INFORMATION FOR YOUNG PEOPLE	
• user friendly introductory leaflet	• Guide planned for future

District	County
I. INDIVIDUAL, SOCIAL AND GROUPWORK SUPPORT AND TRAINING	
• individual project worker	• individual project worker
• drop in centre, open daily	
• social groups	
2. ACCOMMODATION RESOURCE	
• supported lodgings	• supported lodgings
• assistance in securing local authority and housing association tenancies	• protocol agreed with district councils and housing associations
• joint management of housing association properties	• supported accommodation projects
	• semi-independent living projects
3. FINANCIAL ASSISTANCE	
• budgeting help	• budgeting help
• assistance in obtaining DSS, leaving care grants, topping up and rent assistance	• assistance in obtaining DSS, leaving care grants, topping up and rent assistance
4. EDUCATION, EMPLOYMENT AND TRAINING	
• links with local colleges	
• employment training and local employers	Links with TEC's and careers
5. SOCIAL OUTINGS AND HOLIDAYS	
• recent trips include pop concerts, motor cycle racing, Alton Towers	
• holidays including Center Parcs, Belgium	
6. INFORMATION FOR YOUNG PEOPLE	
• 'Taking Steps'	
• user friendly introduction	In preparation

Figure 4 Summary of leaving care procedures (1994)

District: ssd procedures	District (vol) procedures

1. STATUTORY REVIEW FOLLOWING 16TH BIRTHDAY:
Detailed planning, social worker allocated

2. INITIAL LEAVING CARE PLANNING MEETING WITHIN 2 MONTHS OF 1 ABOVE:
To make a detailed and recorded plan including whether to refer to NCH. → → → → →   → 1. REFERRAL BY APPLICATION FORM:
Completed by social worker, in respect of a young person:

3. FUTURE PLANNING MEETINGS:
not less than every 2 months.

- who has been in care or accommodation for more than 3 months after their 16th birthday

4. TENANCY PLANNING MEETING
when young person offered tenancy.

- and approximately 6 months before a major transition is planned
- in exceptional circumstances otherwise.

5. NEW HOME VISITS:
Immediately after they have moved in. Once a week for four weeks.

2. VOL worker will contact the social worker and young person to arrange introduction. At this meeting the young person receives a pack and 'Taking Steps'.

6. PLANNING GROUP MEETING.
Within four weeks of moving into new home, to review progress.

3. VOL carry out a two month assessment with young person, following 'Taking Steps' pack.

7. AFTER CARE REVIEW.
3 months after young person has left care.

4. VOL worker will attend planning and review meetings as outlined in 3–8 opposite. Allocated social worker continues involvement throughout.

8. SOCIAL WORK VISIT AND PLANNING GROUP.
6 months after moving into new home. Decision to continue or close case.

5. A file is kept by VOL. Open access to young person.

6. VOL administer tenancies and supportive lodgings.

7. No further involvement will be notified in writing.

City, ssd procedures	City (vol) and city (ssd)
1. STATUTORY REVIEW Following 16th birthday: detailed planning	
2. INITIAL LEAVING CARE PLANNING MEETING: Within 2 months of 1 above. Detailed and recorded plan including whether to refer to CITY 1 or CITY 2 leaving care teams. → → →	→ 1. REFERRAL BY APPLICATION FORM: • 6 months before transition from care, or at 17, whichever is soonest • in exceptional circumstances otherwise.
3. CORE PLANNING GROUP: To meet within 3 months if not referred to LC Team, (and at 3 monthly intervals if not referred)	2. INTRODUCTORY VISIT
4. FUTURE PLANNING MEETINGS (if referred to a LCT) not less than every 3 months.	3. CORE PLANNING GROUP MEETING: to agree leaving care assessment and programme.
5. TENANCY PLANNING MEETING When young person offered accommodation.	4. PLANNING MEETING: within 2 months of 3 above to consider assessment and programme.
6. NEW HOME VISITS: Immediately after moving in, once a week for four weeks.	5. FUTURE PLANNING MEETINGS: as outlined in 4–9 opposite.
7. PLANNING GROUP MEETING: within 4 weeks of moving.	
8. AFTER CARE REVIEW: 3 months after leaving care	
9. SOCIAL WORK VISIT AND PLANNING GROUP: SW visit after 6 months of moving. Decision to continue or close case.	

County: Leaving Care Team	SSD
1. REFERRALS: By telephone, visit or notification. In respect of young person • In care or accommodation, in their final year at school, considering a move to new accommodation • over school age but under 21, requiring accommodation (including 'Children in Need') • over minimum school leaving age (16), but under 17 and at risk of being 'looked after' 2. AFTER CARE AGREEMENT: Following referral an after care contract is negotiated with the young person, field social worker and leaving care team worker setting out the services to be provided by different partners.	(No published procedures – Leaving Care Team's procedure document in use across the Authority)

Figure 5 Distinctive features (during research period)

Distinctive features	District	County	City (vol)	City (ssd)
1. APPROACH				
i. Perspective	Community based	Social work task centred	Psychodynamic therapeutic	Practical skills based social work
ii. Continuum: Young person demand led to social work planned and led	Balance between young person demand led and social worker planned and led	Social worker planned and led	Structured social worker led	Mix of social worker planned and young person demand led
iii. Methods of work	Individual groupwork social activities	Individual	Individual group work social activities	Individual group work
2. PROVIDER • **Statutory/ voluntary** • **Range**	Voluntary organisation main provider for SSD	Social services main provider for county	Voluntary organisation scheme provider for SSD	Social services main provider in SSD
3. POLICY ROLE	Major advisory role	Major advisory role	Limited policy involvement	Limited policy involvement

Printed in the United Kingdom for HMSO
Dd300764 6/95 C20 G3396 10170